BERLITZ®

FLORENCE

By the staff of Berlitz Guides
A Macmillan Company

Deluxe Guide
1988/1989 Edition

Printed in Austria

Berlitz Trademark Reg. U.S. Patent Office and other countries – Marca Registrada. Library of Congress Catalog Card No. 78-52516.

How to use our guide

- All the practical information, hints and tips that you will need before and during the trip start on page 98.
- For general background, see the sections Florence and the Florentines, p. 6, and A Brief History, p. 10.
- All the sights to see are listed between pages 20 and 72, with suggestions for daytrips from Florence from page 73 to 81. Our own choice of sights most highly recommended is pinpointed by the Berlitz traveller symbol.
- Entertainment, nightlife and all other leisure activities are described between pages 82 and 89, while information on restaurants and cuisine is to be found on pages 90 to 97.
- Finally, there is an index at the back of the book, pp. 126–128.

Although we make every effort to ensure the accuracy of all the information in this book, changes occur incessantly. We cannot therefore take responsibility for facts, prices, addresses and circumstances in general that are constantly subject to alteration. Our guides are updated on a regular basis as we reprint, and we are always grateful to readers who let us know of any errors, changes or serious omissions they come across.

Text: Lyon Benzimra
Photography: Jean Mohr
Layout: Doris Haldemann
We wish to thank Simone Bargellini, Michael H. Sedge, the Italian National Tourist Office and the Azienda Autonoma di Turismo for their assistance with this guide.

Cartography: Falk-Verlag, Hamburg.

Contents

Maps

Cover picture: Entrance to the Palazzo Vecchio

Florence and the Florentines

You must take Florence for what it is: one of History's phenomena. Few nations, let alone cities, can boast such an overpowering array of talent—literary, artistic, political—concentrated over so short a period of time. The names of some of Florence's greatest sons—Dante, Boccaccio, Giotto, Donatello, Botticelli, Leonardo, Michelangelo, Cellini, Machiavelli—are well known the world over. Not a bad achievement for a city whose great period spanned less than 300 years.

Guidebooks often compare Renaissance Florence with 5th-century Athens, but while only spectacular ruins are left of that ancient Greek splendour, Florence is much more than a museum of stone, marble and bronze. Its historic palaces, its great churches, its innumerable works of art are not dry-as-dust relics. They're very much lived-in, worked-in, prayed-in and prized by today's Florentines.

Walking through this amazing city is likely to give you a pain in the neck—literally. There's so much to look at, simultaneously and at every level: a row of shop-windows, a courtyard glimpsed through a *palazzo* gateway, a faded street shrine lit by flickering oil lamps, a worn coat-of-arms, a commemorative plaque, rusted, centuries' old tethering rings and torch-holders. And, higher still, loom the stony masses of the *palazzi*—from medieval fortress dwellings and Renaissance mansions to heavily ornate 17th-century buildings—with names like Acciaiuoli, Rucellai, Strozzi, Pazzi, Salviati, Medici, straight out of history.

You won't feel that time has stood still here. The centre's bustle, its noisy, smelly (though now restricted) traffic, are very much part of the late 20th century. Yet most of the city's main streets are as narrow and their paving as uneven as they've ever been; the *palazzi*

The Arno, once a vital artery, recently brought near disaster.

are little changed and the voices you'll hear, melodious or harsh, with that unique Florentine pronunciation, would still sound familiar to Dante.

Through the centre of the city flows the muddy green Arno, bordered by broad *lungarni,* or embankments, built last century to protect against flooding. Spanning the river is the Ponte Vecchio, one of the oldest and most unusual bridges in the world, known for its goldsmiths' and jewellers' boutiques since the 16th century. Before that it was the domain of the butchers, the Arno being useful for waste disposal.

The craft tradition, a fascinating aspect of Florentine life, is typical of the city's genius for combining art and business. Every district has its artisans—ropemakers, bookbinders, embroiderers, wrought-iron workers or even gold-leaf beaters. In the back streets of the left bank, full of reproduction "factories", the mellow smell of varnish, wax and wood will assail you from many a doorway as you pass.

You may find Florentines disappointingly "un-Italian" in their behaviour. As a whole they're less forthcoming with tourists than, say, Neapolitans or Romans. They're courteous with strangers but refuse to pander to them. You'll experience little of that traditional Italian exuberance, apart maybe from an occasional exchange of street insults in thick Tuscan. But then, the Florentines, like their city, are an exception to the rule.

Hard-working, inventive, sharp-witted: these qualities still describe the natives of Florence. Add to that an inborn sense of dignity and sober elegance, a biting, often cruel wit, a savage pride in their city, a remarkable cockney-like resilience in adversity.

The November 1966 flood disaster (the worst of 50 floods in the city's history) was a supreme example of that resilience. Swollen by heavy rains, the Arno burst its banks one night, carrying all before it. In certain parts of the city, it reached depths of 23 feet. Thick mud, as well as oil from burst central-heating tanks, swirled everywhere. Hundreds of paintings, frescoes, sculptures and over a million priceless old books suffered incalculable damage. The people of Florence rose to the challenge. Before the flood waters had

Young Florentines still rendezvous on medieval Ponte Vecchio.

even receded the city's works of art were being lovingly rescued, and the long, hard job of restoring them immediately begun. It's still going on.

Art lovers from many countries, rallying at the news of the calamity, sent generous donations. But it was the willpower and enterprise of the Florentines that saved this living museum. So now Florence, city of the arts since the 15th century, is once again ready to welcome you.

A Brief History

No one quite knows how Florentia, Fiorenza or Firenze as it's now called came by its name. According to some, it was named after Florinus, a Roman general who encamped in 63 B.C. on the city's future site and from there besieged

Musicians in full regalia for Scoppio del Carro festivities.

the nearby, powerful Etruscan hill town of Fiesole.

Whatever the origin Roman Florence began to develop seriously around 59 B.C., becoming a thriving military and trading town. When you walk along Via Romana and on over Florence's famed Ponte Vecchio towards the city centre, you'll be treading the same ground Roman legions, travellers and merchants trod. And though you'll find no visible Roman remains in Florence (you'll have to visit Fiesole for that), all the trappings of civilized life were to be found here, from baths and a forum to temples and a theatre.

The barbarian invasions and the fall of the Roman empire plunged Europe into a dark, chaotic period. Lombards succeeded Goths, then came a temporary ray of light with Charlemagne's great 8th–9th-century European empire, but by the next century even greater chaos had set in.

Somehow the Carolingian province of Tuscany survived. In the late 11th century, Florence made rapid commercial and political progress under a remarkable ruler, Countess Matilda. The great guilds *(arti)* —wool and silk merchants, spice merchants, apothecaries, etc.—began to develop, and by 1138, 23 years after Matilda's death, Florence was a self-governing republic and a power to be reckoned with.

At that time the city must have presented a strange picture. All the great families had square stone towers (often more than 230 feet high!) built adjoining their houses—impregnable refuges during those ever-recurring feuds. By the end of the 12th century, the city's skyline bristled with over 150 of them (like San Gimignano today). They've all long since disappeared.

Guelphs and Ghibellines

Florence's history might then have been clear sailing but for the savage factional struggles. Sooner or later the interests of an aristocratic caste and a rising merchant class were bound to clash: the nobility opposed the broader based forms of government the merchants sought. Fierce inter-family feuds and continual raids on Florentine trade by "robber barons" did little to help.

Worst of all, powerful foreign interests became involved. The Guelph and Ghibelline parties, which developed in the 13th century, had ties outside Florence: the Guelphs tended to support the Pope, while the

Ghibellines looked to the Holy Roman Emperor. Further complicating matters was the French monarchy; it took a special interest in Florentine developments—ever ready to interfere in and profit from the fratricidal strife.

Other Tuscan cities followed suit with their own Guelph-Ghibelline parties and, for over two centuries, Tuscany was in a state of turmoil as first the aristocratic Ghibellines then the burgher Guelphs gained power. Defeated leaders were exiled with their families and followers, their property confiscated or destroyed. From friendly cities they plotted their return and the whole sorry cycle would begin once more. Pisa, Lucca, Pistoia, Siena, Arezzo, Florence were enemies at one time, allies at another, depending on which party held power.

Yet despite all this, Florentine commerce and banking continued to develop. Its woollen-cloth trade prospered; the first gold florin was minted there in the mid-13th century, and then rapidly adopted everywhere in Europe as a handy unit of coinage. Florence's social evolution over the 13th and 14th centuries was also remarkable: organized "factories" or workshops were opened; hospitals, schools and charitable societies founded; its university (one of Europe's oldest) turned out lawyers, teachers and doctors by the score; streets were paved, laws were passed regulating noise and nuisance; a kind of early Red Cross (the Brotherhood of the Misericordia, see p. 30) was formed. Life was hard, people toiled, but no one was allowed to starve to death. Never a democracy in the modern sense of the term, Florence nonetheless gave its citizens a unique sense of "belonging" that overrode class or party differences.

In spite of their internal divisions, the Guelphs gradually edged the Ghibellines completely out of power. By the late 13th century, the bankers', merchant and craft guilds reigned supreme in the Florentine republic, secure enough to turn their attention to building a fitting seat of government. With a sumptuous cathedral already under way, a mighty People's Palace (Palazzo del Popolo, later Palazzo della Signoria or Palazzo Vecchio) was begun in 1298. It still serves today as Florence's city hall.

Domenico di Michelino's Dante Explaining His Divine Comedy.

Florentine Men of Letters

DANTE ALIGHIERI (1265–1321), member of a Guelph family, was exiled by a faction of his party for the last 19 years of his life. His immortal poem, *The Divine Comedy,* a journey to Paradise via Hell and Purgatory, is one of the great turning points in world literature. In it he presents a double vision: the political and social order as divinely ordained and the ugly reality of the corrupt society around him.

One of the world's most translated authors, Dante wrote his masterpiece not in the usual scholarly Latin but in everyday language for all to understand. His work established the Tuscan vernacular as Italy's literary language.

Dante is especially remembered because of his unrequited love for Beatrice Portinari—yet he was only nine when he first set eyes on her.

GIOVANNI BOCCACCIO (1313–75) was a classical scholar and university lecturer, specializing on Dante. Surviving the Black Death, he used his experiences as the inspired basis for his marvellous, racy prose tales, *The Decameron.* Written in an Italian which is still easily understood, the work is unrivalled for gentle eroticism, humour and vivid characterization.

Dawn of a Golden Age

Florentine bankers now held the purse-strings of Europe, their agents based in every major city. One group headed by the Bardi and Peruzzi families lent Edward III of England a staggering 1,365,000 gold florins, for his campaigns against the French. But Edward's sudden double-dealing declaration of bankruptcy in 1343 had unexpectedly toppled the entire Florentine banking structure.

Yet the resilient Florentines recovered; the merchant interests set out with ruthless zest to regain their lost prestige. Despite continuing social unrest, violent working-class riots, flood, famine and the Black Death of 1347–48 which killed off about half of Florence's population, the city found itself by the early 1400s stronger and richer than it had ever been.

The power of the important business families, the *signori,* had proved greater than that of the guilds. The way now lay open for the Medici, wealthy wool merchants and bankers, who were to dominate every facet of Florentine life and culture for 60 golden years (1434–94). They led the city and its people to unparalleled heights of civilization, while most of Europe struggled to free itself from the coarse, tangled meshes of medieval feudalism.

Yet even before the Medici ushered in this golden age, there were already signs of that great Italian Renaissance which started in Florence. Interest in long-neglected Latin and Greek literature was reviving; Florentine historians were busy recording their city's progress for posterity; merchant guilds and nouveaux-riches with money to burn or consciences to appease found time between business deals and party vendettas to indulge in artistic patronage.

In spite of their factions, the Florentines envisaged ambitious public works and imposing private *palazzi:* the Duomo, Giotto's Campanile, the great monastic churches of Santa Croce and Santa Maria Novella, the Bargello, the Palazzo della Signoria were begun or completed in that tumultuous 14th century.

The Renaissance

The term "Renaissance" was coined by a 16th-century Florentine artist, Giorgio Vasari, whose *Lives of the Painters* still makes fascinating reading and tells us virtually everything we know about the great Italian artists from the 13th century to his own time.

Renaissance means rebirth,

and that's exactly what it was: men appeared to be waking from a long sleep and taking up life where antiquity had left off.

Throughout the Middle Ages the Church had dominated the cultural life of Europe. Literature, architecture, painting, sculpture, music were all geared to glorifying God rather than earthly life and beauty. The Greek and Roman ideal of "art for art's sake" had been forgotten. The Florentines revived this concept. When you visit the Uffizi, compare Cimabue's *Virgin Enthroned* with Botticelli's *Primavera*, painted 200 years later. The two works epitomize the difference between the Middle Ages and the Renaissance.

In those uncertain times the idea took hold that life must be lived to its fullest, that pursuit of earthly knowledge, beauty and pleasure were what really counted in the brief span of life alloted to man. The arts and sciences of the Renaissance were directed to that end.

A 19th-century German scholar wrote it off as "an intellectual bacchanalia"; but Lorenzo de' Medici—*il Magnifico* as his contemporaries dubbed him for his patronage of art and scholarship—summed it up with greater charm:

SCALA, Florence

Lorenzo il Magnifico: merchant, politician, patron of the arts.

Quant'è bella giovinezza,
che si fugge tuttavia!
Chi vuol esser lieto sia:
di doman non c'è certezza.

How fine a thing is youth
but how short-lived.
Let he who wishes to be merry,
be so.
For there's no saying what
tomorrow will bring.

The author of these sentiments had seen his 25-year-old brother Giuliano savagely murdered at his side during mass in the Duomo by members of the rival Pazzi family (1478).

The Medici Hold

Remarkably enough, few of the early Medici ever held office in the city government. Yet Cosimo the Elder (1389–1464), a munificent patron of the arts and letters, who earned himself the title *pater patriae* (father of his country), his son Piero "the Gouty" (1416–69) and his grandson Lorenzo the Magnificent (1449–92) were rulers of Florence in all but name. Ably pulling the strings through supporters elected to the republican Signoria, or government, all three were expert politicians who knew how to woo the Florentine masses.

Poet, naturalist, discerning art collector, would-be architect, a dabbler in philosophy, in other words a typical Renaissance generalist, Lorenzo was perhaps the most outstanding member of the Medici family. His diplomatic skill kept Italy temporarily free of wars and foreign invasion.

On Lorenzo's death in 1492, his son Piero took his place. Loutish and devoid of taste, Piero was totally unworthy of the Medici name; he only lasted two years. When Charles VIII of France invaded Italy in alliance with the Duke of Milan, Piero first opposed them but then, as it became clear that the French were winning, suddenly changed sides. He had to accept humiliating settlement terms. The Florentine people were so enraged that they drove him from the city and set up a republic. It was at this time that Niccolò Machiavelli, author of *The Prince,* held office in Florence, gaining first-hand experience in the art of intrigue and diplomacy.

The spiritual force behind the new republic was a fanatical Dominican friar by the name of Girolamo Savonarola (1452–98). During Lorenzo's last years, he had preached regularly in the Duomo. Audiences of thousands heard him inveigh against the excesses of the Medici and their entourage, prophesying apocalyptic punishments for the city if its people did not turn back to a godlier life. In 1494, he decreed a burning of "vanities", and Florentines rich and poor rushed to Piazza della Signoria with armfuls of books, jewellery, cosmetics and paintings which they hurled upon a huge bonfire in the middle of the square. A repentant Botticelli also joined the crowd, flinging some of his own paintings into the flames. However, Savonarola had powerful enemies within and without Florence (the notorious Borgia pope, for one) who soon brought about his downfall. Arrested, he was sentenced to death for heresy and, ironically, was hanged and burnt on the very spot where the "burning of vanities" had taken place only four years earlier.

In 1512, Piero's two brothers, Giovanni and Giuliano, returned, putting an end to the 18-year-old republic. Michelangelo's Medici tombs in San Lorenzo (one of which is for Giuliano) and his superb Laurentian Library date from this period. Expelled again in 1527, the persistent Medici were back three years later—after a dramatic eight-month siege of

Burning of Savonarola (1498) as seen by a contemporary artist.

Florence—with the help of the Holy Roman Emperor, Charles V.

During the subsequent rule of Duke Cosimo I de' Medici from 1537 to 1574, a rather heavy-handed attempt was made to revive the spirit of the earlier Medicean golden age. Some of Florence's most prominent monuments, the Santa Trinita Bridge, the Boboli Gardens, the Neptune Fountain in the Piazza della Signoria, Cellini's magnificent bronze *Perseus* in the Loggia dei Lanzi, date from this period.

A New Role

Florence now sank into a torpor for over three centuries under the rule of the boring Grand Dukes of Tuscany (Medici until 1743, Habsburg up to 1859). However, Anna Maria Ludovica, last of the Medici

Neptune fountain erected by the Medici on Piazza della Signoria.

line, made a final gesture worthy of her Renaissance forebears. Far-sightedly, she bequeathed the entire Medici art treasure to the city "to attract foreigners" and on condition that none of it ever be removed or sold. And foreigners came, a small but steady trickle of privileged, moneyed young men on the Grand Tour—the 18th-century finish to a gentleman's education.

In the 19th century a new species came, the "Italianate Englishman", led by the poets Byron and Shelley, and followed by the Brownings, John Ruskin and the Pre-Raphaelites. Rapturous Englishmen came or settled there in droves, bringing in their wake French, German and even Russian tourists. Queen Victoria herself visited the city, and Florence Nightingale—named after the city—was born there (see her statue, lamp and all, in Santa Croce cloister).

After the dramatic events of the Risorgimento, Italy's national movement to eject the Austrian occupant and unify the country, the city had a brief moment of glory as temporary capital of the new kingdom of Italy (1865–71). With the capital's permanent transfer to Rome, Florence's story merges into Italian history.

The 20th Century

Despite the excitement at the time of the unification, democracy failed to become firmly established in Italy. Crisis followed crisis, and people lost confidence in the government. During the First World War, Italy fought on the side of Britain and France against Germany and Austria, but afterwards she felt she had been insufficiently rewarded for her sacrifices. As parliamentary democracy disintegrated, Benito Mussolini's fascists seized power in 1922.

With the Rome–Berlin Axis of 1937, Mussolini linked the fate of Italy to that of Hitler's Germany, dragging his country into defeat in the Second World War. The Fascist government fell in 1943, and some of the most heroic battles of the Italian resistance were fought in and around Florence. Fortunately the city's unique art treasures survived.

Present-day Florence is an important, thriving business and university centre. Its vast new suburbs boast a variety of industries by no means all tourist orientated. Conscious heirs of a great creative tradition, today's Florentines keep their city in the forefront in the world of art, fashion and artisan crafts.

What to See

Unless you're on a package tour where decisions are already made for you, it pays to be selective in Florence. Otherwise, you may end up needing another holiday. Florence is a city to be savoured, its finest monuments and works of art lingered over. Don't try to "cover" it all if you're only here for a few days.

To ease your way, we've divided up the city into five geographical areas and described the most interesting sights within them. Each district can be covered on foot (cars, anyway, are banned from the historic centre).

But before exploring on your own, get the feel of the city by investing in a conducted coach tour. Inexpensive, three-hour tours leave daily morning, afternoon and night. Your hotel will have the details.

Florence's museums can be a daunting proposition: there are almost 40, most of them worth visiting. We've noted the more important ones; which you visit will depend on your time and interests. If you've only a few days, better to see two or three at leisure than the lot at a gallop.

Make sure to check with your hotel on the current opening hours and closing days of museums. They're constantly changing.

Florence's churches are best seen and enjoyed in the context of the squares and streets and the life going on around them. On scorching summer afternoons you'll find their interiors a cool refuge and a welcome break from street and museum. But remember, they're places of worship, and shorts and halters are frowned upon.

Officially there are 24 historic churches in Florence, including the Duomo and Baptistery. You probably won't have time to visit a quarter of them, yet all boast architecture, memorials and art treasures of note. Wealthy merchant families vied with one another, and with the Medici, endowing and decorating chapels in their favourite churches, outdoing one another in lavishness and keeping quantities of artists and craftsmen busy for hundreds of years.

Some of the major churches —through which you're free to wander at will—have coin-operated sound-guides with good commentaries in different languages on the church's history and treasures.

The Florence Experience,

Piazzale Michelangelo offers the finest view in town: you can look over the full sweep of the city, from San Miniato to the Duomo and beyond.

screened hourly on the hour in the Cinema Edison on Piazza della Repubblica, provides a fine introduction to the city's past in 45 minutes of multi-vision.

Ponte Vecchio has linked city's two banks for almost 700 years.

Florence's streets are not wide, but their straight, right-angled pattern in its historic centre is a unique example of civilized town planning at a time when even Paris and London were a maze of twisting lanes and alleyways. The one street in central Florence that actually bends (Via Bentaccordi) only does so because it followed the horseshoe-shaped outer wall of the ancient Roman amphitheatre! On a map you can easily follow the line of the old city walls. Pulled down in the 19th century, they were replaced by broad but uninteresting tree-lined residential avenues or *viali*. Some of the original gates still stand forlornly in the middle of huge open squares.

The street names in Florence tell their own story: Via delle Terme (street of the baths) did have real Roman baths, and Via del Campidoglio (street of the capitol) boasted a great temple to Jupiter. Via degli Speziali (street of the spice merchants), Via dei Saponai (of the soap-makers), Corso dei Tintori (of the dyers) were once exclusively occupied by the particular trades. Only their names survive today, but Via de' Calzaiuoli (of the stocking- and shoemakers) is still *the* street for shoes.

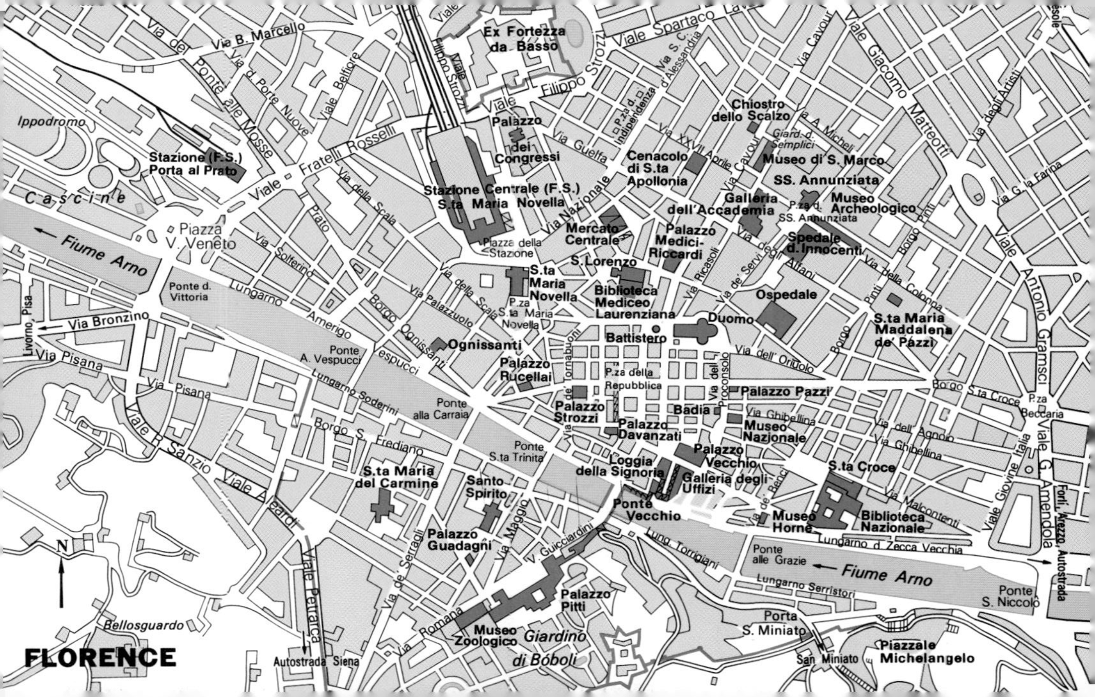
FLORENCE
Ex Fortezza da Basso
Stazione (F.S.) Porta al Prato
Stazione Centrale (F.S.) S.ta Maria Novella
Palazzo dei Congressi
Chiostro dello Scalzo
Cenacolo di S.ta Apollonia
Museo di S. Marco
SS. Annunziata
Museo Archeologico
Galleria dell'Accademia
Spedale d. Innocenti
Mercato Centrale
Palazzo Medici-Riccardi
S. Lorenzo
Biblioteca Mediceo Laurenziana
S.ta Maria Novella
Ospedale
Duomo
Battistero
S.ta Maria Maddalena de' Pazzi
Ognissanti
Palazzo Rucellai
Palazzo Pazzi
Badia
Palazzo Strozzi
Palazzo Davanzati
Museo Nazionale
Palazzo Vecchio
Loggia della Signoria
Galleria degli Uffizi
S.ta Croce
Ponte Vecchio
Museo Horne
Biblioteca Nazionale
S.ta Maria del Carmine
Santo Spirito
Palazzo Guadagni
Palazzo Pitti
Museo Zoologico
Giardino di Bóboli
Piazzale Michelangelo
Fiume Arno
Cascine
Ippodromo
Piazza V. Veneto
Ponte d. Vittoria
Ponte A. Vespucci
Ponte alla Carraia
Ponte S.ta Trinita
Ponte alle Grazie
Ponte S. Niccolò
Porta S. Miniato
San Miniato
Bellosguardo
Autostrada Siena
Livorno, Pisa
Forlí, Arezzo, Autostrada
Viale Filippo Strozzi
Viale Spartaco Lavagnini
Viale Giacomo Matteotti
Viale Antonio Gramsci
Viale G. Amendola
Viale Giovine Italia
Viale Fratelli Rosselli
Viale Petrarca
Viale R. Sanzio
Viale Aleardi
Viale Belfiore
Via B. Marcello
Via d. Porte Nuove
Via del Ponte alle Mosse
Via della Scala
Via Palazzuolo
Borgo Ognissanti
Lungarno Amerigo Vespucci
Lungarno Soderini
Via Bronzino
Via Pisana
Borgo S. Frediano
Via de' Serragli
Via Romana
Via Maggio
V. Guicciardini
Lung. Torrigiani
Lungarno Serristori
Lungarno d. Zecca Vecchia
Via Guelfa
Via Nazionale
Via XXVII Aprile
Via Cavour
Via Ricasoli
Via de' Servi
Via degli Alfani
Via della Colonna
Borgo Pinti
Via dell' Oriuolo
Via del Proconsolo
Via de' Tornabuoni
P.za della Repubblica
Via Ghibellina
Via dell' Agnolo
Via Malcontenti
Borgo S.ta Croce
P.za Beccaria
Via de' Benci
Via degli Artisti
Via G. la Farina
Via A. Micheli
Giard. d. Semplici
P.za d. SS. Annunziata
P.za d. Indipendenza
Via S. C. d'Alessandria
Piazza della Stazione
P.za S.ta Maria Novella
Via Solferino
Prato
N

From the Duomo to the Uffizi

Duomo

Officially known as Santa Maria del Fiore (Our Lady of the Flower), the green, white and pink marble faced Duomo was intended by city-proud Florentines as a cathedral to end all cathedrals (it can hold over 20,000 people!).

The great architect Arnolfo di Cambio designed the Duomo. Work began around 1296 on the site of a far smaller 5th-century church but was not completed until the second half of the 15th century. Its front remained unfaced until the 19th century.

Like most Tuscan churches of the time, the Duomo presents a uniquely local version

Of Crests and Such

Heraldry enthusiasts will find plenty to keep them busy in Florence. Coats of arms of families, trade guilds, city wards, and justices embellish numerous streets and even churches.

The most famous, of course, is the six balls of the Medici. These are said to represent pills, for the Medici, whose name means "doctors", were originally members of the guild of spice merchants and apothecaries. Five balls are coloured red, but the top ball is blue and bears the golden lily of France (a gift from Louis XI of France in the 15th century).

If the Medici coat of arms looks familiar to you, it may be through power of association: the pawnbroker's symbol evolved from it.

The Duomo's majestic cupola rises high above Florence, known from its crest as the city of the lily.

of Gothic, not easily compared with English or French ecclesiastical architecture of the same period.

The mighty **cupola** is a contribution from the Renaissance. First and unquestionably greatest of his talented peers, the architect Filippo Brunelleschi (1377–1446) had marvelled at the dome on Rome's Pantheon, rebuilt for Emperor Hadrian about A.D. 125. No one had subsequently achieved such an engineering feat.

The ambitious Florentines wanted to have a dome on their cathedral. In a public competition held in 1418, Brunelleschi submitted the winning design and a workable building scheme. (You can see his original wooden model in the Museo dell'Opera di Santa Maria del Fiore, see p. 30.) In Florence, where beauty and art were never the preserve of the rich alone, these competitions caused immense popular excitement. Citizens rich and

poor, high or low, often sat together on the juries.

Virtually completed in 1434, the marvellous dome—the first giant cupola since antiquity—was visible for miles around, confirming proud feelings that nothing was beyond a Renaissance man's ingenuity and science, especially a Florentine's. Its 138-foot diameter surpasses the domes of the Pantheon, St. Peter's in Rome, and St. Paul's in London. Climb to the top of its lantern and enjoy yet more breathtaking **panoramic views.**

Most of the original interior and exterior statuary of the Duomo was long ago removed to the Museo dell'Opera di Santa Maria del Fiore. There

Contrasting views—from and of the elegant Campanile by Giotto.

are nevertheless some important works of art on view in the cathedral. Make sure to take a look at Lorenzo Ghiberti's **bronze shrine,** below the high altar, made for the remains of St. Zenobius (one of Florence's first bishops). The Duomo's round stained-glass windows were also designed by the versatile Ghiberti.

Left of the entrance you'll spot unusual *trompe l'œil* frescoed "monuments" to two 15th-century *condottieri* (mercenary captains) who fought in Florentine pay. The right-hand one, painted by a master of perspective, Paolo Uccello, commemorates an Englishman, John Hawkwood, the only foreigner buried in the Duomo.

If you're lucky enough to be in Florence on Easter Sunday, don't miss the famous, centuries'-old Scoppio del Carro ceremony with its added costume pageantry in front of the Duomo. Fireworks on a decorated cart in the piazza are set off by an artificial dove propelled along on a wire from the high altar.

The Duomo's free-standing **Campanile** (bell-tower), one of Florence's most graceful landmarks, has three stories of elegant windows. It was begun in 1334 by that many-sided genius Giotto. It's worth the 414-stair climb to the top and the entrance fee for a highly unusual bird's-eye **view** of the cathedral and the city.

Il Battistero (Baptistery)
Worth leaving till last, this precious gem of Romanesque architecture was built in the early 12th century on the site, traditionally, of a Roman temple of Mars. It served for a time as Florence's cathedral. Salvaged Roman columns were used in its construction. The exterior of the Baptistery remains as it was in the time of Dante.

Byzantine-style, 13th-century **mosaics** inside the cupola include scenes from the *Creation, Life of St. John* and a *Last Judgement*.

The Baptistery's tourist popularity rests on its three sets of bronze doors: those on the south side are by a 14th-century artist, Andrea Pisano; those on the north and east sides were made by Ghiberti in the first half of the 15th century.

Financed by one of the richest merchant guilds, a competition for the north and east doors was held in 1401. Brunelleschi submitted a design, but Ghiberti's was unanimously chosen. See the two artists' bronze models in the Bargello (p. 60), and judge for yourself. Facing the Duomo are the east doors, called the **Doors of Paradise** by an admiring Michelangelo. The name has stuck ever since. Between the little heads and Old Testament figures of the ten main panels, a proud Ghiberti set his own self-portrait. It's on the left door, two panels from the bot-

Scene from John the Baptist's life on Baptistery's south door.

tom, on the right. If you want to study the doors at close quarters, lunchtime or very late afternoon are best.

The simplest landmarks can hide the most dramatic events: the column standing on its own behind the Baptistery commemorates a tree that burst into bloom when the remains of a Florentine bishop, St. Zenobius, were carried past one wintry day centuries ago.

Piazza del Duomo and Piazza San Giovanni

Effectively two piazzas-in-one, this is undoubtedly Florence's religious hub for tourists. Opposite the Baptistery, see the graceful 14th-century Loggia del Bigallo, once part of the headquarters of a society for the care of orphans. On the same side of the piazza lies the seat of Florence's oldest, most respected social institution, the Brotherhood of the Misericordia (mercy). Every day and at most hours, you'll see black-frocked figures dashing out of its doors and roaring off in ambulance vans. They could be going to collect a sick child or comfort a dying old woman. This amazing democratic institution was thought up by the Florentines over 600 years before the existence of the Red Cross or Social Security. Its members, unpaid volunteers from every walk of life, work on rotating shifts round the clock. They now run, among other things, Florence's emergency ambulance service.

Museo dell'Opera di Santa Maria del Fiore (Piazza del Duomo, 9) is the Duomo's own museum, where some of its most precious treasures and original sculptures are kept. See a magnificent 14th–15th-century silver-faced altar from the Baptistery; rich gold and silver reliquaries (one boasting the index finger of St. John); and Brunelleschi's original wooden model for the Duomo cupola. Don't miss Donatello's **Mary Magdalen statue**—a harrowing apparition; or his unforgettable **sculptured choir loft** *(cantoria)*, full of movement and grace. Luca della Robbia's *cantoria* facing it is just as captivating. Here, too, is Michelangelo's unfinished **Pietà;** it is said that he intended it for his own tomb. (See p. 118 for museum opening hours.)

In **Firenze com'era,** "Florence as it was" (Via dell'Oriuolo, 4), you will find paintings, prints and photographs re-

Take a sightseeing break in an unrivalled setting—in front of the Duomo (Santa Maria del Fiore).

tracing the city's physical history. The museum was formerly a monastery.

On the way down Via de' Calzaiuoli to the river you pass **Orsanmichele,** probably the only dual-purpose church in the world. The ground floor was designed for worship, the two upper floors for storing the city's grain reserve. In the church's ceiling you'll be shown the ducts down which grain was poured into waiting sacks below. Mystical and mysterious, the pillared interior is dominated by Orcagna's bulky but splendid 14th-century altarpiece, built around a miracle-working picture of the Madonna.

Adopted by the city's merchant and craft guilds, the church's plain, square, silo-like exterior, was embellished with Gothic-style niches and statues in the late 14th and early 15th centuries. Each guild paid for one of 14 niches and commissioned a statue of its patron or favourite saint for it. On the north side of the church stands Donatello's *St. George* (a copy: the original is in the Bargello, see p. 59). Commissioned by the armourers' guild, this was one of the first great statues of the Renaissance.

Ghiberti statues of *St. Matthew* and *St. Stephen* can be seen on the side of the building facing the 13th-century Palazzo dell'Arte della Lana. Glance up at the impressive upper floors *(Saloni)*, reached via an overhead walkway from this *palazzo,* once the headquarters of the all-powerful wool-merchants' guild. The views alone are worth the climb.

Piazza della Signoria

If the Piazza del Duomo is Florence's religious heart, this is certainly its civic heart. When you first come upon it you'll be amazed at its sheer size, and at the cyclopean dimensions of the piazza.

Tourist attractions abound here—the *palazzo* itself; the Uffizi; a wealth of statuary, to say nothing of open-air cafés. And if you can't get to Venice, don't be disappointed: flocks of tame Florentine pigeons and professional photographers with bags of grain are on hand to make up for it. Some years the piazza serves as the setting on June 24, St. John's Day, for the Giuoco del Calcio, a highly colourful, traditional pageant and football game in 16th-century costume. (Recently, it's been held in the Boboli Gardens.) You should check with your hotel for details of the current year. Repeat performance on June 28.

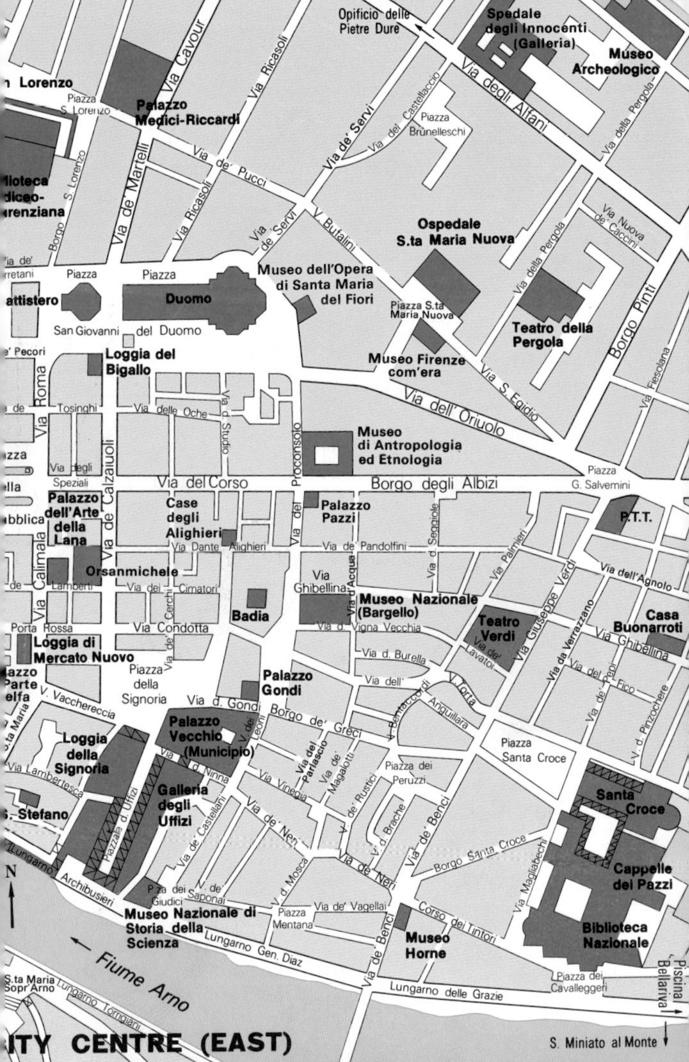
Opificio delle Pietre Dure
Spedale degli Innocenti (Galleria)
Museo Archeologico
Lorenzo
Piazza S. Lorenzo
Palazzo Medici-Riccardi
Via Cavour
Via Ricasoli
Via de' Servi
Via dei Castellaccio
Piazza Brunelleschi
Via degli Alfani
Via della Pergola
Via de' Martelli
Via de' Pucci
Borgo S. Lorenzo
Ospedale S.ta Maria Nuova
Via Nuova de' Caccini
V. Bufalini
Museo dell'Opera di Santa Maria del Fiori
Piazza S.ta Maria Nuova
Teatro della Pergola
Borgo Pinti
Battistero
Piazza San Giovanni
Duomo
Piazza del Duomo
Loggia del Bigallo
Museo Firenze com'era
Via S. Egidio
Via dell' Oriuolo
Via Fiesolana
Via Roma
Via delle Oche
Via d. Studio
Museo di Antropologia ed Etnologia
Via degli Speziali
Via de Calzaiuoli
Via del Corso
Via del Proconsolo
Borgo degli Albizi
Piazza G. Salvemini
Palazzo dell'Arte della Lana
Case degli Alighieri
Palazzo Pazzi
P.T.T.
Via Dante Alighieri
Via de' Pandolfini
Via d. Seggiole
Via Palmieri
Via dell'Agnolo
Via Calimala
Orsanmichele
Via Ghibellina
Via d'Acqua
Via dei Cimatori
Via de' Lamberti
Via dei Cerchi
Badia
Museo Nazionale (Bargello)
Teatro Verdi
Via Giuseppe Verdi
Via da Verrazzano
Casa Buonarroti
Via Porta Rossa
Via Condotta
Via d. Vigna Vecchia
Via de' Lavatoi
Loggia di Mercato Nuovo
Via d. Burella
Via del Fico
Via de' Pepi
Palazzo Parte Guelfa
Piazza della Signoria
Palazzo Gondi
Via dell' Anguillara
V. Torta
Via d. Gondi
V. Vacchereccia
Borgo de' Greci
V. Bentaccordi
Via de' Pinzochere
Palazzo Vecchio (Municipio)
Via dei Leoni
Loggia della Signoria
Via del Parlascio
Via de' Magalotti
Piazza Santa Croce
Via Lambertesca
Via d. Ninna
Piazza dei Peruzzi
Galleria degli Uffizi
Via Vinegia
V. de' Rustici
S. Stefano
Piazzale d. Uffizi
Via de' Castellani
Via de' Neri
V. d. Brache
Via de' Benci
Santa Croce
Borgo Santa Croce
Lungarno Archibusieri
V. d. Mosca
Via Magliabechi
Cappelle dei Pazzi
P.za dei Giudici
V. de' Saponai
Museo Nazionale di Storia della Scienza
Piazza Mentana
Via de' Vagellai
Corso dei Tintori
Biblioteca Nazionale
Museo Horne
Lungarno Gen. Diaz
Fiume Arno
Piazza dei Cavalleggeri
Piscina Bellariva
S.ta Maria Sopr'Arno
Lungarno Torrigiani
Lungarno delle Grazie
N
ITY CENTRE (EAST)
S. Miniato al Monte

Un-medieval in size at a time when only cathedrals were given monumental treatment, the fortress-like Palazzo della Signoria was undertaken at the same time as the Duomo—part of a mammoth public building programme. Designed by Arnolfo di Cambio, the Duomo's architect, this future seat of the city's government (it's still Florence's city hall) went up rather quickly. It was completed in 1314, 120 years before the Duomo.

Its off-centred, 308-foot-high tower helps soften the structure's stony squareness and echoes its off-centre position in the piazza. There's a practical, if unusual reason for this: the area around the 16th-century Neptune Fountain was formerly the site of the Uberti *palazzo*. One of Florence's leading 13th-century Ghibelline families, and one of the most hated, the Uberti were expelled *en masse* from the city, their palace razed to the ground and its site officially cursed for all eternity. The Palazzo della Signoria stands just clear of this tainted land!

Students at Italy's second oldest university confer; right, Giambologna's Rape of the Sabines.

The equally famous **Loggia della Signoria,** or Loggia dei Lanzi, was built in the late 14th century. At first a covered vantage point for city officials at public ceremonies, it took its name later from Cosimo I's Germano-Swiss Landsknechts, or mercenaries, who used it as an open-air guardroom during his nine-year residence in the *palazzo.* When Cosimo moved to the Pitti in 1549, the Palazzo della Signoria became known as the Palazzo Vecchio, the "old palace"; the Landsknechts also moved on, but the Loggia's name stuck.

The first of its celebrated statuary, Cellini's fine bronze *Perseus,* was lodged here on Cosimo's order in the early 1550s; the two Giambologna works *(Rape of the Sabines* and *Hercules and the Centaur)* were added towards the end of the century, while the Roman statues at the back were 18th-century Medici additions.

A masterly feat of bronze-casting, the **Perseus** came within an inch of disaster. Cellini himself, in his lively autobiography, describes the agonizing moments when he had to throw all his pewter vessels into the molten metal—200 plates, goblets and pots—to keep it pouring smoothly into the mould.

And those beautiful little figures embellishing the statue's base might not have been there today if Cosimo's wife Eleonora of Toledo had had her way. Coveting them for herself, she badgered and cajoled Cellini for them. But he, with an eye perpetually cocked on public acclaim, ensured their destiny by soldering them firmly onto the base.

All this statuary was part of Cosimo's ambitious decoration scheme for the piazza, including his own bronze equestrian statue by Giambologna and the massive Neptune Fountain by Ammannati. He'd even toyed with a typically grandiose Michelangelo suggestion to extend the Loggia dei Lanzi round the entire piazza.

Statuary had always stood on the raised stone platform running the length of the *palazzo*'s façade. A *marzocco,* Florence's heraldic lion bearing the city's arms, has been there almost as long as the *palazzo* itself. Donatello's bronze *Judith and Holofernes* (now preserved within the palace) was transferred from the Medici Palace in 1494; Michelangelo's *David* had been there since 1504. Sculpted in just two years out of a giant block of marble on which an earlier artist had made a clumsily unsuccessful start, *David* was moved to the Accademia in 1873 (see p. 52) and replaced by a copy. The present version is a second copy set up this century. The rather grotesque statue of *Hercules and Cacus* balancing it was done by a

Davids Galore

The number of Davids in Florence is no coincidence. A favourite theme with shrewd politicians, artists and the common people, everybody liked to think of Florence as beautiful, young, fearless and divinely ordained for greatness, overcoming her worst enemies as David overcame Goliath.

The Medici commissioned Donatello's bronze *David* for their palace courtyard. Puritanical Savonarola himself didn't hesitate later to have this disturbingly erotic statue moved to the Palazzo della Signoria's courtyard where Verrocchio's bronze *David* already graced a staircase. And Michelangelo's giant *David* was commissioned as a morale-booster for the city —which it undoubtedly was.

Today's young artists strive in the shadow of old Uffizi masters.

16th-century sculptor, Baccio Bandinelli. He was also responsible, among other things, for the seated statue of Cosimo I's father in Piazza San Lorenzo.

The platform *(aringhiera)* served for public speakers or proclamations. A commemorative stone marks the exact spot where Savonarola was executed (see p. 16–17).

The elaborately ornate courtyard of the **Palazzo Vecchio,** or Palazzo della Signoria, comes as a surprise after the austerely medieval exterior. (See section on MUSEUM HOURS on p. 118.) This was part of a 16th-century scheme by Vasari to brighten the place up for his Medici masters. Verrocchio's bronze *putto* (cherub) fountain was specially brought from Lorenzo de' Medici's Careggi villa, as a final softening touch (the original is inside).

Before entering the Palazzo Vecchio, take a look at the right-hand wall close to the corner of the building: you'll see a man's profile cut into one of the lower stones. It's said to have been chiselled in minutes by Michelangelo—working "blind" with his hands behind his back, as a bet! And those dusty old stone lions in the *palazzo*'s gloomy rear courtyard are reminders that real ones were once kept there, liv symbols of Florence's heraldi lion, the *marzocco,* standing o the piazza outside.

The *palazzo*'s highlights in clude the massive first-floor **Sa lone dei Cinquecento.** Built i 1496 for Savonarola's short lived republican Council o 500, it was turned into a gran throne-room by Cosimo I adorned with giant Vasari fres coes of Florentine victories an Michelangelo's *Victory* statu in a niche. Three centuries lat er, the first Italian nationa parliament sat here.

Just off the hall, don't mis the Vasari-designed **Studiolo,** little gem of a study covere from floor to barrel-vaulte ceiling with painted allegorica panels (some on slate), and tw Bronzino portraits of Cosimo and his consort gazing haughti ly down.

The Hall of Leo X (now offices) is frescoed with heroi Medicean themes. On the second floor are the apartments of Eleonora of Toledo (Cosimo I's wife), a riot of gilt, painted ceilings and rich furnishings. Note the frescoes imitating mosaics in the small chapel.

Visit the nearby 15th-century **Sala dei Gigli** (Hall of the Lilies), all blues and golds, lavishly decorated with Florentine ıeraldry, fine gilt-panelled ceil-ng, bright Ghirlandaio fres-:oes and doors superbly inlaid vith figures of Dante and Pe-rarch.

In the next room, see a col-›ured bust of a lifelike, witty-ooking Machiavelli, and Ver-occhio's cuddlesome cherub ıt close quarters; then the plendid **Guardaroba,** a cup-›oard-lined room whose pan-ːls were painted in the 1570s vith 53 maps of Tuscany and he four continents by two earned and artistic Dominican riars. Medici treasures were ›nce stored here.

A dizzying gallery above the Salone connects with the Quar-iere degli Elementi, another et of apartments. Don't miss he loggia and its breathtaking views of San Miniato and the Belvedere.

If you've time, climb up to he gallery below the battle-nents and, a little higher, to he top of the tower itself. Some 300 feet from the ground, you're treated here to one of he most sensational **panoramas** n all Florence. See also the mall cell where Savonarola vas locked up awaiting his ex-ːcution in the piazza below.

To the *palazzo*'s right, the Uffizi museum stretches in a ong U-shape right up to the Arno. Built in the second half of the 16th century by Vasari on Cosimo's order, the building was intended as headquarters for all the various government offices (hence the name), as the official mint and even as workshops for Medici-employed craftsmen. It's now one of the world's most famous art museums.

The Uffizi

A room a day, they say, is the way to see the Uffizi. Most tourists have a morning or even less to do it in. (See p. 118 for the museum's hours and closing days.)

Paintings, in chronological order, cover the cream of Italian and European art from the 13th to the 18th century. To avoid coming away with a blurry impression of the museum, feel no qualms about skipping over some of the 37 or so rooms that lead off two long, glassed-in galleries. Decorated with Roman statuary and sumptuous 16th-century Flemish tapestries, the galleries enjoy unique views over the Arno and Ponte Vecchio.

Start with those early Tuscan "greats", Cimabue and Giotto. In their altarpieces depicting enthroned madonnas

Florentine Art in a Nutshell

Moving away from the Byzantine tradition, Giovanni Cimabue (1240–1302) founded the Florentine school, but it was Giotto (1266–1337), introducing naturalism, who made Florence the first city of Italian art.

The Renaissance was ushered in by Masaccio (1401–28), with his solid well-modelled human figures, followed by Andrea del Castagno (1423–57) and Paolo Uccello (1397–1475), master of perspective, and the melancholy Filippo Lippi (1406–69). In the realm of religious art the outstanding painters were Fra Angelico (1387–1455), noted for the purity of line and colour, Leonardo's teacher Andrea Verrocchio (1435–88), also a fine sculptor, Domenico Ghirlandaio (1449–94), famous for his frescoes, the exquisitely lyrical Botticelli (1444–1510) and Filippino Lippi (c. 1457–1504).

Florentine painting rose to new heights in the 16th century with the versatile artist and scientist Leonardo da Vinci (1452–1519), the magnificent Michelangelo (1475–1564)—sculptor, architect, painter and poet—and Raphael (1483–1520), the epitome of classicism.

The great names in Florentine architecture were Giotto, Brunelleschi (1377–1446), Alberti (1404–72) and Michelozzo (d. 1472); the leading sculptors Lorenzo Ghiberti (1378–1455), Donatello (1386–1466), Luca della Robbia (1400–82), the specialist in terra cottas, and Benvenuto Cellini (1500–71), who excelled as a goldsmith as well.

You can retrace the developmen[t] of Florentine art, starting wit[h] Giotto (above), in Uffizi Gallery

(painted in 1280 and 1310), the mosaic-like stiffness of Cimabue's work contrasts with Giotto's innovating depth and more expressive, realistic figures.*

Greatest painter of the important 14th-century Sienese school was Simone Martini: see the graceful *Annunciation* that he painted for Siena cathedral. And of all the later Italian Gothic masterpieces, Gentile da Fabriano's *Adoration of the Magi* (1423) is the most exquisite.

Nearby, don't miss Masaccio's *Madonna and Child with St. Anne,* an early Renaissance breakthrough because of its new "realism". Enjoy Fra Angelico's *Coronation of the Virgin,* full of light and music; and Paolo Uccello's *Battle of San Romano* (1456), an astounding exercise in perspective and volume. Originally three panels (the others are in Paris and London), they once hung in Lorenzo the Magnificent's bedroom. See also Piero della Francesca's powerful *Duke of Urbino,* warts and all.

Best loved and most reproduced among Renaissance paintings are Botticelli's haunting *Primavera* (spring) and the renowned *Birth of Venus.* Venus is said to represent "la bella Simonetta" Vespucci, mistress of luckless Giuliano de' Medici. Botticelli's lifelike but theatrical *Adoration* features Medici family portraits—Cosimo the Elder, his son Piero the Gouty, grandsons Lorenzo and Giuliano (smugly standing on the extreme left, a few years before his murder). Botticelli himself, in a yellow cloak, gazes out on the far right.

Outstanding among the 15th-century Flemish paintings is Hugo van der Goes' huge *Adoration of the Shepherds* triptych, which was painted in 1478 for the Medici's Flemish agent Tommaso Portinari. The kneeling Portinari are immortalized on its side-panels. In a sunnier, lighter vein is Ghirlandaio's *Adoration* (1487).

One room belongs to Leonardo da Vinci. See the *Baptism of Christ,* painted with his great teacher, Verrocchio. Only the background and left-hand angel were 18-year-old Leonardo's work, but enough, so the story goes, for Verrocchio to swear never to paint again. The exquisite *Annunciation,* painted around the same time, is entirely Leonardo's work, like his barely begun but dramatic *Adoration.*

---

*Because the rooms are rearranged fairly often, we have not given any numbers.

The octagonal Tribuna room, a 1589 Medici extension, symbolizes the four elements; its cupola is encrusted with mother-of-pearl representing water. The superb 17th-century inlaid stone table, specially made for the room, took 16 years to complete! See also Bronzino's portrayals of Cosimo I's Spanish wife *Eleonora of Toledo,* and his chubby smiling baby son—one of the most endearing child portraits ever painted.

The nude marble Medici *Venus,* excavated at Hadrian's Tivoli villa is thought to be a copy of a 4th-century B.C. Greek original by Praxiteles. Said to represent Phryne, notorious Athenian courtesan, it was apparently Thomas Jefferson's favourite statue, for he had a copy of it in his study!

Botticelli's renowned Birth of Venus, *commissioned to decorate the Medici's villa at Castello.*

Among German masterpieces in the Uffizi, don't miss Dürer's *Portrait of His Father* and *Adoration of the Magi;* and Cranach's life-like little portraits of *Luther,* his renegade-nun wife and a solidly Germanic *Adam and Eve.*

In the 15th century Venetian school, be sure to look for Bellini's strange, dream-like *Sacred Allegory* (about 1490).

There is only one work by the great Michelangelo in the Uffizi: a round panel, the *Holy Family,* firmly but humanly treated, his earliest known painting (1503).

Equally notable are Raphael's placid, maternal *Madonna of the Goldfinch* and a wistful self-portrait done in Florence when only 23. In Titian's room, see his voluptuous *Venus of Urbino.*

Not to be missed is Rubens' *Portrait of his Wife.* She is so glowingly alive it's sad to think she died a year after it was painted.

The Niobe Room, built to accommodate Greco-Roman statuary in the centre, is grandly 18th century. Look for two delightful pictures of children by Chardin.

Some fine Dutch landscapes and Caravaggio's splendidly decadent *Bacchus* (1589) and Rembrandt's famous *Portrait of an Old Rabbi,* as well as two self-portraits, bring this orgy of great art to an end.

Stagger into the coffee-bar just beyond, and take a well-deserved drink and rest at an outside table above the Loggia dei Lanzi.

Renaissance art seen at its harmonious best in Raphael's self-portrait. Over a dozen members of the Medici family are buried in San Lorenzo.

From San Lorenzo to San Marco

San Lorenzo

Approached from Borgo San Lorenzo, the rough, unfaced stone façade of this church looks for all the world like a Tuscan barn. Michelangelo was supposed to complete it, but never got started, and, for once, 19th-century architects didn't try to finish the job.

Florence's first entirely Renaissance church and one of Filippo Brunelleschi's earliest architectural triumphs, the building was begun in 1419 on the site of a 4th-century church.

See the town in style by horse and carriage—but negotiate fee first!

Medici money saw the project through, and Cosimo the Elder had his palace built within sight of San Lorenzo. The family arms ostentatiously adorn the ceiling.

The Medici are buried here in force. Cosimo the Elder himself is in the crypt, his father and mother in the Old Sacristy; Cosimo's two sons Piero the Gouty and Giovanni lie here, too, in a sumptuous bronze and porphyry tomb by Verrocchio; Piero's sons Lorenzo the Magnificent and the murdered Giuliano rest with their namesake cousins in Michelangelo's New Sacristy (see p. 47); the later Medici grand dukes are buried here also, as well as that giant of early Renaissance art, Donatello.

The uncluttered interior is a striking example—in an age of soaring Gothic—of new, exciting horizontal perspective effects achieved with the simplest means. Note the purity and elegance of those grey, classical *pietra serena* columns.

Cappelle Medicee (Piazza Madonna degli Aldobrandini; closed Sunday afternoons and Mondays). Once part of the Medici family church of San

Lorenzo but now separated from it, the **Cappella dei Principi** (Chapel of the Princes), a 17th-century Baroque extravaganza of multi-coloured, inlaid marble and semi-precious stones, was intended by Cosimo I as a family burial vault to end all burial vaults. The workmanship is astounding (it took three centuries to complete); the taste more doubtful. But Cosimo and family actually lie in the crypt.

The **New Sacristy** *(Sagrestia Nuova)* is what everybody *really* comes for. An amazing one-man show by Michelangelo who designed the interior and most of the sculptures; it took him more than 14 years.

Commissioned in 1520 by the future Pope Clement VII (illegitimate son of Giuliano de' Medici) as a worthy resting-place for his father and uncle Lorenzo the Magnificent, it was also to accommodate two recently-dead cousins (confusingly named Giuliano and Lorenzo).

The two more illustrious Medici are inconspicuously buried beneath Michelangelo's fine *Virgin and Child* statue, flanked by figures of Medici patron saints Cosmas and Damian (not by Michelangelo). The undistinguished cousins, ironically enough, have been immortalized by Michelangelo in two of the most famous funeral **monuments** of all time. On the right sits an idealized, warlike *Giuliano* above two splendid figures symbolizing Night and Day resting on the elegantly curved sarcophagus. The unfinished face of Day, with the visible marks of Michelangelo's chisel, somehow makes the figure all the more remarkable. Opposite, a thoughtful *Lorenzo* sits above *Dawn* and *Dusk*. The specially foreshortened effect of the upper windows give the cupola a feeling of still greater height. Statues and architecture produce an unforgettable impression.

To the left of the entrance to the church of San Lorenzo is another Michelangelo wonder, the **Biblioteca Mediceo-Laurenziana** (Laurentian Library). Commissioned by Pope Clement VII to house a precious collection of Medici books and manuscripts in 1524, opened to the public in 1571, it's probably one of the most beautiful libraries in the world. Closed Sundays.

It's hard to recapture the Medici atmosphere in the **Palazzo Medici-Riccardi** (Via Cavour, 1; closed Wednesdays), now Florence's Carabinieri-guarded prefecture. But rest awhile in a peaceful little walled garden with orange trees behind the main courtyard. Then climb up to the tiny family chapel to see Benozzo Gozzoli's fresco, the *Procession of the Magi,* that covers its walls. Painted in 1459, in warm, rich colours, it's a lavish pictorial display of everybody who was anybody in Florence—including, of course, the whole Medici clan and their supporters. The chapel remains exactly as the 15th-century Medici knew it. The ground-floor museum of Mediciana features Lorenzo's death mask, some family portraits and other works of art.

In **Chiostro dello Scalzo**

(Cloister of the Bare-footed Order, Via Cavour, 69) are scenes from St. John's life frescoed in chiaroscuro technique by 16th-century painter Andrea del Sarto. Closed for restoration.

From *Last Supper* to *Resurrection,* the best frescoes of Andrea del Castagno (1423–57), a master of vigorous forms and colours, grace the refectory of **Cenacolo di Santa Apollonia** in a former Benedictine nunnery (Via XXVII Aprile, 1). Ring for admittance.

Museo di San Marco

An old monastery re-designed by the Medici palace architect, Michelozzo, and built for the Dominicans with Medici money in 1437, this is one of Florence's most evocative attractions. (See section on MUSEUM HOURS on p. 118.)

Fra Angelico (1387–1455) lived here as a monk, and most of his finest paintings and frescoes, including the great *Deposition* altarpiece, can be seen in this museum. Off the graceful, columned cloister with its venerable cedar tree, you'll find Angelico's luminous paintings; and, in the small refectory, a vivid Ghirlandaio mural of the *Last Supper*—a favourite subject for monastery eating rooms.

Upstairs, visit the simple monks' cells, each one frescoed for religious inspiration by Fra Angelico and his pupils. His famous *Annunciation* fresco

Variations on a devout theme—one of Fra Angelico's movingly simple Annunciation scenes in San Marco.

is located in cell no. 3. At one end of the row of cells see the suite reserved for Cosimo de' Medici's meditations and, at the opposite end, that of the monastery's fiery prior and enemy of the Medici, Girolamo Savonarola. See his haunting portrait by fellow-monk Fra Bartolomeo, the religious banner he carried through Florence's streets and a painting of his execution on Piazza della Signoria.

Walk into Michelozzo's superbly proportioned colonnaded library and you'll be reminded of Fra Angelico's painted backgrounds.

The great bell placidly resting in the cloister has had a chequered career. Donated by Cosimo de' Medici and known as *la piagnona* ("great moaner"), Savonarola's puritanical supporters were nicknamed *i piagnoni* after it. It tolled to alert the monks when Savonarola's enemies came to arrest him. Spitefully condemned for this to 50 years' "exile" outside the city walls, the bell was whipped through the streets all the way to its new home.

Piazza Santissima Annunziata

Set in the most Renaissance of Florence's squares, the church of **Santissima Annunziata** deserves to be savoured in the context of its surroundings. It's best approached from the Via de' Servi (named after the Servite Order for whom the church was rebuilt).

The entire piazza was probably designed by Brunelleschi when he built the Spedale degli Innocenti (see below). Medici money backed the scheme and the church's architect, Michelozzo, stuck to Brunelleschi's original vision, ensuring the piazza's lasting harmony. Even Giambologna's bronze equestrian statue of Grand Duke Ferdinando I (1608) and the two 17th-century fountains add to the unity of the square and the feeling of spaciousness.

Beyond the church's vestibule frescoed by Andrea del Sarto and others, and immediately left of the entrance, is the important 15th-century **shrine** of the Annunziata. It shelters an old fresco that is shown only on special feast days. Said to have miraculous properties, it's been the object of pilgrimages and votive offerings for centuries.

The unusual round choir survives from the 15th century, but many of the over-ornate interior decorations date from the late 17th century.

The **Galleria dello Spedale degli Innocenti** (Piazza Santissima Annunziata, 12) contains sculptures and paintings (15th to 16th century) belonging to this, Florence's foundling hospital, which was built to Brunelleschi's design in the early 1400s. Note the series of 15th-century glazed terracotta roundels of appealing swaddled babes by Andrea della Robbia on its arched façade. Closed Mondays.

One of Italy's most important museums housed in a former grand-ducal palace the **Museo Archeologico** (Via della Colonna) boasts major ancient Egyptian and Etruscan collections. Among its highlights, the famous 6th-century-B.C. Greek *François Vase;* two remarkable Etruscan bronzes, the *Chimera* and *Arringatore* (the orator); remnants of build-

Michelangelo's original David *holds centre-stage in the Accademia.*

ings from Roman Florence. The wonderfully reconstructed Etruscan tombs in its gardens were badly damaged in the 1966 flood. Closed Mondays.

Originally an art school founded by Cosimo I, the **Galleria dell'Accademia,** the exhibition hall (Via Ricasoli, 60), was added in the 18th century for the students' benefit. Its collection of 13th–16th century Florentine School paintings is second only to the Uffizi's. There are tapestries and fine furniture, like the typical Florentine painted marriage chests. (See section on MUSEUM HOURS on p. 118.)

The gallery also boasts seven major Michelangelo sculptures, including the original **David.** Brought here from the Piazza della Signoria in 1873 to preserve it from the elements, this David—unlike its copy—is truly impressive.

The **Conservatorio Musicale Luigi Cherubini** (Via degli Alfani, 80) has an important music library, with composers' original manuscripts and a unique collection of old musical instruments started by Grand Duke Ferdinando de' Medici in the 17th century.

Stroke its nose, throw a coin—and you'll return to Florence!

Mercato Nuovo to Santa Maria Novella

The main attraction of **Mercato Nuovo** (the Straw Market) are the stalls selling leather goods, straw baskets and what-have-you (see p. 86). But don't overlook the 17th-century bronze statue of a boar, known as *Il Porcellino* (the piglet). Tradition has it that if you stroke his nose and throw a coin into the fountain, you will be sure to return to Florence. In the centre of the market is a marble circle, the Batticulo (buttock smacker), where, in the 16th century, welchers and swindlers were soundly beaten.

In the **Palazzo Davanzati** (Via Porta Rossa, 9) you can see how wealthy medieval and Renaissance Florentines really lived. A 14th-century palace with a stern exterior, its rooms are full of colour. See the lavish 14th-century, patterned *trompe l'œil* frescoes (Sala dei Pappagalli) and 15th-century furniture and paintings recreating the atmosphere of each room. Everything from toilets to kitchens, not forgetting amusing graffitti on some of the walls.

On the way to Piazza Santa Trinita, discover one of Florence's most unassuming churches, **Santi Apostoli,** situated on the Piazza del Limbo. Legend has it that Charlemagne himself built it. Inside are some pieces of flint, taken from Jerusalem's Holy Sepulchre centuries ago by a crusader member of the Pazzi family. These are used to light the fireworks for the Scoppio del Carro on Easter Sunday (see p. 28).

After the late 16th-century façade, the Gothic interior of the fine church of **Santa Trinita** comes as a complete surprise. It was built between the 13th and 15th centuries on the site of a far older church whose remains are still visible.

Look for the late 15th-century Sassetti chapel (second on the right from the chancel chapel), with scenes of St. Francis' life by Ghirlandaio. Besides the donor and his family, Lorenzo the Magnificent and his sons are also portrayed against contemporary Florentine backgrounds.

The Strozzi, the Davanzati and the Gianfigliazzi lived in the area and endowed richly frescoed chapels here. So did the Bartolini-Salimbeni family, whose exquisite, early 16th-century *palazzo* (now the French consulate) faces the church, and the Spini family, whose fortress-like 13th-century residence (now Palazzo

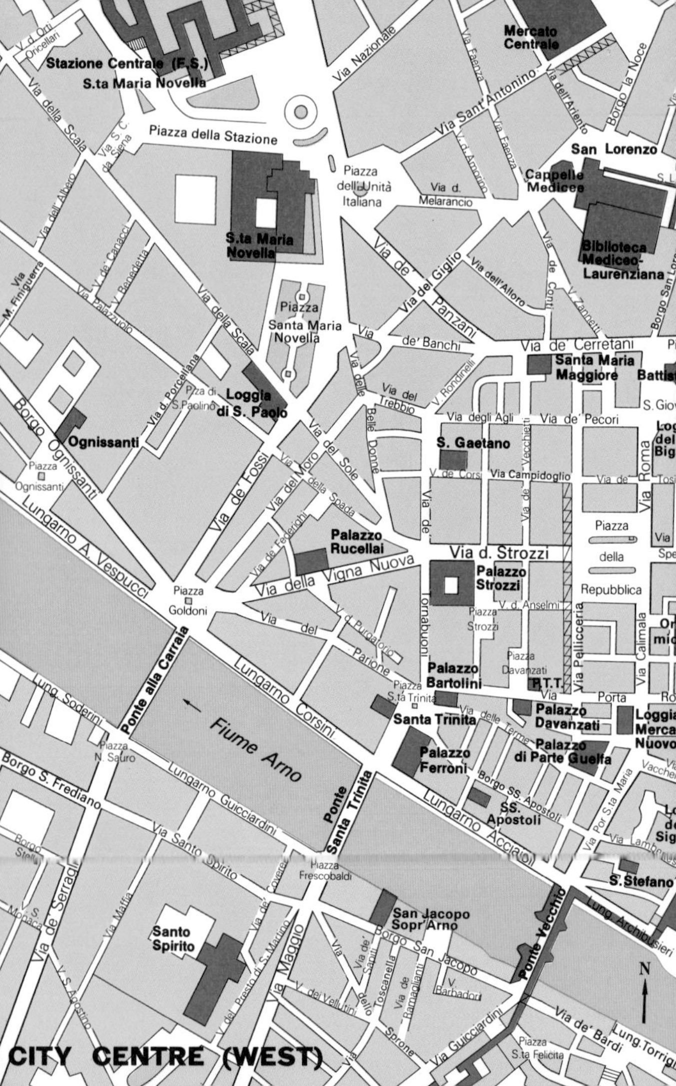

V. d. Orti Oricellari
Stazione Centrale (F.S.)
S.ta Maria Novella
Via Nazionale
Mercato Centrale
Via Faenza
Via Sant'Antonino
Via dell'Ariento
Borgo la Noce
Via della Scala
Via S. C. da Siena
Piazza della Stazione
V. d. Amorino
Via Faenza
San Lorenzo
Cappelle Medicee
Piazza dell'Unità Italiana
Via d. Melarancio
Biblioteca Mediceo-Laurenziana
Via dell'Albero
V. de' Canacci
V. Benedetta
S.ta Maria Novella
Via de' Panzani
Via del Giglio
Via dell'Alloro
Via de Conti
V. Zannetti
Borgo San Lorenzo
Via M. Finiguerra
Via Palazzuolo
Via della Scala
Piazza Santa Maria Novella
Via de' Banchi
Via de' Cerretani
Santa Maria Maggiore
Via delle Belle Donne
Via del Trebbio
V. Rondinelli
Via d. Porcellana
P.zza di S. Paolino
Loggia di S. Paolo
Via degli Agli
Via de' Pecori
Borgo Ognissanti
Ognissanti
Piazza Ognissanti
Via del Sole
S. Gaetano
Via de' Vecchietti
Via de' Fossi
Via del Moro
Via della Spada
V. de Corsi
Via Campidoglio
Via de' Tosinghi
Via Roma
Via de' Tornabuoni
Lungarno A. Vespucci
Via de' Federighi
Palazzo Rucellai
Via d. Strozzi
Piazza della Repubblica
Via della Vigna Nuova
Palazzo Strozzi
V. d. Anselmi
Piazza Strozzi
Via Pellicceria
Via Calimala
Piazza Goldoni
Via del Parione
V. d. Purgatorio
Piazza Davanzati
Ponte alla Carraia
Lungarno Corsini
Palazzo Bartolini
P.T.T.
Via Porta Rossa
Piazza S.ta Trinita
Santa Trinita
Via delle Terme
Palazzo Davanzati
Loggia Mercato Nuovo
Lung. Soderini
Fiume Arno
Palazzo Ferroni
Palazzo di Parte Guelfa
Piazza N. Sauro
Borgo S. Frediano
Lungarno Guicciardini
Ponte Santa Trinita
Borgo SS. Apostoli
SS. Apostoli
Lungarno Acciaioli
Via Por S.ta Maria
Via Lambertesca
Borgo Stella
Via Santo Spirito
Piazza Frescobaldi
S. Stefano
Via de' Serragli
V. S. Monaca
Via de' Coverelli
San Jacopo Sopr'Arno
Lung. Archibusieri
Ponte Vecchio
Santo Spirito
Via Maffia
Via del Presto di S. Martino
Via Maggio
Via de' Michelozzi
Via dello Sprone
Via de' Sapiti
Borgo San Jacopo
V. Toscanella
Via de Ramaglianti
V. Barbadori
N
V. S. Agostino
V. dei Velluti
Via Guicciardini
Via de' Bardi
Lung. Torrigiani
Piazza S.ta Felicita
CITY CENTRE (WEST)

Ferroni) stands at the corner of the piazza. The 15th-century **Palazzo Strozzi,** one of the most beautiful private residences in the whole of Florence, is nearby on Via de' Tornabuoni.

Out on the Piazza Santa Trinita stands the so-called Column of Justice. It is nothing of the kind, but rather a monument set up by Grand Duke Cosimo de' Medici to celebrate his victory over a band of exiled Florentines anxious to overthrow him and re-establish more democratic government.

Despite its fine 17th-century façade and the della Robbia glazed-terracotta relief over the doorway, **Ognissanti** (All Saints Church) actually dates from around 1250. Its builders, the Umiliati ("Humble Ones"), were an industrious monastic community who had a remarkably successful wool business. They were reputed to have been among the first to put Florence on the road to financial prosperity.

See Botticelli's *St. Augustine* and, in the refectory, the famous *The Last Supper* by Ghirlandaio, frescoes commissioned by the Vespucci family of wealthy merchants. Several family members are buried here, as indeed is Botticelli himself.

Florentines at Sea

Amerigo (1454–1512), most famous VESPUCCI of them all, went down in history as the man who gave his name to America. Banker, businessman and navigator, he crossed the Atlantic in Columbus' footsteps, touching the North American coast for the very first time. Columbus believed to the end he'd landed in Asia: Vespucci knew *he* had found a great new continent. America deserves his name.

Over 20 years later, yet another Florentine navigator, GIOVANNI DA VERRAZZANO, searching for the legendary North-West Passage to Asia discovered New York Bay.

Santa Maria Novella

One of Florence's greatest monastic churches, Santa Maria Novella was designed by Dominican architects in the mid-13th century. A Dominican community still resides in its precincts. An unlikely setting for the beginning and end of Boccaccio's *Decameron!*

The bold 15th-century inlaid marble front, begun in Gothic style a century earlier, was completed to Renaissance taste by architect Leon Battista Alberti, also responsible for the graceful Palazzo Rucellai nearby. The Medici *didn't* pay for this church, and the Rucellai donors—to make sure their generosity wouldn't go unnoticed—had their name put up in large Roman letters under the top cornice.

Walk through the mystic gloom of the 328-foot-long nave to a cluster of richly frescoed family chapels around the altar. See the chancel behin the altar with its *Scenes fron the Lives of the Virgin an St. John* **frescoes** by Ghirlandaio and his pupils, paid for b the wealthy Tornabuoni famil (coin-operated floodlamps illuminate them). Don't miss th splendidly inlaid wooden choir stalls.

Ghirlandaio, Florence's to "social" painter in the lat 15th century, peopled the frescoes with Tornabuonis—on of which was Lorenzo the Mag

Obelisk in front of Santa Maria Novella was horse-race turnpost.

nificent's mother—all dressed in the latest fashions.

To the altar's right, a Strozzi family chapel colourfully frescoed by Filippino Lippi, son of the famous painter Fra Filippo; next to it a Bardi chapel with 14th-century frescoes. The Gondi chapel to the left of the altar contains a Brunelleschi altar **crucifix** (his answer to Donatello's "peasant" in Santa Croce; see p. 64); and, on the extreme left, a Strozzi chapel with 14th-century **frescoes** of the *Last Judgement, Heaven* and *Hell*—its donors, of course, depicted in Heaven!

Most striking of all is Masaccio's **Trinity** (c. 1427) on the wall of the left aisle. Amazing for its uncanny spatial depth, the fresco sets the crucifixion, with kneeling husband-and-wife donors, in a purely Renaissance architectural setting, dramatically breaking away from everything that had been painted before. You'll quite likely see someone praying or lighting a votive candle in front of it, just as you may see and hear mass being said in one of those frescoed chapels. It's all part of the beauty of a city whose life, art and history are forever intertwined.

To the left of the church lie part of the surviving monastery buildings (nominal entry fee). The great 14th-century **cloister** with its three giant cypresses is a haven of tranquillity after the noisy piazza. From here you can admire the church's graceful 14th-century campanile at close range. Known as the Chiostro Verde, meaning green cloister for the tint of frescoes once painted here by Paolo Uccello, it leads to the refectory (where some detached surviving frescoes are now kept), to a smaller cloister and to the famous, impressively vaulted chapter-house, the **Cappellone degli Spagnoli** (Spanish Chapel), named in honour of Cosimo I's Spanish wife, Eleonora of Toledo. Gigantic 14th-century frescoes cover its four walls. The artist incorporated a picture of the Duomo with cupola—60 years before its actual completion.

Votive altar in S. Maria Novella.

Bargello, Santa Croce and San Miniato

Museo Nazionale (Bargello)

This forbidding-looking fortress at Via del Proconsolo, 4 is to sculpture what the Uffizi is to painting. Florence's first city hall and one of its earliest public buildings (begun about 1250), it served as the seat of magistrates *(podestà)* responsible for law and order and

later housed the Captain of Justice *(bargello)*, 16th-century equivalent of a police commissioner.

Men were imprisoned, tortured and executed here. Its outer walls were decorated with life-like effigies of traitors and criminals hung by the neck or by one foot—horrific warnings to would-be wrongdoers, often by the best artists. Botticelli himself did the Pazzi conspirators in 1478.

The stern courtyard, softened by the brownish hues of its *pietra forte,* is covered with stone plaques bearing the arms of successive *podestà*. Just off it lies the **Sala Michelangelo e scultura Fiorentina del cinquecento** (Hall of Michelangelo and 16th-Century Florentine Sculptors). Note wall marks recording the 1966 flood level —9½ feet.

Michelangelo was 21 when he finished his early masterpiece *The Drunken Bacchus,* beautifully god-like but just a shade unsteady on his legs! He sculpted the marble *Virgin and Child (Pitti Tondo)* eight years later, while working on his famous *David.* And for a portrait of the artist, see Daniele da Volterra's bronze bust of Michelangelo at his sourest. Don't miss several Cellini bronzes, his handsome bust of Cosimo I de' Medici and the small bronze model for his *Perseus* in the Loggia dei Lanzi.

A 14th-century stone staircase leads to an arcaded loggia on the first floor, where you'll see Giambologna's bronze *Mercury* and his impressionistic series of bronze birds displayed along the parapet. All were garden or fountain decorations for the Medici.

The first floor holds sumptuous, largely Medici-owned collections, ranging from Italian and Tuscan ceramics and old Murano glass, to French Limoges enamels and astonishing sea-shells chiselled like cameos. In the 14th-century chapel's frescoes, painted by a pupil of Giotto, look for the sharp-featured man behind the kneeling figure on the right—supposedly Dante.

If you see nothing else, see the **Great Hall,** which contains the spirit of early Renaissance Florence. Donatello's sturdily human *St. George* (1416), embedded in a huge expanse of blank wall, dominates the high-vaulted room. Commissioned by the armourers' guild as their contribution to the exterior decorations of Orsanmichele (see p. 32), it's generally held to be the first great sculptural breakthrough of the Renaissance.

Donatello's bronze *David,* the first Renaissance nude statue, once graced the Medici palace courtyard. In contrast to the "modern" feeling of the *St.George, David* has an antique sensuality about it, while his delightful bronze *Amore* (cupid) is positively Roman in style. More personal and dramatic are the two marble versions of a youthful and an older *St.John the Baptist.*

Be sure to look at Ghiberti's and Brunelleschi's original bronze models *(The Sacrifice of Abraham)* for the Baptistery doors competition of 1401, clearly a close contest. Don't neglect several sensitive portrait busts of the marble and glazed terracotta reliefs of madonnas. Two of them by Luca della Robbia, white on blue ground, are purity itself.

On the second floor, see Verrocchio's bronze *David* (about 1471); his 19-year-old pupil Leonardo da Vinci is said to have been the model.

Opposite the Bargello you will see the church known as the **Badia Fiorentina,** with its graceful bell-tower part Romanesque, part Gothic. Go inside

Baptistery without the Ghiberti doors shown on old wedding chest.

for a moment to admire Filippino Lippi's delightful *Madonna Appearing to St. Bernard,* on the left as you enter.

Casa Buonarroti (Via Ghibellina, 70; see section on MUSEUM HOURS on p. 117) was bought by bachelor Michelangelo for his closest relatives. It contains letters, drawings, portraits of the great man, plus a collection of 17th-century historical paintings highlighting his long life.

See his famous sculptured relief, the *Madonna of the Staircase,* done before the artist was 16. His astonishing *Battle of Lapiths and Centaurs* dates from around the same time.

Santa Croce

With its vast expanse of open piazza, Santa Croce became one of the city's social and political hubs. Lorenzo and Giuliano de' Medici staged lavish jousts here; and half-starving but defiant Florentines turned out in force during the 1530 siege of their city to watch or take part in a special soccer game.

Santa Croce started off in 1228 as a modest chapel, erected in true Franciscan fashion right in the middle of a working district. Arnolfo di Cambio, the Duomo's architect, drew up the plans for a larger church, which was completed in the 14th century. Its interior is grandly Gothic; the façade, 19th-century Gothic.

Within are buried some of the most illustrious figures in Italian history. Biographer Vasari designed Michelangelo's tomb (first on the right-hand wall). Smuggled out of Rome in a packing-case, his body was given the finest funeral in Florentine memory. The seated statues on the monument represent Sculpture, Painting and Architecture—three domains in which he remains immortal.

The next tomb, Dante's, has no body, much to the Florentine's dismay. His real grave is in Ravenna where he died and the Ravennese have never given in to Florentine pleas for its return. Further along you'll spot Machiavelli's (1469–1527) tomb. Civil servant, political theorist, historian and playwright, his book *The Prince*—advice on how to rule a state—has made his name, fairly or not, a synonym of hypocrisy and devilish cunning.

Further on lies a non-Florentine but a great Italian, Rossini (1792–1868), composer of the beautiful opera *The Barber of Seville*.

Opposite Michelangelo is the Pisan genius Galileo (1564 to 1642) who perfected the earliest astronomical telescope. On the same side lies Lorenzo Ghiberti, creator of the Baptistery doors.

As you walk around this great church, you'll be stepping over any number of fascinating 13th- and 14th-century tomb slabs set in the floor, their effigies badly worn but still visible. Santa Croce was always a popular burial place.

As you progress up the nave, take note of the splendid late 15th-century marble pulpit sculptures with scenes from the

The pure, geometric design of Brunelleschi's Pazzi chapel influenced early Renaissance style.

life of St. Francis and, further on the right, Donatello's sensitive *Annunciation* in grey *pietra serena*. See also a coloured wooden **Christ** on the cross by Donatello. His friend Brunelleschi mockingly called it "a peasant" (see p. 57).

The honeycomb of family chapels on either side of the high altar contains a wealth of frescoes from the 14th to the 16th centuries. Immediately to the right of the altar in the **Bardi Chapel,** you'll find Giotto's finest, most moving paintings: scenes from the life and death of St. Francis, done around 1320.

The adjoining chapel, containing Giotto frescoes of the life of St. John, belonged to the Bardis' partners, the Peruzzi, rich bankers who gave most of the money for the imposing sacristy. Not long afterwards the Peruzzi were ruined by Edward III of England's "bankruptcy" (see p. 14).

If the Pazzi family has an infamous reputation, it's more than redeemed by the small **chapel** bearing their name. One of the earliest, most exquisite Renaissance religious interiors, it was designed for the Pazzi family by Brunelleschi in 1430. Reached by an entry beside the church, you'll see it facing you across a cloister.

The Santa Croce museum contains frescoes and statues removed from the church, but its proudest treasure is Cimabue's massive 13th-century **painted cross,** almost destroyed in the 1966 flood.

Walk into the beautiful second cloister and try to imagine it with the flood waters so high you could only see the tops of its arches.

Museo della Fondazione Horne (Via dei Benci, 6; see p. 118 for museum's hours) is a superb little 15th-century palace, restored, lived-in and bequeathed to Florence in 1916 by an Englishman, H. P. Horne. Within you will see his priceless collection of paintings, drawings, sculptures, ceramics, furniture, coins and medals and old household utensils.

The **Museo di Storia della Scienza** (Museum of the History of Science; Piazza dei Giudici, 1) has a fascinating collection of scientific instruments and unusual curiosities, from Galileo's telescopes and (preserved) middle finger to Torricelli's original "tube" and an Edison phonograph. A change from pure culture.

Green-and-white San Miniato is residence of Benedictine monks

San Miniato and Piazzale Michelangelo

A pleasant walk or bus ride (No. 13 from Piazza dei Giudici) will take you up to the Piazzale Michelangelo with its incomparable **panoramic view** over the city and to the church of San Miniato nearby.

St. Miniato, an early Christian martyred in the 3rd century A.D., is said to have carried his severed head up here from Florence and set it down where the church was later built. All-too-often neglected by tourists in a hurry, San Miniato is one of Florence's most romantic churches and a favourite for weddings.

Rebuilt in the early 11th century, it's a remarkable example of Florentine-style Romanesque architecture. The sight of its superb green and white marble façade glinting golden in the late afternoon sun is something you'll long remember.

The interior has all the splendour of a Byzantine basilica, with its wealth of richly inlaid marble to its mosaic decorations. Note the extraordinary embroidery effect of the nave's

Admire yet another David while taking in the view from Piazzale.

13th-century marble floor—a bit like the bridal train of some fairy-tale princess. See also the fine 15th-century chapel and tomb of the Cardinal of Portugal (who died in Florence), and some well-preserved 14th-century frescoes in the sacristy.

Relax awhile on the great terrace and enjoy the view. Or adjourn to the little shop-cum-bar run by resident Benedictine-Olivetans, where a charming, white-robed father will sell you anything from honey and herb liqueurs to a postcard or a coke.

If it weren't for Michelangelo, San Miniato might not be here today. During the 1530 siege, when the Emperor Charles V's Spanish gunners pounded away at the city, San Miniato was well within range and might have been blown to pieces. But Michelangelo, in charge of the Florentine defences, had a temporary fortress hastily built around the site, while protecting the bell tower with mattresses and wool bales. The fortress (now enclosing a cemetery) was later made permanent. A similar 16th-century fortification, the Forte Belvedere, can be seen to the left.

Pitti Palace to Santa Maria del Carmine

Cross over the Arno on the oldest bridge in Florence, **Ponte Vecchio,** the only one spared in the last war. The present construction, complete with overhanging boutiques, dates back to 1345. Vasari built the covered passageway above the shops

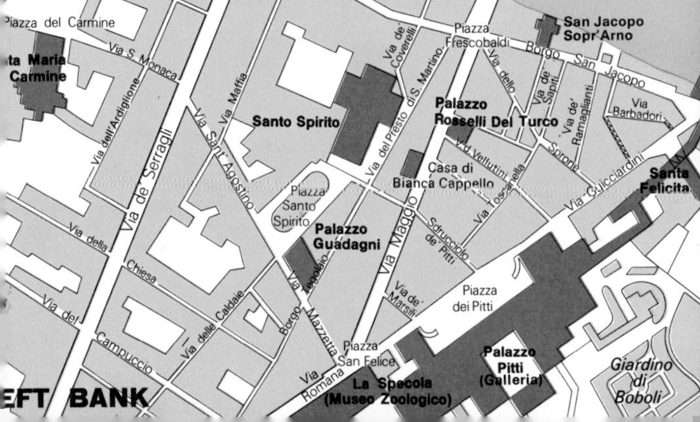

› that Grand Duke Cosimo ·' Medici could go from the ·tti to the Uffizi without get- ng wet.

From the double terrace in ıe middle, admire the elegant, ›ftly curved arches of **Ponte anta Trinita.** Destroyed in ›44, the bridge was carefully ·constructed, exactly as Am- ıannati had built it in the 5th century.

'alazzo Pitti

›fficial Medici and grand-du- ıl residence since 1549, royal ılace of united Italy from 365 to 1871, it's another lorentine "must". The Pitti ılace comprises museums and ılleries, plus some ten acres f ornate Italian gardens and ıany charming surprises. (All ıuseum hours are listed sep- ·rately on p. 118.)

In the sumptuous **Galleria alatina,** you'll feel more like collector's guest than a tour- t. Priceless paintings hang ›ur-high against a lavish gilt, uccoed and frescoed décor. hey've all been left just as the ıst Medici and later grand ukes placed them, according › personal preference rather ıan any historical sequence.

There are splendid works ere by Botticelli, Raphael, itian, Rubens, Velazquez and lurillo, exhibited in grandiose halls, some of which bear the names of their décor (the "Hall of the Iliad" has frescoed scenes from Homer's epic). If time is short, here's what not to miss.

Raphaels abound: make sure to see his *Pregnant Women,* his incisive portrait of *Cardinal Inghirami;* and the famous round painting, the *Madonna of the Chair.* The enigmatic, romantic *Veiled Woman* was, in fact, Raphael's mistress and favourite model.

The "Hall of Mars" is dominated by Rubens' powerful allegory the *Consequences of War,* one of the most striking 17th-century Baroque paintings. See also his *Four Philosophers,* with a ruddy-faced Rubens himself standing on the left.

Most memorable of several fine Titians are *The Magdalen,* the searching *Portrait of a Young Englishman* and *The Concert.*

Look for Fra Filippo Lippi's sensitive *Virgin and Child* (1452), the Virgin's own birth painted in the background.

Though each room is more heavily decorated than the last, Room 29, covered from floor to ceiling with 17th-century frescoes, tops them all for sheer extravagance.

In the 16 sumptuously decorated rooms of the **Museo degli Argenti** (Museum of

Gems), admire some of the Medici's most cherished jewels, cameos, gold, silver, crystal and ivory objects, furniture and porcelain. Truly priceless is Lorenzo the Magnificent's personal collection of 16 exquisite vases in semi-precious stones. The room they're displayed in is the biggest surprise of all: its 17th-century architectural frescoes give you a dizzying, but perfect, optical illusion of extra height and depth; a red-cloaked Lorenzo appears in three of the allegorical murals.

The best of 19th- and 20th-century Italian art, especially Tuscan painting, can be seen in the **Galleria d'Arte Moderna** (Gallery of Modern Art). Discover the exciting Macchiaioli ("blotch-painters"), Tuscany's own Impressionist movement of the 1860s. Look out for paintings by Fattori and Signorini.

Museo delle Carrozze has two rooms of shiny, elegant state coaches. The **Appartamenti Monumentali** (Royal Apartments), a sort of mini-Versailles, were first inhabited by the Medici, later by Italy's royal House of Savoy.

The Palazzo della Meridiana at the south-west corner of the Pitti Palace is given over to the **Collezione Contini Bonacossi,** with its renowned old master paintings, exquisite fu niture and ceramics.

Entrance is free to the **Gia dino di Boboli** (open daily, a.m. to 7 p.m. in summer an Italian pleasure-garden c cypress- and hedge-lined a leys and arbours filled with u usual statuary, lodges, grotto and fountains. Originally quarry where the Pitti's hug stone blocks were extracte the park was built for Cosim I's nature-loving consort Ele nora of Toledo.

The Boboli's highlights i clude a deliciously fat, turtl riding, marble dwarf, Cosim I's court jester; the Grot Grande (near the *palazzo*'s le entrance); the Amphitheat and a fine glimpse of Florenc the Casino del Cavalier housing the Museo delle Po cellane, a fine porcelain co lection; the Vasca del Nettun and unique Piazzale dell'Is lotto, an idyllic island, fountai greenery and statue ensembl

Santo Spirito

A monastic church of the Au gustinian order dating back t the 13th century, Santo Spirit was totally re-designed by Bru nelleschi and built in the sec ond half of the 15th centur after his death.

From its unfinished, unusu ally bare, but dramatic exterio

ɔu'll step into a masterpiece f Renaissance architectural armony. Thirty-eight elegant de altars line the walls, slender rey-stone columns with Conthian capitals and an interlay of arches give the impreson of tremendous depth. The djoining cloister is a 17thntury effort.

Next to the church, in the riginal monastery refectory, e the impressive 14th-cenry frescoes of the *Last Supper* nd *Crucifixion,* and the fine edieval and Renaissance ulptures of the **Museo della ondazione Romano.**

The Augustinians once ran hospital, where young Michelngelo came–with the assent of e prior–to perfect his knowldge of anatomy by dissecting e bodies of dead patients.

anta Maria del Carmine

Mecca of artistic pilgrimage, is unpretentious church shelrs some of the most momenɔus **frescoes** ever painted. ommissioned by the Branacci family, Masaccio and his eacher Masolino worked from 423 to 1427 on fresco decoraions for their chapel here. Masolino's own work is strikng enough but Masaccio's *Triute Money* and the *Expulsion f Adam and Eve from the arden of Eden* lift painting to a completely new plane. His feeling for light and space, his dramatically stage-set figures, the concreteness of their forms are little short of an inspired miracle. Nothing of the kind had been painted before; the Renaissance had come to stay. Masaccio died at 27 before completing his commission.

Florentine artists young and old arrived in never-ending streams to marvel at and learn from his work. Michelangelo himself came as a pupil to sketch the figures. It was here, so the story goes, that Pietro Torrigiani, a fellow-student, broke Michelangelo's nose, goaded by the latter's taunts at his clumsy copying. Torrigiani, fearing Medici retribution for damaging their young protégé, fled abroad, eventually ending up in London where he sculpted Henry VII's ton in Westminster Abbey!

If Masaccio's paintings a miraculous, a miracle sav them from destruction wh the church was gutted by fi in the 18th century. The Bra cacci chapel and a small pa of the main building were t only things saved.

Visit Fiesole's Roman ruins a time of day; a sunny morning best for the Masaccio fresco

Excursions

Many travel agencies offer a wide choice of conducted or unconducted coach tours. The tourist office (see p. 122) also organizes several off-beat local tours—the finest Florentine villa gardens from April to June, nearby vineyards, farms and wine-cellars in September and October.

Regional and long-distance bus lines (see p. 123) cover the whole of Tuscany, while city buses are useful for shorter excursions. Here are a few suggestions less than an hour from Florence by car or bus.

Nearby Attractions

Reached by a winding, villa-bordered road, **Fiesole** (No. 7 bus from Piazza San Marco) is a refreshing little town, pleasant to explore or eat at in the evening, with wonderful views over Florence and the Arno Valley. This former Etruscan hill stronghold has a splendidly situated camping site.

If you can, stop off on the way to see the exquisite **Badia Fiesolana** (signposted to the left), originally Fiesole's cathedral, rebuilt with Medici money in the 15th century.

Apart from wall fragments, Fiesole bears hardly a trace of

the Etruscans, but the Roman ruins are impressive. Off the main piazza lies the well-preserved **Roman theatre.** Built around 100 B.C. and still in use today, it seats some 2,500 spectators. See the Roman bath and temple remains and a small but interesting Archaeological Museum.

Completed in the 13th century, **San Romolo** cathedral has a Byzantine atmosphere within. Its aggressively Tuscan stone turret, visible for miles around, dates back to 1213.

Don't miss a steep but picturesque walk (left of the main piazza) up to **San Francesco** church and its mini-monastery. The views on the way are memorable and the monastery, with its tiny, peaceful cloisters, enchanting.

If you've time, visit Fiesole's Museo Bandini for a well-dis-

Flowering gorse enlivens Tuscan tableau of greenery and vineyards.

played collection of furniture and 14th-century paintings.

A longer way round to Fiesole with a more countrified landscape and still more sights, passes through the village of SETTIGNANO (No. 10 bus from Piazza San Marco), where the baby Michelangelo was put out to nurse—with a stonemason's wife!

Pine liqueur is still distilled in the 13th-century Servite monastery of MONTESENARIO. Breathtaking views over the Arno Valley and surrounding hills from the monastery's terrace.

On the road to SESTO FIORENTINO, visit two grand Medici domiciles, **Villa della Petraia** (closed Mondays) and **Villa di Castello,** with their gardens, fountains and statuary. Just outside Sesto (at Quinto, along the Via Fratelli Rosselli), you'll find a perfectly preserved, remarkably evocative Etruscan tomb, La Montagnola (the Mound).

Another impressive Medici villa is at **Poggio a Caiano** (ring for admittance; closed Mondays). The great hall is richly frescoed with 16th-century allegories especially commemorating Lorenzo the Magnificent who originally bought the place. It's now a pleasant setting for plays and concerts.

Founded in the 14th century and still an active monastery, **Certosa del Galluzzo** (ring for admittance) has some fine frescoes and paintings. Taste or buy the monks' own liqueur, distilled on the spot.

A fine country route leads to a peaceful, centuries' old market town, **Impruneta:** specially interesting in September and October for its famous fairs and various folkloric events. Don't miss the two fine cloisters adjoining the Basilica of Santa Maria dell'Impruneta.

Pisa

The Leaning Tower-cathedral-baptistery trio defies description. The **Piazza del Duomo,** also appropriately known as the Piazza dei Miracoli (the Square of Miracles) is a miracle of human achievement. The **Duomo** was begun around 1063 and finished by 1118 (its fine bronze doors are also 12th century); the **Battistero** took from the 12th to 14th centuries to complete (its acoustics are superb); and the world-famous **bell-tower** with an accidental lean, as beautiful and delicate as carved ivory, was built during the same period. Feel no qualms about climbing up for a fine view. According to the experts the Leaning Tower isn't

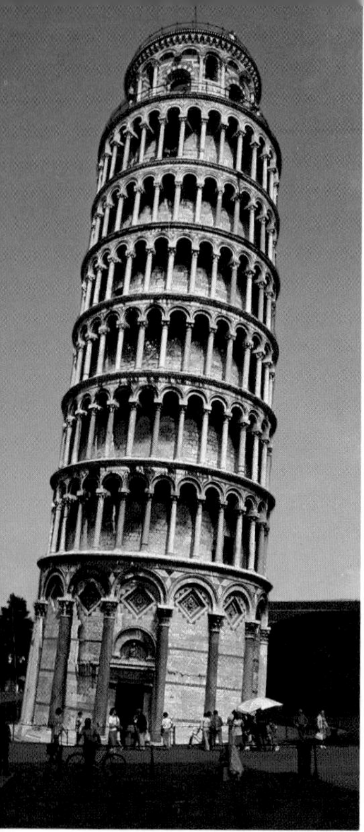

Pisa's tower permitted Galileo to test the principles of gravity.

due to fall for quite a few years, but you'll have to adapt to the slight change in angle!

Behind these mighty monuments lies the walled-in **Camposanto,** a unique 13th-century cloister-like cemetery whose entire walls are covered with remarkable 14th–15th-century frescoes, some by Benozzo Gozzoli.

It's hard to believe today, but Pisa was once the River Arno's estuary (now at Marina di Pisa, 6½ miles away). A flourishing sea-port colonized by the Greeks, settled by the Etruscans, then the Romans, it had become a rich, powerful naval republic by the 12th century, boasting one of Italy's earliest universities. Long desired and fought over as an outlet to the sea by envious Florence, the city was forcibly grabbed in 1406. Yet only 15 years later its harbour lay silted-up and useless!

Pisa is well worth exploring for its numerous fine churches, palaces, picturesque streets and Museo Nazionale di San Matteo (on Lungarno Mediceo).

You can reach Pisa by train or on a half-day conducted tour. If you have time, visit the historic city of **Pistoia,** with its harmonious Piazza del Duomo, the remarkable silver altar of San Iacopo in the cathedral and its elegant, octagonal baptistery. In **Prato,** known for its beautiful cathedral, see the exterior pulpit by Donatello and Michelozzo and the choir frescoes by Filippo Lippi.

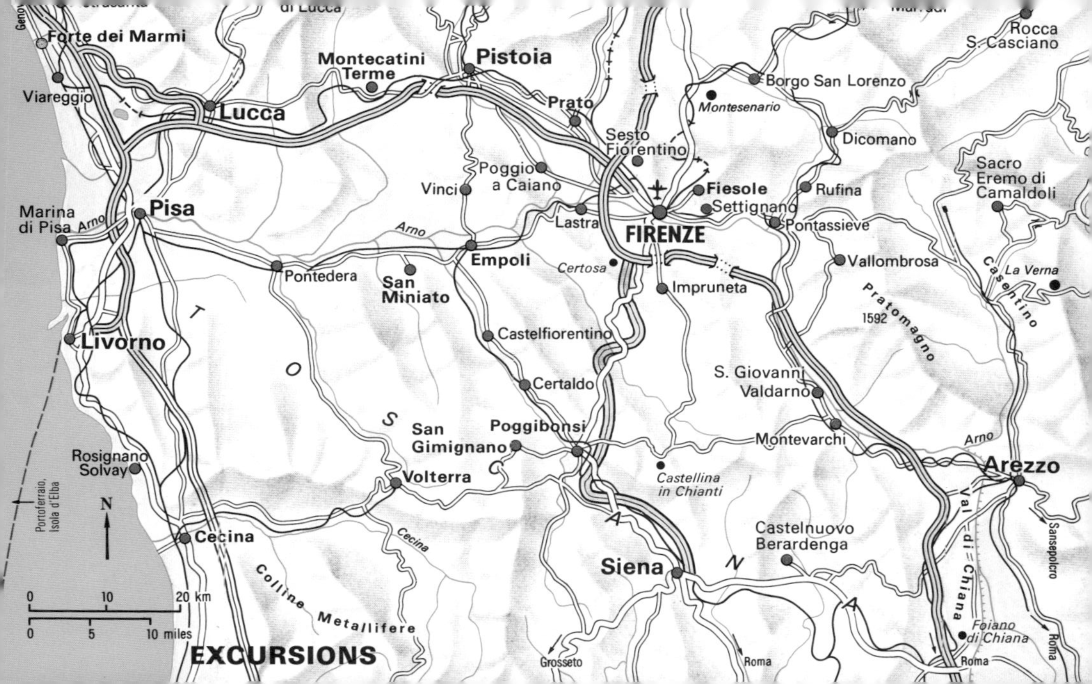
Forte dei Marmi
Viareggio
Lucca
Montecatini Terme
Pistoia
Prato
Sesto Fiorentino
Montesenario
Borgo San Lorenzo
Rocca S. Casciano
Dicomano
Sacro Eremo di Camaldoli
Rufina
Fiesole
Settignano
Pontassieve
Poggio a Caiano
Vinci
Marina di Pisa
Arno
Pisa
Lastra
FIRENZE
Empoli
Certosa
Vallombrosa
Casentino
La Verna
Pontedera
San Miniato
Impruneta
Pratomagno
1592
Livorno
Castelfiorentino
S. Giovanni Valdarno
Certaldo
San Gimignano
Poggibonsi
Montevarchi
Arezzo
Rosignano Solvay
Volterra
Castellina in Chianti
Val di Chiana
Portoferraio, Isola d'Elba
N
Cecina
Castelnuovo Berardenga
Sansepolcro
Siena
TOSCANA
Colline Metallifere
0 10 20 km
0 5 10 miles
Foiano di Chiana
Grosseto
Roma
EXCURSIONS

Siena and San Gimignano

Not to be missed for their incomparable medieval atmosphere, you could spend an entire holiday exploring these two cities and the region.

As you approach **Siena** along a road cut through a succession of undulating ruddy-brown hills, you'll understand how the colour "burnt sienna" got its name. The city itself, contrasting with Florence's browns and greys, is a wonderful marriage of brick and stone—all rich reds and warm pinks.

Imposing Gothic architecture prevails everywhere, from the early 14th-century Palazzo Pubblico and its graceful, slender Torre del Mangia, to the cathedral and the many fine *palazzi.*

The huge, sloping, shell-shaped **Piazza del Campo,** where the exciting Palio horse-race takes place every summer, has all the aristocratic grandeur of the Ghibelline city that Siena was—and secretly still is. Traditionally founded by the family of Remus (whose twin Romulus founded Rome), proudest, most stubbornly independent of Tuscan cities, it only fell under Florentine sway in 1555.

In the **Palazzo Pubblico** se Simone Martini's giant fres coes, the *Maestà* (1315)* an the *Condottiero Guidoriccio d Fogliano* on his richly caparis oned horse (1328); note als Ambrogio Lorenzetti's impres sive fresco cycle *Good and Ba Government* (1339), the larges painting of the Middle Age on a non-religious theme.

---

*Authenticity recently disputed.

Walk through picturesquely winding streets to the great Gothic **cathedral** with its striking black-and-white horizontally striped exterior—an echo of the city's arms. See its expanse of inlaid marble floor, its splendid sculptured pulpit and Pinturicchio's colourful historical frescoes in the adjoining Piccolomini Library. And, by all means, don't overlook the **cathedral museum** with Duccio's splendid *Maestà* (1308).

Continue on past the house where, in the 14th century, the city's patroness, St. Catharine of Siena, was born, to the Basilica of San Domenico where her head is preserved. And, still further, visit the impressive church of San Francesco with its Lorenzetti frescoes and the oratory dedicated to another city patron, San Bernardino.

Siena's richly decorated, marble-covered cathedral dominates town.

The nearby 13th-century Palazzo Tolomei (Via Banchi di Sopra) is a magnificent example of private medieval architecture.

Siena also boasts an important art gallery, the **Pinacoteca** (housed in the Palazzo Buonsignori), exhibiting the finest artists of the Siennese school, and an interesting Archives Museum (Palazzo Piccolomini). But don't neglect some souvenir shopping or that famous *panforte* (see p. 84).

Renowned for its universit (13th century) and its Chi International Music Academ (concerts from July to Sep tember), Siena is also a majc linguistics centre—appropria tely perhaps, since the pure Italian is said to be spoke here.

It's worth going out of you way to see the **Palio,** a hors race run round the piazza i July and August (see p. 88 Try to reserve a seat in a stan or a place on a balcony, as th crush and excitement down o the *campo* can be harrowing After a colourful, stately pro cession of pages, men-at-arms knights and flag-tossers of th city wards *(contrade)* in th most convincing 15th-centur costumes you're ever likely t see, 10 fiercely competing bare back riders race round the piaz za for the coveted Palio— painted silken standard. As yo watch this violent spectacle you'll feel you are taking a ste back into the Renaissance.

The walled medieval tow of **San Gimignano** is one of th most evocative and picturesqu in Italy. Strategically perche on a hill, it looks even highe because of its 15 stone towers At one time there were 72 o them. It was a matter of pres tige to build the tallest towe possible. The town fell unde

‑lorentine sway in the 14th ·entury.

Stroll through streets and quares little changed since)ante himself came here as a ‑lorentine envoy in 1300. See he 12th-century **Collegiata** hurch, filled with impressive rescoes, including a fearsome 4th-century *Last Judgement* nd the *Martyrdom of St. Se-astian* by Benozzo Gozzoli.)on't miss the chapel of Santa ‑ina decorated with Ghirlan-laio's over-elegant frescoes.)nly 15 when she died, this 13th-century mystic was adopted as one of the town's patron saints.

See San Gimignano: living, 14th-entury town preserved intact.

Be sure to visit the 13th–14th-century **Palazzo del Popolo,** with its 177-foot-high tower, its superb little courtyard and unusual frescoes of hunting and courtly love scenes.

Walk up to the **Rocca** or citadel and you'll enjoy a splendid panorama over the town and the valley below. In the 13th-century church of Sant'Agostino, see the fresco in the choir by Benozzo Gozzoli of *Scenes from the Life of St. Augustine,* full of everyday details.

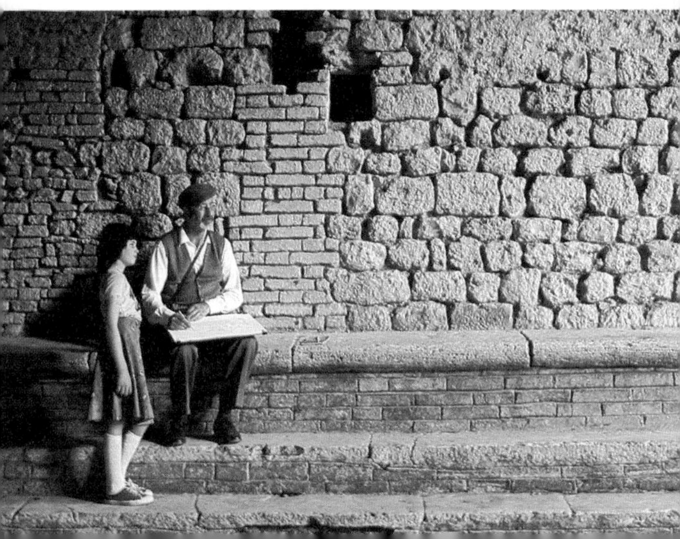

What to Do

Shopping

Shopping attractions compete with the sights for tourists' attention—and deserve all the attention they get. Window-shopping is a pleasure in itself. Fashion boutiques catch the eye along smart, expensive Via de' Tornabuoni and Via de' Calzaiuoli; jewellery, silverware, chinaware and leather shops outdo each other in lavish and original displays; colourfu merchandise is stacked ten fee high on souvenir market stall And almost anywhere yo shop, English is understood

Shops and department store are open from 8.30 or 9 a.m until 1 p.m., and from 4 unti 8 p.m. From June 15 to Sep tember 15 all shops close o Saturday afternoons (on Mon day morning the rest of th year). Hairdressers close year round on Mondays; food shop on Wednesdays.

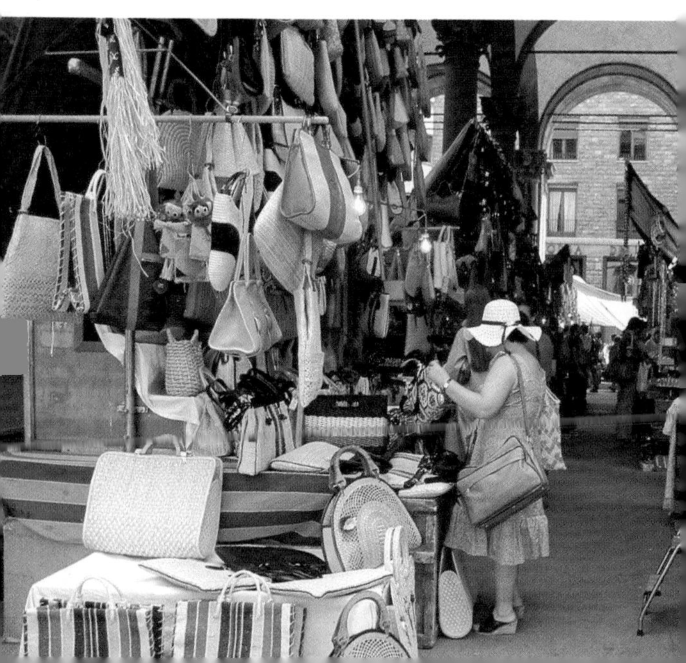

Best Buys

Fashion. Florentine designers share the limelight with Paris, Rome and London. Exclusive dress or coat models are pricey but still far cheaper than they would be at home. There's always a marvellous selection of smaller designer items like blouses, scarves and belts.

Leather. Part of the fashion scene, you'll see it everywhere. Its tell-tale smell around San Lorenzo and especially Santa Croce will lead you to leather factories where you're shown anything from handbags to wallets and bookmarks being made or finished. There's no obligation to buy.

Don't miss the leather school tucked away behind Santa Croce's sacristy in former Franciscan monk's cells. See apprentices from all over the world cutting, tooling, stamp-

Basketfuls of choices await the shopper in Florence straw-market.

ing traditional motifs. A tempting selection of their work is on sale.

The best buys are gloves, belts, purses, wallets and boxes of all shapes and sizes. Handbags are tempting but almost always expensive, shop and market prices varying little here. As a free bonus you can usually have your initials stamped in gold on any purchase.

Gold and silver. Both can be surprisingly cheap in Florence. Creative gold jewellery is expensive, but simpler items like gold or silver charms are very reasonable. You'll want to window-shop along the Ponte Vecchio with its centuries'-old jewellery boutiques, each window more tempting than the last. You won't fail to be impressed by what Florentine designers and craftsmen still produce.

The work of Florentine silversmiths, sometimes inspired by ancient motifs, is invariably beautiful and practical. Look for pill-boxes, napkin rings, photo frames, cruet sets, sugar bowls and candlesticks.

Ceramics and glassware. High quality but expensive table china, ceramic ornaments and innumerable statuettes exist for every taste, largely produced at nearby Sesto Fiorentino. Attractive functional glassware, often very cheap, comes from Empoli or Pisa.

Inlays and mosaics. A Florentine speciality, the art of wood inlay or *intarsio* reached sublime heights in the Renaissance. By the late 16th century semi-precious stones were often used in inlays; the craft still flourishes. You'll see impressive modern examples for sale in Lungarno Torrigiani, Via Guicciardini and Piazza Santa Croce. Larger items like tables are inevitably expensive; small naïve, framed "pictures" of birds, flowers, Tuscan landscapes or views of Florence are charming curiosities and comparatively cheap.

If budding Cellinis are hard to find in Florence today, skilful artisans are not: those colourful, delicate glass mosaic brooches, pendants, bracelets and rings you see everywhere are made at home by armies of patient Florentine women. With no two items identical they're unquestionably the cheapest, best value-for-money trinkets.

To eat and drink. The sweet-toothed should take or send home succulent Italian candied chestnuts; a selection of nutty *torrone* (nougat); delicious ready-boxed biscuits from Siena or the famous Sienese *panforte,* a rich, chewy mixture

of nuts and spiced candied fruits. And don't leave without one of those quaint aromatic monastery liqueurs or a genuine *fiasco* of Chianti to help you remember it all by.

Antiques and Repros

Antiques have been prized in Florence for over five centuries: a major international antique fair is now held biennially at the Palazzo Strozzi (September–October).

Antique shops cluster mainly around Borgo Ognissanti and San Jacopo, Via della Vigna Nuova and della Spada. Specializing largely in furniture, paintings and decorations, none of them are cheap. Bric-à-brac and knicknacks are virtually non-existent.

Flea-market addicts will find a permanent, modest-sized one on Piazza dei Ciompi (open daily in full season).

If you can't afford an old master, treat yourself to a good reproduction, a Florentine speciality. You can get a full-size version of your favourite statue or any piece of "antique" furniture made to order.

Framed reproduction 18th-century prints of Florence are good buys, especially around Piazza del Duomo. Look for unframed prints in San Lorenzo market. Or try one of those little men in the Uffizi busily putting finishing touches to oil copies of Raphaels and Caravaggios. Arms and armour fans can consider inexpensive suits of armour, swords, pistols and conquistador helmets near the Bargello.

Markets

Obvious answers for tourists in a hurry, they're part of the local colour. Conveniently central is the Mercato Nuovo, or Straw Market. Under its loggia (built in 1547), a score of stalls offer masses of attractive straw-work bags, sunhats, semi-precious stone trinkets, glass-mosaic jewellery, reproduction Davids, typical Florentine gilt-patterned wooden articles and so on.

San Lorenzo market caters for tourists and locals selling everything from tools to crocodile handbags. Stretching around Piazza San Lorenzo, its crowded, tempting food-shops add to the bustle and atmosphere. There's clothing, shoes and leatherware here, often at bargain prices. Several stalls even accept credit cards; many take travellers' cheques and will send purchases anywhere.

Haggling, once a tourist must, is fast dying out. With prices more strictly controlled,

there's little need for it, unless buying several items. Shops and boutiques frown on it and often post categorical *prezzi fissi* (fixed prices) notices. At most suggest a "rounding-off" of your bill or expect a small free knicknack if making a sizeable purchase.

Nightlife

Florence boasts many discotheques and dance halls, a few night-clubs, plus some open-air dancing establishments in the summer around the Viale Michelangelo and Fiesole. Hotel receptionists or tourist offices will supply addresses.

After a torrid summer's day spent playing hide-and-seek with the sun, Florentines make the most of the only slightly cooler evenings and take to the streets. Entire family clans, from toddlers to grannies, stroll round the centre, window-shop, sit gossiping in doorways or at crowded open-air café tables, a good-natured, leisurely throng.

Join them. Eat a *gelato,* a slice of piping-hot pizza or cool watermelon, or sit at a café and listen to the babel of voices—foreign and Italian—all around you. Try the cafés on Piazza della Repubblica. One of them offers a regular song-and-band show loud enough to entertain not only its customers but the entire piazza.

If you've a car, drive a few miles out of Florence to discover quaint, unsophisticated country restaurants. One good place to try is Pontassieve (18 km from Florence). Or just take a bus up to Piazzale Michelangelo and see the city by night. You'll never be at a loss for something relaxing to do in the evening.

Events and Festivals

Whatever the time of year, there's bound to be something interesting going on in Florence, whether it's a special art, antique, or handicraft exhibition at the Palazzo Strozzi, a dog or fashion show, a flower show (May and October) or a bit of historic folklore. It's worth obtaining the handy month-by-month *Calendar of Events in Florence and its Province* from the tourist office.

Concerts are a year-round feature: in July and August, open-air evening concerts are given in the Boboli Gardens; organ recitals in historic churches in September and October. During June, July and August nearby Fiesole offers a festival of concerts, ballet, drama and films—much of it in its Roman theatre. In June and September, the beautiful Medici villa at Poggio a Caiano serves as the setting for plays and concerts. The Florentine opera season is in January to February and July.

But if you can, plan to attend the celebrated Maggio Musicale Fiorentino festival (mid-May to end of June) which attracts some of the finest concert, ballet and operatic performers in the world.

Annual events in and around Florence

Annunciation Day (March):	City celebrations.
Easter Sunday:	*Scoppio del Carro.* Noonday fireworks Piazza del Duomo.
Ascension Day (May):	*Festa del Grillo.* Crickets in tiny cages sol at the Cascine to be set free.
June 17:	Historic regatta in Pisa.
St. John's Day (June 24 and 28):	*Giuoco del Calcio.* Traditional rough tough football game in 16th-century cos tume. Fireworks in Piazzale Michelangelo
July 2 and August 16:	*Palio di Siena.* Historic pageant and hors race in Siena's main square.
September 7:	*Festa delle Rificolone.* Impressive bridg (Ponte San Niccolò) and river evenin procession with torches and paper lanterns
September:	Bird Fair at Porta Romana.

See also PUBLIC HOLIDAYS in the Blueprint section of this book.

Sports

Swimming. If walking around Florence isn't enough, you'll certainly find other outlets for your energies. Swim or just sunbathe at the modern Piscina Bellariva (Lungarno Colombo), or Rari Nantes (Lungarno Ferrucci) or Piscina Costoli (Campo di Marte) which offer attractive children's facilities. Or try the more sophisticated, club-like pool at the Cascine. A cross between London's Hyde Park and New York's Central Park in miniature, even boasting a tiny zoo, the Cascine (the name means

"dairies") are pleasant to stroll in—but better avoided after dark.

To enjoy a dip in the sea, you have to travel to Viareggio, Forte dei Marmi, Marina di Pisa or Tirrenia.

Tennis. Would-be tennis players won't get a look-in at the exclusive Cascine tennis club. But there are courts in the Viale Michelangelo, as well as a golf-tennis-swimming complex, the Campi dell'Ugolino, just south of Florence. The tourist office (see p.122), which owns this last establishment, will supply all relevant information.

Riding. Riding facilities are skimpy: you have to go to Impruneta (14 km away). But you can watch trotting or flat racing at the Cascine.

Walking. There are endless possibilities for fascinating walks, hikes or drives that take you right out into those green, undulating hills all around, and to closer places like Bellosguardo park, Piazzale Michelangelo, Certosa del Galluzzo monastery, Poggio Imperiale or the Arcetri observatory—that stands on the very hill from which Galileo gazed at the stars. The tourist office supplies a useful map of Florence province and will advise on routes to take.

Wining and Dining

If measure and simplicity are the keynotes of Tuscan architecture, you could say the same of its cuisine.* Tuscans, and Florentines most of all, have always verged on the fanatical about fresh "country" fare. Fiercely proud of their olive oil, their bread, their wine, they're more likely to wax lyrical over a plateful of tender boiled marrows *(zucchini)*, a *pecorino* cheese or some freshly picked local figs, than over an elaborate dish. Plain-minded or not, well-to-do Florentines of the 16th century commonly ate with knives and forks—perhaps designed by Cellini—while the rest of Europe was still happily using its fingers.

Fussy, yet notoriously unadventurous with exotic or foreign foods, the nearest they get to "disguising" the natural flavour of anything is a fairly generous use of olive oil, sage, rosemary, basil and, of course, tomato in many of their dishes. But you have to admit the raw materials here are superb. Take a morning stroll through the busy markets around San Lorenzo and on Piazza Santo Spirito. See and smell the exhilarating freshness of everything, and you'll be convinced. Meat and poultry in Florence are among the best you'll taste in Italy, but sea-food and fish are likely to be expensive. In season, fresh game (boar, hare, partridge, pheasant, deer) appears on Florentine tables.

From Maestros to Mammas

Restaurants range from expensive establishments to modest family *trattorie*. All restaurants must issue a formal receipt indicating the sales tax or VAT *(I. V. A.)*. A customer may be stopped outside the premises and fined if unable to produce a receipt. The bill usually includes cover *(coperto)* and service *(servizio)* charges as well. Leave about 10 per cent for the waiter.

All but the cheaper *trattorie* offer a "safe" but unimaginative three-course, fixed-price *menu turistico*. Students with international cards can eat cheaply at the Mensa dello Studente (Via San Gallo, 25a). But today's cost-conscious tourists and Florentines are generously catered for by hordes of little sandwich, pizza and coffee bars.

You'll find, too, some counter-service *tavola calda* estab-

---

*For a comprehensive glossary of Italian wining and dining, ask your bookshop for the Berlitz EUROPEAN MENU READER.

lishments, and a handful of pleasant, family-run self-service restaurants offering good cheap food.

If it's atmosphere and Tuscan accents you're after, try the streets around the Ponte Vecchio, Santo Spirito, Santa Croce and San Lorenzo. And if you're feeling fairly adventurous, try a slab of scalding fried *polenta* (purée of maize, or cornmeal), a *crostino* (chopped chicken liver on fried bread) or at least a *bombolone* (doughnut) at a *friggitoría* (fry-shop).

First Courses

Among the usual all-Italian starters, look out for local specialities like *prosciutto crudo con fichi* (raw ham with fresh figs), *crostini, fettunta* (toasted country bread rubbed with garlic and sprinkled with olive oil), *minestra di fagioli* (thick butter-bean soup), *minestrone* (even thicker vegetable soup) and *ribollita* (a bread-based vegetable soup), served hot or cold in summer.

Among the 360 known varieties of Italian pasta, try *pappardelle* (broad noodles, served in season with hare sauce), *paglia e fieno* ("straw and hay"—mixed white and green pasta), *ravioli con panna* (ravioli in fresh cream sauce), as well as the ever-popular *lasagne* or *tortellini*. Remember you can always order a half portion *(mezza porzione)* of pasta.

Meat and Fish

The famous *bistecca alla fiorentina,* a mammoth charcoal-grilled T-bone steak, served with lemon, is a must at least once. It's always expensive: make sure that they show you your meat first and tell you its weight (the price per kilo is normally marked on the menu). It's quite in order for two people to share one *bistecca*. Florentines do it all the time. Try also *arista* (roast loin of pork), *bollito di manzo* or just *lesso* (boiled beef served with a piquant sauce), *trippe alla fiorentina* (tripe cooked with ham, tomato and parmesan), *fritto misto* (deep-fried mixed meats and vegetables) and all kinds of liver *alla fiorentina*, sautéed and flavoured with sage or rosemary.

Chicken *(pollo)* crops up regularly in Tuscan cooking, and you'll probably taste it either *alla cacciatora* (with tomatoes and vegetables), *alla diavola* (charcoal-grilled), *arrosto* (roast) or as *petti di pollo saltati* or *fritti* (chicken breasts sautéed or fried). Hare and rabbit frequently appear *alla cacciatora*.

There's less emphasis on fish dishes in Florentine menus, but two you're almost certain to find are *baccalà alla fiorentina* (a robust cod stew) and the highly tasty Livornese *cacciucco* (red mullet or other fish cooked in tomatoes, onion, garlic and red wine, served on garlic-flavoured croutons).

Vegetables

In Italy vegetables *(contorno)* are usually served and charged for apart. Sample *carciofini fritti* (crisply fried artichokes), *frittata di carciofi* (artichoke omelette) or, in autumn, a plateful of grilled mushrooms *(funghi)*. Try also *fagiolini* or *fagioli all'uccelletto* (boiled green or butter-beans sautéed with tomato and sage), *al fiasco* (same ingredients, baked) or *alla fiorentina* (boiled, simply seasoned with oil, salt and pepper, eaten almost cold) or just settle for an *insalata mista* (mixed salad).

Sweets

For a satisfying dessert, have a slice of *zuccotto,* a large liqueur-soaked, chilled sponge and chocolate cake, a piece of *torta* (cake or tart), or just *frutta di stagione* (fresh fruit). But for a really delightful treat on a warm summer's evening, you can't improve on a cool, juicy slice of watermelon *(anguria* or *cocomero)* bought at one of those colourful street stalls dotted about the city. Ice cream is also a must in Florence (see p. 94).

Doing It Yourself

If you fancy a change from *trattorie* and sandwich bars, take a picnic among the statues in the Loggia dei Lanzi, in the Boboli Gardens, in Fiesole or up on the terrace of San Miniato with all Florence at your feet. Buy fresh fruit and bread, then make for any one of the hundreds of delicatessens *(pizzicheria)*. Crammed with mouthwatering merchandise from floor to ceiling, fun just to browse through, they stock virtually anything edible and drinkable, including wine and soft drinks, and often sell sandwich rolls *(panino ripieno)*. They'll usually oblige by filling your own rolls with whatever you buy, saving you time and mess.

Occasional picnics are the best way to sample specialities you won't find so easily elsewhere. Try *finocchiona,* Tuscany's own garlic- and fennel-flavoured salami, and don't neglect the whole rich Italian range of cured hams, salamis, *mortadella* sausage, etc. As for cheeses, taste *ricotta* (creamy cottage cheese), *stracchino, pecorino* (a tangy ewe's-milk cheese), *caciotta, provola* (smoked or fresh) and, of course, *gorgonzola, parmigiano* or *grana*—the younger variety you eat rather than grate. Delicious with fresh bread and fruit! But don't forget: all food shops are closed on Wednesday afternoons.

Beating the Heat

If the city's summer heat deadens your appetite, you can always fall back on drinks. If Florence as a whole suffers from a shortage of spacious open air cafés to sit and relax in, fashionable ones in the Piazza della Signoria and Piazza della Repubblica are *the* places for aperitifs, appointments, postcard-writing or afternoon tea, while the Via de' Tornabuoni has its share of chic, busy tea-rooms.

In any case, you'll never be at a loss for thirst-quenchers anywhere in Florence—from good Italian beers *(birra),* aperitifs and cocktails, to iced tamarind juice *(tamarindo),* non-alcoholic bitters, fresh fruit juice *(spremuta),* fruit shake *(frullato),* and coffee or lemon poured over crushed ice *(granita).* For children there's always fizzy orange or lemonade *(aranciata* or *limonata)* and, naturally, a bewildering choice of succulent ice-creams *(gelato).* For really off-beat flavours (like fig, chestnut or peach) try the Piazza delle

Cure, Via de' Calzaiuoli, the Ponte Vecchio area or Piazza San Simone.

Wines and Spirits

To a lot of people outside Italy Chianti *is* Italian wine—small wonder, perhaps, since Englishmen were already drinking it at home in the late 17th century. Tuscany's number one wine, it's produced around Florence, Pistoia, Pisa, Siena and Arezzo.

Those picturesque but practical straw-covered *fiaschi*—the most famous wine bottles in the world—conjure up instant visions of Sunny Italy. With rising costs, this bit of real folklore is sadly giving way to ugly plastic imitations. So hoard your *fiasco* for posterity.

Compile your own menu from copious choice at an Italian pizzicheria.

A red, light wine, Chianti can be drunk with almost anything. Quality and price can vary, but it's generally very acceptable and occasionally superlative. If you're bent on trying a really fine Chianti *(Chianti Classico)* straight from Tuscany's top vineyards, make sure the neck of your bottle bears a seal with a black cock on it. Bottles with a cherub on the seal also guarantee absolute authenticity and high quality.

If you've a passion for wine, choose one of several organized coach trips to the finest Chianti cellars with their mighty oak casks and millions of bottles. You'll be taking in some superb sights and countryside at the same time (July to October; details are available from the tourist office; see p. 122). You can buy wines you've tasted on the spot, often at extremely low prices.

The Chianti label extends to the similar *Rufina,* and to another more full-bodied red, *Montalbano*. But Chianti is certainly not on its own. There are other light reds, *Montecarlo* and *Brolio; Aleatico di Portoferraio* (from Elba); an unusual, slightly bitter red, *Nobile di Montepulciano;* and a fine dry red, *Brunello di Montalcino,* all worth trying.

Among the few Tuscan white wines are the excellent dry *Vernaccia di San Gimignano, Montecarlo* and the mellower *bianco dell'Elba* (the Isle of Elba was for long a Tuscan possession, prized for its wine). From Elba, too, comes a range of white *spumante* (sparkling wine), just the thing to round off a celebration meal.

Don't feel compelled to order wine with every meal; there's always a choice of fizzy and still mineral water, or beer. Florence's tap water is heavily chlorinated, but it's drinkable.

Tuscans often like to end their meal with a small glass of *Vinsanto* ("holy wine"), a deep amber-coloured sweet wine. If you're lucky enough to visit a local farmer or family, you'll almost certainly be welcomed with some *Vinsanto,* whatever the time of day. Most bars and cafés serve it by the glass. Or try it as an aperitif.

You'll also find a dizzying array of aperitifs, digestives, bitters *(amari)* of which Italians are so fond, brandies, foreign spirits (Scotch whisky is amazingly cheap) and intriguing herb liqueurs made by monks in nearby monasteries. The trouble is that you won't have time to sample them all!

To Help You Order...

Good evening. I'd like a table.	**Buona sera. Vorrei un tavolo.**
Do you have a set menu?	**Avete un menù a prezzo fisso?**
I'd like a/an/some...	**Vorrei...**

beer	**una birra**	milk	**del latte**
bread	**del pane**	mineral water	**dell'acqua minerale**
butter	**del burro**	napkin	**un tovagliolo**
coffee	**un caffè**	potatoes	**delle patate**
cream	**della panna**	salad	**dell'insalata**
dessert	**un dolce**	soup	**una minestra**
fish	**del pesce**	spoon	**un cucchiaio**
fruit	**della frutta**	sugar	**dello zucchero**
glass	**un bicchiere**	tea	**un tè**
ice-cream	**un gelato**	wine	**del vino**
meat	**della carne**		

...and Read the Menu

aglio	garlic	**maiale**	pork
agnello	lamb	**manzo**	beef
anitra	duck	**melanzana**	aubergine (eggplant)
antipasto	hors d'œuvre	**peperoni**	peppers
arrosto	roast	**pesce**	fish
baccalà	dried cod	**pollo**	chicken
bistecca	steak	**prosciutto**	ham
braciola	chop	**crudo**	cured
calamari	squid	**cotto**	cooked
carciofi	artichokes	**risotto**	rice dish
cipolle	onions	**rognoni**	kidneys
coniglio	rabbit	**salsa**	sauce
fagioli	beans	**sogliola**	sole
fegato	liver	**spinaci**	spinachs
formaggio	cheese	**stufato**	stew
fragole	strawberries	**triglia**	red mullet
frittata	omelette	**trippe**	tripe
frutti di mare	seafood	**uova**	eggs
funghi	mushrooms	**vitello**	veal
gamberi	prawns	**zuppa**	soup

BLUEPRINT for a Perfect Trip

How to Get There

If the choice of ways to go is bewildering, the complexity of fares and regulations can be downright stupefying. A reliable travel agent will have full details of all the latest flight possibilities, fares and regulations.

BY AIR

Scheduled flights

The nearest international airport to Florence is at Pisa. However, Rome and Milan are the main gateways to Italy, both for international and intercontinental flights. From Rome or Milan, you can either transfer to a flight to Pisa and go on by direct train from Pisa airport to Florence, or continue by bus or rail to Florence—or, from Milan, by air to Florence's domestic airport, Peretola.

Charter flights and package tours

If you decide on a package tour or charter, read your contract carefully before you sign. Most tour agents recommend cancellation insurance, a modestly priced safeguard.

From the U.K. and Ireland: Package tours featuring Florence are numerous, ranging from stays of four to 14 nights. It is worth noting that most package tours are on a room-only or just Continental-breakfast basis. A few provide a half-board arrangement but at a supplement. Flights are out of Gatwick or Heathrow, and the prime Italian operator also offers a rail-package deal departing from London Victoria. Florence is heavily featured in two-centre stays in conjunction with Rome and the Tuscan resorts and hills or with the Italian Lakes, although the rail package is not always available for such tours.

From North America: Package deals including hotel, car or other land arrangements can be very good value. In addition to APEX and Excursion fares, there's the Advance Booking Charter (ABC), usually also for flight only, which must be bought at least 30 days in advance.

BY CAR

The main access roads to Florence are: from France via Lyons to Turin, then by A21 and A26 to Genoa and A12 to Pisa, or via the French Riviera through Genoa; from Switzerland via the Grand St. Bernard Pass and by the A5 and A26 to Genoa, or via the Simplon or Gotthard passes to Milan and by A1 through Bologna; from Austria via the Brenner Pass and A22 (E6) through Modena.

BY RAIL

From London or Paris, the Rome Express takes you to Pisa (wher you change for Florence) via Turin and Genoa.

Inter-Rail and Rail Europ Senior cards: The Inter-Rail Card permit 30 days of unlimited rail travel in participating European countries t people under 26. The Rail Europ Senior Card is available for senic citizens and entitles the holder to a discount on European and interna Italian rail journeys.

Eurailpass and Eurail Youthpass: Non-European residents ca travel on these flat-rate, unlimited mileage tickets valid for rail trave anywhere in Western Europe outside of Great Britain. You must bu your pass before leaving home.

The Italian State Railways offer fare reductions in certain cases, par ticularly for large families. The BTLC Tourist Ticket *(Biglietto Turis tico di Libera Circolazione)* is valid for specified periods of unlimite travel within Italy in either first of second class. Inquire, too, abou the advantageous Kilometric Ticket *(Biglietto Chilometrico),* whic may be used by up to 5 people. These tickets can be purchased at hom or in Italy.

When to Go

Despite its central position on the Italian peninsula, Florence is one o the country's hottest cities in summer. The worst period is mid-June tc mid-September, but in early spring and late autumn the weather is more variable.

It's best to visit Florence in April and May, or September anc October, when the city is less crowded. During the fashion shows (October and March/April) hotels tend to be overbooked, so try tc arrange your holidays outside those weeks.

Air temperature		J	F	M	A	M	J	J	A	S	O	N	L
Max.	F	48	53	59	68	75	84	89	88	82	70	57	5
	C	9	12	16	20	24	29	32	31	28	21	14	1
Min.	F	35	36	40	46	53	59	62	61	59	52	43	3
	C	2	2	5	8	12	15	17	17	15	11	6	[illegible]

Figures shown are approximate monthly averages

Planning Your Budget

To give you an idea of what to expect, here are some average prices in Italian lire (L.). However, inflation makes them unavoidably approximate, and there are considerable seasonal differences.

Airport transfer. Train from Pisa airport to Florence L. 4,400.

Baby-sitters. L. 14,000–20,000 per hour.

Bus service. Flat-rate fare for Florence and suburbs L. 600.

Camping (high season). Adults L. 6,000 per person per night, children L. 5,000, caravan (trailer) or camper L. 10,000, car and tent L. 6,500, motorbike L. 2,500.

Car hire (international company). *Fiat Panda 45* L. 38,300 per day, L. 600 per km., L. 592,000 per week with unlimited mileage. *Fiat Regata 70* L. 67,800 per day, L. 816 per km., L. 939,000 per week with unlimited mileage. Add 18% tax.

Cigarettes (packet of 20). Italian brands L. 1,600 and up, imported brands L. 2,500 and up.

Entertainment. Cinema L. 6,000–7,000, discotheque (entry and one drink) L. 20,000–30,000.

Hairdressers. *Woman's* shampoo and set or blow-dry L. 18,000–7,000, permanent wave L. 45,000–70,000. *Man's* haircut L. 12,000–5,000, L. 20,000 with shampoo.

Hotels (double room with bath, including tax and services). ***** L. 400,000–600,000, **** L. 130,000–380,000, *** L. 70,000–240,000, ** L. 45,000–190,000, * L. 30,000–100,000.

Meals and drinks: Continental breakfast L. 7,000–15,000, lunch/dinner in fairly good establishment L. 35,000–80,000, coffee served at a table L. 2,500–4,500, served at the bar L. 600–800, bottle of wine L. 4,000 and up, soft drink L. 1,500 and up, aperitif L. 2,500 and up.

Museums. L. 2,000–7,000.

Shopping bag. 500 g. of bread L. 1,500, 250 g. of butter L. 3,000 and up, 6 eggs L. 1,800, 500 g. of beefsteak L. 8,000–10,000, 250 g. of coffee L. 4,000 and up, bottle of wine L. 3,000 and up.

Youth hostels. L. 12,500 per night with breakfast.

An A–Z Summary of Practical Information and Facts

> A star (*) following an entry indicates that relevant prices are to be found on page 101.
> Listed after most entries is the appropriate Italian translation, usually in the singular, plus a number of phrases that may come in handy during your stay in Italy.

A **ACCOMMODATION** (see also CAMPING). Florence's tourist offic publishes an annual list of hotels *(albergo),* boarding-houses *(pension* and inns *(locanda)* for the city and its immediate environs. It supplie full details on amenities, prices and classification (1 to 5 stars). You ca obtain it in the Florence tourist office or from the Italian State Touri Office (E.N.I.T.) in your country.

During spring, summer and early autumn it's always advisable t book ahead, but for the rest of the year you'll have no problem findin accommodation. In Florence, hotel reservations can be made at th I.T.A. *(Informazioni Turistiche Alberghiere)* counter at the railway sta tion (normally from 9 a.m. to 8.30 p.m. daily).

On page 101 you'll find some average rates for a double room i summer season. Off-season rates are somewhat lower. Single room cost 60 to 70% the price of doubles. Breakfast, which you're expecte to take at the hotel, is not included in the room rate. Unless prices a noted as *tutto compreso* (all inclusive), as much as 20% in tax an service can be added to the bill. A few major hotels have swimmin pools, and some hotels on the outskirts have tennis courts.

Youth Hostels *(ostello della gioventù).* If you're planning to make ex tensive use of youth hostels during your stay in Italy, contact you national youth hostel association before departure to obtain an inter national membership card. The Florence branch of the Associazion Italiana Alberghi per la Gioventù is at:

Viale Augusto Righi, 2; tel. 60 03 15

In full season (especially July) certain religious institutions such a convents or monasteries open their doors to young people. Check wit the tourist office.

ay hotels. Florence has two *alberghi diurni*—"day-time hotels"—one the main railway station, Stazione Centrale (F.S.), where you can ire a room for a few hours' rest. It also provides bathrooms, hairdres-rs, laundry facilities, etc. (open from 6 a.m. to about 8 p.m. with early osing on Sundays).

d like a single/double room.	**Vorrei una camera singola/ matrimoniale.**
ith bath/shower	**con bagno/doccia**
'hat's the rate per night?	**Qual è il prezzo per una notte?**

IRPORT* *(aeroporto)*. Florence has no international airport. The earest one is Pisa's Galileo Galilei (San Giusto), some 80 kilometres way. Florence can be reached either by road or by direct rail service om the airport (a 60-minute ride).

Florence airport, Peretola, handles domestic scheduled flights to ilan, Turin and Venice–Trieste.

orter!	**Facchino!**
ake these bags to the us/train/taxi, please.	**Mi porti queste valige fino all'autobus/al treno/al taxi, per favore.**
Vhat time does the train for lorence leave?	**A che ora parte il treno per Firenze?**

AMPING* *(campeggio)*. Six major camping sites are located in the nmediate vicinity of Florence, two within easy reach of the centre by us. For information on facilities in and around Florence, contact the ourist office (see p. 122).

In Italy, you may camp freely outside of sites if you obtain permis-on either from the owner of the property or from the local authori-es. For your personal safety you should choose sites where there are ther campers.

If you enter Italy with a caravan (trailer) you must be able to show n inventory (with two copies) of the material and equipment in the aravan: dishes, linen, etc.

1ay we camp here?	**Possiamo campeggiare qui?**
there a campsite near here?	**C'è un campeggio qui vicino?**
Ve have a tent/caravan (trailer).	**Abbiamo la tenda/la roulotte.**

AR HIRE* *(autonoleggio)* (see also DRIVING). Your hotel or the ellow pages of the telephone book will supply the addresses of the

C

leading hire firms. You can also arrange immediate hire upon arriv at Florence's railway station.

Firms usually offer a range of Fiats; other Italian and foreig models are less frequently available. Minimum age varies from 1 to 25 according to company. Insurance is mandatory. Normally deposit is charged when hiring a car, but holders of major credit carc are exempt. Special weekend rates and weekly unlimited mileage rate for foreigners may be available. Inquire, too, about any availab seasonal deals.

It's usually possible to have your car delivered to your hotel. Som firms permit you to return your rented car in another Italian or Eurc pean city, for an additional fee.

I'd like to rent a car.	**Vorrei noleggiare una macchina.**

CIGARETTES, CIGARS, TOBACCO* *(sigarette, sigari, tabacco* Sold under state monopoly, tobacco products in Italy are price-cor trolled, foreign brands costing as much as 50% more than domesti Dark and light tobaccos are available, as are most well-known ciga and pipe tobaccos.

Ask for a *toscano* and you'll get a very pungent black cigar that been smoked in Florence for generations. It's better to smell than t smoke, but it's part of the local colour.

The cheapest Italian cigarettes are considered somewhat rough b many foreigners. Most foreign brands are on sale in any tobacco sho *(tabaccheria)* in a hotel district. Foreign menthol cigarettes are als available. Officially, tobacco and matches may be sold only in shop bearing a large white *T* on a dark-blue background—or at certai authorized hotel news-stands and café counters.

I'd like a packet of...	**Vorrei un pacchetto di...**
with/without filter	**con/senza filtro**
I'd like a box of matches, please.	**Per favore, mi dia una scatola di fiammiferi.**

CLOTHING. At least from May to September you'll wear summer weight clothes in Florence; women will find a light wrap useful occa sionally in the evening. A wrap is also handy to cover bare shoulder when visiting churches.

Slacks for women are acceptable everywhere. But miniskirts, short and bare-backed dresses are frowned upon in churches. The tradi tional custom that a woman should cover her head with a scarf or hat in church is giving way to a bare-headed new generation, and most priests don't seem to mind.

COMMUNICATIONS

Post offices *(ufficio postale)* handle telegrams, mail and money transfers, and some have public telephones. Stamps are also sold at tobacconists *(tabaccheria)* and at some hotel desks. Florentine post boxes are red. The slot marked *Per la città* is for local mail only; *Altre destinazioni* for mail going elsewhere.

Post office **hours** are normally from 8.15 a.m. to 1.40 p.m., Monday to Friday, until 12 noon on Saturdays.

The main branches, such as those at Via Pellicceria (off Piazza della Repubblica) and Viale Belfiore, function until 7 p.m. but only for registered mail and other special services. Via Pellicceria has 24-hour telephone and telegram facilities; use the bell outside the main entrance when the doors are locked.

Poste restante (general delivery). It's not worth arranging to receive mail during a brief visit to Florence as Italy's postal system is rather unreliable. Instead, have people cable or telephone your hotel. If you're going to be in Florence for a considerable time and must have things sent to you, there is poste-restante *(fermo posta)* service at the Via Pellicceria post office (see above). Don't forget your passport as identification when you go to pick up mail. Have mail addressed in this way:

Mr. John Smith
Fermo Posta
Palazzo delle Poste
Via Pellicceria
Florence, Italy

Telegrams *(telegramma):* Night letters, or night-rate telegrams, which arrive the next morning, are far cheaper than ordinary cables but can only be sent overseas.

Parcels *(pacco):* Bureaucratic regulations about wrapping and sending packages from Italy—involving different classifications, sealing procedures, insurance, customs requirements, etc.—are so complicated that even immensely knowledgeable hotel concierges don't know them all. Ask at a post office.

Telephone *(telefono).* Here's another challenge in Florence. Glass-enclosed booths are scattered throughout the city, and almost every bar and café has a public telephone, indicated by a yellow sign just outside showing a telephone dial. Older types of public payphones require tokens (*gettoni;* available from machines [generally installed next to the telephone] and at bars, hotels, post offices and tobacconists'), modern ones, with two separate slots, take both *gettoni* and 100- and 200-lira coins.

Calls to other Italian cities and abroad can be dialled directly from local phone boxes. International telephone offices are located at Via Cavour, 21 (Centro Telefonici Pubblici SIP), at the post offices in Via Pellicceria and Via Pietrapiana and at the railway station.

To make a call you insert a coin or token and lift the receiver. A dial tone is a series of regular dash-dash sounds which you may not hear for several minutes. A dot-dot-dot series means Florence's central computer is overloaded—hang up and try again. Or you may finish dialling and then hear nothing at all. When you absolutely must reach a local number but find it engaged, dial 197, wait for a gong and tape-recorded instructions before continuing, then dial your number. This will ensure a message is sent to the desired number to the effect that there is an urgent call waiting to get through.

Some useful numbers:

Domestic directory inquiries (information):	12
International operator	170
Telegrams	186

Give me... *gettoni,* please.	**Per favore, mi dia... gettoni.**
Can you get me this number in...?	**Può passarmi questo numero a...?**
Have you received any mail for...?	**C'è posta per...?**
I'd like a stamp for this letter/ postcard.	**Desidero un francobollo per questa lettera/cartolina.**
airmail	**via aerea**
registered	**raccomandata**
I want to send a telegram to...	**Desidero mandare un telegramma a...**

COMPLAINTS *(reclamo).* Complaining is an Italian national pastime, but can involve elaborate bureaucratic procedures once it passes beyond the verbal stage. In hotels, restaurants and shops, complaints should be made to the manager or proprietor.

If satisfaction is not quickly obtained, mention that you intend to report the matter to the tourist office (see TOURIST INFORMATION

OFFICES), or to the regular police (*Questura*, see POLICE). The threat of a formal declaration to the police should be effective in such cases as overcharging for car repairs, but this will consume hours or even days of your visit.

To avoid problems in all situations, always establish the price in advance—especially when dealing with porters at stations. Any complaint about a taxi fare should be settled by referring to a notice, in four languages, affixed by law in each taxi, specifying extra charges (airport runs, Sunday or holiday rates, night surcharge) in excess of the meter rate.

CONSULATES. Citizens from countries which have no consulate in Florence should get in touch with their embassy in Rome.

Australia: (Rome) Via Alessandria, 215; tel; 84 12 41

Canada: (Rome) Via G. Battista De Rossi, 27; tel. 85 53 41

Eire: (Rome) Via del Pozzetto, 105; tel. 678 25 41

United Kingdom: Lungarno Corsini, 2; tel. 28 41 33

U.S.A.: Lungarno A. Vespucci, 38; tel. 29 82 76/27 25 94

South Africa: (Rome) Piazza Monte Grappa, 4; tel. 360 84 41

Where is the British/American consulate?	**Dov'è il consolato britannico/ americano?**

CONVERTER CHARTS. For distance measures, see p. 112. Italy uses the metric system.

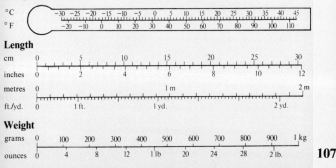

Temperature

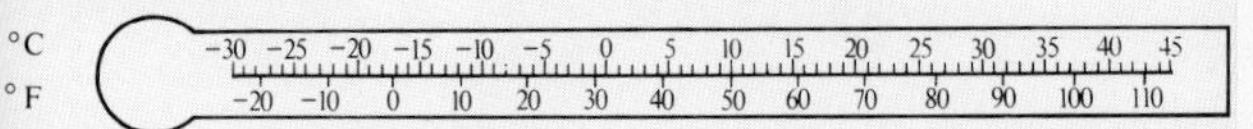

Length

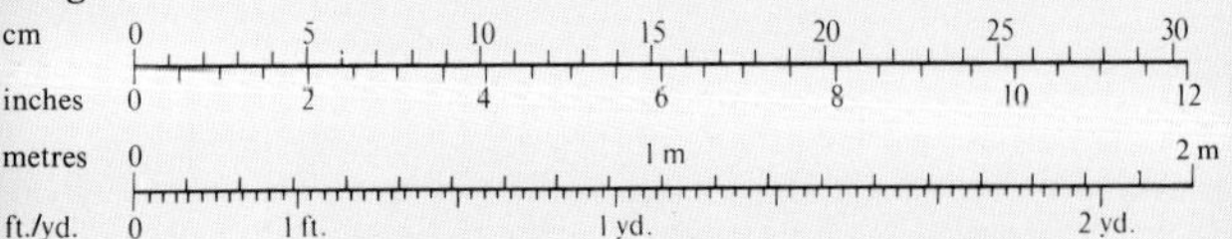

Weight

grams 0 100 200 300 400 500 600 700 800 900 1 kg

ounces 0 4 8 12 1 lb 20 24 28 2 lb.

C

COURTESIES. Although less formal than many other Europeans, Italians do appreciate certain social, courtesies. Upon entering and leaving a shop, restaurant or office, the expected greeting is always *buon giorno* (good morning) or *buona sera* (good evening) from as early as 1 p.m. onwards. When approaching anyone with an inquiry, start with *per favore* (please), and for any service say *grazie* (thanks), to which the reply is *prego* (don't mention it; you're welcome). Introductions to men, women and older children are always accompanied by a handshake, the proper phrase being *piacere* (it's a pleasure). After you know an Italian well, *ciao* is the common phrase of greeting.

How are you?	**Come sta?**
Very well, thanks.	**Molto bene, grazie.**

CRIME and THEFT. Violent crime is, happily, rare in Florence. Though women may be pestered, such attention is unlikely to escalate beyond acceptable bounds. Petty thieves, particularly pickpockets, operate here as in all tourist centres. It's wise to leave your unneeded documents and excess money in the hotel safe.

In the tourist season, shady characters may offer stolen goods (especially transistors, watches, cameras) or "bargain" items which are likely to be of extremely poor workmanship though apparently brand-new. The best thing to do is simply ignore them.

Theft of cars or of their contents can best be avoided by emptying them of everything—not only of valuables. Leave the glove compartments empty and open to discourage prospective thieves. If your hotel has a private garage or guarded parking lot, leave your car there.

I want to report a theft.	**Voglio denunciare un furto.**
My wallet/handbag/passport/ ticket has been stolen.	**Mi hanno rubato il portafoglio/ il passaporto/il biglietto.**

CUSTOMS *(dogana)* **and ENTRY REGULATIONS.** For a stay of up to three months, a valid passport is sufficient for citizens of Australia, Canada, New Zealand and U.S.A. Visitors from Eire and the United Kingdom need only an identity card to enter Italy.

Italian customs officials are unlikely to quibble over smaller points: they are interested mainly in detecting smuggled art treasures, currency or narcotics. If you're exporting archaeological relics, works of art, or gems, you should obtain a bill of sale and a permit from the government (this is normally handled by the dealer).

Here's what you can take into Italy duty-free and, when returning home, into your own country:

Entering Italy from:	Cigarettes		Cigars		Tobacco	Spirits		Wine
1)	200	or	50	or	250 g.	¾ l.	or	2 l.
2)	300	or	75	or	400 g.	1.5 l.	and	4 l.
3)	400	or	100	or	500 g.	¾ l.	or	2 l.
Into:								
Australia	200	or	250 g.	or	250 g.	1 l.	or	1 l.
Canada	200	and	50	and	900 g.	1.1 l.	or	1.1 l.
Eire	200	or	50	or	250 g.	1 l.	and	2 l.
N. Zealand	200	or	50	or	250 g.	1.1 l.	and	4.5 l.
S. Africa	400	and	50	and	250 g.	1 l.	and	2 l.
U.K.	200	or	50	or	250 g.	1 l.	and	2 l.
U.S.A.	200	and	100	and	4)	1 l.	or	1 l.

1) within Europe from non-EEC countries
2) within Europe from EEC countries
3) countries outside Europe
4) a reasonable quantity

Currency restrictions. Non-residents may import or export up to L. 400,000 in local currency. In foreign currencies, tourists may import unlimited amounts, but if you wish to take the equivalent of more than L. 1,000,000 in or out of the country, you must fill out a V2 declaration form at the border upon entry.

DRIVING IN ITALY

Entering Italy. To bring your car into Italy you will need:

- an international driving licence (non-Europeans)
- car registration papers
- Green Card (an extension to your regular insurance policy, making it valid for foreign countries).
- national identity sticker for your car and the red warning triangle in case of breakdown.

Note: Before leaving home, check with your automobile association about the latest regulations concerning *petrol coupons* (that give tourists access to cheaper fuel) in Italy, as they are constantly changing.

Driving conditions. Drive on the right. Pass on the left. Traffic on major roads has the right of way over traffic entering from side roads but this, like all other traffic regulations, is frequently ignored, so beware. At intersections of roads of similar importance, the car on the right theoretically has the right of way. When passing other vehicles or remaining in the left-hand (passing) lane, keep your directional indicator flashing.

The motorways *(autostrada)* and most major national highways are of excellent quality, skilfully designed for fast driving. Florence is a major staging post on the famed Autostrada del Sole which runs the length of Italy, ensuring fast connections with Bologna, Milan, Rome and Naples. Each section of an *autostrada* requires payment of a toll: you collect a card from an automatic machine and pay at the other end for the distance travelled. Try to stock up on coins, since the toll booth attendants don't like making change. Every 2 kilometres on the *autostrada* there's an emergency call box marked SOS. There's often a lane to the extreme right for very slow traffic.

On country roads and even many main highways, you'll encounter bicycles, motorscooters, three-wheeled vehicles, and horse-drawn carts. Very often, such slow-moving vehicles have *no* lights, an obvious danger from dusk to dawn.

Last but not least: cars, buses, lorries (trucks) make use, indiscriminately, of their horns—in fact, blowing one's horn is an Italian attitude—so don't get flustered if it's done at you, and do it wherever it could help to warn of your impending arrival.

Fuel and oil. Fuel, sold at government-set price levels, comes as super (98–100 octane), lead-free (95 octane, still rare) and normal (86–88 octane). Diesel is also usually available. Oil comes in at least three varieties.

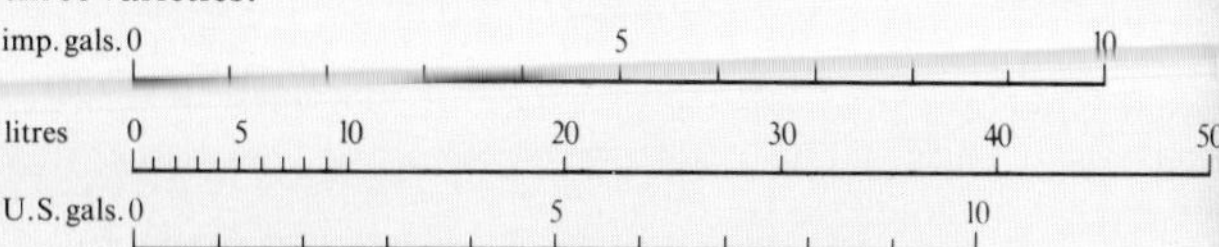

Speed limits. Speed limits in Italy are based on car engine size. The following chart gives the engine size in cubic centimetres and the speed limits (in kilometres per hour):

Engine size	less than 600 cc.	600 to 900 cc.	900 to 1,300 cc. (and motorcycles more than 150 cc.)	more than 1,300 cc.
Main roads	80 kph.	90 kph.	100 kph.	110 kph.
Motorways (Express-ways)	90 kph.	110 kph.	130 kph.	140 kph.

Town speed limits are posted on the entry roads.

Driving in Florence. Most of the streets still open to private traffic are one way. Look out, especially at intersections. Many streets are narrow, and cross-visibility is virtually nil. Treat traffic lights which are theoretically in your favour and white lines across merging sidestreets with caution—don't take your priorities for granted. Unless already familiar with the streets, you'll be far better off sightseeing on foot.

Parking *(posteggio, parcheggio).* There are numerous supervised car parks, including a large one on Piazza della Stazione within walking distance of the centre. Since central Florence is closed to private vehicles, only motorists staying within the restricted zone are allowed to enter and leave. Parking there for any length of time is virtually impossible. Best of all for motorized tourists are the large car parks at Porta Romana (left bank), the Cascine (Piazza Vittorio Veneto) and the Fortezza da Basso (Viale Filippo Strozzi). A bus service from each ensures quick access to the centre.

If you park your car overnight in the centre of Florence, be careful to heed the parking time allowance; when the street-cleaners pass, the car will be towed away if the time limit is not respected. If the worst happens you'll be able to recuperate your vehicle (and pay) at the Parco Macchine Requisite in Via Circondaria, 19.

Traffic police *(polizia stradale):* When they're in evidence, which is rather infrequently, Italian traffic police use motorcycles or Alfa-Romeos. All cities and many towns and villages have signs posted at the outskirts indicating the telephone number of the local traffic police headquarters or *Carabinieri.* In recent years police have become stricter about speeding, an Italian national pastime. They also frown on the widespread practice of "jumping the light". Fines are often paid on the spot. Ask for a receipt.

D

In cases of accidents on the road, call 112 for the *Carabinieri*. If your car is stolen or something is stolen from it, contact the Police Headquarters *(Questura)* in Florence at Via Zara, 2, and get them to draw up a certificate for the insurance.

Breakdowns: In Italy garages abound. Though most dislike dealing with any other make than Fiat, all major towns do have agencies for other models. Out in the country, mechanics in the small towns generally turn out to be very handy repairmen for any minor work.

Dial 116 for breakdown service from the Automobile Club d'Italia.

Distance:

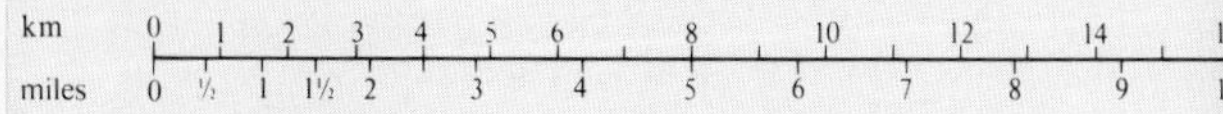

Road signs: Most road signs employed in Italy are international. But there are some written signs you might come across, too:

Accendere le luci	Use headlights
Curva pericolosa	Dangerous bend (curve)
Deviazione	Diversion (Detour)
Discesa pericolosa	Steep hill (with gradient percentage)
Divieto di sorpasso	No overtaking (passing)
Divieto di sosta	No stopping
Lavori in corso	Road works (Men working)
Parcheggio autorizzato	Parking allowed
Passaggio a livello	Level railway crossing
Passaggio limitato in altezza	Height restriction
Passaggio vietato ai pedoni	No pedestrians
Pericolo	Danger
Rallentare	Slow down
Senso vietato/unico	No entry/One-way street
Vietato l'ingresso	No entry
Zona pedonale	Pedestrian zone

(International) Driving Licence	**patente (internazionale)**
car registration papers	**libretto di circolazione**
Green Card	**carta verde**
Can I park here?	**Posso parcheggiare qui?**
Are we on the right road for…?	**Siamo sulla strada giusta per…?**
Fill the tank please…	**Per favore, faccia il pieno de…**
super/normal	**super/normale**
lead-free/diesel	**senza piombo/gasolio**

:heck the oil/tires/battery.	**Controlli l'olio/i pneumatici/ la batteria.**
've had a breakdown.	**Ho avuto un guasto.**
'here's been an accident.	**C'è stato un incidente.**

RUGS. Anyone possessing or selling drugs in Italy faces an unusual- aroused police force and extremely severe legal penalties. No dis- nction is made between soft and hard drugs. Present maximum sen- ence is about eight years in prison and/or extremely stiff fines.

In every sense, drugs are a huge risk in Italy. Because of the monu- nental backlog in the nation's court cases, a person arrested on suspi- ion of a narcotics crime may spend as long as one year in jail before ven being formally charged. Foreign consulates and embassies advise heir citizens that there is no way for them to speed up the legal rocess.

E

LECTRIC CURRENT *(corrente elettrica).* Florence now has 220- olt electric current. Non-Italian appliances may require a special plug) fit the sockets.

d like an adaptor/a battery.	**Vorrei una presa complementare/ una batteria.**

MERGENCIES. The Florence telephone service has several emer- ency numbers. The main ones are listed below. If you don't speak alian, try to find a local resident to help you call, or direct your roblems to the English-speaking operators of the telephone assist- nce service, 116 (see also Tourist Information Offices).

ll-purpose emergency police number	113
ssistance on the road—A.C.I.	116
'ire	222222
mergency medical service, holidays, night	477891
mbulance, first-aid	212222

)epending on the nature of the problem, see also separate entries uch as Consulates, Medical Care, Police, etc.

lease, can you place an mergency call for me to the...?	**Per favore, può fare per me una telefonata d'emergenza...?**
olice	**alla polizia**
re brigade	**ai pompieri**
ospital	**all'ospedale**

G

GUIDES and INTERPRETERS *(guida; interprete).* Most hotels ca arrange for multilingual guides or interpreters for any occasion. If yo prefer, you can contact the Associazione Guide Turistiche:

Viale Gramsci, 9a; tel. 247 81 88

We'd like an English-speaking guide.	**Desideriamo una guida che parla inglese.**
I need an English interpreter.	**Ho bisogno di un interprete d'inglese.**

H

HAIRDRESSERS and BARBERS* *(parrucchiere; barbiere).* It's wis for women to telephone for an appointment, although there are man hairdressers in Florence. Prices range from *haute coiffure* rates to ver reasonable. As in most countries, the owner of a salon should never b tipped. Give the shampooer, manicurist or stylist up to 15% of th bill's total. Many hairdressing salons have facilities for facial treat ments, make-up or massage.

I'd like a shampoo and set.	**Vorrei shampo e messa in piega.**
I want a…	**Voglio…**
haircut	**il taglio**
shave	**la rasatura**
blow-dry (brushing)	**asciugatura al fono**
permanent wave	**la permanente**
colour rinse	**un cachet**
manicure	**la manicure**
Don't cut it too short.	**Non li tagli troppo corti.**
A little more off (here).	**Un po' di più (qui).**

HITCH-HIKING *(autostop).* Hitch-hiking is forbidden on motorway in Italy; there are prominent *No Hitch-hiking* signs at entrances to th *autostrade.* Nonetheless, every summer thousands of young peopl hitch rides all over the country.

Can you give me a lift to…?	**Può darmi un passaggio fino a…**

L

LANGUAGE. Most hotel receptionists and sales staff in the shops an boutiques between the Duomo and Ponte Vecchio speak some English, French or German. Market stall-holders can at least tell you thei prices in English. For the rest, and that includes the *Vigili Urbani* or city police, Italian or sign language is essential. Don't shrink from having a go at the language—Italians appreciate an effort.

There are numerous possibilities for summer language courses for foreigners both in Florence and in Siena (where a pure Italian is spoken). The Italian State Tourist Office in your country will supply information.

The Berlitz phrase book ITALIAN FOR TRAVELLERS covers most situations you are likely to encounter in Italy; also useful is the Italian-English/English-Italian pocket dictionary, containing a special menu-reader supplement.

Do you speak English?	**Parla inglese?**
I don't speak Italian.	**Non parlo italiano.**

LAUNDRY and DRY-CLEANING *(lavanderia; tintoria).* Laundromats and dry-cleaners in the town are worth seeking out because hotels charge extremely high prices for such services. The yellow pages list addresses of establishments under "Lavanderia" and "Tintoria", or your hotel receptionist will tell you where the nearest facilities are to be found. The prices at a launderette are the same whether you do the job yourself or leave it with an attendant.

When will it be ready?	**Quando sarà pronto?**
I must have this for tomorrow morning.	**Mi serve per domani mattina.**

LOST PROPERTY *(oggetti smarriti).* If you've mislaid or lost something away from your hotel, have the receptionist call the Ufficio Oggetti Smarriti, or go yourself to the general lost property office at

Via Circondaria, 19

For property lost on trains: Piazza dell'Unità, 1

Taxi and bus drivers often turn in lost articles to their headquarters.

Lost children. If you lose a child in Florence, don't worry. Italians everywhere adore children, and someone will unfailingly look after your youngster on the way to the nearest police station. Just contact the *Carabinieri* at 212121 immediately.

I've lost my passport/wallet/handbag.	**Ho perso il passaporto/portafoglio/la borsetta.**

MAPS. News-stands and tourist offices have a large selection of maps You can obtain excellent free maps of the city and surrounding area from the tourist offices. The maps in this book were prepared by Falk Verlag, Hamburg, who also publishes a complete map of Florence.

a street plan of...	**un piantina di...**
a road map of this region	**una carta stradale di questa regione**

MEDICAL CARE. Citizens of Common Market countries are entitled to reimbursement for medical treatment in Italy, but ask your trave agent for details. Visitors whose insurance does not cover medical bill in Italy can take out a short-term holiday insurance policy before leav ing home.

Pharmacies. Most chemists' shops *(farmacia)* are open during shop ping hours, but some in Florence and its immediate vicinity are ope all night. There's one in the main hall at Santa Maria Novella railwa station. On weekends or public holidays the addresses of chemists o duty are published in the newspaper *La Nazione* and are also posted o every *farmacia* door. See also EMERGENCIES.

I need a doctor/a dentist.	**Ho bisogno di un medico/ dentista.**
I've a pain here.	**Ho un dolore qui.**
a stomach ache	**il mal di stomaco**
a fever	**la febbre**
a sunburn/sunstroke	**una scottatura di sole/un colpo di sole**

MEETING PEOPLE. Inordinately proud of their city, Florentines are only too pleased to show it off to visitors. Female tourists, however may find they receive too much attention from the male population Once beyond the usual opening line of "You speak English?" the of fers are apt to include a personally conducted tour of Florence, specia bargains in leatherware or taking the tourist's picture next to Michel angelo's *David.* If you're not interested, take no notice. Though Italian girls tend to go about in groups of two or three, they are by no mean shy and retiring and are often pleased to practise their English.

In the *passeggiata,* or evening walk, Florentines of all ages stroll up and down discussing the day's news. The venue is usually a street in the centre of town, and the hour varies according to the season.

IONEY MATTERS

:urrency. Italy's monetary unit is the *lira* (plural *lire*, abbreviated *L.* *r Lit.*).

Coins: L. 50, 100, 200 and 500.

Banknotes: L. 1,000, 2,000, 5,000, 10,000, 50,000 and 100,000.

For currency restrictions, see p. 109.

anking hours are from 8.20 a.m. to 1.20 p.m. and 2.45 to 3.45, Mon-ay to Friday.

:urrency exchange offices *(cambio).* Some exchange offices open on aturday mornings. On Sundays and holidays, the exchange window t the Santa Maria Novella station is always open. Shop around o find the best rate for your cash since banks and exchange offices ary.

:redit cards and traveller's cheques. Most major hotels and many res-aurants and shops now accept credit cards, but these do not entitle ou to any special discounts. Traveller's cheques are welcome almost nywhere, with certain shops advertising a discount (perhaps 10%) on urchases by cheque. However, this advantage may be offset by a oor exchange rate. Paying a hotel bill in foreign currency or by trav-ller's cheque is not wise, since the hotel's exchange rate is usually ower than that of a *cambio.* Eurocheques are easily cashed in Italy.

'rices *(prezzo).* Florence still remains relatively inexpensive for British r North American visitors. The exception is the fashionable centre Via de' Tornabuoni, Via de' Calzaiuoli) where prices compete with hose of New York, Paris or Zurich. In bars or cafés, sitting down and aving a waiter bring your *espresso* may cost you five times as nuch as having it at the counter. Cinemas and horse-drawn carriages re expensive, concerts and taxis reasonable, discotheques and night-lubs often ruinous.

want to change some pounds/ lollars.	**Desidero cambiare delle sterline/ dei dollari.**
)o you accept traveller's cheques?	**Accetta traveller's cheques?**
:an I pay with this credit card?	**Posso pagare con la carta di credito?**

IUSEUM HOURS

:asa Buonarroti. 9 a.m.–2 p.m., Monday and Wednesday to Satur-ay, 9 a.m.–1 p.m. Sundays and holidays, closed on Tuesdays.

M

Firenze com'era. 9 a.m.–2 p.m., Monday to Wednesday and Friday t Saturday, 8 a.m.–1 p.m. on Sundays and holidays, closed on Thurs days.

Galleria dell'Academia. 9 a.m.–2 p.m., Tuesday to Saturday, till 1 p.m on Sundays and holidays, closed on Mondays.

Galleria degli Uffizi. 9 a.m.–7 p.m., Tuesday to Saturday, till 1 p.m. o Sundays and holidays, closed on Mondays.

Museo della Fondazione Horne. 9 a.m.–1 p.m., daily except on Satu days and the second and last Sundays of each month, when it is close

Museo Nazionale (Bargello). 9 a.m.–2 p.m., Tuesday to Saturda 9 a.m.–1 p.m. Sundays and holidays. Closed on Mondays.

Museo dell'Opera di Santa Maria del Fiore. 9 a.m.–8 p.m. in summe 9 a.m.–6 p.m. in winter, 10 a.m.–1 p.m. on Sundays and holidays a year round.

Museo di San Marco. 9 a.m.–2 p.m., Tuesday to Saturday, till 1 p.m on Sundays and holidays, closed on Mondays.

Palazzo Pitti. 9 a.m.–2 p.m., Tuesday to Saturday, till 1 p.m. on Sun days and holidays, closed on Mondays.

Palazzo Vecchio (Palazzo della Signoria). 9 a.m.–7 p.m., Monda to Friday, 8 a.m.–1 p.m. on Sundays and holidays, closed on Satu days.

N

NEWSPAPERS and MAGAZINES *(giornale; rivista).* Many majc British and continental newspapers and magazines are on sale a kiosks—usually a day late—in the centre of Florence, at some hotel and at the station. But English-language periodicals are expensive The Paris-based *International Herald Tribune,* which does arriv the same day, carries news and full U.S. stock-market quotation Florence's most widely read daily, *La Nazione,* carries informatic on events, entertainment and cinemas and even devotes a column t activities for Florence's summer tourists.

P

PHOTOGRAPHY. Central Florence can pose some problems t would-be photographers—there's seldom enough clear distance i which to photograph a church or a monument without cutting part c it out. But don't be discouraged, you can still bring off some first-clas shots with a pocket camera. In summer, Florence's early morning c te afternoon sun is best for panoramic views (from the Piazzale Iichelangelo).

Photography is allowed in all state-owned museums provided you se neither flash nor tripod. In municipal museums you need special ermission.

All major brands and sizes of film are obtainable in Florence, but rices are higher than in most other countries.

d like a film for this camera.	**Vorrei una pellicola per questa macchina fotografica.**
black and white film	**una pellicola in bianco e nero**
colour-slide film	**una pellicola di diapositive**
film for colour prints	**una pellicola per fotografie a colori**
5-mm film	**una pellicola trentacinque millimetri**
iper-8	**super otto**
ow long will it take to develop is film?	**Quanto tempo ci vuole per sviluppare questa pellicola?**
Iay I take a picture?	**Posso fare una fotografia?**

OLICE. Florence's city police, *Vigili Urbani,* handle traffic, hand out arking fines and perform other routine police tasks. While rarely eaking a foreign language, *Vigili Urbani* are courteous and helpful tourists.

The *Carabinieri,* a paramilitary force, wear light brown or blue uni- rms and peaked caps, and deal with violent or serious crimes and emonstrations.

Outside of towns, the *Polizia Stradale* patrol the highways and yways (see under DRIVING).

ome police telephone numbers:

Vigili Urbani H.Q. *(Questura)*	49 66 46
Carabinieri, for emergencies	112
Polizia Stradale	57 77 77
Stolen vehicles department	49 77

here's also the all-purpose emergency number, 113, which will get ou police assistance.

here's the nearest police ation?	**Dov'è il più vicino posto di polizia?**

P

PUBLIC HOLIDAYS *(festa).* Banks, government institutions, mos shops and some museums are closed on all national holidays, as we as at least half a day for the Florentines' special holiday on the 24th c June. This is the day commemorating the town's patron saint, Giovan ni Battista. The week or ten days around August 15 *(Ferragosto)* see almost everything in Florence closed except hotels, a few shop chemists', cafés and restaurants and some of the major sightseein attractions.

January 1	*Capodanno* or *Primo dell'Anno*	New Year's Day
April 25	*Festa della Liberazione*	Liberation Day
May 1	*Festa del Lavoro*	Labour Day
August 15	*Ferragosto*	Assumption Day
November 1	*Ognissanti*	All Saints' Day
December 8	*Immacolata Concezione*	Immaculate Conception
December 25	*Natale*	Christmas Day
December 26	*Santo Stefano*	Saint Stephen's Day
Movable date:	*Lunedì di Pasqua*	Easter Monday

Are you open tomorrow? **È aperto domani?**

R

RADIO and TV *(radio; televisione).* During the tourist season, RA the Italian state radio and TV network, occasionally broadcasts new in English, predominantly about Italian affairs. Vatican Radio carrie foreign-language religious news programmes at various times durin the day. Shortwave radio reception in Florence is excellent throughou the night and part of the day. British (BBC), American (VOA) an Canadian (CBC) programmes are easily obtained on modest transisto radios. The American Southern European Broadcast (SEB) fron Vicenza can be heard on regular AM radio (middle or medium wave RAI television broadcasts only in Italian.

RELIGIOUS SERVICES *(funzione religiosa, messa).* The Duom (Sat. at 5.30 p.m.) and a few other churches celebrate mass in Englisl Confession can be made in English in most churches in the centre.

English-language services for non-Catholic denominations: R

American Episcopalian: St. James', Via B. Rucellai, 13

Anglican: St. Mark's, Via Maggio, 16

Christian Science: Via della Spada, 1

Jewish: synagogue at Via Farini, 4

SIESTA. Florence all but shuts down from 1 to 4 p.m. year-round, for the afternoon meal and a nap or a rest. In full summer it's easy to understand why. Most shops and many offices open again until about 7.30 p.m. Bars, tobacconists and some *farmacie* operate through this dead period, though in low gear. S

TIME DIFFERENCES. Italy follows Central European Time (GMT +1), and from April to September clocks are put one hour ahead (= GMT+2). Summer time chart: T

New York	London	**Italy**	Jo'burg	Sydney	Auckland
6 a.m.	11 a.m.	**noon**	noon	8 p.m.	10 p.m.

What time is it? **Che ore sono?**

TIPPING. Though a service charge is added to most restaurant bills, it is customary to leave an additional tip. It is also in order to hand the bellboys, doormen, hat check attendants, garage attendants, etc., a coin or two for their service.

The chart below gives some suggestions as to what to leave.

Hotel porter, per bag	L. 1,000
Maid, per day	L. 1,000–2,000
Lavatory attendant	L. 300
Waiter	10%
Taxi driver	10%
Haidresser/barber	up to 15%
Tour guide	10%

T

TOILETS. You'll find public toilets in most museums and galleries; restaurants, bars, cafés and large stores usually have facilities; airports and train stations always do. They may be designated in different ways: W.C. (for water closet) with the picture of a man or woman; sometimes the wording will be in Italian—*Uomini* (men) or *Donne* (women). The most confusing label for foreigners is *Signori* (men—with a final *i*) and *Signore* (women—with a final *e*).

Where are the toilets? **Dove sono i gabinetti?**

TOURIST INFORMATION OFFICES. Italian State Tourist Offices (in America called Italian Government Travel Offices) are maintained in many countries throughout the world. Their Italian name: Ente Nazionale Italiano per il Turismo, abbreviated E.N.I.T.

Australia and New Zealand. E.N.I.T., c/o Alitalia, 118 Alfred Street, Milson Point 2061, Sydney; tel. 2921-555

Canada. 3, Place Ville-Marie, Suite 22, Montreal 113, Que.; tel. (514) 849-8351

Eire. 47, Merrion Square, Dublin 2; tel. (01) 766-397

South Africa. E.N.I.T., London House, 21 Loveday Street, P.O. Box 6507, Johannesburg; tel. 838-3247

United Kingdom. 1, Princes Street, London W1 8AY; tel. (01) 408-1254

U.S.A. 500 N. Michigan Avenue, Chicago, IL 60611; tel (312) 644-0990
630 Fifth Avenue, New York, NY 10020; tel. (212) 245-4961/4
St. Francis Hotel, 360 Post Street, Suite 801, San Francisco, CA 94108; tel. (415) 392-5266

In **Florence,** refer to the tourist information office at:

Via de' Tornabuoni, 15; tel. 21 65 44

If you're interested in visiting local farms and Chianti vineyards, contact Agriturist, at:

Via del Proconsolo, 10; tel. 28 78 38

Telephone assistance service:
The English-speaking operators here will answer your questions and give advice. They also serve as trouble shooters, offering help to visitors who have problems. Dial 116 anywhere in Italy.

Where's the tourist office? **Dov'è l'ufficio turistico?**

TRANSPORT

Buses★ *(autobus).* Florence has about 40 main city and suburban bus routes. For all information about buses, and for a useful free bus map, go to the A.T.A.F. office at Piazza del Duomo, 57r.

You must buy your bus ticket in advance at a tobacconist or bar. When you board a bus (always at the rear), punch your ticket in the *red* machine. Long-distance bus companies cover the whole of Tuscany, and go as far as Venice and Rome. Your hotel or any travel agent will supply information.

Taxis *(taxi).* Florence's taxis, which are still fairly cheap by northern European and American standards, may be hailed in the street (a green light tells you when they're free), picked up at a taxi rank or obtained by telephone (4798 and 4390). Cabs are yellow. Fares are indicated on meters, plus extra charges for luggage, station pick-ups and for night rides. A 10% tip is in order, or more if the driver has been especially helpful.

Trains *(treno).* Italian trains *try* to run on time as advertised. If you haven't booked, it is wise to arrive at the station at least 20 minutes before departure to be sure of a seat: Italy's trains are often very crowded. The following list describes the various types of trains:

EuroCity (EC)	International express; first and second class.
Intercity (IC)	Inter-city express with very few stops; a luxury international service with first and second class.
Rapido (R)	Long-distance express train stopping at major cities only; first and second class.
Espresso (EXP)/ Direttissimo	Long-distance train, stopping at main stations.
Diretto (D)	Slower than the *Espresso,* it makes a number of local stops.
Locale (L)	Local train which stops at almost every station.
Accelerato (A)	Same as a *Locale.*

T

Littorina	Small diesel train used on short runs.		
Carozza ristorante	*Vagone letto*	*Carozza cuccette*	*Bagagliaio*
Dining car	Sleeping car with individual compartments and washing facilities	Sleeping berth car (couchette); blankets and pillows	Guard's van (baggage car); normally only registered luggage permitted

When's the next bus/train to...?	**Quando parte il prossimo autobus/treno per...?**
I want a ticket to...	**Vorrei un biglietto per...**
single (one-way)	**andata**
return (round-trip)	**andata e ritorno**
first/second class	**prima/seconda classe**
Will you tell me when to get off?	**Può dirmi quando devo scendere?**
Where can I get a taxi?	**Dove posso trovare un taxi?**
What's the fare to...?	**Qual è la tariffa per...?**

W

WATER *(acqua).* Florence's tap-water is not very tasty, but it's drinkable. One of the only places where water still actually tastes natural is in the inner courtyard of the Palazzo Pitti. You'll see local people filling bottles and other containers at its two fountains.

With meals, take wine and/or bottled mineral water. Mineral waters are popularly believed to help not only digestion, but an incredible array of afflictions, and there's certainly something to it. There'll be a sign reading *acqua non potabile* where water is not for drinking.

a bottle of mineral water	**una bottiglia di acqua minerale**
carbonated/non-carbonated	**gasata/naturale**

SOME USEFUL EXPRESSIONS

yes/no	**sì/no**
please/thank you	**per favore/grazie**
excuse me/you're welcome	**mi scusi/prego**
where/when/how	**dove/quando/come**
how long/how far	**quanto tempo/quanto dista**
yesterday/today/tomorrow	**ieri/oggi/domani**
day/week/month/year	**giorno/settimana/mese/anno**
left/right	**sinistra/destra**
up/down	**su/giù**
good/bad	**buono/cattivo**
big/small	**grande/piccolo**
cheap/expensive	**buon mercato/caro**
hot/cold	**caldo/freddo**
old/new	**vecchio/nuovo**
open/closed	**aperto/chiuso**
free (vacant)/occupied	**libero/occupato**
near/far	**vicino/lontano**
early/late	**presto/tardi**
quick/slow	**rapido/lento**
full/empty	**pieno/vuoto**
easy/difficult	**facile/difficile**
right/wrong	**giusto/sbagliato**
here/there	**qui/là**
Does anyone here speak English?	**C'è qualcuno qui che parla inglese?**
I don't understand.	**Non capisco.**
Please write it down.	**Lo scriva, per favore.**
Waiter/Waitress, please.	**Cameriere!/Cameriera!** (or **Senta!** = "listen")
I'd like…	**Vorrei…**
How much is that?	**Quant'è?**
Have you something less expensive?	**Ha qualcosa di meno caro?**
What time is it?	**Che ore sono?**
Just a minute.	**Un attimo.**
Help me, please.	**Per favore, mi aiuti.**

Index

An asterisk (*) next to a page number indicates a map reference
For index to Practical Information, see also inside front cover.

118/902 RP

Selection of Florence Hotels and Restaurants

BERLITZ®

Where do you start? Choosing a hotel or restaurant in a pla you're not familiar with can be daunting. To help you find yo way amid the bewildering variety, we have made a selecti from the *Red Guide to Italy 1987* published by Micheli the recognized authority on gastronomy and accommodati throughout Europe.

Our own Berlitz criteria have been price and location. In t hotel section, for a double room with bath but witho breakfast, Higher-priced means above L. 250,000, Mediu priced L. 120,000–250,000, Lower-priced below L. 120,000. to restaurants, for a meal consisting of a starter, a main cour and a dessert, Higher-priced means above L. 40,000, Mediu priced L. 30,000–40,000, Lower-priced below L. 30,00 Special features where applicable, plus regular closing days a also given. As a general rule many Florence restaurants a closed in August. For hotels and restaurants, both a check make certain that they are open and advance reservations a advisable. In Florence restaurants, 12–15% service charge w be added to the bill.

In Florence, hotel reservations can be made at the I.T. counter at the railway station.

For a wider choice of hotels and restaurants, we strong recommend you obtain the authoritative Michelin *Red Guide Italy,* which gives a comprehensive and reliable picture of t situation throughout the country.

HOTELS

HIGHER-PRICED
(above L. 250,000)

Excelsior
piazza Ognissanti 3
50123 Florence
Tel. 264201
Tlx. 570022
Summer restaurant service on terrace with view.

Grand Hotel Villa Cora
viale Machiavelli 18, Colli
50125 Florence
Tel. 2298451
Tlx. 570604
Pleasant hotel. Flower-park with outdoor swimming pool. Taverna Machiavelli restaurant.

Regency
piazza Massimo D'Azeglio 3
50121 Florence
Tel. 245247
Tlx. 571058
Pleasant hotel. Charming garden.

Villa La Massa
Candeli
50010 Florence
Tel. 630051
Tlx. 573555
18th-century building, furnished in period style. Quiet hotel. Heated outdoor swimming pool. Garden. Hotel tennis court. Il Verrocchio restaurant.

Villa Medici
via Il Prato 42
50123 Florence
Tel. 261331
Tlx. 570179
Outdoor swimming pool.

MEDIUM-PRICED
(L. 120,000–250,000)

Baglioni
piazza Unità Italiana 6
50123 Florence
Tel. 218441
Tlx. 570225
Roof-garden restaurant with view.

Continental
lungarno Acciaiuoli 2
50123 Florence
Tel. 282392
Tlx. 580525
Flowered terrace with view. No restaurant.

Crest
viale Europa 205
50126 Florence
Tel. 686841
Tlx. 570376
Heated outdoor swimming pool. Garden. La Tegolaia restaurant.

Croce di Malta
via della Scala 7
50123 Florence
Tel. 218351
Tlx. 570540
Outdoor swimming pool. Garden. Il Coccodrillo restaurant.

Della Signoria
via delle Terme 1
50123 Florence
Tel. 214530
Tlx. 571561
No restaurant.

Grand Hotel Minerva
piazza Santa Maria Novella 16
50123 Florence
Tel. 284555
Tlx. 570414
Outdoor swimming pool.

Jolly
piazza Vittorio Veneto 4/a
50123 Florence
Tel. 2770
Tlx. 570191
Outdoor swimming pool on panoramic terrace.

Kraft
via Solferino 2
50123 Florence
Tel. 284273
Tlx. 571523
Roof-garden restaurant with view. Outdoor swimming pool.

Lungarno
borgo Sant'Jacopo 14
50125 Florence
Tel. 264211
Tlx. 570129
View. Collection of modern paintings. No restaurant.

Montebello Splendid
via Montebello 60
50123 Florence
Tel. 298051
Tlx. 574009
Garden.

Plaza Hotel Lucchesi
lungarno della Zecca Vecchia 38
50122 Florence
Tel. 264141
Tlx. 570302
View.

Principe
lungarno Vespucci 34
50123 Florence
Tel. 284848
Tlx. 571400
View. Garden. No restaurant.

Relais Certosa
via Colle Ramole 2, Galluzzo
50124 Florence
Tel. 2047171
Tlx. 574332
View. Heated outdoor swimming pool. Garden. Hotel tennis court.

Villa Belvedere
via Benedetto Castelli 3, Colli
50124 Florence
Tel. 222501
Quiet hotel. View of city and hills. Garden with outdoor swimming pool. Hotel tennis court.

Villa Carlotta
via Michele di Lando 3, Colli
50125 Florence
Tel. 220530
Tlx. 573485
Quiet hotel with charming garden.

Villa le Rondini
via Bolognese Vecchia 224
Trespiano
50139 Florence
Tel. 400081
Quiet, pleasant hotel, set amid olive trees. Outdoor swimming pool. Hotel tennis court.

Villa Liberty
viale Michelangiolo 40
50125 Florence
Tel. 6810581
Garden. No restaurant.

Ville sull'Arno
lungarno Colombo 5
50136 Florence
Tel. 670971
Tlx. 573297
View. Heated outdoor swimming pool. No restaurant.

LOWER-PRICED
(below L. 120,000)

Astor
viale Milton 41
50129 Florence
Tel. 483391
Tlx. 573155

Balestri
piazza Mentana 7
50122 Florence
Tel. 214743
No restaurant.

Calzaiuoli
via Calzaiuoli 6
50122 Florence
Tel. 212456
Tlx. 580589
No restaurant.

Caravel
via Alamanni 9
50123 Florence
Tel. 217651
No restaurant.

Concorde
viale Gori 10
50127 Florence
Tel. 373551
Tlx. 573362

David
viale Michelangiolo 1
50125 Florence
Tel. 6811696
Tlx. 574553
No restaurant.

Fiorino
via Osteria del Guanto 6
50122 Florence
Tel. 210579
No restaurant.

Golf
viale Fratelli Rosselli 56
50123 Florence
Tel. 293088
Tlx. 571630
No restaurant.

Helvetia e Bristol
via de'Pescioni 2
50123 Florence
Tel. 287814
No restaurant.

Jane
via Orcagna 56
50121 Florence
Tel. 677383
No restaurant.

Rapallo
via di Santa Caterina d'Alessandria 7
50129 Florence
Tel. 472412
Tlx. 574251

Royal
via delle Ruote 52
50129 Florence
Tel. 483287
Quiet hotel. Pleasant garden. No restaurant.

Silla
via dei Renai 5
50125 Florence
Tel. 284810
No restaurant.

RESTAURANTS

HIGHER-PRICED
(above L. 40,000)

Cammillo
borgo Sant'Jacopo 57
50125 Florence
Tel. 212427
Notably good cuisine. Typical Florentine trattoria. Closed Wednesday and Thursday.

Da Dante-al Lume di Candela
via delle Terme 23
50123 Florence
Tel. 294566
Reservation essential. Closed Sunday, and Monday lunchtime.

Da Noi
via Fiesolana 46
50122 Florence
Tel. 242917
Notably good cuisine. Reservation essential. Closed Sunday and Monday.

Enoteca Pinchiorri
via Ghibellina 87
50122 Florence
Tel. 242757
Excellent cuisine. Evening service in cool courtyard. Reservation essential. Closed Sunday, and Monday lunchtime.

Gourmet
via II Prato 68
50123 Florence
Tel. 294766
Restaurant with American-style bar. Reservation essential. Closed Sunday.

Harry's Bar
lungarno Vespucci 22
50123 Florence
Tel. 296700
Reservation essential. Closed Sunday.

Sabatini
via de'Panzani 9/a
50123 Florence
Tel. 282802
Elegant traditional decor. Closed Monday.

MEDIUM PRICED
(L. 30,000–40,000)

Al Campidoglio
via del Campidoglio 8
50123 Florence
Tel. 287770
Closed Thursday.

Antico Crespino
largo Enrico Fermi 15, Colli
50125 Florence
Tel. 221155
View. Closed Wednesday.

Barrino
via de'Biffi 2
50122 Florence
Tel. 215180
Restaurant with American-style bar. Reserve. Closed at lunchtime and on Sundays.

Buca Lapi
via del Trebbio 1
50123 Florence
Tel. 213768
Typical taverna. Closed Sunday, and Monday at lunchtime.

Buca Mario
piazza Ottaviani 16
50123 Florence
Tel. 214179
Typical trattoria. Closed Wednesday, and Thursday at lunchtime.

Cafaggi
via Guelfa 35
50129 Florence
Tel. 294989
Closed Sunday evening and Monday.

Cavallino
via delle Farine 6
50122 Florence
Tel. 215818
Typical habitués' restaurant. Outdoor dining in summer with view. Closed Tuesday evening and Wednesday.

Celestino
piazza Santa Felicita 4
50125 Florence
Tel. 296574
Closed Sunday.

Drago Verde
via del Leone 50
50124 Florence
Tel. 224002
Outdoor dining. Closed Saturday lunchtime and Sunday.

---

13 Gobbi
via del Porcellana 9
50123 Florence
Tel. 298769
Tuscan specialities. Closed Sunday and Monday.

Il Profeta
borgo Ognissanti 93
50123 Florence
Tel. 212265
Closed Sunday and Monday.

La Greppia
lungarno Ferrucci 8
50126 Florence
Tel. 6812341
Country-style restaurant and pizzeria. Summer dining on terrace with view. Closed Monday.

La Loggia
piazzale Michelangiolo 1
50125 Florence
Tel. 287032
Outdoor dining in summer with view. Closed Wednesday.

Lo Strettoio
Serpiolle
50142 Florence
Tel. 403044
17th-century villa amid olive grove. Outdoor dining. By reservation only. Closed Sunday and Monday.

Paoli
via dei Tavolini 12
50122 Florence
Tel. 216215
Typical restaurant. Reproduction 14th-century-style decor. Closed Tuesday.

Trattoria Vittoria
via della Fonderia 52
50142 Florence
Tel. 225657
Seafood specialities. Closed Wednesday.

LOWER-PRICED
(below L. 30,000)

Bordino
via Stracciatella 9
50125 Florence
Tel. 213048
Typical trattoria. Reserve. Closed at lunchtime, Sunday and Monday.

Il Caminetto
via dello Studio 34
50122 Florence
Tel. 296274
Closed Tuesday evening and Wednesday.

Il Fagioli
corso Tintori 47
50122 Florence
Tel. 244285
Typical Tuscan trattoria. Closed Sunday and also on Saturday in summer .

Il Tirabuscio
via de' Benci 34
50122 Florence
Tel. 2476225
Reservation essential. Closed Thursday and Friday.

La Carabaccia
via Palazzuolo 190
50123 Florence
Tel. 214782
By reservation only. Closed Sunday and Monday lunchtime.

Le Quattro Stagioni
via Maggio 61
50125 Florence
Tel. 218906
Reservation essential. Closed Sunday.

Omero
via Pian de' Giullari 11
Arcetri
50125 Florence
Tel. 220053
Country trattoria with view. Summer dining on terrace. Closed Tuesday.

Pierot
piazza Taddeo Gaddi 25
50142 Florence
Tel. 702100
Closed Sunday.

BERLITZ®

ITALIAN
for travellers

By the staff of Berlitz Guides

How best to use this phrase book

● We suggest that you start with the **Guide to pronunciatio** (pp. 6–8), then go on to **Some basic expressions** (pp. 9–15). Th gives you not only a minimum vocabulary, but also helps you g used to pronouncing the language. The phonetic transcriptic throughout the book enables you to pronounce every word correctl

● Consult the **Contents** pages (3–5) for the section you need. each chapter you'll find travel facts, hints and useful informatio Simple phrases are followed by a list of words applicable to tl situation.

● Separate, detailed contents lists are included at the beginning (the extensive **Eating out** and **Shopping guide** sections (Menus, p. 3 Shops and services, p. 97).

● If you want to find out how to say something in Italian, yo fastest look-up is via the **Dictionary** section (pp. 164–189). Th not only gives you the word, but is also cross-referenced to its u in a phrase on a specific page.

● If you wish to learn more about constructing sentences, chec the **Basic grammar** (pp. 159–163).

● Note the **colour margins** are indexed in Italian and English help both listener and speaker. And, in addition, there is also a **index in Italian** for the use of your listener.

● Throughout the book, this symbol ☛ suggests phrases yo listener can use to answer you. If you still can't understand, har this phrase book to the Italian-speaker to encourage pointing to a appropriate answer. The English translation for you is just alon side the Italian.

Library of Congress Catalog Card No. 85-81373

Second revised edition—7th printing 1989
Printed in Austria

Contents

cknowledgments

/e are particularly grateful to Francesca Grazzi Rahimi for her elp in the preparation of this book, and to Dr. T.J.A. Bennett who evised the phonetic transcription.

Guide to pronunciation

An outline of the spelling and sounds of Italian

You'll find the pronunciation of the Italian letters and sound explained below, as well as the symbols we're using for ther in the transcriptions. Note that Italian has some diacritica letters—letters with accent marks—which we don't use i English.

The imitated pronunciation should be read as if it wer English except for any special rules set out below. It is base on Standard British pronunciation, though we have tried t take account of General American pronunciation also. C course, the sounds of any two languages are never exact the same; but if you follow carefully the indications supplie here, you'll have no difficulty in reading our transcription in such a way as to make yourself understood.

Letters written in **bold** should be stressed (pronounce louder).

Consonants

Letter	Approximate pronunciation	Symbol	Example	
b, d, f, k, l, m, n, p, q t, v	as in English			
c	1) before **e** and **i**, like **ch** in **ch**ip	ch	**cerco**	**chayr**koa
	2) elsewhere, like **c** in **cat**	k	**conto**	**koan**toa
ch	like **c** in **cat**	k	**che**	kay
g	1) before **e** and **i**, like **j** in **j**et	j	**valigia**	vah**lee**jah
	2) elsewhere, like **g** in **go**	g	**grande**	**grahn**day

h	like **g** in **go**	g	**ghiaccio**	gee**aht**choa
l	like **lli** in mi**lli**on	ly	**gli**	lyee
n	like **ni** in on**i**on	ñ	**bagno**	**bah**ñoa
	always silent		**ha**	ah
	trilled like a Scottish **r**	r	**deriva**	deh**ree**vah
	1) generally like **s** in **s**it	s	**questo**	koo**ay**stoa
	2) sometimes like **z** in **z**oo	z	**viso**	**vee**zoa
c	1) before **e** and **i**, like **sh** in **sh**ut	sh	**uscita**	oo**shee**tah
	2) elsewhere, like **sk** in **sk**in	sk	**scarpa**	**skahr**pah
/zz	1) generally like **ts** in hi**ts**	ts	**grazie**	**graa**tseeay
	2) sometimes like **ds** in roa**ds**	dz	**romanzo**	roa**mahn**dzoa

owels

	1) short, like **a** in c**a**r, but shorter	ah	**gatto**	**gaht**toa
	2) long, like **a** in c**a**r	aa	**casa**	**kaa**sah
	1) can always be pronounced like **ay** in w**ay**, but without moving tongue or lips	ay	**sera**	**say**rah
	2) in correct speech, it is sometimes pronounced like **e** in g**e**t or, when long,	eh	**bello**	**behl**loa
	more like **ai** in h**ai**r	ai	**bene**	**bai**nay
	like **ee** in m**ee**t	ee	**vini**	**vee**nee
	1) can always be pronounced like **oa** in g**oa**t, but without moving tongue or lips	oa	**sole**	**soa**lay
	2) in correct speech, it is sometimes pronounced like **o** in g**o**t, or when long,	o	**notte**	**not**tay
	more like **aw** in l**aw**	aw	**rosa**	**raw**zah
	like **oo** in f**oo**t	oo	**fumo**	**foo**moa

Two or more vowels

In groups of vowels **a, e,** and **o** are strong vowels, and **i** an **u** are weak vowels. When two strong vowels are next to eac other, they are pronounced as two separate syllables, e.g. *beato* = bay**ah**toa. When a strong and weak vowel are nex to each other, the weak one is pronounced more quickly an with less stress (less loudly) than the strong one, e.g., *piede* = pee**ay**day; such sounds are diphthongs and constitute onl one syllable. If the weak vowel is stressed, then it is pro-nounced as a separate syllable, e.g., *due* = **doo**ay. Two wea vowels together are pronounced as a diphthong, and it i generally the second one that is more strongly stressed, e.g. *guida* = goo**ee**dah.

Stressing of words

Generally, the vowel of the next to last syllable is stressed When a final vowel is stressed, it has an accent written ove it *(caffè)*. Normally, when the stress falls on the syllab before the next to last one, it is not indicated by an accent

Pronunciation of the Italian alphabet

A	ah	H	**ahk**kah	O	o	V	vee
B	boo	I	ee	P	pee	W	vee **doa**ppeeah
C	chee	J	ee **loong**gah	Q	koo	X	eeks
D	dee	K	**kah**ppah	R	**eh**rray	Y	ee **gray**kah
E	ay	L	**eh**llay	S	**eh**ssay	Z	**dzay**tah
F	**eh**ffay	M	**eh**mmay	T	tee		
G	jee	N	**eh**nnay	U	oo		

Some basic expressions

Yes.	**Sì.**	see
No.	**No.**	no
Please.	**Per favore/ Per piacere.**	pair fah**voa**ray/ pair peeah**chay**ray
Thank you.	**Grazie.**	**graa**tseeay
Thank you very much.	**Molte grazie/ Tante grazie.**	**moal**tay **graa**tseeay/ **tahn**tay **graa**tseeay
That's all right/ You're welcome.	**Prego.**	**pray**goa

Greetings *Saluti*

Good morning.	**Buon giorno.**	bwon **joar**noa
Good afternoon.	**Buon giorno.**	bwon **joar**noa
Good evening.	**Buona sera.**	**bwo**nah **say**rah
Good night.	**Buona notte.**	**bwo**nah **not**tay
Good-bye.	**Arrivederci.**	ahrreevay**dair**chee
So long!	**Ciao!**	**chaa**oa
See you later.	**A più tardi.**	ah pee**oo** **tahr**dee
This is Mr./Mrs./ Miss …	**Le presento il Signor/la Signora/la Signorina …**	lay pray**zayn**toa eel see**ñoar**/lah see**ñoa**rah/ lah seeñoa**ree**nah
How do you do? (Pleased to meet you.)	**Molto lieto(a).***	**moal**toa lee**ay**toa(ah)
How are you?	**Come sta?**	**koa**may stah
Very well, thanks. And you?	**Molto bene, grazie. E lei?**	**moal**toa **bai**nay **graa**tseeay. ay **la**lee

* In the case where there are masculine and feminine forms of a word, we give the masculine first, with the feminine in brackets afterwards; in this example, a woman would say **Molto lieta.**

How's life?	**Come va?**	koamay vah
Fine.	**Bene.**	bainay
I beg your pardon?	**Prego?**	praygoa
Excuse me.	**Mi scusi.**	mee skoozee
Excuse me. (May I get past?)	**Permesso?**	pairmaissoa
Sorry!	**Mi dispiace.**	mee deespeeahchay

Questions *Domande*

Where?	**Dove?**	doavay
How?	**Come?**	koamay
When?	**Quando?**	kwahndoa
What?	**Che cosa/Che?**	kay kawsah/kay
Why?	**Perchè?**	pehrkay
Who?	**Chi?**	kee
Which?	**Quale?**	kwaalay
Where is ...?	**Dov'è/Dove si trova ...?**	doavai/doavay see trawvah
Where are ...?	**Dove sono/ Dove si trovano ...?**	doavay soanoa/doavay see trawvahnoa
Where can I find/ get ...?	**Dove posso trovare ...?**	doavay possoa trovaaray
How far?	**Quanto dista?**	kwahntoa deestah
How long?	**Quanto tempo?**	kwahntoa tehmpoa
How much/How many?	**Quanto/Quanti?**	kwahntoa/kwahntee
How much does this cost?	**Quanto costa questo?**	kwahntoa kostah kooaystoa
When does ... open/ close?	**A che ora apre/ chiude ...?**	ah kay oarah aapray/ keeooday
What do you call this/that in Italian?	**Come si chiama questo/quello in italiano?**	koamay see keeaamah kooaystoa/kooaylloa een eetahleeaanoa
What does this/that mean?	**Che cosa significa questo/quello?**	kay kawsah seeñeefeekah kooaystoa/kooaylloa

Do you speak ...? *Parla ...?*

Do you speak English?	**Parla inglese?**	**pahr**lah eeng**glay**say
Is there anyone here who speaks ...?	**C'è qualcuno qui che parla ...?**	chai kwahl**koo**noa koo**ee** kay **pahr**lah
I don't speak (much) Italian.	**Non parlo (bene) l'italiano.**	noan **pahr**loa (**bai**nay) leetahlee**aa**noa
Could you speak more slowly?	**Può parlare più lentamente, per favore?**	pwo pahr**laa**ray pee**oo** layntah**mayn**tay pair fah**voa**ray
Could you repeat that?	**Vuol ripetere, per favore?**	vwol ree**pai**tayray pair fah**voa**ray
Could you spell it?	**Può sillabarlo?**	pwo seellah**baar**loa
Please write it down.	**Per favore, me lo scriva.**	pair fah**voa**ray may loa **skree**vah
Can you translate this for me?	**Può tradurmi questo?**	pwo trah**door**mee koo**ay**stoa
Please point to the word/phrase/ sentence in the book.	**Per favore, mi indichi la parola/ l'espressione/ la frase nel libro.**	pair fah**voa**ray mee **een**deekee lah pah**ro**lah/ laysprehssee**oa**nay/ lah **fraa**zay nehl **lee**broa
Just a minute. I'll see if I can find it in this book.	**Un attimo. Guardo se posso trovarla in questo libro.**	oon **aht**teemoa. **gwahr**doa say **pos**soa troa**vaar**lah een koo**ay**stoa **lee**broa
It's on page ...	**È a pagina ...**	ai ah **paa**jeenah
I understand.	**Capisco.**	kah**pee**skoa
I don't understand.	**Non capisco.**	noan kah**pee**skoa
Do you understand?	**Capisce?**	kah**pee**shay

Can/May ...? *Posso ...?*

Can I have ...?	**Posso avere ...?**	**pos**soa ah**vay**ray
Can we have ...?	**Possiamo avere ...?**	possee**aa**moa ah**vay**ray
Can you show me ...?	**Può mostrarmi ...?**	pwo moa**straar**mee
I can't.	**Non posso.**	noan **pos**soa
Can you tell me ...?	**Può dirmi ...?**	pwo **deer**mee

Can you help me?	**Può aiutarmi?**	pwo aheeoo**taar**mee
Can I help you?	**Posso aiutarla?**	**pos**soa aheeoo**taar**lah
Can you direct me to ...?	**Può indicarmi la direzione per ...?**	pwo eendee**kahr**mee lah deeraytsee**oa**nay pair

Wanting ... *Vorrei ...*

I'd like ...	**Vorrei ...**	vorraiee
We'd like ...	**Vorremmo ...**	vor**rehm**moa
What do you want?	**Che cosa desidera?**	kay **kaw**sah day**zee**dayrah
Give me ...	**Mi dia ...**	mee **dee**ah
Give it to me.	**Me lo dia.**	may loa **dee**ah
Bring me ...	**Mi porti ...**	mee **por**tee
Bring it to me.	**Me lo porti.**	may loa **por**tee
Show me ...	**Mi mostri ...**	mee **moa**stree
Show it to me.	**Me lo mostri.**	may loa **moa**stree
I'm looking for ...	**Cerco ...**	**chayr**koa
I'm hungry.	**Ho fame.**	oa **faa**may
I'm thirsty.	**Ho sete.**	oa **say**tay
I'm tired.	**Sono stanco(a).**	**soa**noa **stahng**koa(ah)
I'm lost.	**Mi sono perduto(a).**	mee **soa**noa pehr**doo**toa(ah)
It's important.	**È importante.**	ai eempor**tahn**tay
It's urgent.	**È urgente.**	ai oor**jehn**tay
Hurry up!	**Presto!**	**preh**stoa

It is/There is ... *È/C'è ...*

It is/It's ...	**È ...**	ai
Is it ...?	**È ...?**	ai
It isn't ...	**Non è ...**	noan ai
Here it is. (masc./fem.)	**Eccolo/Eccola.**	**ehk**koaloa/**ehk**koalah
Here they are. (masc./fem.)	**Eccoli/Eccole.**	**ehk**koalee/**ehk**koalay

There it is.	**Eccolo/Eccola.**	**ehk**koaloa/**ehk**koalah
There they are.	**Eccoli/Eccole.**	**ehk**koalee/**ehk**koalay
There is/There are ...	**C'è/Ci sono ...**	chai/chee **soa**noa
Is there/Are there ...?	**C'è/Ci sono ...?**	chai/chee **soa**noa
There isn't/aren't ...	**Non c'è/Non ci sono ...**	noan chai/noan chee **soa**noa
There isn't/aren't any.	**Non ce n'è/Non ce ne sono.**	noan chay nai/noan chay nay **soa**noa

It's ... *È ...*

big/small	**grande/piccolo***	**grahn**day/**peek**koaloa
quick/slow	**rapido/lento**	**raa**peedoa/**lehn**toa
hot/cold	**caldo/freddo**	**kahl**doa/**frayd**doa
full/empty	**pieno/vuoto**	pee**ay**noa/**vwaw**toa
easy/difficult	**facile/difficile**	**faa**cheelay/deef**fee**cheelay
heavy/light	**pesante/leggero**	pay**sahn**tay/layd**jai**roa
open/shut	**aperto/chiuso**	ah**pehr**toa/kee**oo**soa
right/wrong	**giusto/sbagliato**	**joo**stoa/zbahl**yaa**toa
old/new	**vecchio/nuovo**	**vehk**keeoa/**nwaw**voa
old/young	**anziano/giovane**	ahntsee**aa**noa/**joa**vahnay
beautiful/ugly	**bello/brutto**	**bail**loa/**broot**toa
free (vacant)/ occupied	**libero/occupato**	**lee**bayroa/okkoo**paa**toa
good/bad	**buono/cattivo**	**bwaw**noa/kaht**tee**voa
better/worse	**migliore/peggiore**	meel**yoa**ray/payd**joa**ray
here/there	**qui/là**	koo**ee**/**lah**
early/late	**presto/tardi**	**preh**stoa/**tahr**dee
cheap/expensive	**buon mercato/caro**	bwawn mayr**kah**toa/**kaa**roa
near/far	**vicino/lontano**	vee**chee**noa/lon**taa**noa
first/last	**primo/ultimo**	**pree**moa/**ool**teemoa

* For feminine and plural forms, see grammar section page 160 (adjectives).

Quantities *Quantità*

a little/a lot	**un po'/molto**	oon po/**moal**toa
few/a few	**pochi/alcuni**	**po**kee/ahl**koo**nee
much	**molto**	**moal**toa
many	**molti**	**moal**tee
more/less	**più/meno**	pee**oo**/**mai**noa
more than/less than	**più di/meno di**	pee**oo** dee/**mai**noa dee
enough/too	**abbastanza/troppo**	ahbbah**stahn**tsah/**trop**poa
some/any	**del, della, dei, degli, delle**	dayl **dayl**lah **dai**ee **day**lyee **dayl**lay

Some prepositions ... *Alcune preposizioni ...*

at	**a***	ah
on	**su**	soo
in	**in**	een
to	**a**	ah
after	**dopo**	**daw**poa
before (time)	**prima di**	**pree**mah dee
before (place)	**davanti a**	dah**vahn**tee ah
for	**per**	pair
from	**da**	dah
with	**con**	kon
without	**senza**	**sayn**tsah
through	**per, attraverso**	pair ahttrah**vehr**soa
towards	**verso**	**vehr**soa
until	**fino a**	**fee**noa ah
during	**durante**	doo**rahn**tay
next to	**accanto a**	ahk**kahn**toa ah
near	**vicino a**	vee**chee**noa ah
behind	**dietro**	dee**ay**troa

* See also grammar section page 163 (prepositions).

between	**tra, fra**	trah frah
since	**da**	dah
above	**sopra**	**soa**prah
below	**al di sotto**	ahl dee **sot**toa
under	**sotto**	**sot**toa
inside	**dentro**	**dayn**troa
outside	**fuori**	**fwaw**ree
up	**su, in alto**	soo een ahltoa
upstairs	**di sopra**	dee **soa**prah
down	**giù**	joo
downstairs	**di sotto**	dee **sot**toa

... and a few more useful words *... e qualche altra parola utile*

and	**e**	ay
or	**o**	oa
not	**non**	noan
never	**mai**	**ma**hee
nothing	**nulla/niente**	**nool**lah/nee**ayn**tay
something	**qualcosa**	kwahl**kaw**sah
none	**nessuno**	nays**soo**noa
very	**molto**	**moal**toa
too, also	**anche**	**ahng**kay
yet	**ancora**	ahng**koa**rah
but	**ma, però**	mah pay**ro**
at once	**subito**	**soo**beetoa
soon	**presto**	**preh**stoa
now	**adesso**	ah**deh**ssoa
then	**poi, in seguito**	**po**aee een **say**gooeetoa
again	**ancora**	ahng**koa**rah
perhaps	**forse**	**for**say
only	**soltanto**	sol**tahn**toa

Arrival

CONTROLLO DEI PASSAPORTI
PASSPORT CONTROL

Here's my passport.	**Ecco il passaporto.**	ehkkoa eel pahssah**portoa**
I'll be staying ...	**Resterò ...**	raystay**roa**
a few days a week a month	**qualche giorno** **una settimana** **un mese**	**kwahl**kay **joar**noa oonah saytee**maa**nah oon **mai**zay
I don't know yet.	**Non so ancora.**	noan soa ahng**koa**rah
I'm here on holiday.	**Sono qui in vacanza.**	**soa**noa koo**ee** een vah**kahn**tsah
I'm here on business.	**Sono qui per affari.**	**soa**noa koo**ee** pair ahf**faa**ree
I'm just passing through.	**Sono di passaggio.**	**soa**noa dee pahs**sad**joa

If things become difficult:

I'm sorry, I don't understand.	**Mi dispiace, non capisco.**	mee deespee**ah**chay noan kah**pee**skoa
Is there anyone here who speaks English?	**C'è qualcuno qui che parla inglese?**	chai kwahl**koo**noa koo**ee** kay **pahr**lah eeng**glay**say

DOGANA
CUSTOMS

After collecting your baggage at the airport *(l'aeroporto)* you have a choice: follow the green arrow if you have nothing to declare. Or leave via a doorway marked with a red arrow if you have items to declare (in excess of those allowed).

MERCI DA DICHIARARE
GOODS TO DECLARE

NULLA DA DICHIARARE
NOTHING TO DECLARE

The chart below shows what you can bring in duty-free.*

		Cigarettes		Cigars		Tobacco	Spirits		Wine
Italy	1)	400	or	100	or	500 g.	¾ l.	or	2 l.
	2)	300	or	75	or	400 g.	1½ l.	or	5 l.
	3)	200	or	50	or	250 g.	¾ l.	or	2 l.
Switzerland		200	or	50	or	250 g.	1 l.	and	2 l.

1) residents of countries outside Europe
2) residents of countries within Europe and entering from an EEC country
3) residents of countries within Europe and entering from another country

’ve nothing to eclare.	**Non ho nulla da dichiarare.**	noan oa **nool**lah dah deekeeah**raa**ray
’ve a carton f cigarettes/bottle f whisky.	**Ho una stecca di sigarette/bottiglia di whisky.**	oa **oo**nah **stayk**kah dee seegah**rayt**tay/ bot**tee**lyah dee "whisky"
Must I pay on this?	**Devo pagare per questo?**	**day**voa pah**gaa**ray pair koo**ay**stoa
t’s for my personal se.	**È per mio uso personale.**	ai pair **mee**oa **oo**zoa pairsoa**naa**lay

Il passaporto, per favore.	Your passport, please.
Ha qualcosa da dichiarare?	Do you have anything to declare?
Per favore, apra questa borsa.	Please open this bag.
Deve pagare il dazio per questo.	You'll have to pay duty on this.
Ha altri bagagli?	Do you have any more luggage?

* All allowances subject to change without notice.

Baggage—Porter *Bagagli—Facchino*

These days porters are only available at airports or the railway stations of large cities. Where no porters are available you'll find luggage trolleys for the use of the passengers.

Porter!	**Facchino!**	fahk**kee**noa
Please take my ...	**Per favore, prenda ...**	pair fah**voa**ray **prehn**dah
bag	**la mia borsa**	lah **mee**ah **bor**sah
luggage	**i miei bagagli**	ee mee**ai**ee bah**gaa**lyee
suitcase	**la mia valigia**	lah **mee**ah vah**lee**jah
That's mine.	**Quella è mia.**	koo**ayl**lah ai **mee**ah
Take this luggage ...	**Porti questi bagagli ...**	**por**tee koo**ay**stee bah**gaa**lyee
to the bus	**all'autobus**	ahl**low**toabooss
to the luggage lockers	**alla custodia automatica dei bagagli**	**ahl**lah koo**staw**deeah owtoa**maa**teekah **dai**ee bah**gaa**lyee
How much is that?	**Quant'è?**	kwahn**tai**
There's one piece missing.	**Manca un collo.**	**mahng**kah oon **kol**loa
Where are the luggage trolleys (carts)?	**Dove sono i carrelli portabagagli?**	**doa**vay **soa**noa ee kahr**rehl**lee portahbah**gaa**lyee

Changing money *Cambio*

Where's the currency exchange office?	**Dove si trova l'ufficio cambio?**	**doa**vay see **traw**vah loof**fee**choa **kahm**beeoa
Can you change these traveller's cheques (checks)?	**Può cambiare questi traveller's cheques?**	pwo kahmbee**aa**ray koo**ay**stee "traveller's cheques"
I want to change some dollars/pounds.	**Vorrei cambiare dei dollari/delle sterline.**	vor**rai**ee kahmbee**aa**ray **dai**ee **dol**lahree/**dayl**lay stayr**lee**nay
Can you change this into lire/Swiss francs?	**Può cambiare questo in lire/franchi svizzeri?**	pwo kahmbee**aa**ray koo**ay**stoa een **lee**ray/**frahng**kee **sveet**tsayree
What's the exchange rate?	**Qual è il corso del cambio?**	kwahl ai eel **kor**soa dayl **kahm**beeoa

BANK—CURRENCY, see page 129

Vhere is ...? *Dov'è ...?*

Vhere is the ...?	**Dov'è ...?**	doavai
ooking office	**l'ufficio prenotazioni**	looffeechoa praynoatahtseeoanee
ar hire	**l'autonoleggio**	lowtoanoalaydjoa
uty-free shop	**il negozio duty-free**	eel naygotseeoa "duty-free"
ewsstand	**l'edicola**	laydeekolah
estaurant	**il ristorante**	eel reestoarahntay
hopping area	**la zona dei negozi**	lah dzoanah daiee naygotsee
low do I get to ...?	**Come posso andare a ...?**	koamay possoa ahndaaray ah
s there a bus into own?	**C'è un autobus per la città?**	chai oon owtoabooss pair lah cheettah
Vhere can I get a axi?	**Dove posso prendere un taxi?**	doavay possoa prehndayray oon "taxi"
Vhere can I hire a ar?	**Dove posso noleggiare una macchina?**	doavay possoa noalaydjaaray oonah mahkkeenah

lotel reservation *Prenotazione d'albergo*

o you have a hotel uide?	**Ha una guida degli alberghi?**	ah oonah gweedah dailyee ahlbayrgee
ould you reserve room for me t a hotel/boarding-ouse?	**Potrebbe prenotarmi una camera in un albergo/una pensione?**	poatrehbbay praynoataarmee oonah kaamayrah een oon ahlbayrgoa/oonah paynseeoanay
the centre	**in centro**	een chayntroa
ear the railway station	**vicino alla stazione**	veecheenoa ahllah stahtseeoanay
single room	**una camera singola**	oonah kaamayrah seenggoalah
double room	**una camera doppia**	oonah kaamayrah doappeeah
ot too expensive	**non troppo cara**	noan troappoa kaarah
Vhere is the hotel/ oarding house?	**Dov'è l'albergo/la pensione?**	doavai lahlbayrgoa/lah paynseeoanay
o you have a street nap?	**Ha una pianta della città?**	ah oonah peeahntah dayllah cheettah

OTEL/ACCOMMODATION, see page 22

Car hire (rental) *Autonoleggio*

To hire a car you must produce a valid driving licence (held for at least one year) and your passport. Some firms set a minimum age at 21, other 25. Holders of major credit cards are normally exempt from deposit payments, otherwise you must pay a substantial (refundable) deposit for a car. Third party insurance is usually automatically included.

I'd like to hire (rent) a car.	**Vorrei noleggiare una macchina.**	vorr**ai**ee noalayd**jaa**ray oonah **mahk**keenah
small	**piccola**	**peek**koalah
medium-sized	**di media grandezza**	dee **may**deeah grahn**day**tts
large	**grande**	**grahn**day
automatic	**automatica**	owtoa**mah**teekah
I'd like it for a day/a week.	**La vorrei per un giorno/una settimana.**	lah vorr**ai**ee pair oon **joar**noa/oonah saytte**maa**nah
Are there any week-end arrangements?	**Vi sono condizioni speciali per il week-end?**	vee **soa**noa koandeetsee**oa**nee spay**chaa**lee pair eel "week-end"
Do you have any special rates?	**Avete tariffe particolari?**	ah**vay**tay tah**reef**fay pahrteekoa**laa**ree
What's the charge per day/week?	**Qual è la tariffa giornaliera/settimanale?**	kwahl ai lah tah**reef**fah joarnahlee**ay**rah/sayttee-mah**naa**lay
Is mileage included?	**È compreso il chilometraggio?**	ai koam**pray**soa eel keelomay**trahd**joa
What's the charge per kilometre?	**Qual è la tariffa al chilometro?**	kwahl ai lah tah**reef**fah ahl kee**law**maytroa
I want to hire the car here and leave it in ...	**Vorrei noleggiare la macchina qui e renderla a ...**	vorr**ai**ee noalayd**jaa**ray lah **mahk**keenah koo**ee** ay **rayn**dayrlah ah
I want full insurance.	**Voglio l'assicurazione completa.**	**vol**yoa lahsseekooraht-tseeoanay koamplaytah
What's the deposit?	**Quanto è la cauzione?**	**kwahn**toa ai lah kowtsee**oa**nay
I've a credit card.	**Ho una carta di credito.**	oa **oo**nah **kahr**tah dee **kray**deetoa
Here's my driving licence.	**Ecco la mia patente.**	**ehk**koa lah **mee**ah pah**tehn**tay

CAR, see page 75

'axi *Taxi*

'axis are clearly marked and available in all the larger :owns. If the cab is unmetered, or you have a fair distance to ;o, ask the fare beforehand. Special rates for night jourieys, baggage, etc. should be posted on an official fare :hart.

Vhere can I get a axi?	**Dove posso trovare un taxi?**	doavay possoa trawvaaray oon "taxi"
'lease get me a axi.	**Per favore, mi trovi un taxi.**	pair fahvoaray mee trawvee oon "taxi"
Vhat's the fare o ...?	**Qual è il prezzo della corsa fino a ...?**	kwahl ai eel prehttsoa dayllah korsah feenoa ah
łow far is it o ...?	**Quanto dista ...?**	kwahntoa deestah
'ake me to ...	**Mi conduca ...**	mee koandookah
his address	**a questo indirizzo**	ah kooaystoa eendeereettsoa
he airport	**all'aeroporto**	ahllahayroportoa
he town centre	**in centro città**	een chayntroa cheettah
he ... Hotel	**all'albergo ...**	ahllahlbayrgoa
he railway station	**alla stazione**	ahllah stahtseeoanay
'urn ... at the next :orner.	**Al prossimo angolo giri ...**	ahl prosseemoa ahnggoloa jeeree
eft/right	**a sinistra/a destra**	ah seeneestrah/ah dehstrah
3o straight ahead.	**Vada sempre diritto.**	vahdah sehmpray deereettoa
'lease stop here.	**Per favore, si fermi qui.**	pair fahvoaray see fayrmee kooee
'm in a hurry.	**Ho fretta.**	oa frayttah
:ould you drive nore slowly?	**Può andare più lentamente?**	pwo ahndaaray peeoo layntahmayntay
:ould you help me :arry my luggage?	**Può aiutarmi a portare i miei bagagli?**	pwo aheeootaarmee ah portaaray ee meeaiee bahgaalyee
:ould you wait for ne?	**Può aspettarmi?**	pwo ahspehttaarmee
'll be back in 10 ninutes.	**Tornerò fra 10 minuti.**	tornayro frah 10 meenootee

'IPPING, see inside back-cover

Hotel—Other accommodation

Early reservation (and confirmation) is essential in most major tourist centres during the high season. Most towns and arrival points have a tourist information office (*azienda di promozione turistica*—ahdzee**ehn**dah dee proamoatsee**oa**nay too**ree**steekah), or *ufficio turistico* (oof**fee**choa too**ree**steekoa), and that's the place to go if you're stuck without a room.

The Italian tourist organization, E.N.I.T., publishes an annual directory of all hotels in Italy with details of minimum and maximum prices and facilities.

albergo/hotel (ahl**bayr**goa/oa**tehl**)
Hotels in Italy are classified as *di lusso* (international luxury class), or *prima, seconda, terza, quarta categoria* (first, second, third, fourth class).

Note: Especially near railway stations, one often finds *alberghi diurni* (ahl**bayr**gee deeoornee—"daytime hotels"). These have no sleeping accommodation, but provide bathrooms, rest rooms, hairdressers, and other similar services. Most close at midnight.

motel (mo**tehl**)
Increasing in number, improving in service; the Automobile Association of Italy has a list of recommended motels.

locanda (lo**kahn**dah)
A country inn.

pensione (paynsee**oa**nay)
Corresponds to a boarding house; it usually offers *pensione completa* (full board) or *mezza pensione* (half board). Meals are likely to be from a set menu. *Pensioni* are classified first, second or third class.

ostello della gioventù (oas**tehl**loa **dayl**lah joavayn**too**)
Youth hostel. They are open to holders of membership cards issued by the International Youth Hostel Association.

appartamento ammobiliato (ahppahrtah**mayn**toa ahmmoabeelee**ah**toa)
Furnished flat (apartment). Contact a specialized travel agent if this is the type of arrangement you're looking for.

CAMPING, see page 32

Checking in—Reception *Ufficio ricevimento*

∕Iy name is ...	**Mi chiamo ...**	mee keeaamoa
’ve a reservation.	**Ho fatto una prenotazione.**	oa fahttoa oonah praynoatahtseeoanay
∕Ve’ve reserved two ooms.	**Abbiamo prenotato due camere.**	ahbbeeaamoa praynoatahtoa dooay kaamayray
⁞ere’s the ;onfirmation.	**Ecco la conferma.**	ehkkoa lah konfehrmah
)o you have any ′acancies?	**Avete camere libere?**	ahvaytay kaamayray leebayray
’d like a...room...	**Vorrei una camera...**	vorraiee oonah kaamayrah
;ingle	**singola**	seenggoalah
louble	**doppia**	doappeeah
vith twin beds	**con due letti**	kon dooay lehttee
vith a double bed	**con un letto matrimoniale**	kon oon lehttoa mahtreemoaneeaalay
vith a bath	**con bagno**	kon baaño a
vith a shower	**con doccia**	kon dotchah
vith a balcony	**con balcone**	kon bahlkoanay
vith a view	**con vista**	kon veestah
Ve’d like a room ...	**Vorremmo una camera ...**	vorrehmmoa oonah kaamayrah
ı the front	**sul davanti**	sool dahvahntee
ıt the back	**sul retro**	sool raitroa
acing the sea	**sul mare**	sool maaray
: must be quiet.	**Deve essere tranquilla.**	dayvay ehssayray trahngkooeellah
; there ...?	**C’è ...?**	chai
ir conditioning	**l’aria condizionata**	laareeah kondeetseeonaatah
eating	**il riscaldamento**	eel reeskahldahmayntoa
radio/television in the room	**la radio/il televisore nella stanza**	lah raadeeoa/eel taylayveezoaray nayllah stahntsah
ıundry service	**il servizio di lavanderia**	eel sayrveetseeoa dee lahvahndayreeah
›om service	**il servizio nella stanza**	eel sayrveetseeoa nayllah stahntsah
ot water	**l’acqua calda**	lahkkwah kahldah
ınning water	**l’acqua corrente**	lahkkwah korraintay
private toilet	**il gabinetto privato**	eel gahbeenayttoa preevaatoa

HECKING OUT, see page 31

Could you put an extra bed in the room?	**Può mettere un altro letto nella camera?**	pwo mayttehray oon ahltroa lehttoa nayllah kaamayrah

How much? *Quanto?*

What's the price ...?	**Qual è il prezzo ...?**	kwahl ai eel prehttsoa
per night	**per una notte**	pair oonah nottay
per week	**per una settimana**	pair oonah saytteemaanah
for bed and breakfast	**per la camera e la colazione**	pair lah kaamayrah ay lah koalahtseeoanay
excluding meals	**pasti esclusi**	paastee aysklooozee
for full board (A.P.)	**per la pensione completa**	pair lah paynseeoanay koamplaytah
for half board (M.A.P.)	**per mezza pensione**	pair mehdzah paynseeoanay
Does that include ...?	**Il prezzo comprende ...?**	eel prehttsoa koampraynday
breakfast	**la colazione**	lah koalahtseeoanay
service	**il servizio**	eel sayrveetseeoa
value-added tax (VAT)*	**l'I.V.A.**	leevah
Is there any reduction for children?	**C'è una riduzione per i bambini?**	chai oonah reedootseeoanay pair ee bahmbeenee
Do you charge for the baby?	**Fate pagare per il bambino?**	faatay pahgaaray pair eel bahmbeenoa
That's too expensive.	**È troppo caro.**	ai troppoa kaaroa
Haven't you anything cheaper?	**Non ha nulla di meno caro?**	noan ah noollah dee mainoa kaaroa

How long *Quanto tempo?*

We'll be staying ...	**Resteremo ...**	raystayraymoa
overnight only	**una notte**	oonah nottay
a few days	**qualche giorno**	kwahlkay joarnoa
a week (at least)	**una settimana (come minimo)**	oonah saytteemaanah (koamay meeneemoa)
I don't know yet.	**Non ho ancora deciso.**	noan oa ahngkoarah daycheesoa

* Americans note: a type of sales tax in Italy.

NUMBERS, see page 147

Decision *Decisione*

May I see the room?	**Posso vedere la camera?**	possoa vay**day**ray lah **kaa**mayrah
That's fine. I'll take it.	**Va bene, la prendo.**	vah **bai**nay lah **prehn**doa
No, I don't like it.	**No, non mi piace.**	noa noan mee pee**ah**chay
It's too ...	**È troppo ...**	ai **trop**poa
cold/hot	**fredda/calda**	**fray**ddah/**kahl**dah
dark/small	**buia/piccola**	**boo**eeah/**peek**koalah
noisy	**rumorosa**	roomoa**roa**zah
I asked for a room with a bath.	**Ho chiesto una camera con bagno.**	oa kee**eh**stoa **oo**nah **kaa**mayrah kon **baa**ñoa
Do you have anything ...?	**Ha qualcosa ...?**	ah kwahl**kaw**sah
better	**migliore**	mee**lyoa**ray
bigger	**più grande**	pee**oo** **grahn**day
cheaper	**meno caro**	**mai**noa **kaa**roa
quieter	**più tranquillo**	pee**oo** trahngkoo**eel**loa
Do you have a room with a better view?	**Ha una camera con una vista più bella?**	ah **oo**nah **kaa**mayrah kon **oo**nah **vee**stah pee**oo** **bail**lah

Registration *Registrazione*

Upon arrival at a hotel or boarding house you'll be asked to fill in a registration form (*una scheda*—**oo**nah **skay**dah).

Cognome/Nome	Name/First name
Domicilio/Strada/N°	Home address/Street/Number
Cittadinanza/Professione	Nationality/Profession
Data/Luogo di nascita	Date/Place of birth
Proveniente da .../Diretto a ...	From .../To ...
Numero di passaporto	Passport number
Luogo/Data	Place/Date
Firma	Signature

What does this mean?	**Cosa significa questo?**	**kaw**sah see**ñee**feekah koo**ay**stoa

Mi può mostrare il passaporto?	May I see your passport?
Vuol compilare la scheda, per cortesia?	Would you mind filling in this registration form?
Firmi qui, per favore.	Sign here, please.
Quanto tempo si trattiene?	How long will you be staying?

What's my room number?	**Qual è il numero della mia stanza?**	kwahl ai eel **noo**mayroa **day**llah **mee**ah **stahn**tsah
Will you have our luggage sent up?	**Può far portare su i nostri bagagli?**	pwo faar por**taa**ray soo ee **nos**tree bah**gaa**lyee
Where can I park my car?	**Dove posso parcheggiare la macchina?**	**doa**vay **pos**soa pahrkayd**jaa**ray lah **mahk**keenah
Does the hotel have a garage?	**L'albergo ha il garage?**	lahl**bayr**goa ah eel gah**raazh**
I'd like to leave this in your safe.	**Vorrei depositare questo nella vostra cassaforte.**	vor**rai**ee daypozee**taa**ray **kooay**stoa **nay**llah **vos**trah kahssah**for**tay

Hotel staff *Personale d'albergo*

hall porter	**il portiere**	eel pawr**tee**ayray
maid	**la cameriera (nelle camere)**	lah kahmayree**ay**rah (**nay**llay **kaa**mayray)
manager	**il direttore**	eel deereht**toa**ray
page (bellboy)	**il fattorino**	eel fahttor**ee**noa
porter	**il facchino**	eel fahk**kee**noa
receptionist	**il capo ricevimento**	eel **kah**poa reechayvee**mayn**toa
switchboard operator	**il (la) centralinista**	eel (lah) chayntrahlee**nee**stah
waiter	**il cameriere**	eel kahmayree**ay**ray
waitress	**la cameriera**	lah kahmayree**ay**rah

General requirements *Richieste generali*

The key, please.	**La chiave, per favore.**	lah **keeaa**vay pair fah**voa**ray
Will you please wake me at ...?	**Potrebbe svegliarmi alle ...?**	poa**treh**bbay zvay**lyaar**mee **ahl**lay

TELLING THE TIME, see page 153

Is there a bath on this floor?	**C'è un bagno a questo piano?**	chai oon **baa**ñoa ah koo**ay**stoa pee**aa**noa
What's the voltage?	**Qual è il voltaggio?**	kwahl ai eel voal**tahd**joa
Where's the socket (outlet) for the shaver?	**Dov'è la presa per il rasoio?**	doa**vai** lah **pray**zah pair eel rah**zoa**eeoa
Can we have breakfast in our room?	**Possiamo avere la colazione in camera?**	possee**aa**moa ah**vay**ray lah koalahtsee**oa**nay een **kaa**mayrah
Can you find me a ...?	**Può trovarmi ...?**	pwo traw**vahr**mee
babysitter	**una babysitter**	**oo**nah "babysitter"
secretary	**una segretaria**	**oo**nah saygray**taa**reeah
typewriter	**una macchina per scrivere**	**oo**nah **mahk**keenah pair **skree**vayray
May I have a/an/some ...?	**Posso avere ...?**	**pos**soa ah**vay**ray
ashtray	**un portacenere**	oon portah**chay**nayray
bath towel	**un asciugamano**	oon ahshoogah**maa**noa
(extra) blanket	**una coperta (in più)**	**oo**nah ko**pehr**tah (een pee**oo**)
envelopes	**delle buste**	**dayl**lay **boo**stay
(more) hangers	**degli attaccapanni (in più)**	**day**lyee ahttahkkah**pahn**nee (een pee**oo**)
hot-water bottle	**una borsa dell'acqua calda**	**oo**nah **boar**sah dehl**lahk**kwah **kahl**dah
ice cubes	**dei cubetti di ghiaccio**	**dai**ee koo**beht**tee dee gee**aht**choa
needle and thread	**un ago e del filo**	oon **aa**goa ay dayl **fee**loa
(extra) pillow	**un guanciale (in più)**	oon gwahn**chaa**lay (een pee**oo**)
reading-lamp	**una lampada**	**oo**nah **lahm**pahdah
soap	**una saponetta**	**oo**nah sahpoa**neht**tah
writing-paper	**della carta da lettere**	**dayl**lah **kahr**tah dah **leht**tayray
Where's the ...?	**Dov'è ...?**	doa**vai**
bathroom	**il bagno**	eel **baa**ñoa
dining-room	**la sala da pranzo**	lah **saa**lah dah **prahn**dzoa
emergency exit	**l'uscita di sicurezza**	loo**shee**tah dee seekoo**reh**tsah
hairdresser's	**il parrucchiere**	eel pahrrookkee**ay**ray
lift (elevator)	**l'ascensore**	lahshayn**soa**ray
Where are the toilets?	**Dove sono i gabinetti?**	**doa**vay **soa**noa ee gahbee**neht**tee

BREAKFAST, see page 38

Telephone—Post (mail) *Telefono—Posta*

Can you get me Rome 123-45-67?	**Può passarmi Roma 123-45-67?**	pwo pah**ssahr**mee **roa**mah 123-45-67
How much are my telephone charges?	**Quanto devo pagare per la telefonata?**	**kwahn**toa **day**voa pah**gaa**ray pair lah taylayfoa**naa**tah
Do you have stamps?	**Ha dei francobolli?**	ah **dai**ee frahngkoa**boal**lee
Would you please mail this for me?	**Può spedirmi questo, per favore?**	pwo spay**deer**mee koo**ay**stoa pair fah**voa**ray
Are there any messages for me?	**Vi sono messaggi per me?**	vee **soa**noa may**ssahd**jee pair mai
Is there any mail for me?	**C'è posta per me?**	chai **pos**tah pair mai

Difficulties *Difficoltà*

The ... doesn't work.	**... non funziona.**	... noan foontsee**oa**nah
air conditioner	**il condizionatore d'aria**	eel koandeetseeoanah**toa**ray **daa**reeah
fan	**il ventilatore**	eel vaynteelah**toa**ray
heating	**il riscaldamento**	eel reeskahldah**mayn**toa
light	**la luce**	lah **loo**chay
radio	**la radio**	lah **raa**deeoa
television	**il televisore**	eel taylayvee**zoa**ray
The tap (faucet) is dripping.	**Il rubinetto sgocciola.**	eel roobee**neht**toa **zgot**choalah
There's no hot water.	**Non c'è acqua calda.**	noan chai **ahk**kwah **kahl**dah
The wash-basin is blocked.	**Il lavabo è otturato.**	eel lah**vaa**boa ai ottoo**raa**toa
The window is jammed.	**La finestra è incastrata.**	lah fee**neh**strah ai eengkah**straa**tah
The curtains are stuck.	**Le tende sono bloccate.**	lay **tayn**day **soa**noa blok**kaa**tay
The bulb is burned out.	**La lampadina è bruciata.**	lah lahmpah**dee**nah ai broo**chaa**tah
My room has not been made up.	**La mia camera non è stata rifatta.**	lah **mee**ah **kaa**mayrah noan ai **staa**tah ree**faht**tah

POST OFFICE AND TELEPHONE, see page 132

The ... is broken.	**... è rotto(a).**	... ai **rott**oa(ah)
blind	**la persiana**	lah pairsee**aa**nah
lamp	**la lampada**	lah **lahm**pahdah
plug	**la spina**	lah **spee**nah
shutter	**l'imposta**	leem**poa**stah
switch	**l'interruttore**	leentayrroot**toa**ray
Can you get it repaired?	**Può ripararlo(la)?**	pwo reepah**rahr**loa(lah)

Laundry—Dry cleaner's *Lavanderia—Lavanderia a secco*

I want these clothes ...	**Voglio far ... questi abiti.**	**vo**lyoa faar ... koo**ay**stee **aa**beetee
cleaned	**pulire**	poo**lee**ray
ironed	**stirare**	stee**raa**ray
pressed	**stirare a vapore**	stee**raa**ray ah vah**poa**ray
washed	**lavare**	lah**vaa**ray
When will they be ready?	**Quando saranno pronti?**	**kwahn**doa sah**rahn**noa **proan**tee
I need them ...	**Ne ho bisogno ...**	nay oa bee**zoa**ñoa
tonight	**stasera**	stah**say**rah
tomorrow	**domani**	doa**maa**nee
before Friday	**prima di venerdì**	**pree**mah dee vaynayr**dee**
Can you ... this?	**Mi può ... questo?**	mee pwo ... koo**ay**stoa
mend	**rammendare**	rahmmayn**daa**ray
patch	**rappezzare**	rappeht**tsaa**ray
stitch	**cucire**	koo**chee**ray
Can you sew on this button?	**Può attaccare questo bottone?**	pwo ahttahk**kaa**ray koo**ay**stoa boat**toa**nay
Can you get this stain out?	**Mi può togliere questa macchia?**	mee pwo **to**lyayray koo**ay**stah **mahk**keeah
Can this be invisibly mended?	**Mi può fare un rammendo invisibile?**	mee pwo **faa**ray oon rahm**mayn**doa eenvee**zee**beelay
Is my laundry ready?	**È pronta la mia biancheria?**	ai **pron**tah lah **mee**ah beeahngkay**ree**ah
This isn't mine.	**Questo non è mio.**	koo**ay**stoa noan ai **mee**oa
There's something missing.	**Manca un capo.**	**mahng**kah oon **kaa**poa
There's a hole in this.	**C'è un buco in questo.**	chai oon **boo**koa een koo**ay**stoa

Hairdresser—Barber *Parrucchiere—Barbiere*

Is there a hairdresser/ beauty salon in the hotel?	**C'è il parrucchiere/ l'istituto di bellezza nell'albergo?**	chai eel pahrrookk**eeay**ray/ leestee**too**toa dee behl**leh**ttsah nayllahl**bayr**goa
Can I make an appointment for Thursday?	**Posso avere un appuntamento per giovedì?**	**pos**soa ah**vay**ray oon ahppoontah**mayn**toa pair joavay**dee**
I'd like it cut and shaped.	**Vorrei il taglio e la messa in piega.**	vor**rai**ee eel **taa**lyoa ay lah **mays**sah een pee**ay**gah
I want a haircut, please.	**Voglio il taglio dei capelli, per favore.**	**vo**lyoa eel **taa**lyoa **da**iee kah**pehl**lee pair fah**voa**ray
bleach	**una decolorazione**	**oo**nah daykoaloaraht-see**oa**nay
blow-dry	**l'asciugatura col fono**	lashoogah**too**rah kol **faw**no
colour rinse	**un cachet**	oon kah**shay**
dye	**una tintura**	**oo**nah teen**too**rah
face-pack	**la maschera di bellezza**	lah **mah**skayrah dee behl**leh**ttsah
manicure	**la manicure**	lah mahnee**koor**
permanent wave	**la permanente**	lah pairmah**nayn**tay
setting lotion	**un fissatore**	oon feessah**toa**ray
shampoo and set	**shampoo e messa in piega**	"shampoo" ay **mays**sah een pee**ay**gah
with a fringe (bangs)	**con la frangia**	kon lah **frahn**jah
I'd like a shampoo for ... hair.	**Vorrei uno shampoo per capelli ...**	vor**rai**ee **oo**noa "shampoo" pair kah**pehl**lee
normal/dry/ greasy (oily)	**normali/secchi/ grassi**	noar**maa**lee/**sayk**kee/ **grahs**see
Do you have a colour chart?	**Avete una tabella dei colori?**	ah**vay**tay **oo**nah tah**bayl**lah **da**iee koa**loa**ree
Don't cut it too short.	**Non li tagli troppo corti.**	noan lee **taa**lyee **trop**poa **koar**tee
A little more off the ...	**Ancora un po'**	ahng[illegible]rah [illegible] po
back	**dietro**	dee**ay**troa
neck	**sul collo**	sool **kol**loa
sides	**ai lati**	**ah**ee **laa**tee
top	**in cima**	een **chee**mah
I don't want any hairspray.	**Non voglio lacca.**	noan **vo**lyoa **lahk**kah

DAYS OF THE WEEK, see page 151

I'd like a shave.	**Vorrei che mi radesse.**	vor**rai**ee kay mee rah**days**say
Would you please trim my ...?	**Per favore, vuole spuntarmi ...?**	pair fah**voa**ray **vwaw**lay spoon**tahr**mee
beard	**la barba**	lah **bahr**bah
moustache	**i baffi**	ee **bahf**fee
sideboards (sideburns)	**le basette**	lay bah**zayt**tay

Checking out *Partenza*

May I please have my bill?	**Posso avere il conto, per favore?**	**pos**soa ah**vay**ray eel **koan**toa pair fah**voa**ray
I'm leaving early in the morning. Please have my bill ready.	**Partirò domani mattina presto. Mi prepari il conto, per favore.**	pahrtee**roa** doa**maa**nee maht**tee**nah **preh**stoa. mee pray**paa**ree eel **koan**toa pair fah**voa**ray
We'll be checking out around noon.	**Partiremo verso mezzogiorno.**	pahrtee**ray**moa **vehr**soa mehdzoa**joar**noa
I must leave at once.	**Devo partire immediatamente.**	**day**voa pahr**tee**ray eemmaydeeahtah**mayn**tay
Is everything included?	**È tutto incluso?**	ai **toot**toa eeng**kloo**zoa
Can I pay by credit card?	**Posso pagare con la carta di credito?**	**pos**soa pah**gaa**ray kon lah **kahr**tah dee **kray**deetoa
You've made a mistake in this bill, I think.	**Ha fatto un errore nel conto, credo.**	ah **faht**toa oon ehr**roa**ray nayl **koan**toa **kray**doa
Can you get us a taxi?	**Può chiamarci un taxi?**	pwo keeah**mahr**chee oon "taxi"
Would you send someone to bring down our luggage?	**Può mandare qualcuno a portare giù i nostri bagagli?**	pwo mahn**daa**ray kwahl**koo**noa ah por**taa**ray joo ee **nos**tree bah**gaa**lyee
Here's the forwarding address.	**Ecco il mio prossimo indirizzo.**	**ehk**koa eel **mee**oa **pros**seemoa eendee**reet**tsoa
You have my home address.	**Avete il mio indirizzo abituale.**	ah**vay**tay eel **mee**oa eendee**reet**tsoa ahbeetoo**aa**lay
It's been a very enjoyable stay.	**È stato un soggiorno molto piacevole.**	ai **staa**toa oon soad**joar**noa **moal**toa peeah**chay**voalay

TIPPING, see inside back-cover

Camping *Campeggio*

In Italy there are many authorized camping sites with excellent facilities. Most camp sites are equipped with water, electricity and toilets. You will find them listed in the telephone directory, under *Campeggio*. The local tourist office has a list of sites, tariffs and facilities available. The Touring Club Italiano also publish a list of campsites and touristic villages. It is on sale in bookshops.

Is there a camp site near here?	**C'è un campeggio qui vicino?**	chai oon kahmpaydjoa kooee veecheenoa
Can we camp here?	**Possiamo campeggiare qui?**	posseeaamoa kahmpaydjaaray kooee
Have you room for a tent/caravan (trailer)?	**C'è posto per una tenda/una roulotte?**	chai poastoa pair oonah taindah/oonah roolot
What's the charge...?	**Quanto si paga ...?**	kwahntoa see paagah
per day	**al giorno**	ahl joarnoa
per person	**per persona**	pair payrsoanah
for a car	**per una macchina**	pair oonah mahkkeenah
for a tent	**per una tenda**	pair oonah taindah
for a caravan (trailer)	**per una roulotte**	pair oonah roolot
Is the tourist tax included?	**È compresa la tassa di soggiorno?**	ai koampraysah lah tahssah dee soadjoarnoa
Is there/Are there (a) ...?	**C'è/Ci sono ...?**	chai/chee soanoa
drinking water	**l'acqua potabile**	lahkkwah poataabeelay
electricity	**l'elettricità**	laylehttreecheetah
playground	**il parco giochi**	eel pahrkoa joakee
restaurant	**il ristorante**	eel reestoarahntay
shopping facilities	**dei negozi**	daiee naygotsee
swimming pool	**la piscina**	lah peesheenah
Where are the showers/toilets?	**Dove sono le docce/i gabinetti?**	doavay soanoa lay dotchay ee gahbeenayttee
Where can I get butane gas?	**Dove posso trovare del gas butano?**	doavay possoa trovaaray dayl gahz bootaanoa
Is there a youth hostel near here?	**C'è un ostello della gioventù qui vicino?**	chai oon oastehlloa dayllah joavayntoo kooee veecheenoa

CAMPING EQUIPMENT, see page 106

Eating out

There are various types of places to eat and drink in Italy. Here are some of them:

Autogrill (owtoagreel) — large restaurant on a motorway (expressway); usually table and cafeteria service available.

Bar (bahr) — bar; can be found on virtually every street corner; coffee and drinks served. In most of them you first have to get a ticket from the cashier. Then you go to the counter and order what you want. Only a few bars have tables and chairs. If you want to be served at a table, the charge for your drinks and food will be somewhat higher.

Caffè (kahffai) — coffee shop; generally food isn't served there except for breakfast. If it offers *panini o toasts* you'll be able to get a snack. Coffee shops always serve alcoholic beverages.

Gelateria (jaylahtayreeah) — ice-cream parlour; Italian ice-cream is very tasty, rich and creamy, often reminiscent of old-fashioned, homemade ice-cream.

Locanda (lokahndah) — simple restaurants serving local dishes.

Osteria (oastayreeah) — inn; wine and simple food are served.

Paninoteca (pahneenoataykah) — a sort of coffee shop where you can find a great variety of sandwiches *(panini)* served hot or cold.

Pizzeria (peettsayreeah) — pizza parlour; often other dishes are served, too.

Ristorante (reestoarahntay) — You'll encounter restaurants classified by stars, forks and knives and endorsed by everyone including travel agencies, automobile associations and gastronomic guilds. Bear in mind that any form of classification is relative. Some restaurants are judged according to their fancy décor while others—linen and chandeliers aside—are rated merely by the quality of their cooking.

Rosticceria (roasteetchay**ree**ah) — originally, it was a shop specializing in grilled meats, chicken and fish. But today *rosticcerie* often have tables where you eat grilled food on the premises.

Sala da tè (**saa**lah dah tai) — serves ice-cream and pastries.

Taverna (tah**vehr**nah) — a more modest type of *trattoria.*

Tavola calda (**taa**voalah **kahl**dah) — "hot table"; a cafeteria-style restaurant serving hot dishes at fairly low prices. They're usually crowded but quick; you may have to eat standing up.

Trattoria (trahttoa**ree**ah) — a medium-priced restaurant serving meals and drink. The food is simple but can be surprisingly good if you happen to hit upon the right place.

Most restaurants display a menu in the window. Many offer a tourist menu *(menù turistico),* a fixed-price three- or four-course meal with limited choice, or the speciality of the day *(piatto del giorno).*

All restaurants, no matter how modest, must now issue a formal bill *(la ricevuta fiscale)* with VAT, or sales tax *(I.V.A.).* A customer may actually be stopped outside the premises and fined if he cannot produce this receipt. The bill usually includes cover *(il coperto)* and service *(il servizio)* charges as well.

Meal times *Orari dei pasti*

Breakfast (*la colazione*—lah kolahtsee**oa**nay) at the hotel is normally served from 7 to 10 a.m. (See page 38 for a breakfast menu.)

Lunch (*il pranzo*—eel **prahn**dzoa) is served from 12.30 to 2 p.m.

Dinner (*la cena*—lah **chay**nah) begins at 7 or 8 p.m., but hotels tend to open their dining rooms earlier for the foreign tourists.

TIPPING, see inside back-cover

Note: The names of meals can be confusing. Lunch is sometimes called *colazione* and dinner *pranzo,* especially in towns. If you are invited out, make sure of the time, so you don't turn up at the wrong meal.

Italian cuisine *Cucina italiana*

To many foreigners, Italian cooking means *spaghetti, macaroni, tagliatelle*... in other words, pasta. In fact, you will be amazed at the rich variety available: tasty hors d'œuvres, long-simmered soups, traditional meat dishes, fresh fish and shellfish, high-quality poultry, an incredible number of cheeses, not to mention the magnificent cakes and ice-cream.

Each region has its own speciality, never lacking in flavour or originality, inspired by sun-drenched fruit and vegetables. Italian cooking is like the country itself: colourful, happy, generous, exuberant.

Cosa desidera?	What would you like?
Le consiglio questo.	I recommend this.
Cosa desidera da bere?	What would you like to drink?
Non abbiamo ...	We haven't got ...
Vuole ...?	Do you want ...?

Hungry? *Ha fame?*

I'm hungry/I'm thirsty.	**Ho fame/Ho sete.**	oa **faa**may/oa **say**tay
Can you recommend a good restaurant?	**Può consigliarmi un buon ristorante?**	pwo koanseel**yaar**mee oon bwon reestoa**rahn**tay
Are there any inexpensive restaurants around here?	**Vi sono dei ristoranti economici qui vicino?**	vee **soa**noa **dai**ee reestoa**rahn**tee aykoa**naw**meechee **koo**ee vee**chee**noa

If you want to be sure of getting a table in a well-known restaurant, it may be better to telephone in advance.

I'd like to reserve a table for 4.	**Vorrei riservare un tavolo per 4.**	vorraiee reesehrvaaray oon taavoala pair 4
We'll come at 8.	**Verremo alle 8.**	vayrraymoa ahllay 8
Could we have a table ...?	**Potremmo avere un tavolo ...?**	poatraymmoa ahvayray oon taavoaloa
in the corner	**d'angolo**	dahnggoaloa
by the window	**vicino alla finestra**	veecheenoa ahllah feenaystrah
outside	**all'aperto**	ahllahpehrtoa
on the terrace	**sulla terrazza**	soollah tayrrahttsah
in a non-smoking area	**nel settore per non fumatori**	nayl sehttoaray pair noan foomahtoaree

Asking and ordering *Chiedere e ordinare*

Waiter/Waitress!	**Cameriere/ Cameriera!**	kahmayreeairay/kahmay-reeairah
I'd like something to eat/drink.	**Vorrei mangiare/bere qualcosa.**	vorraiee mahnjaaray/bayray kwahlkawsah
May I have the menu, please?	**Posso avere il menù?**	possoa ahvayray eel maynoo
Do you have a set menu/local dishes?	**Avete un menù a prezzo fisso/dei piatti locali?**	ahvaytay oon maynoo ah prehttsoa feessoa/daiee peeahttee loakaalee
What do you recommend?	**Cosa consiglia?**	kawsah konseelyah
I'd like ...	**Vorrei ...**	vorraiee
Could we have a/an ..., please?	**Potremmo avere ..., per favore?**	poatraymmoa ahvayray ... pair fahvoaray
ashtray	**un portacenere**	oon portahchaynayray
cup	**una tazza**	oonah tahttsah
extra chair	**una sedia in più**	oonah saideeah een peeoo
fork	**una forchetta**	oonah forkehttah
glass	**un bicchiere**	oon [illegible]
knife	**un coltello**	oon koaltehlloa
napkin (serviette)	**un tovagliolo**	oon toavahlyawloa
plate	**un piatto**	oon peeahttoa
spoon	**un cucchiaio**	oon kookkeeaaeeoa
May I have some ...?	**Potrei avere ...?**	poatraiee ahvayray
bread	**del pane**	dayl paanay
butter	**del burro**	dayl boorroa

NUMBERS, see page 147

emon	**del limone**	dayl leemoanay
mustard	**della senape**	dayllah saynahpay
oil	**dell'olio**	dayllolyoa
pepper	**del pepe**	dayl paypay
salt	**del sale**	dayl saalay
seasoning	**del condimento**	dayl koandeemayntoa
sugar	**dello zucchero**	daylloa tsookkayroa
vinegar	**dell'aceto**	dayllahchaytoa

Some useful expressions for dieters or those with special requirements:

I'm on a diet.	**Sono a dieta.**	soanoa ah deeaytah
mustn't eat food containing ...	**Non devo mangiare cibi che contengono ...**	noan dayvoa mahnjaaray cheebee kay koan-taynggoanoa
flour/fat	**farina/grasso**	fahreenah/grahssoa
salt/sugar	**sale/zucchero**	saalay/tsookkayroa
Do you have ... for diabetics?	**Avete ... per diabetici?**	ahvaytay ... pair deeahbaiteechee
cakes	**dei dolci**	daiee doalchee
fruit juice	**del succo di frutta**	dayl sookkoa dee froottah
special menu	**un menù speciale**	oon maynoo spaychaalay
Do you have vege-tarian dishes?	**Avete dei piatti vegetariani?**	ahvaytay daiee peeahttee vayjaytahreeaanee
Could I have ... instead of the dessert?	**Potrei avere ... invece del dessert?**	potraiee ahvayray ... eenvaychay dayl dayssehr
Can I have an artificial sweetener?	**Posso avere del dolcificante?**	possoa ahvayray dayl doalcheefeekahntay

And ...

I'd like some more.	**Ne vorrei ancora.**	nai vorraiee ahngkoarah
Can I have more ..., please.	**Posso avere ancora un po' di ...?**	possoa ahvayray ahngkoarah oon po dee
Just a small portion.	**Una piccola porzione.**	oonah peekkoalah poartsee-oanay
Nothing more, thanks.	**Nient'altro, grazie.**	neeayntahltroa graatseeay
Where are the toilets?	**Dove sono i gabinetti?**	doavay soanoa ee gahbee-nayttee

Breakfast *Colazione*

Italians just have a *cappuccino* and a brioche for breakfast Hotels usually propose coffee or tea, bread, butter and jam You can ask for fruit juice, an egg and toast, if you like a more copious breakfast.

I'd like breakfast, please.	**Vorrei fare colazione.**	vorr**aiee** f**aa**ray kolah-tsee**oa**nay
I'll have a/an/ some ...	**Desidero ...**	day**zee**dayroa
bacon and eggs	**uova e pancetta**	**waw**vah ay pahn**cheht**tah
boiled egg	**un uovo alla coque**	oon **waw**voa **ahl**lah kok
soft/hard	**molle/sodo**	**mol**lay/**so**doa
cereal	**dei cereali**	**dai**ee chehreh**aa**lee
eggs	**delle uova**	**day**llay **waw**vah
fried eggs	**delle uova fritte**	**day**llay **waw**vah **freet**tay
scrambled eggs	**delle uova strapazzate**	**day**llay **waw**vah strahpaht**tsaa**tay
fruit juice	**un succo di frutta**	oon **sook**koa dee **froot**tah
grapefruit	**pompelmo**	pom**payl**moa
orange	**arancia**	ah**rahn**chah
ham and eggs	**uova e prosciutto**	**waw**vah ay proa**shoot**toa
jam	**della marmellata**	**day**llah mahrmay**llaa**tah
marmalade	**della marmellata d'arance**	**day**llah mahrmay**llaa**tah dah**rahn**chay
toast	**del pane tostato**	dayl **paa**nay tos**taa**toa
May I have some ...?	**Posso avere ...?**	**pos**soa ah**vay**ray
bread	**del pane**	dayl **paa**nay
butter	**del burro**	dayl **boor**roa
(hot) chocolate	**una cioccolata (calda)**	**oo**nah choakkoa**laa**tah (**kahl**dah)
coffee	**un caffè**	oon kahf**fai**
decaffeinated	**decaffeinato**	daykahffeh**ee**n**aa**toa
black	**nero**	**nay**roa
with milk	**macchiato**	mahkkee**aa**toa
honey	**del miele**	dayl mee**ay**lay
milk	**del latte**	dayl **laht**tay
cold/hot	**freddo/caldo**	**frayd**doa/**kahl**doa
rolls	**dei panini**	**dai**ee pah**nee**nee
tea	**del tè**	dayl tai
with milk	**con latte**	kon **laht**tay
with lemon	**con limone**	kon lee**moa**nay
(hot) water	**dell'acqua (calda)**	day**llahk**kwah (**kahl**dah)

What's on the menu? *Che c'è sul menù?*

Under the headings below you'll find alphabetical lists of dishes that might be offered on an Italian menu with their English equivalent. You can simply show the book to the waiter. If you want some cheese, for instance, let *him* point to what's available on the appropriate list. Use pages 36 and 37 for ordering in general.

Note: Italian cooking remains essentially regional. Each of the nation's 18 regions has its own specialities. There are, of course, many well-known dishes that are common to all Italy. But here again the terminology may vary from place to place. (There are at least half a dozen names for octopus or squid!) So in the lists that follow, be prepared for regional variations.

Reading the menu *Per leggere il menù*

Menù a prezzo fisso	Set menu
Piatto del giorno	Dish of the day
Lo chef consiglia ...	The chef recommends ...
Specialità della casa	Specialities of the house
Specialità locali	Local specialities
Contorno a scelta	Choice of vegetables
I nostri piatti di carne sono serviti con contorno	Our meat dishes are accompanied by vegetables
Su ordinazione	Made to order
Supplemento	Extra charge
Verdure di stagione	Vegetables in season
Attesa: 15 minuti	Waiting time: 15 minutes
Pane, grissini e coperto L. ...	Bread, *grissini* and cover L. ...
A scelta	Choice
Piatti freddi	Cold dishes

antipasti	ahntee**pah**stee	hors d'œuvres
bevande	bay**vahn**day	drinks
cacciagione	kahtchah**joa**nay	game
carne	**kahr**nay	meat
carne ai ferri	**kahr**nay **ahee fehr**ree	grilled meat
crostacei	kroa**stah**chayee	shellfish
dessert	days**sehr**	dessert
formaggi	foar**mah**djee	cheese
frutta	**froot**tah	fruit
frutti di mare	**froot**tee dee **maa**ray	seafood
gelati	jay**laa**tee	ice-cream
insalate	eensah**laa**tay	salads
minestre	mee**neh**stray	soups
pastasciutta	pahstah**shoot**tah	pasta
pesci	**pay**shee	fish
pollame	poal**laa**may	poultry
primi piatti	**pree**mee pee**ah**ttee	first course
riso	**ree**zoa	rice
secondi piatti	say**koan**dee pee**ah**ttee	second (main) course
verdure	vehr**doo**ray	vegetables
vini	**vee**nee	wines

Appetizers *Antipasti*

I'd like an appetizer.	**Vorrei un antipasto.**	vorraiee oon ahnteepahstoa
acciughe	ahtchoogay	anchovies
affettati misti	ahffayttaatee meestee	cold cuts of pork
antipasto assortito	ahnteepahtoa ahssoar-teetoa	assorted appetizer
carciofi	kahrchofee	artichokes
caviale	kahveeaalay	caviar
coppa	koappah	cured pork shoulder
frutti di mare	froottee dee maaray	mixed seafood
gamberetti	gahmbayrayttee	shrimps
mortadella	moartahdehllah	Bologna sausage
olive	oleevay	olives
ostriche	ostreekay	oysters
prosciutto	proashoottoa	ham
cotto	kottoa	cooked ham
crudo di Parma	kroodoa dee pahrmah	cured ham from Parma
salame	sahlaamay	salami
salmone affumicato	sahlmoanay affoomee-kaatoa	smoked salmon
sardine all'olio	sahrdeenay ahllolyoa	sardines in oil
sottaceti	soattahchaytee	pickled vegetables
tonno	tonnoa	tunny in oil

bagna cauda (baañah kahoodah) — raw vegetables accompagnied by a hot sauce made from anchovies, garlic, oil, butter and sometimes truffles (Northern Italy)

carciofini sottolio (kahrchofeenee soattolyoa) — artichoke hearts in olive oil

insalata di frutti di mare (eensahlaatah dee froot-tee dee maaray) — prawns and squid with lemon, pickles and olives

insalata di pollo (eensahlaatah dee poalloa) — chicken salad with green salad, lemon, cream

insalata russa (eensahlaatah roossah) — diced boiled vegetables in mayonnaise

mozzarella con pomodori (motsahrayllah kon poamoadawree) — mozzarella cheese with tomatoes, basilic, pepper and olive oil

prosciutto crudo con melone (proa**shoot**toa **kroo**doa kon may**loa**nay)	sliced melon with cured ham from Parma

Pizza

Pizza (plural *pizze*) is surely one of Italy's best-known culinary exports. And the variety of toppings is endless, from simple cheese and tomato to assorted seafood. A *calzone* has basically the same ingredients, but the pastry forms a sort of sealed sandwich, with the filling inside.

Here are the best known variations on the theme:

capricciosa (kahpreet**choa**sah)	the cook's speciality
margherita (mahrgay**ree**tah)	named after Italy's first queen, the *pizza* ingredients, tomato, cheese and basil, reflect the national colours
napoletana (nahpoalay**taa**nah)	the classic *pizza* with anchovies, ham, capers, tomatoes, cheese and oregano
quattro stagioni (**kwaht**troa stah**joa**nee)	"four seasons" – containing a variety of vegetables: tomatoes, artichoke, mushrooms, olives, plus cheese, ham and bacon
siciliana (seecheelee**aa**nah)	with black olives, capers and cheese

Omelets *Frittate*

I'd like an omelet.	**Vorrei una frittata.**	vor**rai**ee **oo**nah freet**taa**tah
frittata	freet**taa**tah	omelet
di asparagi	dee ah**spaa**rahjee	asparagus
di carciofi	dee kahr**cho**fee	artichokes
di cipolle	dee chee**poal**lay	onions
di spinaci	dee spee**naa**chee	spinach
di zucchine	dee tsook**kee**nay	dried baby marrow (zucchini)
frittata campagnola	freet**taa**tah kahmpah**ñoa**lah	an omelet with onion, grated cheese, milk and cream
frittata primaverile	freet**taa**tah preemahvay**ree**lay	omelet with vegetables

Soups *Minestre, zuppe*

In Italy, soup goes by many names, as the following list shows. Some of them are sufficient for a main course. An Italian meal always includes a soup or a dish of *pastasciutta*.

brodo	**braw**doa	bouillon, broth, soup
di manzo	dee **mahn**dzoa	meat broth
di pollo	dee **poal**loa	chicken broth
busecca	boo**zayk**kah	thick tripe, vegetable and bean soup
cacciucco	kaht**chook**koa	spicy seafood stew (chowder)
crema di legumi	**kreh**mah dee lay**goo**mee	vegetable cream soup
crema di pomodori	**kreh**mah dee poamoa**daw**ree	tomato cream soup
minestra	mee**neh**strah	soup
in brodo	een **braw**doa	bouillon with noodles or rice
di funghi	dee **foong**gee	cream of mushroom
minestrone	meeneh**stroa**nay	a thick vegetable soup (sometimes with noodles) sprinkled with parmesan cheese
passato di verdura	pahs**saa**toa dee vehr**doo**rah	mashed vegetable soup, generally with croutons
pasta e fagioli	**pah**stah ay fah**joa**lee	noodles and beans
pastina in brodo	pah**stee**nah een **braw**doa	broth with little noodles
zuppa	**tsoop**pah	soup
alla cacciatora	**ahl**lah kahtchah**toa**rah	meat with mushrooms
alla marinara	**ahl**lah mahree**naa**rah	spicy fish stew (chowder)
alla pavese	**ahl**lah pah**vay**zay	consommé with poached egg, croutons and grated cheese
alla veneta	**ahl**lah **vay**naytah	vegetables with white wine and noodles
di datteri di mare	dee **daht**tayree dee **maa**ray	sea dates (kind of mussel)
di frutti di mare	dee **froot**tee dee **maa**ray	seafood
di pesce	dee **pay**shay	spicy fish stew (chowder)
di vongole	dee **vong**goalay	clams and white wine

Pasta

Pasta (or *pastasciutta*), the generic name for a wide range of noodles and noodle-related dishes, constitutes the traditional Italian first course. In addition to the well-known *spaghetti*, pasta comes in a bewildering variety of sizes and shapes—ribbons, strings, tubes, shells or stars—known under as many different appellations. It can be served on its own, in broth, with butter or tomato sauce, stuffed with meat, cheese or vegetables, and is often accompanied by a highly flavoured sauce such as those described below.

agnolotti (ahñoa**lot**tee)	a round pasta parcel with a filling of chopped meat, vegetables and cheese
cannelloni (kahnnay**llaw**nee)	tubular dough stuffed with meat, cheese or vegetables, covered with a white sauce and baked
cappelletti (kahppay**llayt**tee)	small ravioli filled with meat, herbs, ham, cheese and eggs
fettuccine (fayttoot**chee**nay)	narrow flat noodles
lasagne (lah**zaa**ñay)	thin layers of white or green *(lasagne verdi)* dough alternating with tomato sauce and sausage meat, white sauce and grated cheese; baked in the oven
rigatoni (reegah**taw**nee)	large macaroni, similar to *cannelloni* but smaller and ridged
tagliatelle (tahlyah**tehl**lay)	flat noodles
tortellini (toartehl**lee**nee)	rings of dough filled with seasoned minced meat and served in broth or with a sauce

Sauces *Salse*

It's the sauce that makes spaghetti and macaroni so delicious—Italian cooks are masters of the art.

aglio, olio, peperoncino (ahlyoa olyoa paypayroan**chee**noa)	garlic, olive oil, sweet peppers, anchovies and parmesan

al burro (ahl **boor**roa)	with butter and grated parmesan
al sugo (ahl **soo**goa)	with tomato sauce and grated parmesan
amatriciana (ahmahtree**chaa**nah)	tomatoes, red peppers, bacon, onions, garlic and white wine
bolognese (boaloa**ñay**zay)	tomatoes, minced meat, onions and herbs
carbonara (kahrboa**naa**rah)	smoked ham, cheese, eggs and olive oil
carrettiera (kahrraytte**eay**rah)	tuna, mushrooms, tomato purée, freshly ground pepper
marinara (mahree**naa**rah)	tomatoes, olives, garlic, clams and mussels
pesto (**pay**stoa)	basil leaves, garlic, cheese, and sometimes pine kernels and marjoram
pommarola (poammah**raw**lah)	tomatoes, garlic, basil
puttanesca (poottah**nay**skah)	capers, black olives, parsley, garlic, olive oil, black pepper
ragù (rah**goo**)	like *bolognese*
con le vongole (kon lay **voan**goalay)	clams, garlic, parsley, pepper, olive oil, sometimes tomatoes

Rice *Riso*

In Northern Italy, a rice dish is often offered as a first course to replace pasta. Cooked on its own or together with vegetables, meat, herbs, fish and/or seafood, rice may also be served with a sauce.

risi e bisi	**ree**see ay **bee**see	rice with peas and bacon
riso in bianco	**ree**soa een bee**ahng**koa	boiled rice with butter and grated parmesan
risotto	reesottoa	rice casserole
con fegatini	kon faygah**tee**nee	with chicken livers
con funghi	kon **foong**gee	with mushrooms
alla milanese	**ahl**lah meelah**nai**say	marrow, white wine, saffron and parmesan

Fish and seafood *Pesci e frutti di mare*

Don't miss the opportunity to sample some of the wide variety of fresh fish and seafood in coastal areas. Some inland regions offer special preparations of fish from their rivers lakes and streams. Fish is most commonly baked or poached until just done, then dressed with a delicate sauce.

I'd like some fish.	**Vorrei del pesce.**	vorr**aiee** dayl **pay**shay
What kind of seafood do you have?	**Che genere di frutti di mare avete?**	kay **jeh**nayray dee **froot**tee dee **maa**ray ahv**ay**tay
acciughe	aht**choo**gay	anchovies
aguglie	ah**goo**lyay	garfish
anguilla	ahnggoo**eel**lah	eel
aragosta	ahrah**goa**stah	lobster
aringa	ah**reeng**gah	herring
arselle	ahr**sehl**lay	scallops
baccalà	bahkkah**lah**	dried salt cod
bianchetti	beeahng**kayt**tee	whitebait
branzino	brahn**dzee**noa	(sea) bass
calamaretti	kahlahmah**rayt**tee	baby squid
calamari	kahlah**maa**ree	squid
carpa	**kahr**pah	carp
cozze	**koat**say	mussels
dentice	**dehn**teechay	type of sea bream
eperlano	aypayr**laa**noa	smelt
gamberetti	gahmbay**rayt**tee	shrimps
gamberi	**gahm**bayree	crayfish
granchi	**grahng**kee	crabs
gronghi	**groang**gee	conger eel
lamprede	lahm**pray**day	lampreys
luccio	**loot**choa	pike
lumache di mare	loo**maa**kay dee **maa**ray	sea snails
merlano	mayr**laa**noa	whiting
merluzzo	mayr**loot**tsoa	cod
nasello	nah**sehl**loa	coal-fish
orata	oa**raa**tah	type of sea bream
ostriche	**o**streekay	oysters
pesce persico	**pay**shay **pehr**seekoa	perch
pesce spada	**pay**shay **spaa**dah	swordfish
polpo	**poal**poa	octopus
razza	**raht**tsah	ray
ricci	**reet**chee	sea urchins
rombo	**roam**boa	turbot
salmone	sahl**moa**nay	salmon

sardine	sahr**dee**nay	sardines
scampi	**skahm**pee	prawns
scorfano	**skoar**fahnoa	sea-scorpion, sculpin
sgombro	**zgoam**broa	mackerel
seppia	**sayp**peeah	cuttlefish
sogliola	**saw**lyoalah	sole
spigola	**spee**goalah	sea bass
storione	stoaree**oa**nay	sturgeon
tonno	**toan**noa	tunny (tuna)
triglie	**tree**lyay	red mullet
trota	**traw**tah	trout
vongole	**vong**goalay	clams

baked	**al forno**	ahl **for**noa
boiled	**lesso**	**lays**soa
(deep) fried	**(ben) fritto**	(bain) **freet**toa
grilled	**alla griglia**	**ahl**lah **gree**lyah
marinated	**marinato**	mahree**naa**toa
poached	**affogato**	ahffoa**gaa**toa
smoked	**affumicato**	ahffoomee**kaa**toa
steamed	**cotto a vapore**	**kot**toa ah vah**poa**ray
stewed	**in umido**	een **oo**meedoa

Fish specialities *Specialità di pesce*

anguilla alla veneziana (ahnggoo**eel**lah **ahl**lah vaynaytsee**aa**nah) — eel cooked in sauce made from tunny (tuna) and lemon

baccalà alla vicentina (bahkkah**lah ahl**lah veechayn**tee**nah) — cod cooked in milk with onion, garlic, parsley, anchovies and cinnamon

fritto misto (**freet**toa **mee**stoa) — a fry of various small fish and shellfish

pesci in carpione (**pay**shee een kahrpoo**oa**nay) — boiled fish, cooked in vinegar, served cold with lemon

pesci al cartoccio (**pay**shee ahl kahr**tot**choa) — baked in a parchment envelope with onions, parsley and herbs

sgombri in umido (**zgoam**bree een **oo**meedoa) — stewed mackerel in white wine with green peas

stoccafisso (stoakkah**fees**soa) — dried cod cooked with tomatoes, olives and artichoke

sogliole alla mugnaia (sawlyolay ahllah mooñaaeeah)	sole sautéed in butter, garnished with parsley and lemon
triglie alla livornese (treelyay ahllah leevoarnaysay)	baked red mullet

Meat *Carne*

I'd like some ...	**Vorrei ...**	vorraiee
beef	**del manzo**	dayl mahndzoa
lamb	**dell'agnello**	dayllahñehlloa
mutton	**del montone**	dayl moantoanay
pork	**del maiale**	dayl maaeeaalay
veal	**del vitello**	dayl veetehlloa
animelle di vitello	ahneemehllay dee veetehlloa	sweetbreads
arrosto	ahrroastoa	roast
bistecca	beestaykkah	steak
di filetto	dee feelehttoa	rib steak
braciola	brahchoalah	chop
cervello	chayrvehlloa	brains
cosciotto	koashawttoa	leg
costola	kostoalah	rib
costoletta	koastoalayttah	cutlet
fegato	faygahtoa	liver
fesa	faysah	round cut from rump
filetto	feelayttoa	fillet
lingua	leenggwah	tongue
lombata/lombo	loambaatah/loamboa	loin
medaglioni	maydahlyoanee	round fillet
midollo	meedoalloa	marrow
nodini	noadeenee	veal chops
pancetta affumicata	pahnchehttah ahffoomeekaatah	bacon
polpette	poalpayttay	meatballs
polpettone	poalpayttoanay	meat loaf of seasoned beef or veal
porcellino da latte/ porchetta	poarchaylleenoa dah lahttay/poarkayttah	suck(l)ing pig
prosciutto	proashoottoa	ham
rognoni	roañoanee	kidneys
rosbif	rosbeef	roast beef
salsicce	sahlseetchay	sausages
salumi	sahloomee	assorted pork products

scaloppina	skahloap**pee**nah	escalope
spalla	**spahl**lah	shoulder
tripe	**treep**pay	tripe

Meat dishes *Piatti di carne*

abbacchio (ahb**bahk**keeoa)	roast lamb, often served in a casserole with anchovies
bistecca alla fiorentina (bee**stayk**kah **ahl**lah feeoarayn**tee**nah)	a grilled steak flavoured with pepper, lemon juice and parsley
cima alla genovese (**chee**mah **ahl**lah jaynoa**vay**say)	rolled veal stuffed with eggs, sausage and mushrooms
costata al prosciutto (koa**staa**tah ahl proa**shoot**toa)	a chop filled with ham, cheese and truffles; breaded and fried until golden brown
costoletta alla milanese (koastoa**layt**tah **ahl**lah meelah**nay**say)	breaded veal cutlet, flavoured with cheese
fegato alla veneziana (**fay**gahtoa **ahl**lah vaynaytsee**aa**nah)	thin slices of calf's liver fried with onions
involtini (eenvoal**tee**nee)	thin slices of meat (beef, veal or pork) rolled and stuffed
ossi buchi (**os**see **boo**kee)	veal or beef knuckle braised and served in a highly flavoured sauce
iccata al marsala (peek**kaa**tah ahl mahr**saa**lah)	thin veal escalope braised in marsala sauce
altimbocca alla romana (sahlteem**boak**kah **ahl**lah roa**maa**nah)	veal escalope braised in marsala wine with ham and sage
caloppina alla Valdostana (skahloap**pee**nah **ahl**lah vahldoa**staa**nah)	veal escalope filled with cheese and ham
spezzatino (spaytsah**tee**noa)	meat or poultry stew
spiedino (speeay**dee**noa)	pieces of meat grilled or roasted on a skewer

stracotto (strah**ko**ttoa)	meat stew slowly cooked for several hours
trippe alla fiorentina (**tree**ppay **ah**llah feeorayn**tee**nah)	tripe and beef braised in a tomato sauce, served with cheese
vitello tonnato (veetayl**lo**a toan**naa**toa)	cold veal with tuna fish sauce
zampone (tsahm**poa**nay)	pig's trotter filled with seasoned pork, boiled and served in slices

How do you like your meat? *Come vuole la carne?*

baked	**al forno**	ahl **for**noa
barbecued	**alla graticola/alla griglia**	**ah**llah grahtee**koa**lah/ **ah**llah **gree**lyah
boiled	**lesso**	**lay**ssoa
braised	**brasato**	brah**saa**toa
broiled	**allo spiedo**	**ah**lloa spee**eh**doa
casseroled	**in casseruola**	een kassay**rwo**lah
fried	**fritto**	**free**ttoa
grilled	**ai ferri**	**ahee feh**rree
roast(ed)	**arrosto**	ah**rroa**stoa
spit-roasted	**allo spiedo**	**ah**lloa spee**eh**doa
stewed	**in umido**	een **oo**meedoa
stuffed	**farcito**	fahr**chee**toa
underdone (rare)	**al sangue**	ahl **sahng**gooay
medium	**a puntino**	ah poon**tee**noa
well-done	**ben cotto**	bain **ko**ttoa

Game and poultry *Cacciagione e pollame*

Many small fowl not regarded as game birds in America or Britain are served as first or main courses in Italy. They're usually grilled or roasted. Among small fowl considered as gourmet dishes are lark, plover, thrush and ortolan.

I'd like some game.	**Vorrei della cacciagione.**	vorraiee **day**llah kahtchah**joa**nay
What poultry dishes do you serve?	**Che piatti di pollame servite?**	kay pee**ah**ttee dee poa**llaa**may sayr**vee**tay

allodola	ahl**lo**doalah	lark
anatra	**aa**nahtrah	duck
beccaccia	bayk**kaht**chah	woodcock
beccaccino	baykkaht**chee**noa	snipe
camoscio	kah**mo**shoa	chamois
cappone	kahp**poa**nay	capon
capretto	kah**prayt**toa	kid goat
capriolo	kahpree**o**loa	roebuck
cervo	**chehr**voa	deer
cinghiale	cheengee**aa**lay	wild boar
coniglio	koa**nee**lyoa	rabbit
fagiano	fah**jaa**noa	pheasant
faraona	fahrah**oa**nah	guinea fowl
gallina	gahl**lee**nah	stewing fowl
gallo cedrone	**gahl**loa cheh**droa**nay	grouse
lepre	**lai**pray	hare
oca	**o**kah	goose
ortolano	oartoa**laa**noa	ortolan
pernice	payr**nee**chay	partridge
piccione	peet**choa**nay	pigeon
piviere	peevee**eh**ray	plover
pollo	**poal**loa	chicken
pollo novello	**poal**loa noa**vehl**loa	spring chicken
quaglia	**kwah**lyah	quail
selvaggina	saylvahd**jee**nah	venison
tacchino	tahk**kee**noa	turkey
tordo	**toar**doa	thrush

capretto ripieno al forno (kah**prayt**toa reepee**ay**noa ahl **for**noa) — stuffed kid, oven-roasted

galletto amburghese (gahl**layt**toa ahmboor**gay**say) — young tender chicken, oven-roasted

palombacce allo spiedo (pahloam**baht**chay **ahl**loa spee**eh**doa) — wood pigeon, spit-roasted

polenta e coniglio (poa**lehn**tah ay koa**nee**lyoa) — rabbit stew served with a mush made from maize flour (cornmeal mush)

polenta e uccelli (poa**lehn**tah ay oot**chehl**lee) — various small birds roasted on a spit and served with polenta (see immediately above)

pollo alla diavola (**poal**loa **ahl**lah dee**aa**voalah) — highly spiced and grilled chicken

Vegetables—Salads *Verdure—Insalate*

What kind of vegetables have you got?	**Che genere di verdure avete?**	kay **jeh**nayray dee vehr**doo**ray ah**vay**tay
I'd like a (mixed) salad.	**Vorrei un'insalata (mista).**	vor**rai**ee ooneensah**laa**tah (**mee**stah)

asparagi	ah**spaa**rahjee	asparagus
barbabietola	bahrbah**beeeh**toalah	beetroot
broccoli	**brok**kolee	broccoli
carciofi	kahr**cho**fee	artichokes
carote	kah**raw**tay	carrots
cavolfiore	kahvoalfee**oa**ray	cauliflower
cavolo	**kaa**voaloa	cabbage
cavolini di Bruxelles	kahvoa**lee**nee dee broos**sayl**	brussels sprouts
ceci	**chay**chee	chick-peas
cetriolini	chaytreeoa**lee**nee	gherkins
cetriolo	chaytree**o**loa	cucumber
cicoria	chee**ko**reeah	endive (Am. chicory)
cipolle	chee**pol**lay	onions
fagioli	fah**joa**lee	haricot beans
fagiolini	fahjoa**lee**nee	French (green) beans
fave	**faa**vay	broad beans
finocchio	fee**nok**keeoa	fennel
funghi	**foong**gee	mushrooms
indivia	een**dee**veeah	chicory (Am. endive)
insalata (verde)	eensah**laa**tah (**vayr**day)	(green) salad
lattuga	laht**too**gah	lettuce
lenticchie	layn**teek**keeay	lentils
melanzane	maylahn**tsaa**nay	aubergine (eggplant)
patate	pah**taa**tay	potatoes
peperoni	paypay**roa**nee	sweet peppers
piselli	pee**sehl**lee	peas
pomodoro	poamoa**daw**roa	tomato
porcini	poar**chee**nee	boletus mushrooms
porro	**por**roa	leeks
radicchio	rah**deek**keeoa	a kind of bitter, red and white lettuce
ravanelli	rahvah**nehl**lee	radishes
sedano	**seh**dahnoa	celery
spinaci	spee**naa**chee	spinach
tartufi	tahr**too**fee	truffles
verdura mista	vehr**doo**rah **mee**stah	mixed vegetables
verza	**vehr**dzah	green cabbage
zucca	**tsook**kah	pumpkin, gourd
zucchini	tsook**kee**nee	zucchini

Spices and herbs *Spezie e odori*

aglio	ah**l**yoa	garlic
basilico	bah**zee**leekoa	basil
cannella	kahn**nehl**lah	cinnamon
capperi	**kahp**pehree	capers
chiodi di garofano	keeodee dee gah**ro**fahnoa	cloves
cipollina	cheepoal**lee**nah	chive
cumino	koo**mee**noa	cumin
lauro	**lah**ooroa	bay
maggiorana	madjoa**raa**nah	marjoram
menta	**mayn**tah	mint
noce moscata	**noa**chay moa**skaa**tah	nutmeg
origano	oa**ree**gahnoa	origan
prezzemolo	preht**tsay**moaloa	parsley
rosmarino	roazmah**ree**noa	rosemary
salvia	**sahl**veeah	sage
scalogno	skah**loa**ñoa	shallot
timo	**tee**moa	thyme
zafferano	dzahffeh**raa**noa	saffron
zenzero	**dzehn**dzehroa	ginger

Cheese *Formaggio*

Italy produces a great variety of cheese, many of them little known outside the locality in which they're made.

Bel Paese (behl pahayzay)	smooth cheese with delicate taste
caciocavallo (kahchoakah**vahl**loa)	firm, slightly sweet cheese from cow's or sheep's milk
gorgonzola (goargoan**dzo**lah)	most famous of the Italian blue-veined cheese, rich with a tangy flavour
mozzarella (motsah**rehl**lah)	soft, unripened cheese with a bland, slightly sweet flavour, made from buffalo's milk in southern Italy, elsewhere with cow's milk
parmigiano (-reggiano) (pahrmee**jaa**noa-ray**djaa**noa)	parmesan (also called *grana*), a hard cheese generally grated for use in hot dishes and pasta but also eaten alone
pecorino (paykoa**ree**noa)	a hard cheese made from sheep's milk
ricotta (reekottah)	soft cow's or sheep's milk cheese

Fruit *Frutta*

Do you have fresh fruit?	**Avete della frutta fresca?**	ahvaytay dayllah froottah frayskah
I'd like a fresh fruit cocktail.	**Vorrei una macedonia di frutta.**	vorraiee oonah mahchaydoneeah dee froottah

albicocca	ahlbeekokkah	apricot
ananas	ahnahnahss	pineapple
anguria	ahnggooreeah	watermelon
arachide	ahrahkeeday	peanuts
arancia	ahrahnchah	orange
banana	bahnaanah	banana
caco	kaakoa	persimmon
castagna	kahstaañah	chestnut
cedro	chaydroa	lime
ciliege	cheeleeayjay	cherries
cocomero	koakoamayroa	watermelon
cotogna	koatoañah	quince
datteri	dahttayree	dates
fico	feekoa	fig
fragole	fraagoalay	strawberries
lamponi	lahmpoanee	raspberries
limone	leemoanay	lemon
mandarino	mahndahreenoa	tangerine
mandorle	mahndoarlay	almonds
mela	maylah	apple
melone	mayloanay	melon
mirtilli	meerteellee	blueberries
more	moray	blackberries
nocciole	noatcholay	hazelnuts
noce di cocco	noachay dee kokkoa	coconut
noci	noachee	walnuts
pera	payrah	pear
pesca	pehskah	peach
pinoli	peenolee	pine kernels
pompelmo	poampaylmoa	grapefruit
prugna	prooñah	plum
prugna secca	prooñah saykkah	prune
ribes	reebays	redcurrants
ribes nero	reebays nayroa	blackcurrants
susina	soozeenah	plum
uva	oovah	grapes
bianca/nera	beeahngkah/nayrah	white/black
uva passa	oovah pahssah	raisins
uva spina	oovah speenah	gooseberries

Dessert *Dolce*

You'll find a profusion of cakes and tarts to round off the meal. Among the more interesting is the *zuppa inglese*—not a soup at all but a kind of trifle (see below). *Granita* is a partially frozen dessert made with coffee or fruit juice. Or try some of the delicious ice-cream for which Italy is renown.

I'd like a dessert, please.	**Vorrei un dessert, per favore.**	vorr**ai**ee oon dayss**ehr** pair fah**voa**ray
What do you recommend?	**Cosa consiglia?**	**kaw**sah koan**see**lyah
Something light, please.	**Qualcosa di leggero, per favore.**	kwahl**kaw**sah dee laydj**ai**roa pair fah**voa**ray
I'd like a slice of cake.	**Vorrei una fetta di torta.**	vorr**ai**ee **oo**nah **feh**ttah dee **toa**rtah
with/without (whipped) cream	**con/senza panna (montata)**	kon/**sayn**tsah **pahn**nah (moan**taa**tah)

budino	boo**dee**noa	pudding
crema	**krai**mah	custard
crostata di mele	kroa**staa**tah dee **may**lay	apple pie
dolce	**doal**chay	cake
gelato	jay**laa**toa	ice-cream
alla fragola	**ahl**lah **fraa**goalah	strawberry
al limone	ahl lee**moa**nay	lemon
alla vaniglia	**ahl**lah vah**nee**lyah	vanilla
misto	**mee**stoa	mixed
tartufi di cioccolata	tahr**too**fee dee choakkoa**laa**tah	chocolate truffles
torta	**toa**rtah	cake
di cioccolata	dee choakkoa**laa**tah	chocolate cake
di frutta	dee **froo**ttah	fruit cake

cassata (kas**saa**tah)	ice cream with candied fruit (Am. spumoni)
cassata siciliana (kas**saa**tah seecheelee**aa**nah)	sponge cake garnished with sweet cream cheese, chocolate and candied fruit
zabaglione (dzahbah**lyoa**nay)	a mixture of eggyolks, sugar and Marsala wine; served warm
zuppa inglese (dzooppah eeng**glay**say)	sponge cake steeped in rum with candied fruit and custard or whipped cream

Drinks *Bevande*

Aperitifs *Aperitivi*

The average Italian is just as fond of his favourite *aperitivo* (ahpehreeteevoa) as we are of our cocktail or highball. Often bittersweet, some aperitifs have a wine and brandy base with herbs and bitters while others may have a vegetable base. Here are some aperitifs you may want to try:

Americano (ahmayreekaanoa)	despite its name, one of the most popular Italian aperitifs; a vermouth to which bitters, brandy and lemon peel are added
Aperol (ahpayroal)	a non-alcoholic bitters
Campari (kahmpaaree)	reddish-brown bitters, flavoured with orange peel and herbs, it has a quinine taste
Cynar (cheenaar)	produced from artichoke
Martini (mahrteenee)	a brand-name vermouth not to be confused with a martini cocktail

neat (straight)	**liscio**	leeshoa
on the rocks	**con ghiaccio**	kon geeahtchoa
with (seltzer) water	**con acqua (di seltz)**	kon ahkkwah (dee sehltz)

SALUTE!/CIN-CIN!
(sahlootay/cheen cheen)
YOUR HEALTH!/CHEERS!

Wine *Vino*

Italy is one of the most important wine producers in Europe. Vineyards are found all over the Italian peninsula and islands.

Some of the country's most reputed wines (like *Barbaresco, Barbera* and *Barolo*) come from the Piedmont in northwestern Italy. But most other regions have noted wine, too. This is your opportunity to sample local wine, some of which is of surprisingly good quality.

Chianti is doubtless Italy's best-known wine outside of its borders. The best of it is produced between Florence and Siena. The term *Chianti classico* on the label indicates that the production of this wine has been carefully supervised. A *Chianti* of superior quality carries the term *riserva* on the label.

Some restaurants list their wines in a corner of the menu while others have them marked up on the wall. As much of the nation's wine doesn't travel well, don't expect a *trattoria* to offer more than a few types of wine. Most of the wine must be drunk young so don't look too hard for vintage labels. In smaller places you might get *vino aperto* (open wine) or *vino della casa* (house wine) at a moderate price, served in one-quarter, one-half or one-litre carafes.

May I have the wine list, please.	**Per favore, mi porti la lista dei vini.**	pair fah**voa**ray mee **por**tee lah **lee**stah **daiee vee**nee
I'd like a bottle of white/red wine.	**Vorrei una bottiglia di vino bianco/ rosso.**	vor**raiee oo**nah bot**tee**lyah dee **vee**noa bee**ahng**koa/ **roas**soa
half a bottle	**mezza bottiglia**	**meh**dzah bot**tee**lyah
a carafe	**una caraffa**	**oo**nah kah**rahf**fah
half a litre	**mezzo litro**	**meh**dzoa **lee**troa
a glass	**un bicchiere**	oon beek**keeai**ray
A bottle of champagne, please.	**Una bottiglia di champagne, per favore.**	**oo**nah bot**tee**lyah dee sham**pahñ** pair fah**voa**ray
Where does this wine come from?	**Da dove viene questo vino?**	dah **doa**vay vee**ay**nay koo**ay**stoa **vee**noa

red	**rosso**	**roas**soa
white	**bianco**	bee**ahng**koa
rosé	**rosatello**	rawzah**tehl**loa
dry	**secco**	**sehk**koa
full-bodied	**pieno**	pee**ay**noa
light	**leggero**	lay**djai**roa
sparkling	**spumante**	spoo**mahn**tay
sweet	**dolce**	**doal**chay

The following chart will help you to choose your wine if you want to do some serious wine-tasting.

Type of wine	Examples	Accompanies
sweet white wine	*Orvieto* from Umbria (the export variety is usually dry), *Aleatico* and *Vino Santo* from Tuscany and the famed *Marsala* from Sicily.	desserts, especially custard, pudding, cake
dry white wine	*Frascati* from Latium or *Verdicchio dei Castelli di Jesi* from the Adriatic Marches; local white wine generally falls into this category	fish, seafood, cold or boiled meat, fowl (the unconventional Romans enjoy drinking *Frascati* with a heavy meal)
rosé	*Lagrein* from Trentino-Alto Adige	goes with almost anything but especially cold dishes, eggs, pork and lamb
light-bodied red wine	*Bardolino* and *Valpolicella* from the Lake of Garda; local red wine, including Italian- Swiss *Merlot,* usually fits this category	roast chicken, turkey, veal, lamb, steaks, ham, liver, quail, pheasant, soft-textured cheeses, stews and pasta
full-bodied red wine	*Barolo, Barbera* and *Barbaresco* from Piedmont	duck, goose, kidneys, most game, tangy cheese like *gorgonzola*—in short, any strong-flavoured dishes
sparkling white wine	*Asti spumante* (Italians like to refer to it as champagne but it's slightly sweet)	goes nicely with dessert and pastry; if it's dry, you might try *spumante* as an aperitif or with shellfish, nuts or dried fruit

Beer *Birra*

Beer is always available and growing in popularity. Italian brands are weaker than northern European beers.

I'd like a beer, please.	**Vorrei una birra, per favore.**	vor**rai**ee **oo**nah **beer**rah pair fah**voa**ray
Do you have ... beer?	**Avete della birra ...?**	ah**vay**tay **dayl**lah **beer**rah
bottled	**in bottiglia**	een bot**tee**lyah
draught	**alla spina**	**ahl**lah **spee**nah
foreign	**straniera**	strahnee**ay**rah
light/dark	**bionda/scura**	bee**oan**dah/**skoo**rah

Other alcoholic drinks *Altre bevande alcoliche*

Coffee shops and bars usually have a good stock of foreign and domestic liquor—even some of your favourite brands.

aperitif	**un aperitivo**	oon ahpayree**tee**voa
brandy	**un brandy**	oon "brandy"
cognac	**un cognac**	oon "cognac"
gin and tonic	**un gin e tonico**	oon "gin" ay **to**neekoa
liqueur	**un liquore**	oon look**woa**ray
port	**un porto**	oon **por**toa
rum	**un rum**	oon room
vermouth	**un vermouth**	oon **vehr**moot
vodka	**una vodka**	**oo**nah **vod**kah
whisky (and soda)	**un whisky (e soda)**	oon "whisky" (ay **so**dah)

glass	**un bicchiere**	oon beekkee**ai**ray
bottle	**una bottiglia**	**oo**nah bot**tee**lyah
double (a double shot)	**doppio**	**doap**peeoa
neat (straight)	**liscio**	**lee**shoa
on the rocks	**con ghiaccio**	kon gee**aht**choa

You'll certainly want to take the occasion to sip an after-dinner drink. If you'd like something which approaches French cognac try *Vecchia Romagna*. If you feel a digestive is called for ask for an *amaro* (bitter), or a glass of *Fernet-Branca* should fit the bill.

I'd like to try a glass of ..., please.	**Vorrei assaggiare un bicchiere di ...**	vorraiee ahssahdjaaray oon beekkeeairay dee
Are there any local specialities?	**Avete specialità locali?**	ahvaytay spaychahleetah loakaalee

Nonalcoholic drinks *Bevande analcoliche*

The Italian *caffè espresso* has a rich aroma and is excellent everywhere. Served in demi-tasses, it's stronger than what we're used to at home. However, if you'd like to try a more concentrated cup of espresso coffee, ask for a *ristretto* (reestrayttoa). As against this, a *caffè lungo* (kahffay loonggoa) is a slightly weaker cup of espresso coffee.

For breakfast don't miss the opportunity to drink a *cappuccino* (kahppootcheenoa), a delicious mixture of coffee and hot milk, dusted with cocoa. In summer, iced tea and coffee are popular.

I'd like a/an ...	**Vorrei ...**	vorraiee
chocolate	**un cioccolato**	oon choakkoalaatoa
coffee	**un caffè**	oon kahffai
with cream	**con panna**	kon pahnnah
iced coffee	**un caffè freddo**	oon kahffay frayddoa
fruit juice	**un succo di frutta**	oon sookkoa dee froottah
grapefruit	**di pompelmo**	dee poampaylmoa
lemon	**di limone**	dee leemoanay
orange	**d'arancia**	dahrahnchah
herb tea	**una tisana**	oonah teezaanah
lemonade	**una limonata**	oonah leemoanaatah
milk	**del latte**	dayl lahttay
milkshake	**un frullato di latte**	oon froollaatoa dee lahttay
mineral water	**dell'acqua minerale**	dayllahkkwah meenayraalay
fizzy (carbonated)	**gasata**	gahzaatah
still	**naturale**	nahtooraalay
orangeade	**un'aranciata**	oonahrahnchaatah
tea	**un tè**	oon tai
with milk/lemon	**con latte/limone**	kon lahttay/leemoanay
iced tea	**un tè freddo**	oon tai frayddoa
tomato juice	**un succo di pomodoro**	oon sookkoa dee poamoadawroa
tonic water	**dell'acqua tonica**	dayllahkkwah toneekah

Complaints *Reclami*

There is a plate/glass missing.	**Manca un piatto/un bicchiere.**	mahngkah oon peeahttoa/oon beekkeeairay
I have no knive/fork/spoon.	**Non ho il coltello/la forchetta/il cucchiaio.**	noan oa eel koltehlloa/lah forkehttah/eel kookkeeaaeeoa
That's not what I ordered.	**Non è ciò che avevo ordinato.**	noan ai cho kay ahvayvoa oardeenaatoa
I asked for ...	**Avevo chiesto ...**	ahvayvoa keeehstoa
There must be some mistake.	**Ci deve essere un errore.**	chee dayvay ehssayray oon ehrroaray
May I change this?	**Posso cambiare questo?**	possoa kahmbeeaaray kooaystoa
I asked for a small portion (for the child).	**Avevo chiesto una piccola porzione (per il bambino).**	ahvayvoa keeehstoa oonah peekkoalah poartseeoanay (pair eel bahmbeenoa)
The meat is ...	**La carne è ...**	lah kahrnay ai
overdone	**troppo cotta**	troppoa kottah
underdone	**poco cotta**	pokoa kottah
too rare	**troppo al sangue**	troppoa ahl sahnggooay
too tough	**troppo dura**	troppoa doorah
This is too ...	**Questo è troppo ...**	kooaystoa ai troppoa
bitter/salty	**amaro/salato**	ahmaaroa/sahlaatoa
sweet	**dolce**	doalchay
I don't like it.	**Non mi piace.**	noan mee peeahchay
The food is cold.	**Il cibo è freddo.**	eel cheeboa ai frayddoa
This isn't fresh.	**Questo non è fresco.**	kooaystoa noan ai frayskoa
What's taking you so long?	**Perchè impiegate tanto tempo?**	pehrkai eempeeaygaatay tahntoa tehmpoa
Have you forgotten our drinks?	**Ha dimenticato le nostre bevande?**	ah deemaynteekaatoa lay nostray bayvahnday
The wine tastes of cork.	**Il vino sa di tappo.**	eel veenoa sah dee tahppoa
This isn't clean.	**Questo non è pulito.**	kooaystoa noan ai pooleetoa
Would you ask the head waiter to come over?	**Vuole chiedere al capo cameriere di venire qui?**	vwolay keeaydayray ahl kaapoa kahmayreeehray dee vayneeray kooee

The bill (check) *Il conto*

Though the bill usually includes the service charge *(il servizio),* it is customary to leave a tip *(la mancia)* for the waiter. Note that you will occasionally also find one or both of the following items added to your bill: *coperto* (cover charge), *supplemento* (surcharge).

I'd like to pay.	**Vorrei pagare.**	vorraiee pahgaaray
We'd like to pay separately.	**Vorremmo pagare separatamente.**	vorrehmmoa pahgaaray saypahrahtahmayntay
I think you've made a mistake in this bill.	**Penso che abbiate fatto un errore nel conto.**	pehnsoa kay ahbbeeaatay fahttoa oon ayrroaray nayl koantoa
What is this amount for?	**Per che cos'è questo importo?**	pair kay kozai kooaystoa eemportoa
Is service included?	**È compreso il servizio?**	ai koampraysoa eel sayrveetseeoa
Is the cover charge included?	**È compreso il coperto?**	ai koampraysoa eel kopairtoa
Is everything included?	**È tutto compreso?**	ai toottoa koampraysoa
Do you accept traveller's cheques?	**Accettate i traveller's cheques?**	ahtchayttaatay ee "traveller's cheques"
Can I pay with this credit card?	**Posso pagare con questa carta di credito?**	possoa pahgaaray kon kooaystah kahrtah dee kraydeetoa
Thank you, this is for you.	**Grazie, questo è per lei.**	graatseeay kooaystoa ai pair lehee
Keep the change.	**Tenga il resto.**	taynggah eel rehstoa
That was a delicious meal.	**È stato un pasto delizioso.**	ai staatoa oon paastoa dayleetseeoasoa
We enjoyed it, thank you.	**Ci è piaciuto grazie.**	chee ai peeahchootoa graatseeay

SERVIZIO COMPRESO
SERVICE INCLUDED

TIPPING, see inside back-cover

Snacks—Picnic *Spuntini—Picnic*

Bars and snack bars stay open from early morning till late at night. Most have a selection of sandwiches *(panini imbottiti)* and pastries *(pasticcini),* inexpensive if you eat at the counter. There are, of course, *pizzerie* for a sit-down pizza or, if you're in a hurry, places selling pizza by the slice. In a *paninoteca,* you can find all sorts of *panini* to eat on the spot or to bring away. The same in a *rosticceria,* plus a great variety of food ready to eat at home or in a picnic.

I'll have one of those, please.	**Per favore, vorrei uno di quelli.**	pair fahvoaray vorraiee oonoa dee kooayllee
Give me two of these and one of those.	**Mi dia due di questi e uno di quelli.**	mee deeah dooay dee kooaystee ay oonoa dee kooayllee
to the left/right	**a sinistra/a destra**	ah seeneestrah/a dehstrah
above/below	**sopra/sotto**	soaprah/soattoa
It's to take away.	**È da portare via.**	ai dah poartaaray veeah
How much is that?	**Quant'è?**	kwahntai
I'd like a/some ...	**Vorrei ...**	vorraiee
chicken	**un pollo**	oon poalloa
half a roasted chicken	**metà pollo arrosto**	maytah poalloa ahrroastoa
chips	**delle patatine fritte**	dayllay pahtahteenay freettay
(slice of) pizza	**una (fetta di) pizza**	oonah (fayttah dee) peettzah
sandwich	**un panino imbottito**	oon pahneenoa eembot-teetoa
cheese	**al formaggio**	ahl foarmadjoa
ham	**al prosciutto cotto**	ahl proashoottoa kottoa
Parma ham	**al prosciutto crudo**	ahl proashoottoa kroodoa
salami	**al salame**	ahl sahlaamay

Here's a basic list of food and drink that might come in useful when shopping for a picnic.

Please give me a/an/ some ...	**Per favore, mi dia ...**	pair fahvoaray mee deeah
apples	**delle mele**	dayllay maylay
bananas	**delle banane**	dayllay bahnaanay

biscuits (Br.)	**dei biscotti**	daiee beeskoattee
beer	**della birra**	dayllah beerrah
bread	**del pane**	dayl paanay
butter	**del burro**	dayl boorroa
cake	**una torta**	oonah toartah
cheese	**del formaggio**	dayl foarmahdjoa
chips (Am.)	**delle patatine fritte**	dayllay pahtahteenay freettay
chocolate bar	**una stecca di cioccolato**	oonah staykkah dee chokkoalaatoa
coffee	**del caffè**	dayl kahffai
instant	**solubile**	soaloobeelay
cold cuts	**degli affettati**	daylyee ahffehttaatee
cookies	**dei biscotti**	daiee beeskoattee
crackers	**dei cracker**	daiee "cracker"
crisps	**delle patatine fritte**	dayllay pahtahteenay freettay
eggs	**delle uova**	dayllay wawvah
frankfurters	**dei Würstel**	daiee "würstel"
gherkins (pickles)	**dei cetriolini**	daiee chaytreeoaleenee
grapes	**dell'uva**	daylloovah
ham	**del prosciutto**	dayl proashoottoa
ice-cream	**del gelato**	dayl jaylaatoa
lemon	**un limone**	oon leemoanay
milk	**del latte**	dayl lahttay
mustard	**della senape**	dayllah saynahpay
(olive) oil	**dell'olio (d'oliva)**	dayllolyoa (doleevah)
oranges	**delle arance**	dayllay ahrahnchay
pastries	**dei pasticcini**	daiee pahsteetcheenee
peaches	**delle pesche**	dayllay payskay
peppers	**dei peperoni**	daiee paypayroanee
pickles	**dei sottaceti**	daiee soattahchaytee
plums	**delle prugne**	dayllay prooñay
rolls	**dei panini**	daiee pahneenee
salad	**dell'insalata**	dayleensahlaatah
salami	**del salame**	dayl sahlaamay
salt	**del sale**	dayl saalay
sausages	**delle salsicce**	dayllay sahlseetchay
soft drink	**una bibita**	oonah beebeetah
sugar	**dello zucchero**	daylloa tsookkayroa
tea	**del tè**	dayl tai
tomatoes	**dei pomodori**	daiee poamoadawree
vinegar	**dell'aceto**	dayllahchaytoa
(mineral) water	**dell'acqua (minerale)**	dayllahkkwah (meenayraalay)
wine	**del vino**	dayl veenoa
yoghurt	**uno yogurt**	oonoa eeoagoort

Travelling around

Plane *Aereo*

Is there a flight to Naples?	**C'è un volo per Napoli?**	chai oon **voa**loa pair **naa**poalee
Is it a direct flight?	**È un volo diretto?**	ai oon **voa**loa dee**ray**ttoa
When's the next flight to Palermo?	**A che ora è il prossimo volo per Palermo?**	ah kay **oa**rah ai eel **pross**eemoa **voa**loa pair pah**lehr**moa
Do I have to change planes?	**Devo cambiare aereo?**	**day**voa kahmbee**aa**ray ahairayoa
Is there a connection to Venice?	**C'è una coincidenza per Venezia?**	chai **oo**nah koeenchee**dehn**tsah pair vay**nay**tseeah
I'd like a ticket to Milan.	**Vorrei un biglietto per Milano.**	vor**rai**ee oon bee**lyay**ttoa pair mee**laa**noa
single (one-way)	**andata**	ahn**daa**tah
return (roundtrip)	**andata e ritorno**	ahn**daa**tah ay ree**tor**noa
What time do we take off?	**A che ora si parte?**	ah kay **oa**rah see **pahr**tay
What time should I check in?	**A che ora devo presentarmi?**	ah kay **oa**rah **day**voa prayzehn**taar**mee
Is there a bus to the airport?	**C'è un autobus per l'aeroporto?**	chai oon **ow**toabooss pair lahayro**por**toa
What's the flight number?	**Qual è il numero del volo?**	kwahl ai eel **noo**mayroa dayl **voa**loa
What time do we arrive?	**A che ora arriveremo?**	ah kay **oa**rah ahrreevay**ray**moa
I'd like to ... my reservation on flight no ...	**Vorrei ... la mia prenotazione sul volo ...**	vor**rai**ee ... lah **mee**ah praynoatahtsee**oa**nay sool **voa**loa
cancel	**annullare**	ahnnool**laa**ray
change	**cambiare**	kahmbee**aa**ray
confirm	**confermare**	koanfayr**maa**ray

ARRIVO
ARRIVAL

PARTENZA
DEPARTURE

Train *Treno*

Italian trains *try* to run on time as advertised. If you haven' booked, it's wise to arrive at the station at least 20 minute before departure to be sure of a seat: Italy's trains are ofte very crowded.

The following list describes the various types of trains:

TEE (teh-eh-eh)	Trans Europ Express; a luxury, internationa service with first class only; additional far and reservation required
Rapido (R) (**raa**peedoa)	Long-distance express train stopping a major cities only; first and second class
Intercity (IC) ("intercity")	Inter-city express with very few stops; luxury, international service with first an second class
Espresso (EXP)/ Direttissimo (ay**sprehs**soa/ deereht**tees**seemoa)	Long-distance train, stopping at main station
Diretto (D) (dee**reht**toa)	Slower than the *Espresso*, it makes a numbe of local stops
Locale (L) (loa**kaa**lay)	A local train which stops at almost every sta tion
Accelerato (A) (ahtchaylay**raa**toa)	Same as a *Locale*
Littorina (leettoa**ree**nah)	Small diesel used on short runs

Here are some more useful terms which you may need.

Carrozza ristorante (kahr**rot**tsah reesto**rahn**tay)	Dining-car
Vagone letto (vah**goa**nay **leht**toa)	Sleeping-car with individual compartment and washing facilities
Carrozza cuccette (kahr**rot**tsah koot**cheht**tay)	A berth with blankets and pillows
Bagagliaio (bahgah**lyaa**eeoa)	Guard's van (baggage car): normally onl registered luggage permitted

To the railway station *Per andare alla stazione*

Where's the railway station?	**Dove si trova la stazione (ferroviaria)?**	**doa**vay see **traw**vah lah stahtsee**oa**nay (fehrrovee**aa**reeah)
Taxi, please!	**Taxi, per favore!**	"taxi" pair fah**voa**ray
Take me to the railway station.	**Mi porti alla stazione.**	mee **por**tee **ahl**lah stahtsee**oa**nay
What's the fare?	**Quant'è?**	kwahn**tai**

ENTRATA	ENTRANCE
USCITA	EXIT
AI BINARI	TO THE PLATFORMS
INFORMAZIONI	INFORMATION

Where's the ...? *Dov'è ...?*

Where is/are the ...?	**Dov'è ...?**	doa**vai**
bar	**il bar**	eel "bar"
booking office	**l'ufficio prenotazioni**	loof**fee**choa praynoatahtsee**oa**nee
currency-exchange office	**l'ufficio cambio**	loof**fee**choa **kahm**beeoa
left-luggage office (baggage check)	**il deposito bagagli**	eel day**paw**zeetoa bah**gaa**lyee
lost property (lost-and-found) office	**l'ufficio oggetti smarriti**	loof**fee**choa od**jeht**tee smahr**ree**tee
luggage lockers	**la custodia automatica dei bagagli**	lah koo**staw**deeah owtoa**maa**teekah **dai**ee bah**gaa**lyee
newsstand	**l'edicola**	lay**dee**koalah
platform 7	**il binario 7**	eel bee**naa**reeoa 7
reservations office	**l'ufficio prenotazioni**	loof**fee**choa praynoatahtsee**oa**nee
restaurant	**il ristorante**	eel reesto**rahn**tay
snack bar	**lo "snack bar"**	loa "snack bar"
ticket office	**la biglietteria**	lah beelyayttay**ree**ah
waiting room	**la sala d'aspetto**	lah **saa**lah dahs**peht**toa
Where are the toilets?	**Dove sono i gabinetti?**	**doa**vay **soa**noa ee gahbee**nayt**tee

TAXI, see page 21

Inquiries *Informazioni*

When is the ... train to Rome?	**Quando parte ... treno per Roma?**	**kwahn**doa **pahr**tay ... **tray**noa pair **roa**mah
first/last	**il primo/l'ultimo**	eel **pree**moa/**lool**teemoa
next	**il prossimo**	eel **pros**seemoa
What time does the train for Milan leave?	**A che ora parte il treno per Milano?**	ah kay **oa**rah **pahr**tay eel **tray**noa pair mee**laa**noa
What's the fare to Ancona?	**Quanto costa il biglietto per Ancona?**	**kwahn**toa **kos**tah eel bee**lyayt**toa pair ahng**koa**nah
Is it a through train?	**È un treno diretto?**	ai oon **tray**noa dee**reht**toa
Is there a connection to ...?	**C'è una coincidenza per ...?**	chai **oo**nah koaeenchee**dayn**tsah pair
Do I have to change trains?	**Devo cambiare treno?**	**day**voa kahmbee**aa**ray **tray**noa
How long will the train stop at ...?	**Quanto tempo si fermerà il treno a ...?**	**kwahn**toa **tehm**poa see fayrmay**rah** eel **tray**noa ah
Is there sufficient time to change?	**C'è il tempo per cambiare?**	chai eel **tehm**poa pair kahmbee**aa**ray
Will the train leave on time?	**Partirà in orario il treno?**	pahrtee**rah** een oa**raa**reeoa eel **tray**noa
What time does the train arrive at Florence?	**A che ora arriverà a Firenze il treno?**	ah kay **oa**rah ahrreevay**rah** ah fee**rehn**tsay eel **tray**noa
Is there a dining-car/sleeping-car on the train?	**C'è una carrozza ristorante/un vagone letto sul treno?**	chai **oo**nah kahr**rot**tsah reesto**rahn**tay/oon vah**goa**nay **leht**toa sool **tray**noa
Does the train stop at Lugano?	**Il treno si fermerà a Lugano?**	eel **tray**noa see fayrmay**rah** ah loo**gaa**noa
What platform does the train for Verona leave from?	**Da che binario parte il treno per Verona?**	dah kay bee**naa**reeoa **pahr**tay eel **tray**noa pair vay**roa**nah
What platform does the train from Bari arrive at?	**A che binario arriva il treno proveniente da Bari?**	ah kay bee**naa**reeoa ahr**ree**vah eel **tray**noa provaynee**ehn**tay dah **baa**ree
I'd like to buy a timetable.	**Vorrei comprare un orario ferroviario.**	vor**rai**ee koam**praa**ray oon oa**raa**reeoa fehrrovee**aa**reeoa

È un treno diretto.	It's a through train.
Deve cambiare a ...	You have to change at ...
Cambi a ... e prenda un treno locale.	Change at ... and get a local train.
Il binario 7 è ...	Platform 7 is ...
laggiù/su dalle scale a sinistra/a destra	over there/upstairs on the left/on the right
C'è un treno per ... alle ...	There's a train to ... at ...
Il suo treno partirà dal binario 8.	Your train will leave from platform 8.
Ci sarà un ritardo di ... minuti.	There'll be a delay of ... minutes.
Prima classe in testa/ nel mezzo/in coda.	First class at the front/ in the middle/at the end.

Tickets *Biglietti*

I want a ticket to Rome.	**Desidero un biglietto per Roma.**	day**zee**dayroa oon bee**lyayt**toa pair **roa**mah
single (one-way)	**andata**	ahn**daa**tah
return (roundtrip)	**andata e ritorno**	ahn**daa**tah ay ree**tor**noa
first/second class	**prima/seconda classe**	**pree**mah/say**koan**dah **klahs**say
half price	**metà tariffa**	may**tah** tah**reef**fah

Reservation *Prenotazione*

I want to book a ...	**Vorrei prenotare ...**	vor**raiee** praynoa**taa**ray
seat (by the window)	**un posto (vicino al finestrino)**	oon **pos**toa (vee**chee**noa ahl feenay**stree**noa)
berth	**una cuccetta**	**oo**nah koot**cheht**tah
upper	**superiore**	soopayree**oa**ray
middle	**nel mezzo**	nayl **mehd**zoa
lower	**inferiore**	eenfayree**oa**ray
berth in the sleeping car	**un posto nel vagone letto**	oon **pos**toa nayl vah**goa**nay **leht**toa

All aboard *In vettura!*

Is this the right platform for the train to Bellinzona?	**È il binario giusto per il treno che va a Bellinzona?**	ai eel beenaareeo joostoa pair eel traynoa kay vah ah behlleendzoanah
Is this the right train to Genoa?	**È il treno giusto per Genova?**	ai eel traynoa joostoa pair jainoavah
Excuse me. May I get by?	**Mi scusi. Posso passare?**	mee skoozee. possoa pahssaaray
Is this seat taken?	**È occupato questo posto?**	ai oakkoopaatoa kooaystoa postoa

FUMATORI
SMOKER

NON FUMATORI
NONSMOKER

I think that's my seat.	**Penso che questo sia il mio posto.**	paynsoa kay kooaystoa seeah eel meeoa postoa
Would you let me know before we get to Milan?	**Può avvisarmi prima di arrivare a Milano?**	pwo ahvveezaarmee preemah dee ahrreevaaray ah meelaanoa
What station is this?	**Che stazione è?**	kay stahtseeoanay ai
How long does the train stop here?	**Quanto tempo si ferma qui il treno?**	kwahntoa tehmpoa see fayrmah kooee eel traynoa
When do we get to Pisa?	**Quando arriveremo a Pisa?**	kwahndoa ahrreevay-raymoa ah peezah

Sleeping *Nel vagone letto*

Are there any free compartments in the sleeping-car?	**Ci sono degli scompartimenti liberi nel vagone letto?**	chee soanoa dailyee skoampahrteemayntee leebayree nail vahgoanay lehttoa
Where's the sleeping-car?	**Dov'è il vagone letto**	doavai eel vahgoanay lehttoa
Where's my berth?	**Dov'è la mia cuccetta?**	doavai lah meeah kootchehttah
I'd like a lower berth.	**Vorrei la cuccetta inferiore.**	vorraiee lah kootchehttah eenfayreeoaray

Would you make up our berths?	**Può preparare le nostre cuccette?**	pwo praypah**raa**ray lay **no**stray koot**cheht**tay
Would you call me at 7 o'clock?	**Può svegliarmi alle 7?**	pwo svay**lyahr**mee **ahl**lay 7
Would you bring me some coffee in the morning?	**Può portarmi un caffè domani mattina?**	pwo por**tahr**mee oon kahf**fai** doa**maa**nee maht**tee**nah

Eating *Nella carrozza ristorante*

You can get snacks and drinks in the buffet-car and in the dining-car when it isn't being used for main meals. On some trains an attendant comes around with snacks, tea, coffee and soft drinks.

Where's the dining-car?	**Dov'è la carrozza ristorante?**	doa**vai** lah kahr**rott**sah reesto**rahn**tay

Baggage and porters *Bagagli e facchini*

Porter!	**Facchino!**	fahk**kee**noa
Can you help me with my luggage?	**Può prendere il mio bagaglio?**	pwo **prehn**dayray eel **mee**oa bah**gaa**lyoa
Where are the luggage trolleys (carts)?	**Dove sono i carrelli portabagagli?**	**doa**vay **soa**noa ee kahr**rehl**lee portahbah**gaa**lyee
Where are the luggage lockers?	**Dove sono le custodie automatiche dei bagagli?**	**doa**vay **soa**noa lay koo**staw**deeay owtoa**maa**teekay **dai**ee bah**gaa**lyee
Where's the left-luggage office (baggage check)?	**Dov'è il deposito bagagli?**	doa**vai** eel day**paw**zeetoa bah**gaa**lyee
I'd like to leave my luggage, please.	**Vorrei depositare i miei bagagli, per favore.**	vor**rai**ee daypozee**taa**ray ee mee**ai**ee bah**gaa**lyee pair fah**voa**ray
I'd like to register (check) my luggage.	**Vorrei far registrare i miei bagagli.**	vor**rai**ee fahr rayjee**straa**ray ee mee**ai**ee bah**gaa**lyee

REGISTRAZIONE BAGAGLI
REGISTERING (CHECKING) BAGGAGE

PORTERS, see also page 18

Coach (long-distance bus) *Pullman/Corriera*

You'll find information on destinations and timetables at the coach terminals, usually situated near railway stations. Many travel agencies offer coach tours.

When's the next coach to ...?	**A che ora parte il prossimo pullman per ...?**	ah kay **oa**rah **pahr**tay eel **pros**seemoa **pool**mahn pair
Does this coach stop at ...?	**Questa corriera si ferma a ...?**	koo**ay**stah korree**ay**rah see **fayr**mah ah
How long does the journey (trip) take?	**Quanto tempo dura il percorso?**	**kwahn**toa **tehm**poa **doo**rah eel payr**koar**soa

Note: Most of the phrases on the previous pages can be used or adapted for travelling on local transport.

Bus–Tram (streetcar) *Autobus–Tram*

Many cities have introduced an automatic system of fare-paying: either you insert the exact change into a ticket dispenser at the bus or tram stop or you punch your ticket in the machine.

If you're planning to get around a lot in one city by bus, tram, or *metropolitana* (see next page), enquire about a booklet of tickets or special runabout tickets, such as *biglietto giornaliero* (one-day ticket).

I'd like a booklet of tickets.	**Vorrei un blocchetto di biglietti.**	vor**rai**ee oon blok**keht**toa dee bee**lyayt**tee
Where can I get a bus to the Vatican?	**Dove posso prendere l'autobus per il Vaticano?**	**doa**vay **pos**soa **prehn**dayray **low**toabooss pair eel vahtee**kaa**noa
What bus do I take for the Colosseum?	**Quale autobus devo prendere per andare al Colosseo?**	**kwaa**lay **ow**toabooss **day**voa **prehn**dayray pair ahn**daa**ray ahl koaloas**sai**oa
Where's the bus stop?	**Dove si trova la fermata dell'autobus?**	**doa**vay see **traw**vah lah fehr**maa**tah day**llow**toabooss

When is the ... bus to the Lido?	**A che ora parte ... autobus per il Lido?**	ah kay **oa**rah **pahr**tay ... **ow**toabooss pair eel **lee**doa
first/last	**il primo/l'ultimo**	eel **pree**moa/**lool**teemoa
next	**il prossimo**	eel **pros**seemoa
How much is the fare to ...?	**Quanto costa il biglietto per ...?**	**kwahn**toa **kos**tah eel bee**lyayt**toa pair
Do I have to change buses?	**Devo cambiare autobus?**	**day**voa kahmbee**aa**ray **ow**toabooss
How many bus stops are there to ...?	**Quante fermate ci sono fino a ...?**	**kwahn**tay fayr**maa**tay chee **soa**noa **fee**noa ah
Will you tell me when to get off?	**Può dirmi quando devo scendere?**	pwo **deer**mee **kwahn**doa **day**voa **shayn**dayray
I want to get off at Piazza di Spagna.	**Voglio scendere a Piazza di Spagna.**	**vo**lyoa **shayn**dayray ah pee**ah**tsah dee **spah**ñah

FERMATA D'AUTOBUS	REGULAR BUS STOP
FERMATA A RICHIESTA	STOPS ON REQUEST

Underground (subway) *Metropolitana*

The *metropolitana* in Rome and Milan corresponds to the London underground or the New York subway. In both cities, the fare is always the same, irrespective of the distance you travel. Big maps in every *Metro* station make the system easy to use.

Where's the nearest underground station?	**Dove si trova la più vicina stazione della metropolitana?**	**doa**vay see **traw**vah lah pee**oo** vee**chee**nah stahtsee**oa**nay **dayl**lah maytroapoalee**taa**nah
Does this train go to ...?	**Questo treno va a ...?**	koo**ay**stoa **tray**noa vah ah
Where do I change for ...?	**Dove cambio per andare a ...?**	**doa**vay **kahm**beeoa pair ahn**daa**ray ah
Is the next station ...?	**La prossima stazione è ...?**	lah **pros**seemah stahtsee**oa**nay ai
Which line should I take for ...?	**Che linea devo prendere per ...?**	kay **lee**nayah **day**voa **prehn**dayray pair

Boat service *Battello*

When does the next boat for ... leave?	**A che ora parte il prossimo battello per ...?**	ah kay **oa**rah **pahr**tay eel **pros**seemoa baht**tehl**loa pair
Where's the embarkation point?	**Dove ci si imbarca?**	**doa**vay chee see eem**bahr**kah
How long does the crossing take?	**Quanto tempo dura la traversata?**	**kwahn**toa **tehm**poa **doo**rah lah trahvayr**saa**tah
At which ports do we stop?	**A che porti si ferma?**	ah kay **por**tee see **fayr**mah
I'd like to take a cruise.	**Vorrei fare una crociera.**	vor**rai**ee **faa**ray **oo**nah kroa**chay**rah
boat	**il battello/la nave**	eel baht**tehl**loa/lah **naa**vay
cabin	**la cabina**	lah kah**bee**nah
single/double	**a un letto/a due letti**	ah oon **leht**toa/ah **doo**ay **leht**tee
deck	**il ponte**	eel **poan**tay
ferry	**il traghetto**	eel trah**geht**toa
hydrofoil	**l'aliscafo**	lahlee**skaa**foa
life belt/boat	**la cintura/il canotto di salvataggio**	lah cheen**too**rah/eel kah**not**toa dee sahlvah**tahd**joa
ship	**la nave**	lah **naa**vay

Bicycle hire *Noleggio biciclette*

In many cities of Italy there is the possibility to hire a bicycle. Ask any tourist office for the address of a rental firm.

I'd like to hire a bicycle.	**Vorrei noleggiare una bicicletta.**	vor**rai**ee noalay**djaa**ray **oo**nah beechee**kleht**tah

Other means of transport *Altri mezzi di trasporto*

cable car	**la funivia**	lah fooneeveeah
helicopter	**l'elicottero**	laylee**kot**tayroa
moped	**il motorino**	eel moatoa**ree**noa
motorbike/scooter	**la moto/la motoretta**	lah **mo**toa/lah motoa**reht**tah

Or perhaps you prefer:

to hitchhike	**fare l'autostop**	**faa**ray lowtoa**stop**
to walk	**camminare**	kahmmee**naa**ray

Car *Macchina*

In general roads are good in Italy and Switzerland. Motorways (expressways) are subject to tolls *(il pedaggio)* in Italy. If you use the motorways in Switzerland you must purchase a sticker (valid for one year) to be displayed on the windscreen.

A red reflector warning triangle must be carried for use in case of a breakdown, and seat-belts *(le cinture di sicurezza)* are obligatory in Switzerland.

Where's the nearest filling station?	**Dov'è la stazione di rifornimento più vicina?**	doa**vai** lah stahtsee**oa**nay dee reeforneе**mayn**toa pee**oo** vee**chee**nah
Full tank, please.	**Il pieno, per favore.**	eel pee**ai**noa pair fah**voa**ray
Give me ... litres of petrol (gasoline).	**Mi dia ... litri di benzina.**	mee **dee**ah ... **lee**tree dee bayn**dzee**nah
super (premium)/ regular/unleaded/ diesel	**super/normale/ senza piombo/ gasolio**	**soo**payr/noar**maa**lay/ **sayn**tsah pee**oam**boa/ gah**zo**lyoa
Please check the ...	**Per favore, controlli ...**	pair fah**voa**ray koan**troa**llee
battery	**la batteria**	lah bahttay**ree**ah
brake fluid	**l'olio dei freni**	**lo**lyoa **da**iee **fray**nee
oil/water	**l'olio/l'acqua**	**lo**lyoa/**lahk**kwah
Would you check the tyre pressure?	**Può controllare la pressione delle gomme?**	pwo koantroa**llaa**ray lah praysssee**oa**nay **dayl**lay **goam**may
1.6 front, 1.8 rear.	**1,6 davanti, 1,8 dietro.**	**oo**noa ay **se**hee dah**vahn**tee **oo**noa ay **o**ttoa dee**eh**troa
Please check the spare tyre, too.	**Per favore, controlli anche la ruota di scorta.**	pair fah**voa**ray koan**troa**llee **ahng**kay lah **rwaw**tah dee **skor**tah
Can you mend this puncture (fix this flat)?	**Può riparare questa foratura?**	pwo reepah**raa**ray koo**ay**stah forah**too**rah
Would you please change the ...?	**Potrebbe cambiare ...**	poa**trehb**bay kahmbee**aa**ray
bulb	**la lampadina**	lah lahmpah**dee**nah
fan belt	**la cinghia del ventilatore**	lah **cheeng**geeah dayl vaynteelah**toa**ray

CAR HIRE, see page 20

spark(ing) plugs	**le candele**	lay kahn**day**lay
tyre	**la gomma**	lah **goam**mah
wipers	**i tergicristalli**	ee tayrjeekree**stahl**lee
Would you clean the windscreen (windshield)?	**Mi pulisca il parabrezza, per favore.**	mee poo**lees**kah eel pahrah**braydz**ah pair fah**voa**ray

Asking the way *Per chiedere la strada*

Can you tell me the way to ...?	**Può dirmi qual è la strada per ...?**	pwo **deer**mee kwahl ai lah **straa**dah pair
How do I get to ...?	**Come si va a ...?**	**koa**may see vah ah
Are we on the right road for ...?	**Siamo sulla strada giusta per ...?**	see**aa**moa **sool**lah **straa**dah **joo**stah pair
How far is the next village?	**Quanto dista il prossimo villaggio?**	**kwahn**toa **dee**stah eel **pros**seemoa veel**lahd**joa
How far is it to ... from here?	**Quanto dista ... da qui?**	**kwahn**toa **dee**stah ... dah koo**ee**
Is there a motorway (expressway)?	**C'è un'autostrada?**	chai oonowtoa**straa**dah
Is there a road with little traffic?	**C'è una strada con poco traffico?**	chai **oo**nah **straa**dah kon **po**koa **trahf**feekoa
How long does it take by car/on foot?	**Quanto tempo ci vuole in macchina/ a piedi?**	**kwahn**toa **tehm**poa chee **vwo**lay een **mahk**keenah/ ah pee**ay**dee
Can I drive to the centre of town?	**Si può andare in macchina nel centro città?**	see pwo ahn**daa**ray een **mahk**keenah nayl **chayn**troa cheet**tah**
Can you tell me, where ... is?	**Può dirmi dove si trova ...?**	pwo **deer**mee **doa**vay see **traw**vah
How can I find this place?	**Come posso trovare questo posto?**	**koa**may **pos**soa tro**vaa**ray koo**ay**stoa **poa**stoa
Where can I find this address?	**Dove posso trovare questo indirizzo?**	**doa**vay **pos**soa tro**vaa**ray koo**ay**stoa eendee**reet**tsoa
Where's this?	**Dov'è questo?**	doa**vai** koo**ay**stoa
Can you show me on the map where I am?	**Può indicarmi sulla carta dove mi trovo?**	pwo eendee**kaar**mee **sool**lah **kahr**tah **doa**vay mee **traw**voa

☞	☜
Lei è sulla strada sbagliata.	You're on the wrong road.
Vada diritto.	Go straight ahead.
È laggiù a ...	It's down there on the ...
sinistra/destra **di fronte/dietro ...** **accanto a/dopo ...**	left/right opposite/behind ... next to/after ...
nord/sud **est/ovest**	north/south east/west
Vada fino al primo/ secondo incrocio.	Go to the first/second crossroad (intersection).
Al semaforo, giri a sinistra.	Turn left at the traffic lights.
Giri a destra al prossimo angolo.	Turn right at the next corner.
Prenda la strada per ...	Take the road for ...
Segua la direzione per Stresa.	Follow the sign for "Stresa".
Deve tornare indietro ...	You have to go back to ...

Parking *Parcheggio*

In town centres, most street parking is limited. The blue zones require the *disco di sosta* or parking disc (obtainable from petrol stations), which you set to show when you arrived and when you must leave.

Where can I park?	**Dove posso parcheggiare?**	doavay possoa pahrkaydjaaray
Is there a car park nearby?	**C'è un parcheggio qui vicino?**	chai oon pahr**kaydj**oa kooee veecheenoa
May I park here?	**Posso parcheggiare qui?**	possoa pahrkaydjaaray kooee
How long can I park here?	**Quanto tempo posso restare qui?**	kwahntoa tehmpoa possoa raystaaray kooee
What's the charge per hour?	**Quanto si paga all'ora?**	kwahntoa see paagah ahlloarah
Do you have some change for the parking meter?	**Ha della moneta per il parchimetro?**	ah **dayl**lah moa**nay**tah pair eel pahr**kee**maytroa

Breakdown—Road assistance *Guasti—Assistenza stradale*

Where's the nearest garage?	**Dov'è il garage più vicino?**	doa**vai** eel gah**raazh** pee**oo** vee**chee**noa
Excuse me. My car has broken down.	**Mi scusi. Ho un guasto all'automobile.**	mee **skoo**zee. oa oon **gwaa**stoa ahllowtoa**maw**beelay
May I use your phone?	**Posso usare il suo telefono?**	**pos**soa oo**zaa**ray eel **soo**a tay**lay**foanoa
I've had a breakdown at ...	**Ho avuto un guasto a ...**	oa ah**voo**toa oon **gwaa**stoa ah
Can you send a mechanic?	**Può mandare un meccanico?**	pwo mahn**daa**ray oon mayk**kaa**neekoa
My car won't start.	**La mia macchina non parte.**	lah **mee**ah **mahk**keenah noan **pahr**tay
The battery is dead.	**La batteria è scarica.**	lah bahttay**ree**ah ai **skaa**reekah
I've run out of petrol (gasoline).	**Sono rimasto(a) senza benzina.**	**soa**noa ree**mah**stoa(ah) **sayn**tsah bayn**dzee**nah
I have a flat tyre.	**Ho una gomma sgonfia.**	oa **oo**nah **goam**mah **sgoan**feeah
The engine is overheating.	**Il motore è surriscaldato.**	eel moa**toa**ray ai soorreeskahl**daa**toa
There is something wrong with ...	**Qualcosa non va con ...**	kwahl**kaw**sah noan vah kon
brakes	**i freni**	ee **fray**nee
carburettor	**il carburatore**	eel kahrboorah**toa**ray
exhaust pipe	**il tubo di scappamento**	eel **too**boa dee skahppah**mayn**toa
radiator	**il radiatore**	eel rahdeeah**toa**ray
wheel	**la ruota**	lah **rwaw**tah
Can you send a breakdown van (tow truck)?	**Può mandare un carro attrezzi?**	pwo mahn**daa**ray oon **kahr**roa at**treht**tsee
How long will you be?	**Quanto tempo impiegherete?**	**kwahn**toa **tehm**poa eempeeaygay**ray**tay

Accident—Police *Incidenti—Polizia*

Please call the police.	**Per favore, chiami la polizia.**	pair fah**voa**ray kee**aa**mee lah poalee**tsee**ah

There's been an accident.	**C'è stato un incidente.**	chai **staa**toa oon eenchee**dayn**tay
Where's the nearest telephone?	**Dov'è il telefono più vicino?**	doa**vai** eel tay**lay**foanoa pee**oo** vee**chee**noa
Call a doctor/an ambulance quickly.	**Chiami un medico/ un'ambulanza, presto.**	kee**aa**mee oon **mai**deekoa/ oonahmboo**lahn**tsah **preh**stoa
There are people injured.	**Ci sono dei feriti.**	chee **soa**noa **dai**ee fay**ree**tee
What's your name and address?	**Qual è il suo nome e indirizzo?**	kwahl ai eel **soo**oa **noa**may ay eendee**reet**soa
What's your insurance company?	**Qual è la sua assicurazione?**	kwahl ai lah **soo**ah ahsseekoorahtsee**oa**nay

Road signs *Segnali stradali*

ACCENDERE I FARI IN GALLERIA	Switch on headlights before entering tunnel
ACCOSTARE A DESTRA (SINISTRA)	Keep right (left)
ALT	Stop
AREA DI SERVIZIO	Service area
CADUTA MASSI	Falling rocks
CARABINIERI	Police
CIRCONVALLAZIONE	Ring road (belt highway)
CORSIA D'EMERGENZA	Emergency parking zone
CURVE PER 5 KM.	Bends (curves) for 5 km.
DEVIAZIONE	Diversion/detour
DIVIETO DI SOSTA	No parking
DIVIETO DI SORPASSO	No overtaking (passing)
LAVORI IN CORSO	Road works ahead (men working)
PASSAGGIO A LIVELLO	Level (railroad) crossing
PERICOLO	Danger
POLIZIA STRADALE	Highway police
RALLENTARE	Reduce speed
SENSO UNICO	One way
SOCCORSO A.C.I.	A.C.I. emergency road service
STRADA DISSESTATA	Poor road surface
TRANSITO CON CATENE	Chains required
VICOLO CIECO	Dead end
VIETATO L'ACCESSO	No entry
VIGILI URBANI	City police
ZONA PEDONALE	Pedestrian zone

Sightseeing

Where's the tourist office?	**Dov'è l'ufficio turistico?**	doavai looffeechoa tooreesteekoa
What are the main points of interest?	**Quali sono i principali punti di interesse?**	kwaalee soanoa ee preencheepaalee poontee dee eentayrayssay
We're here for ...	**Siamo qui per ...**	seeaamoa kooee pair
only a few hours	**alcune ore soltanto**	ahlkoonay oaray soltahntoa
a day	**un giorno**	oon joarnoa
a week	**una settimana**	oonah saytteemaanah
Can you recommend a sightseeing tour/an excursion?	**Può consigliare un giro turistico/una gita?**	pwo konseelyaaray oon jeeroa tooreesteekoa/ oonah jeetah
What's the point of departure?	**Da dove si parte?**	dah doavay see pahrtay
Will the bus pick us up at the hotel?	**Il pullman passerà a prenderci all'hotel?**	eel poolmahn pahssayrah ah prehndehrchee ahllotehl
How much does the tour cost?	**Quanto costa il giro?**	kwahntoa koastah eel jeeroa
What time does the tour start?	**A che ora inizia il giro?**	ah kay oarah eeneetseeah eel jeeroa
Is lunch included?	**Il pranzo è compreso?**	eel prahndzoa ai koampraysoa
What time do we get back?	**A che ora si ritorna?**	ah kay oarah see reetoarnah
Do we have free time in ...?	**Avremo del tempo libero a ...?**	ahvraymoa dayl tehmpoa leebayroa ah
Is there an English-speaking guide?	**C'è una guida che parla inglese?**	chai oonah gooeedah kay pahrlah eengglaysay
I'd like to hire a private guide for ...	**Vorrei avere una guida privata per ...**	vorraiee ahvayray oonah gooeedah preevaatah pair
half a day	**mezza giornata**	mehddzah joarnaatah
a full day	**una giornata intera**	oonah joarnaatah eentayrah

Where is/Where are the ...?	**Dove si trova/Dove si trovano ...?**	**doa**vay see **traw**vah/ **doa**vay see **traw**vahnoa
abbey	**l'abbazia**	lahbbaht**see**ah
art gallery	**la galleria d'arte**	lah gahllay**ree**ah **dahr**tay
artists' quarter	**il quartiere degli artisti**	eel kwahrtee**ay**ray **day**lyee ahr**tee**stee
botanical gardens	**i giardini botanici**	ee jahr**dee**nee botaa-neechee
building	**l'edificio**	laydee**fee**choa
business district	**il quartiere degli affari**	eel kwahrtee**ay**ray **day**lyee ahf**faa**ree
castle	**il castello**	eel kah**stehl**loa
catacombs	**le catacombe**	lay kahtah**kom**bay
cathedral	**la cattedrale**	lah kahttay**draa**lay
cave	**la grotta**	lah **grot**tah
cemetery	**il cimitero**	eel cheemee**tai**roa
city centre	**il centro città**	eel **chayn**troa chee**ttah**
chapel	**la cappella**	lah kahp**pehl**lah
church	**la chiesa**	lah kee**ay**zah
concert hall	**la sala dei concerti**	lah **saa**lah **dai**ee kon-**chehr**tee
convent	**il convento**	eel kon**vayn**toa
court house	**il palazzo di giustizia**	eel pah**laht**tsoa dee joo**stee**tseeah
downtown area	**il centro (città)**	eel **chayn**troa (chee**ttah**)
exhibition	**l'esposizione**	layspozeetsee**oa**nay
factory	**la fabbrica**	lah **fahb**breekah
fair	**la fiera**	lah fee**ay**rah
flea market	**il mercato delle pulci**	eel mehr**kaa**toa **dayl**lay **pool**chee
fortress	**la fortezza**	lah for**teht**tsah
fountain	**la fontana**	lah foan**taa**nah
gardens	**i giardini**	ee jahr**dee**nee
harbour	**il porto**	eel **por**toa
lake	**il lago**	eel **laa**goa
library	**la biblioteca**	lah beebleeo**tai**kah
market	**il mercato**	eel mayr**kaa**toa
memorial	**il memoriale**	eel maymoaree**aa**lay
monastery	**il monastero**	eel moanah**stai**roa
monument	**il monumento**	eel moanoo**mayn**toa
museum	**il museo**	eel moo**zai**oa
old town	**la città vecchia**	lah chee**ttah vehk**keeah
opera house	**il teatro dell'opera**	eel tay**aa**troa dayl**lo**payrah
palace	**il palazzo**	eel pah**laht**tsoa
park	**il parco**	eel **pahr**koa
parliament building	**il Parlamento**	eel pahrlah**mayn**toa

planetarium	**il planetario**	eel plahnay**taa**reeoa
royal palace	**il palazzo reale**	eel pah**laht**tsoa ray**aa**lay
ruins	**le rovine**	lay ro**vee**nay
shopping area	**la zona dei negozi**	lah **dzo**nah **dai**ee nay**go**tsee
square	**la piazza**	lah pee**aht**sah
stadium	**lo stadio**	loa **staa**deeoa
statue	**la statua**	lah **staa**tooah
stock exchange	**la borsa valori**	lah **bor**sah vah**loa**ree
theatre	**il teatro**	eel tay**aa**troa
tomb	**la tomba**	lah **toam**bah
tower	**la torre**	lah **toar**ray
town hall	**il municipio**	eel mooneeche**ee**peeoa
university	**l'università**	looneevayrsee**tah**
zoo	**lo zoo**	loa dzoo

Admission *All'entrata*

Is ... open on Sundays?	**È aperto la domenica il ...?**	ai ah**pehr**toa lah doa**may**neekah eel
When does it open?	**Quando apre?**	**kwahn**doa **aa**pray
When does it close?	**Quando chiude?**	**kwahn**doa kee**oo**day
How much is the entrance fee?	**Quanto costa l'entrata?**	**kwahn**toa **ko**stah layn**traa**tah
Is there any reduction for ...?	**C'è una riduzione per ...?**	chai **oo**nah reedootsee**oa**nay pair
children	**i bambini**	ee bahm**bee**nee
disabled	**gli andicappati**	lyee ahndeekahp**paa**tee
groups	**i gruppi**	ee **groop**pee
pensioners	**i pensionati**	ee paynseeoa**naa**tee
students	**gli studenti**	lyee stoo**dayn**tee
Have you a guidebook (in English)?	**Avete una guida turistica (in inglese)?**	ah**vay**tay **oo**nah goo**ee**dah too**ree**steekah (een eeng**glay**say)
Can I buy a catalogue?	**Posso comprare un catalogo?**	**pos**soa koam**praa**ray oon kah**taa**loagoa
Is it all right to take pictures?	**È permesso fare delle fotografie?**	ai pehr**mays**soa **faa**ray **dayl**lay foatoagrah**fee**ay

ENTRATA LIBERA	ADMISSION FREE
VIETATO FOTOGRAFARE	NO CAMERAS ALLOWED

Who—What—When? *Chi—Cosa—Quando?*

What's that building?	**Che cos'è quest'edificio?**	kay ko**sai** koo**ay**staydee**fee**choa
Who was the ...?	**Chi è stato ...?**	kee ai **staa**toa
architect	**l'architetto**	lahrkee**teht**toa
artist	**l'artista**	lahr**tee**stah
painter	**il pittore**	eel peet**toa**ray
sculptor	**lo scultore**	loa skool**toa**ray
Who built it?	**Chi lo costruì?**	kee loa koastroo**ee**
Who painted that picture?	**Chi dipinse questo quadro?**	kee dee**peen**say koo**ay**stoa **kwaa**droa
When did he live?	**Quando è vissuto?**	**kwahn**doa ai vees**soo**toa
When was it built?	**Quando fu costruito?**	**kwahn**doa foo koastroo**ee**toa
Where's the house where ... lived?	**Dove si trova la casa in cui visse ...?**	**doa**vay see **traw**vah lah **kaa**sah een **koo**ee **vees**say
We're interested in ...	**Ci interessiamo di ...**	chee eentayrays**seeaa**moa dee
antiques	**antichità**	ahnteekee**tah**
archaeology	**archeologia**	ahrkayoaloa**jee**ah
art	**arte**	**ahr**tay
botany	**botanica**	bo**taa**neekah
ceramics	**ceramiche**	chay**raa**meekay
coins	**monete**	mo**nai**tay
fine arts	**belle arti**	**behl**lay **ahr**tee
furniture	**mobilio**	mo**beel**yoa
geology	**geologia**	jayoaloa**jee**ah
handicrafts	**artigianato**	ahrteejah**naa**toa
history	**storia**	**sto**reeah
medicine	**medicina**	maydee**chee**nah
music	**musica**	**moo**zeekah
natural history	**storia naturale**	**sto**reeah nahtoo**raa**lay
ornithology	**ornitologia**	oarneetoaloa**jee**ah
painting	**pittura**	peet**too**rah
pottery	**terrecotte**	tehrray**kot**tay
prehistory	**preistoria**	prayee**sto**reeah
religion	**religione**	raylee**joa**nay
sculpture	**scultura**	skool**too**rah
zoology	**zoologia**	dzoaoaloa**jee**ah
Where's the ... department?	**Dov'è il reparto di/del ...?**	doa**vai** eel ray**pahr**toa dee/dayl

It's ...	**È ...**	ai
amazing	**sorprendente**	soarprayn**dehn**tay
awful	**orribile**	or**ree**beelay
beautiful	**bello**	**behl**loa
excellent	**eccellente**	ehtcheh**llayn**tay
gloomy	**malinconico**	mahleeng**kaw**neekoa
impressive	**impressionante**	eempraysseeoa**nahn**tay
interesting	**interessante**	eentayrays**sahn**tay
magnificent	**magnifico**	mah**ñee**feekoa
nice	**bello**	**behl**loa
overwhelming	**sbalorditivo**	sbahloardee**tee**voa
strange	**strano**	**straa**noa
superb	**superbo**	soo**pehr**boa
terrifying	**terrificante**	tayrreefee**kahn**tay
tremendous	**fantastico**	fahn**tah**steekoa
ugly	**brutto**	**broot**toa

Religious services *Funzioni religiose*

Most churches and cathedrals are open to the public, except, of course, during mass.

If you are interested in taking pictures, you should obtain permission first. Shorts and backless dresses are definitely out when visiting churches.

Is there a/an ... near here?	**C'è una ... qui vicino?**	chai **oo**nah ... koo**ee** vee**chee**noa
Catholic church	**chiesa cattolica**	kee**ay**zah kaht**toa**leekah
Protestant church	**chiesa protestante**	kee**ay**zah proatay**stahn**tay
synagogue	**sinagoga**	seenah**gaw**gah
mosque	**moschea**	moa**skai**ah
At what time is ...?	**A che ora è ...?**	ah kay **oa**rah ai
mass	**la messa**	lah **mays**sah
the service	**la funzione**	lah foontseeoanay
Where can I find a ... who speaks English?	**Dove posso trovare un ... che parla inglese?**	**doa**vay **pos**soa tro**vaa**ray oon ... kay **pahr**lah eeng**glay**say
priest/minister	**prete/pastore**	**prai**tay/pah**stoa**ray
rabbi	**rabbino**	rahb**bee**noa
I'd like to visit the church.	**Vorrei visitare la chiesa.**	vor**rai**ee veezee**taa**ray lah kee**ay**zah

In the countryside *In campagna*

Is there a scenic route to ...?	**C'è una strada panoramica per ...?**	chai **oo**nah **straa**dah pahnoa**raa**meekah pair
How far is it to ...?	**Quanto dista ...?**	**kwahn**toa **dee**stah
Can we walk?	**Possiamo andare a piedi?**	possee**aa**moa ahn**daa**ray ah pee**ay**dee
How high is that mountain?	**Quanto è alta quella montagna?**	**kwahn**toa ai **ahl**tah koo**ayl**lah moan**taa**ñah
What's the name of that ...?	**Come si chiama questo ...?**	**koa**may see kee**aa**mah koo**ay**stoa
animal/bird	**animale/uccello**	ahnee**maa**lay/oot**chehl**loa
flower/tree	**fiore/albero**	fee**oa**ray/**ahl**bayroa

Landmarks *Punti di riferimento*

bridge	**il ponte**	eel **poan**tay
cliff	**la scogliera**	lah skoa**lyay**rah
farm	**la fattoria**	lah fahttoa**ree**ah
field	**il campo**	eel **kahm**poa
footpath	**il sentiero**	eel saynteea**yay**roa
forest	**la foresta**	lah faw**reh**stah
garden	**il giardino**	eel jahr**dee**noa
hamlet	**il gruppo di casolari**	eel **groop**poa dee kahsoa**laa**ree
hill	**la collina**	lah koal**lee**nah
house	**la casa**	lah **kaa**sah
lake	**il lago**	eel **laa**goa
meadow	**il prato**	eel **praa**toa
mountain	**la montagna**	lah moan**taa**ñah
(mountain) pass	**il passo**	eel **pahs**soa
peak	**il picco**	eel **peek**koa
pond	**lo stagno**	loa **staa**ñoa
river	**il fiume**	eel fee**oo**may
road	**la strada**	lah **straa**dah
sea	**il mare**	eel **maa**ray
spring	**la sorgente**	lah soar**jayn**tay
valley	**la valle**	lah **vahl**lay
village	**il villaggio/il paese**	eel veel**lahd**joa/eel pah**ay**zay
vineyard	**la vigna**	lah **vee**ñah
wall	**il muro**	eel **moo**roa
waterfall	**la cascata**	lah kah**skaa**tah
well	**il pozzo**	eel **poat**soa
wood	**il bosco**	eel **boas**koa

ASKING THE WAY, see page 76

Relaxing

Cinema (movies)—Theatre *Cinema—Teatro*

You can find out what's playing from newspapers and billboards. In Rome and in the main towns in Italy look for the weekly entertainment guides available at major newsstands, at the tourist office and the hotel reception.

What's showing at the cinema tonight?	**Cosa danno al cinema questa sera?**	**kaw**sah **dahn**noa ahl **chee**naymah koo**ay**stah **say**rah
What's playing at the ... theatre?	**Che spettacolo c'è al teatro ...?**	kay spayt**taa**koaloa chai ahl tay**aa**troa
What sort of play is it?	**Che genere di commedia è?**	kay **jai**nayray dee koam**mai**deeah ai
Who's it by?	**Di chi è?**	dee kee ai
Can you recommend (a) ...?	**Può consigliarmi ...?**	pwo konsee**lyaar**mee
good film	**un buon film**	oon bwawn "film"
comedy	**una commedia**	**oo**nah koam**mai**deeah
musical	**una commedia musicale**	**oo**nah koam**mai**deeah moozee**kaa**lay
Where's that new film by ... being shown?	**In che cinema danno il nuovo film di ...?**	een kay **chee**naymah **dahn**noa eel **nwo**voa "film" dee
Who's in it?	**Chi sono gli attori?**	kee **soa**noa lyee aht**toa**ree
Who's playing the lead?	**Chi interpreta il ruolo principale?**	kee een**tehr**prehtah eel **rwo**loa preenchee**paa**lay
Who's the director?	**Chi è il regista?**	kee ai eel ray**jee**stah
At what theatre is that new play by ... being performed?	**In quale teatro viene rappresentata la nuova commedia di ...?**	een **kwaa**lay tay**aa**troa vee**ay**nay rahppraysayn**taa**tah lah **nwo**vah koam**mai**deeah dee
Is there a sound-and-light show on somewhere?	**C'è uno spettacolo suoni e luci da qualche parte?**	chai **oo**noa spayt**taa**koaloa **swo**nee ay **loo**chee dah **kwahl**kay **paar**tay

What time does it begin?	**A che ora incomincia?**	ah kay **oa**rah eengkoa**meen**chah
Are there any seats for tonight?	**Ci sono posti per questa sera?**	chee **soa**noa **pos**tee pair kooa**ys**tah **say**rah
How much are the seats?	**Quanto costano i posti?**	**kwahn**toa **ko**stahnoa ee postee
I want to reserve 2 seats for the show on Friday evening.	**Desidero prenotare 2 posti per lo spettacolo di venerdì sera.**	day**zee**dayroa praynoa**taa**ray 2 **pos**tee pair loa spayt**taa**koaloa dee vaynayr**dee say**rah
Can I have a ticket for the matinée on Tuesday?	**Posso avere un biglietto per lo spettacolo del pomeriggio di martedì?**	**pos**soa ah**vay**ray oon bee**lyayt**toa pair loa spayt**taa**koaloa dayl poamay**reed**joa dee mahrtay**dee**
I want a seat in the stalls (orchestra).	**Desidero una poltrona.**	day**zee**dayroa **oo**nah poal**troa**nah
Not too far back.	**Non troppo indietro.**	noan **trop**poa eendee**ay**troa
Somewhere in the middle.	**A metà circa.**	ah may**tah cheer**kah
How much are the seats in the circle (mezzanine)?	**Quanto costano i posti in galleria?**	**kwahn**toa **ko**stahnoa ee **pos**tee een gahllay**ree**ah
May I please have a programme?	**Per favore, posso avere un programma?**	pair fah**voa**ray **pos**soa ah**vay**ray oon pro**grahm**mah
Where's the cloakroom?	**Dov'è il guardaroba?**	doa**vai** eel gwahrdah**ro**bah

Sono spiacente, è tutto esaurito.	I'm sorry, we're sold out.
Vi sono solo alcuni posti in galleria.	There are only a few seats left in the circle (mezzanine).
Posso vedere il suo biglietto?	May I see your ticket?*
Questo è il suo posto.	This is your seat.

* It's customary to tip usherettes *(la maschera)* in most Italian theatres.

DAYS OF THE WEEK, see page 151

Opera—Ballet—Concert *Opera—Balletto-Concerto*

Can you recommend a ...?	**Può consigliarmi ...?**	pwo konsee**lyahr**mee
ballet	**un balletto**	oon bahl**leht**toa
concert	**un concerto**	oon koan**chehr**toa
opera	**un'opera**	oon**o**payrah
operetta	**un'operetta**	oonopay**rayt**tah
Where's the opera house/the concert hall?	**Dov'è il teatro dell'opera/la sala dei concerti?**	doa**vai** eel tay**aa**troa dayl**lo**payrah/lah **saa**lah **dai**ee koan**chehr**tee
What's on at the opera tonight?	**Cosa danno all'Opera questa sera?**	**kaw**sah **dahn**noa ahl**lo**payrah koo**ay**stah **say**rah
Who's singing/dancing?	**Chi canta/balla?**	kee **kahn**tah/**bahl**lah
What orchestra is playing?	**Che orchestra suona?**	kay oar**kay**strah **swo**nah
What are they playing?	**Cosa suonano?**	**kaw**sah **swo**nahnoa
Who's the conductor/soloist?	**Chi è il maestro/il solista?**	kee ai eel mah**eh**stroa/eel so**lee**stah

Nightclub *Night-club*

Can you recommend a good nightclub?	**Può consigliarmi un buon night-club?**	pwo konsee**lyahr**mee oon bwon "night-club"
Is there a floor show?	**C'è il varietà?**	chai eel vahreeay**tah**
What time does the floor show start?	**A che ora inizia il varietà?**	ah kay **oa**rah ee**neet**seeah eel vahreeay**tah**
Is evening dress necessary?	**È necessario l'abito da sera?**	ai naychays**saa**reeoa **laa**beetoa dah **say**rah

Discos *Discoteche*

Where can we go dancing?	**Dove possiamo andare a ballare?**	**doa**vay possee**aa**moa ahn**daa**ray ah bahl**laa**ray
Is there a discotheque in town?	**C'è una discoteca in città?**	chai **oo**nah deeskoa**tay**kah een cheet**tah**
Would you like to dance?	**Vuole ballare?**	**vwo**lay bahl**laa**ray

Sports *Sport*

Football (soccer), tennis, boxing, wrestling and bicycle, car and horse racing are among popular spectator sports. If you like sailing, fishing, horseback riding, golf, tennis, hiking, cycling, swimming, golf or trap shooting, you'll find plenty of opportunity to satisfy your recreational bent.

Is there a football (soccer) match anywhere this Saturday?	**C'è una partita di calcio da qualche parte, sabato?**	chai **oo**nah pahr**tee**tah dee **kahl**choa dah **kwahl**kay **pahr**tay **saa**bahtoa
Which teams are playing?	**Che squadre giocano?**	kay **skwaa**dray **joa**kahnoa
Can you get me a ticket?	**Mi può procurare un biglietto?**	mee pwo proakoo**raa**ray oon bee**lyayt**toa

basketball	**la pallacanestro**	lah pahllahkah**neh**stroa
boxing	**il pugilato**	eel poojee**laa**toa
car racing	**la corsa automobilistica**	lah **koar**sah owtoamoabee**lee**steeka
cycling	**il ciclismo**	eel chee**klee**zmoa
football (soccer)	**il calcio**	eel **kahl**choa
horse racing	**la corsa di cavalli**	lah **koar**sah dee kah**vahl**lee
skiing	**lo sci**	loa shee
swimming	**il nuoto**	eel **nwo**toa
tennis	**il tennis**	eel "tennis"
volleyball	**la pallavolo**	lah pahllah**voa**loa

I'd like to see a boxing match.	**Vorrei vedere un incontro di pugilato.**	vor**rai**ee vay**day**ray oon eeng**koan**troa dee poojee**laa**toa
What's the admission charge?	**Quanto costa l'entrata?**	**kwahn**toa **ko**stah layn**traa**tah
Where's the nearest golf course?	**Dove si trova il campo da golf più vicino?**	**doa**vay see **traw**vah eel **kahm**poa dah golf pee**oo** vee**chee**noa
Where are the tennis courts?	**Dove sono i campi da tennis?**	**doa**vay **soa**noa ee **kahm**pee dah "tennis"
What's the charge per ...?	**Qual è il prezzo per ...?**	kwahl ai eel **preht**tsoa pair
day/round/hour	**un giorno/una partita/un'ora**	oon **joar**noa/**oo**nah pahr**tee**tah/oo**noa**rah

Can I hire (rent) rackets?	**Posso noleggiare le racchette?**	possoa noalay**djaa**ray lay rahk**keht**tay
Where is the race course (track)?	**Dov'è l'ippodromo?**	doa**vai** leeppoa**draw**moa
Is there any good fishing around here?	**Ci sono buone possibilità di pesca in questa zona?**	chee **soa**noa **bwaw**nay posseebeelee**tah** dee **pay**skah een koo**ay**stah **dzoa**nah
Do I need a permit?	**È necessario il permesso?**	ai naychays**saa**reeoa eel payr**mays**soa
Where can I get one?	**Dove posso procurarmene uno?**	**doa**vay **pos**soa proakoo**rahr**maynay **oo**noa
Can one swim in the lake/river?	**Si può nuotare nel lago/fiume?**	see pwo nwaw**taa**ray nayl **laa**goa/fee**oo**may
Is there a swimming pool here?	**C'è una piscina qui?**	chai **oo**nah pee**shee**nah koo**ee**
Is it open-air or indoor?	**È una piscina all'aperto o coperta?**	ai **oo**nah pee**shee**nah ahllah**pehr**toa oa koa**pehr**tah
Is it heated?	**È riscaldata?**	ai reeskahl**daa**tah
What's the temperature of the water?	**Qual è la temperatura dell'acqua?**	kwahl ai lah taympayrah**too**rah day**llahk**kwah
Is there a sandy beach?	**C'è una spiaggia di sabbia?**	chai **oo**nah spee**ahd**jah dee **sahb**beeah

On the beach *In spiaggia*

Is it safe for swimming?	**Si può nuotare senza pericolo?**	see pwo nwaw**taa**ray **sayn**tsah pay**ree**koaloa
Is there a lifeguard?	**C'è un bagnino?**	chai oon bah**ñee**noa
There are some big waves.	**Ci sono cavalloni.**	chee **soa**noa kahvahl**loa**nee
Is it safe for children?	**È sicuro per i bambini?**	ai see**koo**roa pair ee bahm**bee**nee
Are there any dangerous currents?	**Vi sono correnti pericolose?**	vee **soa**noa koar**rayn**tee payreekoa**loa**say
What time is high tide/low tide?	**A che ora è l'alta marea/la bassa marea?**	ah kay **oa**rah ai **lahl**tah mah**ray**ah/lah **bahs**sah mah**ray**ah

I want to hire a/an/ some ...	**Vorrei noleggiare ...**	vorraiee noalaydjaaray
bathing hut (cabana)	**una cabina**	oonah kahbeenah
deck-chair	**una sedia a sdraio**	oonah saydeeah ah sdraaeeoa
motorboat	**una barca a motore**	oonah bahrkah ah motoaray
rowing-boat	**una barca a remi**	oonah bahrkah ah raymee
sailboard	**una tavola a vela**	oonah taavolah ah vailah
sailing-boat	**una barca a vela**	oonah bahrkah ah vailah
sunshade (umbrella)	**un ombrellone**	oon oambraylloanay
surfboard	**un sandolino**	oon sahndoaleenoa
water-skis	**degli sci nautici**	daylyee shee nowteechee

SPIAGGIA PRIVATA	PRIVATE BEACH
DIVIETO DI BALNEAZIONE	NO SWIMMING

Winter sports *Sport invernali*

Is there a skating rink near here?	**C'è una pista di pattinaggio qui vicino?**	chai oonah peestah dee pahtteenadjoa kooee veecheenoa
I'd like to ski.	**Vorrei sciare.**	vorraiee sheeaaray
downhill/cross-country skiing	**sci di pista/sci di fondo**	shee dee peestah/shee dee foandoa
Are there any ski runs for ...?	**Vi sono delle piste per ...?**	vee soanoa dayllay peestay pair
beginners	**principianti**	preencheepeeahntee
average skiers	**sciatori medi**	sheeahtoaree maydee
good skiers	**buoni sciatori**	bwawnee sheeahtoaree
Can I take skiing lesson there?	**Posso prendere delle lezioni di sci?**	possoa prehndayray dayllay laytseeoanee dee shee
Are there ski lifts?	**Ci sono delle sciovie?**	chee soanoa dayllay sheeoveeai
I want to hire a/ some ...	**Vorrei noleggiare ...**	vorraiee noalaydjaaray
poles	**dei bastoni**	daiee bahstoanee
skates	**dei pattini**	daiee pahtteenee
ski boots	**degli scarponi da sci**	daylyee skahrpoanee dah shee
skiing equipment	**una tenuta da sci**	oonah taynootah dah shee
skis	**degli sci**	daylyee shee

Making friends

Introductions *Presentazioni*

May I introduce ...?	**Posso presentarle ...?**	possoa prayzayntaarlay
John, this is ...	**Giovanni, ti presento ...**	jovahnnee tee prayzayntoa
My name is ...	**Mi chiamo ...**	mee keeaamoa
Pleased to meet you.	**Piacere.**	peeahchayray
What's your name?	**Come si chiama?**	koamay see keeaamah
How are you?	**Come sta?**	koamay stah
Fine, thanks. And you?	**Bene, grazie. E lei?**	bainay graatseeay. ay laiee

Follow-up *Per rompere il ghiaccio*

How long have you been here?	**Da quanto tempo è qui?**	dah kwahntoa tehmpoa ai kooee
We've been here a week.	**Siamo qui da una settimana.**	seeaamoa kooee dah oonah saytteemaanah
Is this your first visit?	**È la prima volta che viene?**	ai lah preemah voltah kay veeaynay
No, we came here last year.	**No, siamo già venuti l'anno scorso.**	noa seeaamoa jah vaynootee lahnnoa skoarsoa
Are you enjoying your stay?	**Le piace il suo soggiorno?**	lay peeaachay eel sooo soadjoarnoa
Yes, I like it very much.	**Sì, mi piace molto.**	see mee peeaachay moaltoa
I like the landscape a lot.	**Mi piace molto il paesaggio.**	mee peeaachay moaltoa eel pahayzahdjoa
Do you travel a lot?	**Viaggia molto?**	veeahdjah moaltoa
Where do you come from?	**Da dove viene?**	dah doavay veeaynay
I'm from ...	**Sono di ...**	soanoa dee
What nationality are you?	**Di che nazionalità è?**	dee kai nahtseeoanahleetah ai

COUNTRIES, see page 146

I'm ...	**Sono ...**	**soa**noa
American	**americano(a)**	ahmayree**kaa**noa(ah)
British	**britannico(a)**	bree**tahn**neekoa(ah)
Canadian	**canadese**	kahnah**day**say
English	**inglese**	eeng**glay**say
Irish	**irlandese**	eerlahn**day**say
Scottish	**scozzese**	skot**say**say
Where are you staying?	**Dove soggiorna?**	**doa**vay soad**joar**nah
Are you on your own?	**È solo(a)?**	ai **soa**loa(ah)
I'm with my ...	**Sono con ...**	**soa**noa kon
wife	**mia moglie**	**mee**ah **moa**lyay
husband	**mio marito**	**mee**oa mah**ree**toa
family	**la mia famiglia**	lah **mee**ah fah**mee**lyah
parents	**i miei genitori**	ee mee**aiee** jaynee**toa**ree
boyfriend	**il mio ragazzo**	eel **mee**oa rah**gaht**tsoa
girlfriend	**la mia ragazza**	lah **mee**ah rah**gaht**tsah

grandfather/ grandmother	**il nonno/la nonna**	eel **non**noa/la **non**nah
father/mother	**il padre/la madre**	eel **paa**dray/lah **maa**dray
son/daughter	**il figlio/la figlia**	eel **fee**lyoa/lah **fee**lyah
brother/sister	**il fratello/la sorella**	eel frah**tehl**loa/lah so**rehl**lah
uncle/aunt	**lo zio/la zia**	loa **dzee**oa/lah **dzee**ah
nephew/niece	**il nipote/la nipote**	eel nee**poa**tay/lah nee**poa**tay
cousin	**il cugino/la cugina**	eel koo**jee**noa/lah koo**jee**nah

Are you married/ single?	**È sposato(a)/scapolo (nubile)?**	ai spo**zaa**toa(ah)/**skaa**poa-loa (**noo**beelay)
Do you have children?	**Ha dei bambini?**	ah **dai**ee bahm**bee**nee
What do you think of the country/people?	**Cosa pensa del paese/della gente?**	**kaw**sah **payn**sah dayl pah**ay**say/**dayl**lah **jayn**tay
What do you do?	**Che lavoro fa?**	kay lah**voa**roa fah
I'm a student.	**Sono studente.**	**soa**noa stoo**dehn**tay
I'm here on a business trip.	**Sono qui in viaggio d'affari.**	**soa**noa koo**ee** een vee**ahd**-joa dah**ffaa**ree
Do you play cards/ chess?	**Gioca a carte/a scacchi?**	**joa**kah ah **kahr**tay/ah **skahk**kee

The weather *Il tempo*

What a lovely day!	**Che bella giornata!**	kay behllah joarnaatah
What awful weather!	**Che tempo orribile!**	kay tehmpoa orreebeelay
Isn't it cold/hot today?	**Che freddo/caldo fa oggi!**	kay frehddoa/kahldoa fah odjee
Is it usually as warm as this?	**Fa sempre caldo così?**	fah sehmpray kahldoa kawsee
Do you think it's going to ... tomorrow?	**Pensa che domani ...?**	paynsah kay domaanee
be a nice day	**sarà una bella giornata**	sahrah oonah behllah joarnaatah
rain	**pioverà**	peeovayrah
snow	**nevicherà**	nayveekayrah
What is the weather forecast?	**Come sono le previsioni del tempo?**	koamay soanoa lay prehveezeeoanee dayl tehmpoa

cloud	**la nuvola**	lah noovolah
fog	**la nebbia**	lah nehbbeeah
frost	**il gelo**	eel jayloa
ice	**il ghiaccio**	eel geeahtchoa
lightning	**il lampo**	eel lahmpoa
moon	**la luna**	lah loonah
rain	**la pioggia**	lah peeodjah
sky	**il cielo**	eel chayloa
snow	**la neve**	lah nayvay
star	**la stella**	lah stayllah
sun	**il sole**	eel soalay
thunder	**il tuono**	eel twonoa
thunderstorm	**il temporale**	eel tehmpoaraalay
wind	**il vento**	eel vayntoa

Invitations *Inviti*

Would you like to have dinner with us on ...?	**Vorrebbe cenare con noi ...?**	vorrehbbay chaynaaray kon noaee
May I invite you for lunch?	**Posso invitarla a pranzo?**	possoa-eenveetaarlah ah prahndzoa

DAYS OF THE WEEK, see page 151

Can you come over for a drink this evening?	**Può venire a bere un bicchiere da me questa sera?**	pwo vay**nee**ray ah **bay**ray oon beekkee**ay**ray dah mai koo**ay**stah **say**rah
There's a party. Are you coming?	**C'è un ricevimento. Viene?**	chai oon reechayvee**mayn**toa. vee**ay**nay
That's very kind of you.	**È molto gentile da parte sua.**	ai **moal**toa jayn**tee**lay dah **pahr**tay **soo**ah
I'd love to come.	**Verrò con piacere.**	vayr**ro** kon peeah**chay**ray
What time shall we come?	**A che ora dobbiamo venire?**	ah kay **oa**rah doab**bee**aamoa vay**nee**ray
May I bring a friend?	**Posso portare un amico (un'amica)?**	**pos**soa por**taa**ray oon ah**mee**koa (oonah**mee**kah)
I'm afraid we've got to go now.	**Mi dispiace, ma adesso dobbiamo andare.**	mee deespee**aa**chay mah ah**dehs**soa doabbee**aa**moa ahn**daa**ray
Next time you must come to visit us.	**La prossima volta dovete venire da noi.**	lah **pros**seemah **vol**tah doa**vay**tay vay**nee**ray dah **noa**ee
Thanks for the evening. It was great.	**Grazie per la serata. È stata splendida.**	**graa**tseeay pair la say**raa**tah. ai **staa**tah **splehn**deedah

Dating *Appuntamento*

Do you mind if I smoke?	**La disturbo se fumo?**	lah dee**stoor**boa say **foo**moa
Would you like a cigarette?	**Posso offrirle una sigaretta?**	**pos**soa of**free**rlay **oo**nah seegah**rayt**tah
Do you have a light, please?	**Ha un fiammifero, per favore?**	ah oon feeahm**mee**fayroa pair fah**voa**ray
Why are you laughing?	**Perchè ride?**	pay**rkai** **ree**day
Is my Italian that bad?	**È così cattivo il mio italiano?**	ai ko**see** kaht**tee**voa eel **mee**oa eetahlee**aa**noa
Do you mind if I sit down here?	**Permette che mi sieda qui?**	pehr**mayt**tay kay mee see**ay**dah koo**ee**
Can I get you a drink?	**Posso offrirle qualcosa da bere?**	**pos**soa of**free**rlay kwahl**kaw**sah dah **bay**ray
Are you waiting for someone?	**Aspetta qualcuno?**	ah**spayt**tah kwahl**koo**noa

Are you free this evening?	**È libera stasera?**	ai **lee**bayrah stah**say**rah
Would you like to go out with me tonight?	**Uscirebbe con me stasera?**	oosheer**ehb**bay kon mai stah**say**rah
Would you like to go dancing?	**Le piacerebbe andare a ballare?**	lay peeahchay**rehb**bay ahn**daa**ray ah bahl**laa**ray
I know a good discotheque.	**Conosco una buona discoteca.**	koa**noa**skoa **oo**nah **bwaw**nah deeskoa**tay**kah
Shall we go to the cinema (movies)?	**Andiamo al cinema?**	ahndee**aa**moa ahl **chee**naymah
Would you like to go for a drive?	**Andiamo a fare un giro in macchina?**	ahndee**aa**moa ah **faa**ray oon **jee**roa een **mahk**keenah
Where shall we meet?	**Dove possiamo incontrarci?**	**doa**vay possee**aa**moa eengkon**traar**chee
I'll pick you up at your hotel.	**Passerò a prenderla all'albergo.**	pahssay**roa** ah **prayn**dayrlah ahllahl**behr**goa
I'll call for you at 8.	**Passerò da lei alle 8.**	pahssay**roa** dah **laiee** **ahl**lay 8
May I take you home?	**Posso accompagnarla a casa?**	**pos**soa ahkkoampah**ñaar**lah ah **kaa**sah
Can I see you again tomorrow?	**Posso rivederla domani?**	**pos**soa reevay**dayr**lah doa**maa**nee
What's your telephone number?	**Qual è il suo numero di telefono?**	kwahl ai eel **soo**oa **noo**mayroa dee tay**lai**foanoa

... and you might answer:

I'd love to, thank you.	**Con piacere, grazie.**	kon peeah**chay**ray **graa**tseeay
Thank you, but I'm busy.	**Grazie, ma sono impegnato(a).**	**graa**tseeay mah **soa**noa eempạy**ñaa**toa(ah)
No, I'm not interested, thank you.	**No, non mi interessa, grazie.**	no noan mee eentay**rehs**sah **graa**tseeay
Leave me alone!	**Mi lasci in pace!**	mee **lah**shee een **paa**chay
Thank you, it's been a wonderful evening.	**Grazie, è stata una magnifica serata.**	**graa**tseeay ai **staa**tah **oo**nah mah**ñee**feekah sayr**aa**tah
I've enjoyed myself.	**Mi sono divertito(a) molto.**	mee **soa**noa deevayr**tee**toa(ah) **moal**toa

Shopping guide

This shopping guide is designed to help you find what you want with ease, accuracy and speed. It features:

1. A list of all major shops, stores and services (p. 98);
2. Some general expressions required when shopping to allow you to be specific and selective (p. 100);
3. Full details of the shops and services most likely to concern you. Here you'll find advice, alphabetical lists of items and conversion charts listed under the headings below.

LAUNDRY, see page 29/HAIRDRESSER, see page 30

Shops, stores and services *Negozi e servizi*

Shop hours in Italy differ from summer to winter. In winter the shops are generally open from 8 a.m. to 7 p.m. with a lunch break between 1 and 3 p.m. During the tourist season, shops open and close later in the afternoon (4 to 8 p.m.). Some remain open on Sundays but most close a half day during the week—often Monday morning or Thursday afternoon.

Swiss shops are open from 8 a.m. to noon or 12.30 p.m. and from 1.30 to 6.30 or 7 p.m. (Saturdays until 5 p.m.) with half-day closings similar to Italy.

Where's the nearest ...?	**Dove si trova ... più vicino(a)?**	doavay see trawvah ... peeoo veecheenoa(ah)
antique shop	**l'antiquario**	lahnteekwaareeoa
art gallery	**la galleria d'arte**	lah gahllayreeah dahrtay
baker's	**la panetteria**	lah pahnehttayreeah
bank	**la banca**	lah bahngkah
barber's	**il barbiere**	eel bahrbeeayray
beauty salon	**l'istituto di bellezza**	leesteetootoa dee behllehttsah
bookshop	**la libreria**	lah leebrayreeah
butcher's	**la macelleria**	lah mahchayllayreeah
cake shop	**la pasticceria**	lah pahsteetchayreeah
camera shop	**il negozio d'apparecchi fotografici**	eel naygotseeoa dahppahrehkkee foatoagraafeeche
chemist's	**la farmacia**	lah fahrmahcheeah
confectioner's	**la pasticceria**	lah pahsteetchayreeah
dairy	**la latteria**	lah lahttayreeah
delicatessen	**la salumeria**	lah sahloomayreeah
department store	**il grande magazzino**	eel grahnday mahgahdzeenoa
drugstore	**la farmacia**	lah fahrmahcheeah
dry cleaner's	**la lavanderia a secco**	lah lahvahndayreeah ah saykkoa
electrician	**l'elettricista**	laylehttreecheestah
fishmonger's	**la pescheria**	lah payskayreeah
flower shop	**il fiorista**	eel feeoareestah
furrier's	**la pellicceria**	lah paylleetchayreeah
greengrocer's	**il negozio di frutta e verdura**	eel naygotseeoa dee froottah ay vehrdoorah
grocery	**il negozio di alimentari**	eel naygotseeoa dee ahleemayntaaree
hairdresser's	**il parrucchiere**	eel pahrrookkeeayray

hardware store	**il negozio di ferramenta**	eel nay**go**tseeoa dee fehrrah**mayn**tah
health food shop	**il negozio di cibi dietetici**	eel nay**go**tseeoa dee **chee**beeh deeay**tay**teechee
ironmonger's	**il negozio di ferramenta**	eel nay**go**tseeoa dee fehrrah**mayn**tah
jeweller's	**la gioielleria**	lah joeeayllay**ree**ah
launderette	**la lavanderia automatica**	lah lahvahnday**ree**ah owtoa**maa**teekah
laundry	**la lavanderia**	la lahvahnday**ree**ah
library	**la biblioteca**	lah beebleeoa**tay**kah
market	**il mercato**	eel mayr**kaa**toa
newsagent's	**il giornalaio**	eel joarnah**laa**eeoa
newsstand	**l'edicola**	lay**dee**koalah
optician	**l'ottico**	**lot**teekoa
pastry shop	**la pasticceria**	lah pahsteetchay**ree**ah
photographer	**il fotografo**	eel foa**toa**grahfoa
police station	**il posto di polizia**	eel **poa**stoa dee poalee**tsee**ah
post office	**l'ufficio postale**	loof**fee**choa poa**staa**lay
shoemaker's (repairs)	**il calzolaio**	eel kahltsoa**laa**eeoa
shoe shop	**il negozio di scarpe**	eel nay**go**tseeoa dee **skahr**pay
souvenir shop	**il negozio di ricordi**	eel nay**go**tseeoa dee ree**kor**dee
sporting goods shop	**il negozio di articoli sportivi**	eel nay**go**tseeoa dee ahr**tee**koalee spor**tee**vee
stationer's	**la cartoleria**	lah kahrtoalay**ree**ah
supermarket	**il supermercato**	eel soopairmayr**kaa**toa
tailor's	**la sartoria**	lah sahrto**ree**ah
tobacconist's	**la tabaccheria**	lah tahbahkkay**ree**ah
toy shop	**il negozio di giocattoli**	eel nay**go**tseeoa dee joa**kaht**toalee
travel agency	**l'agenzia di viaggi**	lahjayn**tsee**ah dee vee**ah**djee
vegetable store	**il negozio di frutta e verdura**	eel nay**go**tseeoa dee **froot**tah ay vehr**doo**rah
watchmaker's	**l'orologiaio**	loaroaloa**jaa**eeoa
wine merchant	**il vinaio**	eel vee**naa**eeoa

ENTRATA	ENTRANCE
USCITA	EXIT
USCITA DI SICUREZZA	EMERGENCY EXIT

General expressions *Espressioni generali*

Where? *Dove?*

Where's a good ...?	**Dov'è un buon ...?**	doavai oon bwawn
Where can I find ...?	**Dove posso trovare ...?**	doavay possoa trovaaray
Where's the main shopping area?	**Dov'è la zona principale dei negozi?**	doavai lah dzoanah preencheepaalay daiee naygotsee
How far is from here?	**Quanto dista da qui?**	kwahntoa deestah dah kooee
How do I get there?	**Come ci si può arrivare?**	koamay chee see pwo ahrreevaaray

SALDI SALE

Service *Servizio*

Can you help me?	**Può aiutarmi?**	pwo aheeootaarmee
I'm just looking.	**Do soltanto un'occhiata.**	doa soaltahntoa oonokkeeaatah
I want ...	**Desidero ...**	dayzeedayroa
Can you show me some ...?	**Può mostrarmi dei ...?**	pwo moastraarmee daiee
Do you have any ...?	**Ha dei ...?**	ah daiee
Where is the ... department?	**Dove si trova il reparto ...?**	doavay see trawvah eel raypahrtoa
Where is the lift (elevator)/escalator?	**Dov'è l'ascensore/ la scala mobile?**	doavai lahshaynsoaray/ lah skahlah mobeelay
Where do I pay?	**Dov'è la cassa?**	doavai lah kahssah

That one *Quello là*

Can you show me ...?	**Mi può mostrare ...?**	mee pwo moastraaray
this/that	**questo/quello**	kooaystoa/kooaylloa
the one in the window/on the shelf	**quello in vetrina/ sullo scaffale**	kooaylloa een vaytreenah/ soolloa skahffaalay

Defining the article *Descrizione dell'articolo*

I'd like a ... one.	**Ne vorrei un ...**	nay vor**rai**ee oon
big	**grande**	**grahn**day
cheap	**economico**	aykoa**naw**meekoa
dark	**scuro**	**skoo**roa
good	**buono**	**bwaw**noa
heavy	**pesante**	pay**sahn**tay
large	**grande**	**grahn**day
light (weight)	**leggero**	lay**djai**roa
light (colour)	**chiaro**	kee**aa**roa
oval	**ovale**	ov**aa**lay
rectangular	**rettangolare**	rehttahngo**laa**ray
round	**rotondo**	roto**an**doa
small	**piccolo**	**peek**koaloa
square	**quadrato**	kwah**draa**toa
sturdy	**solido**	**soa**leedoa
I don't want anything too expensive.	**Non voglio qualcosa di troppo caro.**	noan **vol**yoa kwahl**kaw**sah dee **trop**poa **kaa**roa

Preference *Preferenze*

Can you show me some more?	**Me ne può mostrare degli altri?**	may nay pwo moa**straa**ray **day**lyee **ahl**tree
Haven't you anything ...?	**Non ha qualcosa ...?**	noan ah kwahl**kaw**sah
better	**migliore**	mee**lyoa**ray
cheaper	**meno caro**	**may**noa **kaa**roa
larger	**più grande**	pee**oo** **grahn**day
smaller	**più piccolo**	pee**oo** **peek**koaloa

How much? *Quanto?*

How much is this?	**Quanto costa questo?**	**kwahn**toa **kos**tah koo**ay**stoa
How much are they?	**Quanto costano?**	**kwahn**toa **kos**tahnoa
I don't understand.	**Non capisco.**	noan kah**pee**skoa
Please write it down.	**Per favore, me lo scriva.**	pair fah**voa**ray may loa **skree**vah
I don't want to spend more than ... lire.	**Non voglio spendere più di ... lire.**	noan **vol**yoa **spehn**dayray pee**oo** dee ... **lee**ray

COLOURS, see page 113

Decision *Decisione*

It's not quite what I want.	**Non è ciò che volevo.**	noan ai choa kay voa**lay**voa
No, I don't like it.	**No, non mi piace.**	noa noan mee pee**aa**chay
I'll take it.	**Lo prendo.**	loa **prayn**doa

Ordering *Ordinazione*

Can you order it for me?	**Può ordinarmelo?**	pwo oardee**naar**mayloa
How long will it take?	**Quanto tempo ci sarà da aspettare?**	**kwahn**toa **tehm**poa chee sah**rah** dah ahspeht**taa**ray

Delivery *Consegna*

I'll take it with me.	**Lo porto via.**	loa **poar**toa **vee**ah
Deliver it to the ... Hotel.	**Lo consegni all'Albergo ...**	loa kon**say**ñee ahllahl**bayr**goa
Please send it to this address.	**Per favore, lo mandi a questo indirizzo.**	pair fah**voa**ray loa **mahn**dee ah koo**ay**stoa eendee**reet**tsoa
Will I have any difficulty with the customs?	**Avrò delle difficoltà alla dogana?**	ah**vroa dayl**lay deeffeekoal**tah ahl**lah doa**gaa**nah

Paying *Pagamento*

How much is it?	**Quant'è?**	kwahn**tai**
Can I pay by traveller's cheque?	**Accettate i traveller's cheque?**	ahtcheht**taa**tay ee "traveller's cheque"
Do you accept dollars/pounds?	**Accettate dei dollari/delle sterline?**	ahtcheht**taa**tay **daiee dol**lahree/**dayl**lay stayr**lee**nay
Do you accept credit cards?	**Accettate carte di credito?**	ahtcheht**taa**tay **kahr**tay dee **kray**deetoa
Do I have to pay the VAT (sales tax)?	**Devo pagare l'I.V.A.?**	**day**voa pah**gaa**ray **lee**vah
Haven't you made a mistake in the bill?	**Non vi siete sbagliati nel fare il conto?**	noan vee see**ay**tay sbah**lyaa**tee nayl **faa**ray eel **koan**toa

Anything else? *Qualcos'altro?*

No, thanks, that's all.	**No, grazie, è tutto.**	no **graa**tseeay ai **too**ttoa
Yes. I want ...	**Sì, desidero ...**	see day**zee**dayroa
Show me ...	**Mi mostri ...**	mee **moa**stree
May I have a bag, please?	**Può darmi un sacchetto, per favore?**	pwo **daar**mee oon sahk**keht**toa pair fah**voa**ray

Dissatisfied *Scontento*

Can you please exchange this?	**Può cambiare questo, per favore?**	pwo kahmbee**aa**ray koo**ay**stoa pair fah**voa**ray
I want to return this.	**Desidero rendere questo.**	day**zee**dayroa **rayn**dayray koo**ay**stoa
I'd like a refund. Here's the receipt.	**Desidero essere rimborsato. Ecco la ricevuta.**	day**zee**dayroa **ehs**sayray reemboar**saa**toa. **ehk**koa lah reechay**voo**tah

Posso aiutarla?	Can I help you?
Cosa desidera?	What would you like?
Che ... desidera?	What ... would you like?
colore/forma qualità/quantità	colour/shape quality/quantity
Mi dispiace, non ne abbiamo.	I'm sorry, we haven't any.
L'abbiamo esaurito.	We're out of stock.
Dobbiamo ordinarglielo?	Shall we order it for you?
Lo porta via o dobbiamo mandarglielo?	Will you take it with you or shall we send it?
Qualcos'altro?	Anything else?
Sono ... lire, per favore.	That's ... lire, please.
La cassa è laggiù.	The cashier's over there.

Bookshop—Stationer's *Libreria—Cartoleria*

In Italy, bookshops and stationer's are usually separate shops, though the latter will often sell paperbacks. Newspapers and magazines are sold at newsstands.

Where's the nearest ...?	**Dov'è ... più vicina?**	doa**vai** ... pe**eoo** vee**chee**nah
bookshop	**la libreria**	lah leebray**ree**ah
stationer's	**la cartoleria**	lah kahrtoalay**ree**ah
newsstand	**l'edicola**	lay**dee**koalah
Where can I buy an English-language newspaper?	**Dove posso comprare un giornale in inglese?**	**doa**vay **pos**soa kom**praa**ray oon joar**naa**lay een eeng**glay**say
Where's the guidebook section?	**Dov'è il reparto delle guide turistiche?**	doa**vai** eel ray**pahr**toa **dayl**lay goo**ee**day too**ree**steekay
Where do you keep the English books?	**Dov'è il reparto dei libri inglesi?**	doa**vai** eel ray**pahr**toa **dai**ee **lee**bree eeng**glay**see
Do you have second-hand books?	**Avete libri d'occasione?**	ah**vay**tay **lee**bree dokkahzee**oa**nay
I'd like a/an/some ...	**Vorrei ...**	vor**rai**ee
address book	**un'agenda per gli indirizzi**	oonah**jayn**dah pair lyee eendee**reet**tsee
ball-point pen	**una biro**	**oo**nah **bee**roa
book	**un libro**	oon **lee**broa
calendar	**un calendario**	oon kahlayn**daa**reeoa
carbon paper	**della carta carbone**	**dayl**lah **kahr**tah kahr**boa**nay
cellophane tape	**del nastro adesivo**	dayl **nah**stroa ahday**zee**voa
crayons	**dei pastelli**	**dai**ee pah**stehl**lee
dictionary Italian-English	**un dizionario italiano-inglese**	oon deetseeoa**naa**reeoa eetahlee**aa**noa/ eeng**glay**say
pocket	**tascabile**	tah**skaa**beelay
drawing paper	**della carta da disegno**	**dayl**lah **kahr**tah dah dee**say**ñoa
drawing pins	**delle puntine**	**dayl**lay poon**tee**nay
envelopes	**delle buste**	**dayl**lay **boo**stay
eraser	**una gomma**	**oo**nah **goam**mah
exercise book	**un quaderno**	oon kwah**dair**noa
felt-tip pen	**un pennarello**	oon paynnah**rehl**loa
fountain pen	**una penna stilografica**	**oo**nah **payn**nah steeloa**graa**feekah

glue	**della colla**	day**l**lah **kol**lah
grammar book	**una grammatica**	**oo**nah grahm**mah**teekah
guidebook	**una guida turistica**	**oo**nah goo**ee**dah tooreesteekah
ink	**dell'inchiostro**	daylleengkee**o**stroa
(adhesive) labels	**delle etichette (adesive)**	day**l**lay aytee**keh**ttay (ahday**zee**vay)
magazine	**una rivista**	**oo**nah ree**vee**stah
map	**una carta geografica**	**oo**nah **kahr**tah jayoa**graa**feekah
map of the town	**una pianta della città**	**oo**nah pee**ahn**tah **dayl**lah cheet**tah**
road map of ...	**una carta stradale di ...**	**oo**nah **kahr**tah strah**daa**lay dee
mechanical pencil	**un portamine**	oon poartah**mee**nay
newspaper	**un giornale**	oon joar**naa**lay
notebook	**un taccuino**	oon tahkkoo**ee**noa
note paper	**della carta da lettere**	**dayl**lah **kahr**tah dah **leht**tayray
paintbox	**una scatola di colori**	**oo**nah **skaa**toalah dee koa**loa**ree
paper	**della carta**	**dayl**lah **kahr**tah
paperback	**un libro tascabile**	oon **lee**broa tah**skaa**beelay
paperclips	**dei fermagli**	**dai**ee fayr**mah**lyee
paste	**della colla**	**dayl**lah **kol**lah
pen	**una penna**	**oo**nah **payn**nah
pencil	**una matita**	**oo**nah mah**tee**tah
pencil sharpener	**un temperamatite**	oon taympayrahmah**tee**tay
playing cards	**delle carte da gioco**	**dayl**lay **kahr**tay dah **jo**koa
pocket calculator	**una calcolatrice tascabile**	**oo**nah kahlkoalah**tree**chay tah**skaa**beelay
postcard	**una cartolina**	**oo**nah kahrtoa**lee**nah
propelling pencil	**un portamine**	oon poartah**mee**nay
refill (for a pen)	**un ricambio (per biro)**	oon ree**kahm**beeoa (pair **bee**roa)
rubber	**una gomma**	**oo**nah **goam**mah
ruler	**una riga**	**oo**nah **ree**gah
staples	**delle graffette**	**dayl**lay grah**ffeh**ttay
string	**dello spago**	**dayl**loa **spaa**goa
thumbtacks	**delle puntine**	**dayl**lay poon**tee**nay
tissue paper	**della carta velina**	**dayl**lah **kahr**tah vay**lee**nah
typewriter ribbon	**un nastro per macchina da scrivere**	oon **nah**stroa pair **mahk**keenah dah **skree**vayray
typing paper	**della carta per macchina da scrivere**	**dayl**lah **kahr**tah pair **mahk**keenah dah **skree**vayray
writing pad	**un blocco per appunti**	oon **blok**koa pair ap**poon**tee

COLOURS, see page 113

Camping equipment *Materiale da campeggio*

I'd like a/an/some ...	**Vorrei ...**	vor**rai**ee
bottle-opener	**un apribottiglia**	oon ahpreebot**tee**lyah
bucket	**un secchio**	oon **sayk**keeoa
butane gas	**del gas butano**	dayl gahz boo**taa**noa
campbed	**un letto da campo**	oon **leht**toa dah **kahm**poa
can opener	**un apriscatole**	oon ahprees**kaa**toalay
candles	**delle candele**	**dayl**lay kahn**day**lay
(folding) chair	**una sedia (pieghevole)**	oonah **say**deeah (peeay**gay**voalay)
charcoal	**della carbonella**	**dayl**lah kahrboa**nayl**lah
clothes pegs	**delle mollette da bucato**	**dayl**lay mol**leht**tay dah boo**kaa**toa
compass	**una bussola**	**oo**nah **boos**soalah
cool box	**una ghiacciaia**	**oo**nah geeaht**chaa**eeah
corkscrew	**un cavatappi**	oon kahvah**tahp**pee
dishwashing detergent	**del detersivo per lavare i piatti**	dayl dehtehr**see**voa pair lah**vaa**ray ee pee**aht**tee
first-aid kit	**una cassetta del pronto soccorso**	**oo**nah kahs**seht**tah dayl **proan**toa soak**koar**soa
fishing tackle	**degli arnesi da pesca**	**day**lyee ahr**nay**zee dah **pay**skah
flashlight	**una lampadina tascabile**	**oo**nah lahmpah**dee**nah tah**skaa**beelay
food box	**un contenitore per il cibo**	oon koantaynee**toa**ray pair eel **chee**boa
frying-pan	**una padella**	**oo**nah pah**dehl**lah
groundsheet	**un telo per il terreno**	oon **tay**loa pair eel tayr**ray**noa
hammer	**un martello**	oon mahr**tehl**loa
hammock	**un'amaca**	oo**naa**mahkah
ice-pack	**un elemento refrigerante**	oon aylay**mayn**toa rayfree-jay**rahn**tay
kerosene	**del petrolio**	dayl pay**tro**lyo
knapsack	**uno zaino**	**oo**noa **dzaa**eenoa
lamp	**una lampada**	**oo**nah **lahm**pahdah
lantern	**una lanterna**	**oo**nah lahn**tehr**nah
matches	**dei fiammiferi**	**da**iee feeahm**mee**fayree
mattress	**un materasso**	oon mahtay**rahs**soa
methylated spirits	**dell'alcool metilico**	dayl**lahl**koal may**tee**leekoa
mosquito net	**una zanzariera**	**oo**nah dzahndzahree**ay**rah
pail	**un secchio**	oon **sayk**keeoa
paper napkins	**dei tovagliolo di carta**	**da**iee toavah**lyoa**lee dee **kahr**tah
paraffin	**del petrolio**	dayl pay**tro**lyo

penknife	**un temperino**	oon taympay**ree**noa
picnic basket	**un cestino da picnic**	oon chay**stee**noa dah "picnic"
plastic bag	**un sacchetto di plastica**	oon sahk**keht**toa dee **plah**steekah
rope	**della corda**	**dayl**lah **koar**dah
rucksack	**uno zaino**	**oo**noa **dzaa**eenoa
saucepan	**una casseruola**	**oo**nah kahssay**rwoa**lah
scissors	**un paio di forbici**	oon **paa**eeoa dee **foar**beechee
screwdriver	**un cacciavite**	oon kahtchah**vee**tay
sleeping bag	**un sacco a pelo**	oon **sahk**koa ah **pay**loa
(folding) table	**una tavola (pieghevole)**	**oo**nah **taa**voalah (peeay**gay**voalay)
tent	**una tenda**	**oo**nah **tayn**dah
tent pegs	**dei picchetti per tenda**	**dai**ee peek**keht**tee pair **tayn**dah
tent pole	**un palo per tenda**	oon **paa**loa pair **tayn**dah
tinfoil	**un foglio di alluminio**	oon **foa**lyoa dee ahlloo**mee**neeoa
tin opener	**un apriscatole**	oon ahpree**skaa**toalay
tongs	**un paio di tenaglie**	oon **paa**eeoa dee tay**naa**lyay
torch	**una lampadina tascabile**	**oo**nah lahmpah**dee**nah tah**skaa**beelay
vacuum flask	**un thermos**	oon **tair**moas
washing powder	**del detersivo**	dayl daytehr**see**voa
water flask	**una borraccia**	**oo**nah boar**rat**chah
wood alcohol	**dell'alcool metilico**	dayl**lahl**koal may**tee**leekoa

Crockery *Stoviglie*

cups	**delle tazze**	**dayl**lay **taht**tsay
mugs	**dei boccali**	**dai**ee boak**kaa**lee
plates	**dei piatti**	**dai**ee pee**aht**tee
saucers	**dei piattini**	**dai**ee peeaht**tee**nee
tumblers	**dei bicchieri**	**dai**ee beekee**ay**ree

Cutlery *Posate*

forks	**delle forchette**	**dayl**lay for**keht**tay
knives	**dei coltelli**	**dai**ee koal**tehl**lee
spoons	**dei cucchiai**	**dai**ee kookkee**aa**ee
teaspoons	**dei cucchiaini**	**dai**ee kookkeeah**ee**nee
(made of) plastic	**(di) plastica**	(dee) **plah**steekah
(made of) stainless steel	**(di) acciaio inossidabile**	(dee) aht**chaa**eeoa eenossee**daa**beelay

Chemist's (drugstore) *Farmacia*

The Italian chemists' normally don't stock the great range of goods that you'll find in England or in the U.S. For example, they don't sell photographic equipment or books. For perfume, make-up, etc., you can also go to a *profumeria* (proafoomay**ree**ah).

You can recognize a chemist's by the sign outside—a green or red cross, illuminated at night. In the window you'll see a notice telling where the nearest all-night chemist's is.

This section is divided into two parts:

1. Pharmaceutical—medicine, first-aid, etc.
2. Toiletry—toilet articles, cosmetics

General *Generalità*

Where's the nearest (all-night) chemist's?	**Dov'è la farmacia (di turno) più vicina?**	doa**vai** lah fahrmah**chee**ah (dee **toor**noa) pee**oo** vee**chee**nah
What time does the chemist's open/ close?	**A che ora apre/ chiude la farmacia?**	ah kay **oa**rah **aa**pray/ kee**oo**day lah fahrmah**chee**ah

1 – Pharmaceutical *Medicine, primi soccorsi, ecc.*

I want something for a ...	**Desidero qualcosa per ...**	day**zee**dayroa kwahl**kaw**sah pair
cold	**il raffreddore**	eel rahffrayd**doa**ray
cough	**la tosse**	lah **toas**say
hay fever	**la febbre del fieno**	lah **fayb**bray dayl fee**ay**noa
insect bites	**le punture d'insetti**	lay poon**too**ray deen**seht**tee
hangover	**il mal di testa**	eel mahl dee **teh**stah
sunburn	**una scottatura solare**	**oo**nah skoattah**too**rah soa**laa**ray
travel sickness	**il mal d'auto**	eel mahl **dow**toa
upset stomach	**il mal di stomaco**	eel mahl dee **sto**mahkoa
Can you make up this prescription for me?	**Può prepararmi questa ricetta?**	pwo praypah**raar**mee koo**ay**stah ree**cheht**tah
Can I get it without a prescription?	**Può darmi questa medicina senza ricetta?**	pwo **daar**mee koo**ay**stah maydee**chee**nah **sayn**tsah ree**cheht**tah

DOCTOR, see page 137

Can I have a/an/ some ...?	**Mi può dare ...?**	mee pwo **daa**ray
analgesic	**un analgesico**	oon ahnahl**jai**zeekoa
antiseptic cream	**della crema antisettica**	day**l**lah **krai**mah ahntee**seht**teekah
aspirin	**delle aspirine**	day**l**lay ahspee**ree**nay
bandage	**una benda**	**oo**nah **bayn**dah
elastic bandage	**una benda elastica**	**oo**nah **bayn**dah ay**lah**steekah
Band-Aids	**dei cerotti**	da**i**ee chay**rot**tee
contraceptives	**degli antifecondativi**	day**l**yee ahnteefaykoandah**tee**vee
corn plasters	**dei cerotti callifughi**	da**i**ee chay**rot**tee kahllee**foo**gee
cotton wool (absorbent cotton)	**del cotone idrofilo**	dayl koa**toa**nay ee**droa**feeloa
cough drops	**delle pasticche per la tosse**	day**l**lay pah**steek**kay pair lah **toa**ssay
disinfectant	**del disinfettante**	dayl deeseenfeht**tahn**tay
ear drops	**delle gocce per le orecchie**	day**l**lay **goat**chay pair lay o**rayk**keeay
Elastoplast	**dei cerotti**	da**i**ee chay**rot**tee
eye drops	**delle gocce per gli occhi**	day**l**lay **goat**chay pair lyee **ok**kee
gauze	**della garza**	day**l**lah **gahr**dzah
insect repellent/ spray	**una crema contro gli insetti/uno spray insetticida**	**oo**nah **krai**mah **koan**troa lyee een**seh**ttee/**oo**noa "spray" eensehttee**chee**dah
iodine	**della tintura di iodio**	day**l**lah teen**too**rah dee ee**o**deeoa
laxative	**un lassativo**	oon lahssah**tee**voa
mouthwash	**un gargarismo**	oon gahrgah**reez**moa
nose drops	**delle gocce nasali**	day**l**lay **goat**chay naa**saa**lee
sanitary towels (napkins)	**degli assorbenti igienici**	day**l**yee ahssoar**bayn**tee ee**jay**neechee
sleeping pills	**dei sonniferi**	da**i**ee soan**nee**fayree
suppositories	**delle supposte**	day**l**lay soop**po**stay
... tablets	**delle pastiglie ...**	day**l**lay pah**stee**lyay
tampons	**dei tamponi igienici**	da**i**ee tahm**poa**nee ee**jay**neechee
thermometer	**un termometro**	oon tayr**moa**maytroa
throat lozenges	**delle pasticche per la gola**	day**l**lay pah**steek**kay pair lah **goa**lah
tranquillizers	**dei tranquillanti**	da**i**ee trahnkooeel**lahn**tee
vitamin pills	**delle vitamine**	day**l**lay veetah**mee**nay

2—Toiletry *Articoli da toilette*

I'd like a/an/some ...	**Desidero ...**	day**zee**dayroa
after-shave lotion	**una lozione dopobarba**	oonah loatsee**oa**nay dawpoa**bahr**bah
bath salts	**dei sali da bagno**	daiee **saa**lee dah **baa**ñoa
bubble bath	**un bagnoschiuma**	oon baañoaskee**oo**mah
cream	**una crema**	oonah **krai**mah
cleansing cream	**una crema detergente**	oonah **krai**mah daytehr**jayn**tay
foundation cream	**un fondo tinta**	oon **foan**doa **teen**tah
moisturizing cream	**una crema idratante**	oonah **krai**mah eedrah**tahn**tay
night cream	**una crema da notte**	oonah **krai**mah dah **not**tay
cuticle remover	**un prodotto per togliere le pellicine**	oon proa**doat**toa pair **tol**yayray lay pehllee**chee**nay
deodorant	**un deodorante**	oon dayoadoa**rahn**tay
emery board	**una limetta per unghie**	oonah lee**meht**tah pair **oong**geeay
eye liner	**un eye-liner**	oon "eye-liner"
eye pencil	**una matita per occhi**	oonah mah**tee**tah pair **ok**kee
eye shadow	**un ombretto**	oon oam**brayt**toa
face powder	**della cipria**	**dayl**lah **chee**preeah
foot cream	**una crema per i piedi**	oonah **krai**mah pair ee pee**ay**dee
hand cream	**una crema per le mani**	oonah **krai**mah pair lay **maa**nee
lipsalve	**un burro cacao**	oon **boor**roa kah**kaa**oa
lipstick	**un rossetto**	oon roas**seht**toa
make-up remover pads	**dei tamponi per togliere il trucco**	daiee tahm**poa**nee pair **tol**yayray eel **trook**koa
nail brush	**uno spazzolino da unghie**	oonoa spahtsoa**lee**noa dah **oong**geeay
nail file	**una lima da unghie**	oonah **lee**mah dah **oong**geeay
nail polish	**uno smalto**	oonoa **smahl**toa
nail polish remover	**un solvente per le unghie**	oon soal**vayn**tay pair lay **oong**geeay
nail scissors	**un paio di forbicine per le unghie**	oon pahyoa dee forbee**chee**nay pair lay **oong**geeay
perfume	**un profumo**	oon proa**foo**moa
powder	**della cipria**	**dayl**lah **chee**preeah
razor	**un rasoio**	oon rah**soa**eeoa
razor blades	**delle lamette**	**dayl**lay lah**mayt**tay
rouge	**del fard**	dayl "fard"

safety pins	**delle spille di sicurezza**	**day**llay **speel**lay dee seekoo**ray**ttsah
shaving cream	**una crema da barba**	**oo**nah **krai**mah dah **bahr**bah
soap	**una saponetta**	**oo**nah sahpoa**nayt**tah
sun-tan cream	**una crema solare**	**oo**nah **krai**mah soa**laa**ray
sun-tan oil	**un olio solare**	oon **o**lyoa soa**laa**ray
talcum powder	**del talco**	dayl **tahl**koa
tissues	**dei fazzolettini di carta**	**dai**ee fahttsoaleht**tee**nee dee **kahr**tah
toilet paper	**della carta igienica**	**day**llah **kahr**tah ee**jay**neekah
toilet water	**dell'acqua di colonia**	dayll**ahk**kwah dee koa**lo**neeah
toothbrush	**uno spazzolino da denti**	**oo**noa spahttsoa**lee**noa dah **dehn**tee
toothpaste	**un dentifricio**	oon daynteef**ree**choa
tweezers	**delle pinzette**	**day**llay peen**tseht**tay

For your hair *Per i vostri capelli*

bobby pins	**delle mollette**	**day**llay mol**layt**tay
colour shampoo	**uno shampoo colorante**	**oo**noa **shahm**poa koaloa**rahn**tay
comb	**un pettine**	oon **payt**teenay
dry shampoo	**uno shampo secco**	**oo**noa **shahm**poa **sehk**koa
hairbrush	**una spazzola per capelli**	**oo**nah **spaht**tsoalah pair kah**payl**lee
hair slide	**un fermaglio**	oon fayr**maa**lyoa
hairgrips	**delle mollette**	**day**llay mol**layt**tay
hair lotion	**una lozione per capelli**	**oo**nah loatsee**oa**nay pair kah**pehl**lee
hairspray	**della lacca**	**day**llah **lahk**kah
setting lotion	**una lozione fissativa**	**oo**nah loatsee**oa**nay feessah**tee**vah
shampoo	**dello shampoo**	**day**lloa **shahm**poa
for dry/greasy (oily) hair	**per capelli secchi/grassi**	pair kah**pehl**lee **sayk**kee/**grahs**see

For the baby *Per il vostro bambino*

baby food	**degli alimenti per bebè**	**day**lyee ahlee**main**tee pair bay**bay**
dummy (pacifier)	**un succhiotto**	oon sookkee**ot**toa
feeding bottle	**un biberon**	oon beebay**roan**
nappies (diapers)	**dei pannolini**	**dai**ee pahnnoa**lee**nee

Clothing *Abbigliamento*

If you want to buy something specific, prepare yourself in advance. Look at the list of clothing on page 116. Get some idea of the colour, material and size you want. They're all listed on the next few pages.

General *Generalità*

I'd like ...	**Vorrei ...**	vor**rai**ee
I want ... for a 10-year-old boy/girl.	**Desidero ... per un bambino/una bambina di 10 anni.**	day**zee**dayroa ... pair oon bahm**bee**noa/**oo**nah bahm**bee**nah dee 10 **ahn**nee
I want something like this.	**Voglio qualcosa come questo.**	**vol**yoa kwahl**kaw**sah **koa**may koo**ay**stoa
I like the one in the window.	**Mi piace quello in vetrina.**	mee pee**aa**chay koo**ayl**loa een vay**tree**nah
How much is that per metre?	**Quanto costa al metro?**	**kwahn**toa **kos**tah ahl **may**troa

1 centimetre (cm.)	= 0.39 in.	1 inch	= 2.54 cm.
1 metre (m.)	= 39.37 in.	1 foot	= 30.5 cm.
10 metres	= 32.81 ft.	1 yard	= 0.91 m.

Colour *Colore*

I want something in ...	**Voglio qualcosa di colore ...**	**vol**yoa kwahl**kaw**sah dee koa**loa**ray
I'd like a darker/lighter shade.	**Desidero una tonalità più scura/più chiara.**	day**zee**dayroa **oo**nah toanahlee**tah** pee**oo** skoorah/peeoo keeaarah
I want something to match this.	**Voglio qualcosa per ravvivare questo.**	**vol**yoa kwahl**kaw**sah pair rahvvee**vaa**ray koo**ay**stoa
I'd like the same colour as ...	**Vorrei lo stesso colore che ...**	vor**rai**ee loa **stays**soa koa**loa**ray kai
I don't like the colour.	**Non mi piace il colore.**	noan mee pee**aa**chay eel koa**loa**ray

beige	**beige**	baizh
black	**nero**	**nay**roa
blue	**blu**	bloo
light blue	**azzurro**	ah**dzoor**roa
brown	**marrone**	mahr**roa**nay
golden	**dorato**	doa**raa**toa
green	**verde**	**vayr**day
grey	**grigio**	**gree**joa
mauve	**lilla**	**leel**lah
orange	**arancio**	ah**rahn**choa
pink	**rosa**	**raw**zah
purple	**viola**	vee**o**lah
red	**rosso**	**roas**soa
silver	**argentato**	ahrjayn**taa**toa
turquoise	**turchese**	toor**kay**zay
white	**bianco**	bee**ahng**koa
yellow	**giallo**	**jahl**loa
light ...	**... chiaro**	kee**aa**roa
dark ...	**... scuro**	**skoo**roa

tinta unita
(**teen**tah oo**nee**tah)

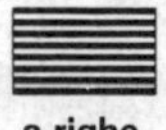

a righe
(ah **ree**gay)

a pallini
(ah pahl**lee**nee)

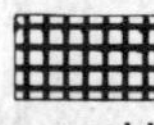

a quadri
(ah **kwaa**dree)

fantasia
(fahntah**zee**ah)

Material *Tessuto*

Do you have anything in ...?	**Ha qualcosa in ...?**	ah kwahl**kaw**sah een
I want a cotton blouse.	**Voglio una blusa di cotone.**	**vol**yoa **oo**nah **bloo**sah dee koa**toa**nay
Is that ...?	**È un prodotto ...?**	ai oon proa**doat**toa
handmade	**fatto a mano**	**faht**toa ah **maa**noa
imported	**importato**	eempoar**taa**toa
made here	**nazionale**	nahtseeoa**naa**lay
I want something thinner.	**Desidero qualcosa di più fine.**	day**zee**dayroa kwahl**kaw**sah dee pee**oo** **fee**nay
Do you have any better quality?	**Ha una qualità migliore?**	ah **oo**nah kwahlee**tah** mee**lyoa**ray
What's it made of?	**Di che cos'è?**	dee kay kosai

cambric	**la tela battista**	lah **tay**lah baht**tee**stah
camel-hair	**il pelo di cammello**	eel **pay**loa dee kahm**mehl**loa
chiffon	**lo chiffon**	loa sheef**foan**
corduroy	**il velluto a coste**	eel vayl**loo**toa ah **koa**stay
cotton	**il cotone**	eel koa**toa**nay
crepe	**il crespo**	eel **kray**spoa
denim	**la tela di cotone**	lah **tay**lah dee koa**toa**nay
felt	**il feltro**	eel **fayl**troa
flannel	**la flanella**	lah flah**nehl**lah
gabardine	**il gabardine**	eel gahbahr**deen**
lace	**il pizzo**	eel **peet**tsoa
leather	**la pelle**	lah **pehl**lay
linen	**il lino**	eel **lee**noa
poplin	**il popeline**	eel poapay**leen**
satin	**il raso**	eel **raa**soa
silk	**la seta**	lah **say**tah
suede	**la renna**	lah **rehn**nah
towelling (terrycloth)	**il tessuto di spugna**	eel tays**soo**toa dee **spoo**ñah
velvet	**il velluto**	eel vayl**loo**toa
velveteen	**il velluto di cotone**	eel vayl**loo**toa dee koa**toa**nay
wool	**la lana**	lah **laa**nah
worsted	**il pettinato**	eel payttee**naa**toa

Is it ...?	**È ...?**	ai
pure cotton/wool	**puro cotone/pura lana**	**poo**roa koa**toa**nay/**poo**rah **laa**nah
synthetic	**sintetico**	seen**tay**teekoa
colourfast	**di colore solido**	dee koa**loa**ray **so**leedoa
wrinkle resistant	**ingualcibile**	eengwahl**chee**beelay
Is it hand washable/ machine washable?	**Si può lavare a mano/ in lavatrice?**	see pwo lah**vaa**ray ah **maa**noa/een lahvah**tree**chay
Will it shrink?	**Si restringe al lavaggio?**	see ray**streen**jay ahl lah**vahd**joa

Size *Taglia*

I take size 38.	**La mia taglia è il 38.**	lah **mee**ah **tahl**yah ai eel 38
Could you measure me?	**Può prendermi le misure?**	pwo **prehn**dayrmee lay mee**zoo**ray
I don't know the Italian sizes.	**Non conosco le misure italiane.**	noan koa**noa**skoa lay mee**zoo**ray eetahlee**aa**nay

Sizes can vary somewhat from one manufacturer to another, so be sure to try on shoes and clothing before you buy.

Women *Donne*

Dresses/Suits						
American	8	10	12	14	16	18
British	10	12	14	16	18	20
Continental	36	38	40	42	44	46

Stockings							Shoes			
American / British	8	8½	9	9½	10	10½	6 / 4½	7 / 5½	8 / 6½	9 / 7½
Continental	0	1	2	3	4	5	37	38	40	41

Men *Uomini*

Suits/Overcoats							Shirts			
American / British	36	38	40	42	44	46	15	16	17	18
Continental	46	48	50	52	54	56	38	41	43	45

Shoes								
American / British	5	6	7	8	8½	9	9½	10	11
Continental	38	39	41	42	43	43	44	44	45

A good fit? *Una buona prova?*

Can I try it on?	**Posso provarlo?**	possoa provahrloa
Where's the fitting room?	**Dov'è la cabina di prova?**	doavai lah kahbeenah dee prawvah
Is there a mirror?	**C'è uno specchio?**	chai oonoa spaykkeeoa
It fits very well.	**Va molto bene.**	vah moaltoa bainay
It doesn't fit.	**Non va bene.**	noan vah bainay
It's too ...	**È troppo ...**	ai troppoa
short/long	**corto/lungo**	koartoa/loonggoa
tight/loose	**stretto/largo**	strayttoa/lahrgoa

NUMBERS, see page 147

How long will it take to alter?	**Quanto tempo ci vuole per le modifiche?**	**kwahn**toa **tehm**poa chee **vwo**lay pair lay moa**dee**feekay

Clothes and accessories *Indumenti e accessori*

I'd like a/an/some ...	**Vorrei ...**	vor**raiee**
anorak	**una giacca a vento**	**oo**nah **jahk**kah ah **vayn**toa
bathing cap	**una cuffia da bagno**	**oo**nah **koof**feeah dah **baa**ñoa
bathing suit	**un costume da bagno**	oon koa**stoo**may dah **baa**ñoa
bathrobe	**un accappatoio**	oon ahkkahppah**toa**eeoa
blouse	**una blusa**	**oo**nah **bloo**zah
bow tie	**una cravatta a farfalla**	**oo**nah krah**vaht**tah ah fahr**fahl**lah
bra	**un reggiseno**	oon raydjee**say**noa
braces	**delle bretelle**	**dayl**lay bray**tehl**lay
briefs	**uno slip**	**oo**noa "slip"
cap	**un berretto**	oon bayr**rayt**toa
cardigan	**un cardigan**	oon "cardigan"
coat	**un cappotto**	oon kahp**pot**toa
dress	**un abito**	oon **aa**beetoa
dressing gown	**una vestaglia**	**oo**nah veh**stahl**yah
evening dress (woman's)	**un abito da sera**	oon **aa**beetoa dah **say**rah
frock	**un abito**	oon **aa**beetoa
garter belt	**un reggicalze**	oon raydjee**kahl**tsay
girdle	**un busto**	oon **boo**stoa
gloves	**dei guanti**	**dai**ee **gwahn**tee
handbag	**una borsetta**	**oo**nah boar**sayt**tah
handkerchief	**un fazzoletto**	oon fahtsoa**leht**toa
hat	**un cappello**	oon kahp**pehl**loa
jacket	**una giacca**	**oo**nah **jahk**kah
jeans	**dei jeans**	**dai**ee "jeans"
jersey	**una maglietta**	**oo**nah mahl**yeht**tah
jumper (Br.)	**un maglione**	oon mahl**yoa**nay
kneesocks	**dei calzettoni**	**dai**ee kahltsay**ttoa**nee
nightdress	**una camicia da notte**	**oo**nah kah**mee**chah dah **not**tay
overalls	**una tuta**	**oo**nah **too**tah
pair of ...	**un paio di ...**	oon **paa**eeoa dee
panties	**uno slip**	**oo**noa "slip"
pants (Am.)	**dei pantaloni**	**dai**ee pahntah**loa**nee
panty girdle	**una guaina**	**oo**nah **gwaa**eenah
panty hose	**dei collant**	**dai**ee **kol**lahnt

pullover	**un pullover**	oon "pullover"
roll-neck (turtle-neck)	**a collo alto**	ah **kol**loa **ahl**toa
round	**a girocollo**	ah jeeroa**kol**loa
V-neck	**con scollatura a punta**	kon skollah**too**rah ah **poon**tah
pyjamas	**un pigiama**	oon pee**jaa**mah
raincoat	**un impermeabile**	oon eempayrmay**aa**beelay
scarf	**una sciarpa**	**oo**nah **shahr**pah
shirt	**una camicia**	**oo**nah kah**mee**chah
shorts	**uno short**	**oo**noa "short"
skirt	**una gonna**	**oo**nah **goan**nah
slip	**una sottoveste**	**oo**nah soattoa**veh**stay
socks	**dei calzini**	**dai**ee kahl**tsee**nee
stockings	**delle calze da donna**	**day**llay **kahl**tsay dah **don**nah
suit (man's)	**un completo**	oon koam**play**toa
suit (woman's)	**un tailleur**	oon "tailleur"
suspenders (Am.)	**delle bretelle**	**day**llay bray**teh**llay
sweater	**un maglione**	oon mah**lyoa**nay
sweatshirt	**una blusa**	**oo**nah **bloo**zah
swimming trunks/ swimsuit	**un costume da bagno**	oon koa**stoo**may dah **baa**ñoa
T-shirt	**una maglietta di cotone**	**oo**nah mah**lyeh**ttah dee koa**toa**nay
tie	**una cravatta**	**oo**nah krah**vah**ttah
tights	**dei collant**	**dai**ee **kol**lahnt
tracksuit	**una tuta sportiva**	**oo**nah **too**tah sport**ee**vah
trousers	**dei pantaloni**	**dai**ee pahntah**loa**nee
umbrella	**un ombrello**	oon oam**brehl**loa
underpants	**delle mutande/uno slip**	**day**llay moo**tahn**day/**oo**noa "slip"
undershirt	**una canottiera**	**oo**nah kahnottee**ay**rah
vest (Am.)	**un panciotto**	oon pahn**chot**toa
vest (Br.)	**una canottiera**	**oo**nah kahnottee**ay**rah
waistcoat	**un panciotto**	oon pahn**chot**toa

belt	**la cintura**	lah cheen**too**rah
button	**il bottone**	eel boat**toa**nay
pocket	**la tasca**	lah **tah**skah
press stud (snap fastener)	**il bottone a pressione**	eel boat**toa**nay ah praysseeoanay
sleeve	**la manica**	lah **maa**neekah
zip (zipper)	**la cerniera**	lah chehrnee**ay**rah

Shoes *Scarpe*

I'd like a pair of ...	**Vorrei un paio di ...**	vorraiee oon paaeeoa dee
boots	**stivali**	steevaalee
moccasins	**mocassini**	moakahsseenee
plimsolls (sneakers)	**scarpe da tennis**	skahrpay dah tainnees
sandals	**sandali**	sahndahlee
shoes	**scarpe**	skahrpay
flat	**basse**	bahssay
with a heel	**con i tacchi**	koan ee tahkkee
slippers	**pantofole**	pahntofoalay
These are too ...	**Queste sono troppo ...**	kwaystay soanoa troppoa
narrow/wide	**strette/larghe**	strayttay/lahrgay
large/small	**grandi/piccole**	grahndee/peekkoalay
Do you have a larger/smaller size?	**Ha un numero più grande/più piccolo?**	ah oon noomayroa peeoo grahnday/peeoo peekkoaloa
Do you have the same in black?	**Ha le stesse in nero?**	ah lay stehssay een nayroa
cloth/leather/rubber/suede	**in tela/pelle/gomma/camoscio**	een taylah/pehllay/goammah/kahmoshoa
Is it genuine leather?	**È vera pelle?**	ai vayrah pehllay
I need some shoe polish/shoelaces.	**Mi serve del lucido/dei lacci.**	mee sairvay dayl loocheedoa/daiee lahtchee

Shoes worn out? Here's the key to getting them fixed again:

Can you repair these shoes?	**Mi può riparare queste scarpe?**	mee pwo reepahraaray kooaystay skahrpay
Can you stitch this?	**Può attaccare questo?**	pwo ahttahkkaaray kooaystoa
I want new soles and heels.	**Desidero suole e tacchi nuovi.**	dayzeedayroa swoalay ay tahkkee nwawvee
When will they be ready?	**Quando saranno pronte?**	kwahndoa sahrahnnoa proantay
I need them ...	**Ne ho bisogno ...**	nay oa beezoañoa
as soon as possible	**il più presto possibile**	eel peeoo prehstoa posseebeelay
tomorrow	**domani**	doamaanee

COLOURS, see page 113

Electrical appliances *Apparecchi elettrici*

In Italy you will usually find 220-volt current, though some older buildings, particularly in Rome, have 125-volt outlets.

What's the voltage?	**Qual è il voltaggio?**	kwahl ai eel voal**tahd**joa
Do you have a battery for this?	**Ha una pila per questo?**	ah **oo**nah **pee**lah pair koo**ay**stoa
This is broken. Can you repair it?	**È rotto. Me lo può riparare?**	ai **roat**toa. may loa pwo reepah**raa**ray
Can you show me how it works?	**Può mostrarmi come funziona?**	pwo moa**straar**mee **koa**may foontsee**oa**nah
I'd like (to hire) a video cassette.	**Vorrei (noleggiare) una video cassetta.**	vor**rai**ee (noalayd**jaa**ray) **oo**nah **vee**dayoa kahs**seht**tah
I'd like a/an/some ...	**Vorrei ...**	vor**rai**ee
adaptor	**una presa multipla**	**oo**nah **pray**zah **mool**teeplah
amplifier	**un amplificatore**	oon ahmpleefeekah**toa**ray
bulb	**una lampadina**	**oo**nah lahmpah**dee**nah
clock-radio	**una radio-sveglia**	**oo**nah **raa**deeoa-**svay**lyah
electric toothbrush	**uno spazzolino da denti elettrico**	**oo**noa spatsoa**lee**noa dah **dayn**tee ay**leht**treekoa
extension lead (cord)	**una prolunga**	**oo**nah proa**loong**gah
hair dryer	**un asciugacapelli**	oon ashoogahkah**pay**llee
headphones	**una cuffia (d'ascolto)**	**oo**nah **koof**feeah (dahs**koal**toa)
(travelling) iron	**un ferro da stiro (da viaggio)**	oon **fehr**roa dah **stee**roa (dah vee**ahd**joa)
lamp	**una lampada**	**oo**nah **lahm**pahdah
plug	**una spina**	**oo**nah **spee**nah
portable ...	**... portatile**	... poar**taa**teelay
radio	**una radio**	**oo**nah **raa**deeoa
car radio	**un'autoradio**	oonowtoa**raa**deeoa
record player	**un giradischi**	oon jeerah**dee**skee
shaver	**un rasoio elettrico**	oon rah**soa**eeoa ay**leht**treekoa
speakers	**degli altoparlanti**	**day**lyee ahltoapahr**lahn**tee
(cassette) tape recorder	**un registratore (a cassette)**	oon rayjeestrah**toa**ray (ah kas**seht**tay)
(colour) television	**un televisore (a colori)**	oon taylayvee**zoa**ray (ah koa**loa**ree)
transformer	**un trasformatore**	oon trahsfoarmah**toa**ray
video-recorder	**un video registratore**	oon **vee**dayoa rayjeestrah**toa**ray

Grocery *Negozio di alimentari*

I'd like some bread, please.	**Vorrei del pane, per favore.**	vorr**ai**ee dayl **paa**nay pair fah**voa**ray
What sort of cheese do you have?	**Che formaggi avete?**	kay foar**mahd**jee ah**vay**tay
A piece of that one/ the one on the shelf.	**Un pezzo di quello/ quello sullo scaffale.**	oon **peht**soa dee koo**ayl**loa/ koo**ayl**loa **sool**loa skahf**faa**lay
I'll have one of those, please.	**Vorrei uno di quelli, per favore.**	vorr**ai**ee **oo**noa dee koo**ayl**lee pair fah**voa**ray
May I help myself?	**Posso servirmi?**	**pos**soa sayr**veer**mee
I'd like ...	**Vorrei ...**	vorr**ai**ee
a kilo of apples	**un chilo di mele**	oon **kee**loa dee **may**lay
half a kilo of tomatoes	**mezzo chilo di pomodori**	**mehd**zoa **kee**loa dee pomo**daw**ree
100 grams of butter	**100 grammi (un etto) di burro**	**chehn**toa **grahm**mee (oon **eht**toa) dee **boor**roa
a litre of milk	**un litro di latte**	oon **lee**troa dee **laht**tay
half a dozen eggs	**mezza dozzina di uova**	**mehd**zah doad**zee**nah dee **waw**vah
4 slices of ham	**4 fette di prosciutto**	4 **feht**tay dee proa**shoot**toa
a packet of tea	**un pacchetto di tè**	oon pahk**keht**toa dee tai
a jar of jam	**un vasetto di marmellata**	oon vah**zeht**toa dee marmehl**laa**tah
a tin (can) of peaches	**una scatola di pesche**	**oo**nah **skaa**toalah dee **pay**skay
a tube of mustard	**un tubetto di mostarda**	oon too**beht**toa dee moa**stahr**dah
a box of chocolates	**una scatola di cioccolatini**	**oo**nah **skaa**toalah dee ch[illegible]koalah**tee**nee

1 kilogram or kilo (kg.) = 1000 grams (g.)

100 g. = 3.5 oz. ½ kg. = 1.1 lbs.
200 g. = 7.0 oz. 1 kg. = 2.2 lbs.

1 oz. = 28.35 g.
1 lb. = 453.60 g.

1 litre (l.) = 0.88 imp. quarts = 1.06 U.S. quarts

1 imp. quart = 1.14 l. 1 U.S. quart = 0.95 l.
1 imp. gallon = 4.55 l. 1 U.S. gallon = 3.8 l.

FOOD, see also page 63

Jeweller's—Watchmaker's *Gioielleria—Orologeria*

Could I please see that?	**Potrei vedere quello, per favore?**	potraiee vay**day**ray kooayl-loa pair fah**voa**ray
Do you have anything in gold?	**Avete qualcosa in oro?**	ah**vay**tay kwahl**kaw**sah een **oa**roa
How many carats is this?	**Di quanti carati è?**	dee **kwahn**tee kah**raa**tee ai
Is this real silver?	**È vero argento?**	ai **vay**roa ahr**jayn**toa
Can you repair this watch?	**Può riparare questo orologio?**	pwo reepah**raa**ray kooay-stoa oaroa**lo**joa
I'd like a/an/some ...	**Vorrei ...**	vor**rai**ee
alarm clock	**una sveglia**	**oo**nah **svay**lyah
bangle	**un braccialetto**	oon brahtchah**leht**toa
battery	**una pila**	**oo**nah **pee**lah
bracelet	**un braccialetto**	oon brahtchah**leht**toa
chain bracelet	**un braccialetto a catena**	oon brahtchah**leht**toa ah kah**tay**nah
charm bracelet	**un braccialetto a ciondoli**	oon brahtchah**leht**toa ah **choan**doalee
brooch	**una spilla**	**oo**nah **speel**lah
chain	**una catenina**	**oo**nah kahtay**nee**nah
charm	**un ciondolo**	oon **choan**doaloa
cigarette case	**un portasigarette**	oon portahseegah**rayt**tay
cigarette lighter	**un accendino**	oon ahtchayn**dee**noa
clip	**un fermaglio**	oon fayr**maa**lyoa
clock	**un orologio**	oon oaroa**lo**joa
cross	**una croce**	**oo**nah **kroa**chay
cuckoo clock	**un orologio a cucù**	oon oaroa**lo**joa ah koo**koo**
cuff links	**dei gemelli**	**dai**ee jay**mehl**lee
cutlery	**delle posate**	**dayl**lay poa**saa**tay
earrings	**degli orecchini**	**day**lyee oarayk**kee**nee
gem	**una pietra preziosa**	**oo**nah pee**ay**trah pray-tsee**oa**sah
jewel box	**un portagioielli**	oon portahjoee**ehl**lee
music box	**un carillon**	oon kahree**yon**
necklace	**una collana**	**oo**nah koal**laa**nah
pendant	**un pendente**	oon payn**dayn**tay
pocket watch	**un orologio da tasca**	oon oaroa**lo**joa dah **tah**skah
powder compact	**un portacipria**	oon portah**chee**preeah
ring	**un anello**	oon ah**nehl**loa
engagement ring	**un anello di fidanzamento**	oon ah**nehl**loa dee feedahntsah**mayn**toa

signet ring	**un anello con stemma**	oon ah**neh**lloa kon **stehm**mah
wedding ring	**una fede nuziale**	oonah **fay**day nootsee**aa**lay
rosary	**un rosario**	oon rawz**aa**reeoa
silverware	**dell'argenteria**	dayllahrjayntay**ree**ah
tie clip	**un fermacravatte**	oon fayrmahkrah**vaht**tay
tie pin	**uno spillo per cravatta**	**oo**noa **speel**loa pair krah**vaht**tah
watch	**un orologio**	oon oaroa**lo**joa
automatic	**automatico**	owtoa**maa**teekoa
digital	**digitale**	deejee**taa**lay
quartz	**al quarzo**	ahl **kwahr**tsoa
with a second hand	**con lancetta dei secondi**	kon lahn**cheht**tah **daiee** say**koan**dee
watchstrap	**un cinturino per orologio**	oon cheentoo**ree**noa pair oaroa**lo**joa
wristwatch	**un orologio braccialetto**	oon oaroa**lo**joa brahtchah**leht**toa

alabaster	**l'alabastro**	lahlah**bah**stroa
amber	**l'ambra**	**lahm**brah
amethyst	**l'ametista**	lahmay**tee**stah
copper	**il rame**	eel **raa**may
coral	**il corallo**	eel koa**rahl**loa
crystal	**il cristallo**	eel kree**stahl**loa
cut glass	**il vetro tagliato**	eel **vay**troa tah**lyaa**toa
diamond	**il diamante**	eel deeah**mahn**tay
emerald	**lo smeraldo**	loa smay**rahl**doa
enamel	**lo smalto**	loa **smahl**toa
gold	**l'oro**	**lo**roa
gold plate	**placcato d'oro**	plahk**kaa**toa **do**roa
ivory	**l'avorio**	lah**vo**reeoa
jade	**la giada**	lah **jaa**dah
onyx	**l'onice**	**lo**neechay
pearl	**la perla**	lah **pehr**lah
pewter	**il peltro**	eel **payl**troa
platinum	**il platino**	eel **plaa**teenoa
ruby	**il rubino**	eel roo**bee**noa
sapphire	**lo zaffiro**	loa dzahf**fee**roa
silver	**l'argento**	lahr**jayn**toa
silver plate	**placcato d'argento**	plahk**kaa**toa dahr**jayn**toa
stainless steel	**l'acciaio inossidabile**	lah**tchaa**eeoa eenoas**see**daabeelay
topaz	**il topazio**	eel toa**paat**seeoa
turquoise	**il turchese**	eel toor**kay**zay

Optician *Ottico*

I've broken my glasses.	**Ho rotto gli occhiali.**	oa **roat**toa lyee okkee**aa**lee
Can you repair them for me?	**Può ripararmeli?**	pwo reepah**raar**maylee
When will they be ready?	**Quando saranno pronti?**	**kwahn**doa sah**rahn**noa **proan**tee
Can you change the lenses?	**Può cambiare le lenti?**	pwo kahmbee**aa**ray lay **lehn**tee
I want tinted lenses.	**Desidero delle lenti colorate.**	day**zee**dayroa **dayl**lay **lehn**tee koaloa**raa**tay
The frame is broken.	**La montatura è rotta.**	lah moantah**too**rah ai **roat**tah
I'd like a spectacle case.	**Vorrei un astuccio per occhiali.**	vor**rai**ee oon ah**stoot**choa pair okkee**aa**lee
I'd like to have my eyesight checked.	**Vorrei farmi controllare la vista.**	vor**rai**ee **fahr**mee koantroal**laa**ray lah **vee**stah
I'm short-sighted/long-sighted.	**Sono miope/presbite.**	**soa**noa **mee**oapay/**preh**zbeetay
I want some contact lenses.	**Desidero delle lenti a contatto.**	day**zee**dayroa **dayl**lay **lehn**tee ah koan**taht**toa
I've lost one of my contact lenses.	**Ho perso una lente a contatto.**	oa **pehr**soa **oo**nah **lehn**tay ah koan**taht**toa
Could you give me another one?	**Può darmene un'altra?**	pwo **daar**mehneh oo**nahl**trah
I have hard/soft lenses.	**Ho delle lenti a contatto dure/morbide.**	oa **dayl**lay **lehn**tee ah koan**taht**toa **doo**ray/**mor**beeday
Have you any contact-lens liquid?	**Avete del liquido per lenti a contatto?**	ah**vay**tay dayl **lee**kooeedoa pair **lehn**tee ah koan**taht**toa
I'd like to buy a pair of sunglasses.	**Vorrei degli occhiali da sole.**	vor**rai**ee **day**lyee okkee**aa**lee dah **soa**lay
May I look in a mirror?	**Posso guardarmi in uno specchio?**	**pos**soa gwahr**daar**mee een **oo**noa **spehk**keeoa
I'd like to buy a pair of binoculars.	**Vorrei acquistare un binocolo.**	vor**rai**ee akkooee**staa**ray oon bee**no**koaloa

Photography *Fotografia*

I want a(n) ... camera.	**Voglio una macchina fotografica ...**	volyoa **oo**nah **mahk**keenah foatoa**graa**feekah
automatic	**automatica**	owtoa**maa**teekah
inexpensive	**economica**	aykoa**no**meekah
simple	**semplice**	**saym**pleechay
Show me some cine (movie) cameras, please.	**Per favore, mi faccia vedere alcune cineprese.**	pair fah**voa**ray mee **faht**chah vay**day**ray ahl**koo**nay cheenay**pray**zay
I'd like to have some passport photos taken.	**Vorrei che mi facesse delle fotografie d'identità.**	vor**rai**ee kay mee faht**chays**say **dayl**lay foatoa**grah**fee**ay** deedaynteetah

Film *Pellicola*

I'd like a film for this camera.	**Vorrei una pellicola per questa macchina fotografica.**	vor**rai**ee **oo**nah pehl**lee**koalah pair koo**ay**stah **mahk**keenah foatoa**graa**feekah
black and white	**in bianco e nero**	een bee**ahng**koa ay **nay**roa
colour	**a colori**	ah koa**loa**ree
colour negative	**per negativo a colori**	pair naygah**tee**voa ah koa**loa**ree
colour slide	**per diapositive**	pair deeahpoazee**tee**vay
cartridge	**un rotolo**	oon **ro**toaloa
roll film	**una bobina**	**oo**nah boa**bee**nah
video cassette	**una video cassetta**	**oo**nah **vee**dayoa kahs**sayt**tah
24/36 exposures	**ventiquattro/trentasei pose**	vaynteek**waht**troa/trayntah**seh**ee **poa**zay
this size	**questo formato**	koo**ay**stoa foar**maa**toa
this ASA/DIN number	**questo numero ASA/DIN**	koo**ay**stoa **noo**mayroa aasah/deen
artificial light type	**per luce artificiale**	pair **loo**chay ahrteefee**chaa**lay
daylight type	**par luce naturale**	pair **loo**chay nahtoo**raa**lay
fast (high-speed)	**rapida**	**raa**peedoa
fine grain	**a grana fine**	ah **graa**nah **fee**nay

Processing *Sviluppo*

How much do you charge for developing?	**Quanto fate pagare per lo sviluppo?**	**kwahn**toa **faa**tay pahgaaray pair loa svee**loop**poa

NUMBERS, see page 147

I want ... prints of each negative.	**Voglio ... stampe per ogni negativa.**	**vol**yoa ... **stahm**pay pair **oa**ñee naygah**tee**vah
with a mat finish	**su carta opaca**	soo **kahr**tah oa**paa**kah
with a glossy finish	**su carta lucida**	soo **kahr**tah **loo**cheedah
Will you please enlarge this?	**Mi può ingrandire questo, per favore?**	mee pwo eenggrahn**dee**ray koo**ay**stoa pair fah**voa**ray
When will the photos be ready?	**Quando saranno pronte le fotografie?**	**kwahn**doa sah**rahn**noa **pron**tay lay foatoagrah**fee**ay

Accessories and repairs *Accessori e riparazioni*

I want a/an/some ...	**Vorrei ...**	vor**rai**ee
battery	**una pila**	**oo**nah **pee**lah
cable release	**uno scatto**	**oo**noa **skaht**toa
camera case	**un astuccio (per macchina fotografica)**	oon ah**stoot**choa (pair **mahk**keenah foatoa**graa**feekah)
(electronic) flash	**un flash (elettronico)**	oon "flash" (aylayt**tro**neekoa)
filter	**un filtro**	oon **feel**troa
for black and white	**per bianco e nero**	pair bee**ahng**koa ay **nay**roa
for colour	**per foto a colori**	pair **foa**toa ah koa**loa**ree
lens	**un obiettivo**	oon oabeeayt**tee**voa
telephoto lens	**un teleobiettivo**	oon taylayoabeeayt**tee**voa
wide-angle lens	**un grandangolare**	oon grahndahngoa**laa**ray
lens cap	**un cappuccio (per obiettivo)**	oon kah**ppoot**choa (pair oabeeayt**tee**voa)
Can you repair this camera?	**Può riparare questa macchina fotografica?**	pwo reepah**raa**ray koo**ay**stah **mahk**keenah foatoa**graa**feekah
The film is jammed.	**La pellicola è bloccata.**	lah pehl**lee**koalah ai bloak**kaa**tah
There's something wrong with the ...	**... non funziona.**	noan foont**see**oanah
exposure counter	**il contatore di esposizioni**	eel koantah**toa**ray dee ayspoazeetsee**oa**nee
film winder	**la leva d'avanzamento della pellicola**	lah **lay**vah dahvahntsah**mayn**toa **dayl**lah pehl**lee**koalah
flash attachment	**l'attaccatura del flash**	lahttahkkah**too**rah dayl "flash"
light meter	**l'esposimetro**	layspoa**zee**maytroa
rangefinder	**il telemetro**	eel tay**lay**maytroa
shutter	**l'otturatore**	loattoorah**toa**ray

Tobacconist's *Tabaccheria*

Tobacco is a state monopoly in Italy. You recognize licensed tobacconist's by a large white "T" on a black background. Cigarettes are also sold in some cafés and newsstands.

A packet of cigarettes, please.	**Un pacchetto di sigarette, per favore.**	oon pahk**kayt**toa dee seegah**rayt**tay pair fah**voa**ray
Do you have any American/English cigarettes?	**Avete sigarette americane/inglesi?**	ah**vay**tay seegah**rayt**tay ahmayree**kaa**nay/eeng**glay**see
I'd like a carton.	**Ne vorrei una stecca.**	nay vor**rai**ee **oo**nah **stayk**kah
Give me a/some ..., please.	**Per favore, mi dia ...**	pair fah**voa**ray mee **dee**ah
candy	**delle caramelle**	**dayl**lay kahrah**mail**lay
chewing gum	**della gomma da masticare**	**dayl**lah **goam**mah dah mahstee**kaa**ray
chocolate	**del cioccolato**	dayl choakkoa**laa**toa
cigarette case	**un portasigarette**	oon portahseegah**rayt**tay
cigarette holder	**un bocchino**	oon boak**kee**noa
cigarettes	**delle sigarette**	**dayl**lay seegah**rayt**tay
filter-tipped/ without filter	**con filtro/ senza filtro**	kon **feel**troa/ **sayn**tsah **feel**troa
light/dark tobacco	**tabacco chiaro/ scuro**	tah**bahk**koa kee**aa**roa/ **skoo**roa
mild/strong	**leggere/forti**	lay**djay**ray/**for**tee
menthol	**al mentolo**	ahl mayn**toa**loa
king-size	**formato lungo**	foar**maa**toa **loong**goa
cigars	**dei sigari**	**dai**ee **see**gahree
lighter	**un accendino**	oon ahtchayn**dee**noa
lighter fluid/gas	**della benzina/del gas per accendino**	**dayl**lah bayn**dzee**nah/ dayl gahz pair ahtchayn**dee**noa
matches	**dei fiammiferi**	**dai**ee feeahm**mee**fayree
pipe	**una pipa**	**oo**nah **pee**pah
pipe cleaners	**dei nettapipe**	**dai**ee nayttah**pee**pay
pipe tobacco	**del tabacco da pipa**	dayl tah**bahk**koa dah **pee**pah
pipe tool	**un curapipe**	oon koorah**pee**pay
postcard	**una cartolina**	**oo**nah kahrtoa**lee**nah
stamps	**dei francobolli**	**dai**ee frahngkoa**boal**lee
sweets	**delle caramelle**	**dayl**lay karah**mail**lay
wick	**uno stoppino**	**oo**noa stop**pee**noa

Miscellaneous *Diversi*

Souvenirs *Oggetti ricordo*

Here are some suggestions for articles you might like to bring back as a souvenir or a gift. Italy is particularly noted for its top fashions for men and women, for articles made of silk, leather, olive wood and alabaster, for pottery and embroidered clothes and accessories. Hand-made jewellery of amber, gold and silver are particularly appreciated.

antiques	**l'antichità**	lahnteekee**tah**
ceramics	**la ceramica**	lah chay**raa**meekah
doll	**la bambola**	lah **bahm**boalah
flask of Chianti	**il fiasco di Chianti**	eel fee**aa**skoa dee kee**ahn**tee
glassware	**gli articoli di vetro**	lyee ahr**tee**koalee dee **veh**troa
jewellery	**i gioielli**	ee joee**eh**llee
knitwear	**la maglieria**	lah mahlyay**ree**ah
leather work	**la pelletteria**	lah payllayttay**ree**ah
needlework	**il ricamo**	eel ree**kaa**moa
porcelain	**la porcellana**	lah poarchay**llaa**nah
silk	**la seta**	lah **sai**tah
woodwork	**il lavoro in legno**	eel lah**voa**roa een **leh**ñoa

Some typical products of Switzerland are:

chocolate	**il cioccolato**	eel choakkoa**laa**toa
cuckoo clock	**l'orologio a cucù**	loaroa**lo**joa ah koo**koo**
fondue forks/pot	**le forchette/il pentolino per la fonduta**	lay foar**kayt**tay/eel payntoa**lee**noa pair lah foan**doo**tah
watch	**l'orologio**	loaroa**lo**joa

Records—Cassettes *Dischi—Cassette*

Do you have any records by ...?	**Avete dischi di ...?**	ah**vay**tay **dee**skee dee
I'd like a ...	**Vorrei ...**	vor**rai**ee
cassette	**una cassetta**	**oo**nah kahs**sayt**tah
video cassette	**una video cassetta**	**oo**nah **vee**dayoa kahs**sayt**tah
compact disc	**un disco compatto**	oon **dee**skoa koam**paht**toa

Have you any songs by ...?	**Avete delle canzoni di ...?**	ahv**ay**tay **dayl**lay kahn**tsoa**nee dee
Can I listen to this record?	**Posso ascoltare questo disco?**	**pos**soa ahskoal**taa**ray koo**ay**stoa **dee**skoa

L.P. (33 rpm)	**33 giri**	trayntah**tray jee**ree
E.P. (45 rpm)	**super 45 giri**	**soo**pair kwahrahntah**cheeng**kooay **jee**ree
single	**45 giri**	kwahrahntah**cheeng**kooay **jee**ree

chamber music	**musica da camera**	**moo**zeekah dah **kaa**mayrah
classical music	**musica classica**	**moo**zeekah **klahs**seekah
folk music	**musica folcloristica**	**moo**zeekah folk**loree**steekah
instrumental music	**musica strumentale**	**moo**zeekah stroomayn**taa**lay
jazz	**jazz**	"jazz"
light music	**musica leggera**	**moo**zeekah lay**djai**rah
orchestral music	**musica sinfonica**	**moo**zeekah seen**fo**neekah
pop music	**musica pop**	**moo**zeekah pop

Toys *Giocattoli*

I'd like a toy/ game ...	**Vorrei un giocattolo/ un gioco ...**	vor**rai**ee oon joa**kaht**toaloa/oon **joa**koa
for a boy	**per un bambino**	pair oon bahm**bee**noa
for a 5-year-old girl	**per una bambina di 5 anni**	pair **oo**nah bahm**bee**nah dee 5 **ahn**nee
beach ball	**un pallone (da spiaggia)**	oon pahl**loa**nay (dah spee**ahd**jah)
bucket and spade (pail and shovel)	**un secchiello e una paletta**	oon sayk**keeayl**loa ay **oo**nah pah**layt**tah
building blocks (bricks)	**un gioco di costruzioni**	oon **joa**koa dee koastroo**tseeoa**nee
card game	**delle carte da gioco**	**dayl**lay **kahr**tay dah **joa**koa
chess set	**degli scacchi**	**day**lyee **skahk**kee
doll	**una bambola**	**oo**nah **bahm**boalah
electronic game	**un gioco elettronico**	oon **joa**koa aylayt**tro**neekoa
flippers	**delle pinne**	**dayl**lay **peen**nay
roller skates	**dei pattini a rotelle**	**dai**ee **paht**teenee ah ro**tehl**lay
snorkel	**la maschera da subacqueo**	lah **mah**skayrah dah soo**bahk**kooayoa

Your money: banks—currency

Italy's monetary unit is the *lira* (**lee**rah), plural *lire* (**lee**ray), abbreviated to *L.* or *Lit.* There are coins of 10, 20, 50, 100, 200 and 500 lire. Banknotes come in denomination of 500, 1,000, 2,000, 5,000, 10,000, 50,000 and 100,000 lire.

In Switzerland, the basic unit currency is the *franco* (**frahng**koa) divided into 100 *centesimi* (chayn**tay**zeemee). There are coins of 5, 10, 20 and 50 centimes and of 1, 2 and 5 francs. There are banknotes of 10, 20, 50, 100, 500 and 1,000 francs.

Though hours can vary, banks in Italy are generally open from 8.30 to 1 p.m. and from 2.30 to 3.30 p.m., Monday to Friday.

In Switzerland banks are generally open from 8.30 or 9 a.m. to noon and from 1.30 or 2 to 4.30 or 5 p.m., Monday to Friday. Main branches often remain open during the lunch hours.

In both countries you will find currency-exchange offices *(uffici cambio)* which are often open outside regular banking hours.

Credit cards may be used in an increasing number of hotels, restaurants, shops, etc. Signs are posted indicating which cards are accepted.

Traveller's cheques are accepted by hotels, travel agents and many shops, although the exchange rate is invariably better at a bank. Don't forget to take your passport when going to cash a traveller's cheque. Eurocheques are also accepted.

Where's the nearest bank?	**Dov'è la banca più vicina?**	doa**vai** lah **bahng**kah pee**oo** vee**chee**nah
Where is the currency exchange office?	**Dov'è l'ufficio cambio?**	doa**vai** looff**ee**choa **kahm**beeoa

At the bank *In banca*

I want to change some dollars/pounds.	**Desidero cambiare dei dollari/delle sterline.**	day**zee**dayroa kahmbee**aa**ray **daiee dol**lahree/**dayl**lay stayr**lee**nay
I want to cash a traveller's cheque/Eurocheque.	**Voglio incassare un traveller's cheque/un eurocheque.**	**vol**yoa eengkahs**saa**ray oon "traveller's cheque"/oon "eurocheque"
What's the exchange rate?	**Qual è il corso del cambio?**	kwahl ai eel **koar**soa dayl **kahm**beeoa
How much commission do you charge?	**Quanto trattiene di commissione?**	**kwahn**toa trahttee**ay**nay dee koammeessee**oa**nay
Can you cash a personal cheque?	**Può cambiare un assegno personale?**	pwo kahmbee**aa**ray oon ahs**say**ñoa payrsoa**naa**lay
Can you telex my bank in London?	**Può mandare un telex alla mia banca a Londra?**	pwo mahn**daa**ray oon "telex" **ahl**lah **mee**ah **bahng**kah ah **loan**drah
I have a/an/some ...	**Ho ...**	oa
bank card	**una carta d'identità bancaria**	**oo**nah **kahr**tah deedayntee**tah** bahng**kaa**reeah
credit card	**una carta di credito**	**oo**nah **kahr**tah dee **kray**deetoa
introduction from ...	**una lettera di presentazione di ...**	**oo**nah **leht**tayrah dee prayzayntahtsee**oa**nay dee
letter of credit	**una lettera di credito**	**oo**nah **leht**tayrah dee **kray**deetoa
I'm expecting some money from New York. Has it arrived?	**Aspetto del denaro da New York. È arrivato?**	ah**speht**toa dayl day**naa**roa dah "New York". ai ahrree**vaa**toa
Please give me ... notes (bills) and some small change.	**Per favore, mi dia ... banconote e della moneta.**	pair fah**voa**ray mee **dee**ah ... bahngkoa**no**tay ay **dayl**lah moa**nay**tah

Depositing—Withdrawing *Depositi—Prelevamenti*

I want to credit this to my account.	**Desidero accreditare questo sul mio conto.**	day**zee**dayroa ahkkraydee**taa**ray koo**ay**stoa sool **mee**oa **koan**toa
I want to ...	**Desidero ...**	day**zee**dayroa
open an account	**aprire un conto**	ah**pree**ray oon **koan**toa
withdraw ... lire	**prelevare ... lire**	praylay**vaa**ray ... **lee**ray

NUMBERS, see page 147

I want to credit this to Mr...'s account.	**Desidero accreditare questo sul conto del signor ...**	day**zee**dayroa ahkkraydee**taa**ray koo**ay**stoa sool **koan**toa dayl see**ñoar**
Where should I sign?	**Dove devo firmare?**	**doa**vay **day**voa feer**maa**ray

Business terms *Termini d'affari*

My name is ...	**Mi chiamo ...**	mee kee**aa**moa
Here's my card.	**Ecco il mio bigliettino.**	**eh**kkoa eel **mee**oa beelyayt**tee**noa
I have an appointment with ...	**Ho un appuntamento con ...**	oa oon appoontah**mayn**toa kon
Can you give me an estimate of the cost?	**Può farmi un preventivo?**	pwo **faar**mee oon prayvayn**tee**voa
What's the rate of inflation?	**Qual è il tasso di inflazione?**	kwahl ai eel **tah**ssoa dee eenflahtsee**oa**nay
Can you provide me with an interpreter/ a secretary?	**Può procurarmi un interprete/una segretaria?**	pwo prokoo**raar**mee oon een**tehr**prehtay/**oo**nah saygray**taa**reeah
Where can I make photocopies?	**Dove posso fare delle fotocopie?**	**doa**vay **po**ssoa **faa**ray **dayl**lay foto**kaw**peeay

amount	**l'importo**	leem**poar**toa
balance	**il bilancio**	eel bee**lahn**choa
capital	**il capitale**	eel kahpee**taa**lay
cheque book	**il libretto d'assegni**	eel lee**breht**toa dahs**say**ñee
contract	**il contratto**	eel koan**traht**toa
expenses	**le spese**	lay **spay**say
interest	**l'interesse**	leentay**rehs**say
investment	**l'investimento**	leenvaystee**mayn**toa
invoice	**la fattura**	lah faht**too**rah
loss	**la perdita**	lah **payr**deetah
mortgage	**l'ipoteca**	leepoa**tay**kah
payment	**il pagamento**	eel pahgah**mayn**toa
percentage	**la percentuale**	lah payrchayntoo**aa**lay
profit	**il profitto**	eel proa**feet**toa
purchase	**l'acquisto**	lahkoo**ee**stoa
sale	**la vendita**	lah **vayn**deetah
share	**l'azione**	lahtsee**oa**nay
transfer	**il trasferimento**	eel trahsfayree**mayn**toa
value	**il valore**	eel vah**loa**ray

At the post office

Post offices in Italy bear the sign *PT* and are normally open from 8.15 a.m. to 1 or 2 p.m., Monday to Friday, Saturday till 12 noon or 1 p.m. Offices in major towns and tourist resorts stay open longer, but often for urgent matters only. Stamps are also sold at tobacconist's *(tabaccaio)* and at some hotel desks. Letter boxes (mailboxes) are red in Italy, and yellow in Switzerland.

Swiss post offices are recognized by a *PTT* sign and are open from 7.30 a.m. to noon and from 1.45 to 6.30 p.m., Monday to Friday, Saturday till 11 a.m.

Note that telephone service in Italy is generally separated from the post office.

Where's the nearest post office?	**Dov'è l'ufficio postale più vicino?**	doa**vai** looff**ee**choa poa**staa**lay peeoo vee**chee**noa
What time does the post office open/close?	**A che ora apre/chiude l'ufficio postale?**	ah kay **oa**rah **aa**pray/kee**oo**day looff**ee**choa poa**staa**lay
A stamp for this letter/postcard, please.	**Un francobollo per questa lettera/cartolina, per favore.**	oon frahngkoa**boal**loa pair koo**ay**stah **leht**tayrah/kahrtoa**lee**nah pair fah**voa**ray
I want 2 ... -lire stamps.	**Vorrei 2 francobolli da ... lire.**	vor**rai**ee 2 frahngkoa**boal**lee dah ... **lee**ray
What's the postage for a letter to London?	**Qual è l'affrancatura per una lettera per Londra?**	kwahl ai lahffrahngkah**too**rah pair **oo**nah **leht**tayrah pair **loan**drah
What's the postage for a postcard to Los Angeles?	**Qual è l'affrancatura per una cartolina per Los Angeles?**	kwahl ai lahffrahngkah**too**rah pair **oo**nah kahrtoa**lee**nah pair "Los Angeles"
Where's the letter box (mailbox)?	**Dov'è la cassetta delle lettere?**	doa**vai** lah kahs**seht**tah **dayl**lay **leht**tayray
I want to send this parcel.	**Vorrei spedire questo pacco.**	vor**rai**ee spay**dee**ray koo**ay**stoa **pahk**koa

I want to send this by ...	**Desidero inviare questo per ...**	day**zee**dayroa eenvee**aa**ray koo**ay**stoa pair
airmail	**via aerea**	**vee**ah ah**ay**rayah
express (special delivery)	**espresso**	ay**sprehs**soa
registered mail	**raccomandata**	rahkkoamahn**daa**tah
At which counter can I cash an international money order?	**A quale sportello posso riscuotere un vaglia internazionale?**	ah **kwaa**lay spor**tehl**loa **pos**soa rees**kwo**tayray oon **vaa**lyah eentayr-nahtseeoa**naa**lay
Where's the poste restante (general delivery)?	**Dov'è lo sportello del fermo posta?**	doa**vai** loa spoar**tehl**loa dayl **fayr**moa **pos**tah
Is there any mail for me? My name is ...	**C'è della posta per me? Mi chiamo ...**	chai **dayl**lah **pos**tah pair may? mee kee**aa**moa

FRANCOBOLLI	STAMPS
PACCHI	PARCELS
VAGLIA POSTALI	MONEY ORDERS

Telegrams *Telegrammi*

In Italy and Switzerland, you can either go directly to the post-office to send a telegram or phone it in. Some telegraph offices are open 24 hours a day.

I want to send a telegram/telex.	**Vorrei inviare un telegramma/telex.**	vor**raiee** eenvee**aa**ray oon taylay**grahm**mah/"telex"
May I please have a form?	**Può darmi un modulo?**	pwo **daar**mee oon **mo**dooloa
How much is it per word?	**Quanto costa ogni parola?**	**kwahn**toa **kos**tah oñee pah**ro**lah
How long will a cable to Boston take?	**Quanto tempo ci vorrà per inviare un telegramma a Boston?**	**kwahn**toa **tehm**poa chee vor**rah** pair eenvee**aa**ray oon taylay**grahm**mah ah **bos**ton
How much will this telex cost?	**Quanto costerà questo telex?**	**kwahn**toa koastay**rah** koo**ay**stoa "telex"

Telephoning *Per telefonare*

The telephone system in Italy and Switzerland is virtually entirely automatic. International or long-distance calls can be made from phone boxes, or ask at your hotel. Local calls in Italy can also be made from cafés, where you might have to pay after the call or to buy a *gettone* (token) to put into the phone.

Telephone numbers are given in pairs in Italy so that 12 34 56 would be expressed in Italian, twelve, thirty-four, fifty-six.

Where's the telephone?	**Dov'è il telefono?**	doa**vai** eel tay**lay**foanoa
I'd like a telephone token.	**Vorrei un gettone (telefonico).**	vor**rai**ee oon jayt**toa**nay (taylay**fo**neekoa)
Where's the nearest telephone booth?	**Dov'è la cabina telefonica più vicina?**	doa**vai** lah kah**bee**nah taylay**fo**neekah pee**oo** vee**chee**nah
May I use your phone?	**Posso usare il suo telefono?**	**pos**soa oo**zaa**ray eel **soo**oa tay**lay**foanoa
Do you have a telephone directory for Rome?	**Ha un elenco telefonico di Roma?**	ah oon ay**layng**koa taylay**fo**neekoa dee **roa**mah
What's the dialling (area) code for ...?	**Qual è il prefisso di ...?**	kwahl ai eel pray**fees**soa dee
How do I get the international operator?	**Come si ottiene il servizio internazionale?**	**koa**may see ottee**ay**nay eel sayr**vee**tseeoa eentayrnahtseeoa**naa**lay

Operator *Centralinista*

Good morning, I want Venice 12 34 56.	**Buon giorno. Desidero il 12 34 56 di Venezia.**	bwon **joar**noa. day**zee**dayroa eel 12 34 56 dee vay**nai**tseeah
Can you help me get this number?	**Mi può aiutare a ottenere questo numero?**	mee pwo aheeoo**taa**ray ah oattay**nay**ray koo**ay**stoa **noo**mayroa

NUMBERS, see page 147

I want to place a ...	**Vorrei fare ...**	vorr**aiee** f**aa**ray
personal (person-to-person) call	**una telefonata con preavviso**	**oo**nah taylayfoa**naa**tah kon prayahv**vee**zoa
reversed charge (collect) call	**una telefonata a carico del destinatario**	**oo**nah taylayfoa**naa**tah ah **kaa**reekoa dayl daysteenah**taa**reeoa

Speaking *Al telefono*

Hello. This is ... speaking.	**Pronto. Qui parla ...**	**pron**toa. koo**ee** **pahr**lah
I want to speak to ...	**Vorrei parlare a ...**	vorr**aiee** pahr**laa**ray ah
I want extension ...	**Mi dia la linea interna ...**	mee **dee**ah lah **lee**nayah een**tehr**nah
Speak louder/more slowly, please.	**Parli più forte/più lentamente, per favore.**	**pahr**lee pee**oo** **for**tay/pee**oo** layntah**mayn**tay pair fah**voa**ray

Bad luck *Sfortuna*

Would you please try again later?	**Per favore, vuol provare di nuovo più tardi?**	pair fah**voa**ray vwawl proa**vaa**ray dee **nwaw**voa pee**oo** **tahr**dee
Operator, you gave me the wrong number.	**Signorina, mi ha dato il numero sbagliato.**	seeñoa**ree**nah mee ah **daa**toa eel **noo**mayroa zbah**lyaa**toa
Operator, we were cut off.	**Signorina, la comunicazione si è interrotta.**	seeñoa**ree**nah lah komooneekahtsee**oa**nay see ai eentehr**roat**tah

Telephone alphabet

A	**Ancona**	ahng**koa**nah	N	**Napoli**	**naa**poalee
B	**Bari**	**baa**ree	O	**Otranto**	**oa**trahntoa
C	**Catania**	kah**taa**neeah	P	**Palermo**	pah**lehr**moa
D	**Domodossola**	doamoa**dos**soalah	Q	**Quarto**	**kwahr**toa
E	**Empoli**	**aym**poalee	R	**Roma**	**roa**mah
F	**Firenze**	fee**rehn**tsay	S	**Sassari**	**sahs**sahree
G	**Genova**	**jai**noavah	T	**Torino**	taw**ree**noa
H	**Hotel**	oa**tehl**	U	**Udine**	**oo**deenay
I	**Imperia**	eem**pay**reeah	V	**Venezia**	vay**nait**seeah
J	**i lunga**	ee **loong**gah	W	**v doppia**	vee **doap**peeah
K	**kappa**	**kahp**pah	X	**ix**	eekss
L	**Livorno**	lee**voar**noa	Y	**i greca**	ee **gray**kah
M	**Milano**	mee**laa**noa	Z	**zeta**	**dzai**tah

Not there *La persona è assente*

When will he/she be back?	**Quando ritornerà?**	**kwahn**doa reetoarneh**rah**
Will you tell him/her I called? My name is ...	**Vuol dirgli/dirle che ho telefonato? Mi chiamo ...**	vwawl **deer**lyee/**deer**lay kay oa taylayfoa**naa**toa. mee kee**aa**moa
Would you ask him/her to call me?	**Può chiedergli/ chiederle di telefonarmi?**	pwo kee**ai**dayrlyee/ kee**ai**dayrlay dee taylay-foa**naar**mee
Would you please take a message?	**Per favore, può trasmettere un messaggio?**	pair fah**voa**ray pwo trahz**mayt**tayray oon mays**sahd**joa

Charges *Costo della telefonata*

What was the cost of that call?	**Quanto è costata la telefonata?**	**kwahn**toa ai kos**taa**tah lah taylayfoa**naa**tah
I want to pay for the call.	**Desidero pagare la telefonata.**	dayzee**e**dayroa pah**gaa**ray lah taylayfoa**naa**tah

C'è una telefonata per lei.	There's a telephone call for you.
Che numero chiama?	What number are you calling?
La linea è occupata.	The line's engaged.
Non risponde.	There's no answer.
Ha chiamato il numero sbagliato	You've got the wrong number.
Il telefono non funziona.	The phone is out of order.
Un momento!	Just a moment.
Resti in linea.	Hold on, please.
Egli/Ella è fuori in questo momento.	He's/She's out at the moment.

Doctor

To be at ease, make sure your health insurance policy covers any illness or accident while on holiday. If not, ask your insurance representative, automobile association or travel agent for details of special health insurance.

General *Generalità*

Can you get me a doctor?	**Può chiamarmi un medico?**	pwo keeah**maar**mee oon **mai**deekoa
Is there a doctor here?	**C'è un medico qui?**	chai oon **mai**deekoa koo**ee**
I need a doctor, quickly!	**Mi serve un medico— presto!**	mee **sayr**vay oon **mai**deekoa— **preh**stoa
Where can I find a doctor who speaks English?	**Dove posso trovare un medico che parla inglese?**	**doa**vay **pos**soa troa**vaa**ray oon **mai**deekoa kay **pahr**lah eeng**glay**say
Where's the surgery (doctor's office)?	**Dov'è l'ambulatorio del medico?**	doa**vai** lahmboolah**to**reeoa dayl **mai**deekoa
What are the surgery (office) hours?	**Quali sono le ore di consultazione?**	**kwah**lee **soa**noa lay **oa**ray dee koansooltahtsee**oa**nay
Could the doctor come to see me here?	**Il medico può venire a visitarmi qui?**	eel **mai**deekoa pwo vay**nee**ray ah veezee**taar**mee koo**ee**
What time can the doctor come?	**Quando può venire il medico?**	**kwahn**doa pwo vay**nee**ray eel **mai**deekoa
Can you recommend a/an ...?	**Può consigliarmi ...?**	pwo koansee**lyaar**mee
general practitioner	**un medico generico**	oon **mai**deekoa jeh**nay**reekoa
children's doctor	**un pediatra**	oon paydee**aa**trah
eye specialist	**un oculista**	oon okoo**lee**stah
gynaecologist	**un ginecologo**	oon jeenay**ko**loagoa
Can I have an appointment ...?	**Può fissarmi un appuntamento ...?**	pwo fees**saar**mee oon ahppoontah**mayn**toa
right now	**subito**	**soo**beetoa
tomorrow	**domani**	doa**maa**nee
as soon as possible	**il più presto possibile**	eel pee**oo** **preh**stoa pos**see**beelay

CHEMIST'S (PHARMACY), see page 108

Parts of the body *Parti del corpo*

appendix	**l'appendice**	lahppayn**dee**chay
arm	**il braccio**	eel **braht**choa
artery	**l'arteria**	lahr**tai**reeah
back	**la schiena**	lah skee**ai**nah
bladder	**la vescica**	lah vay**shee**kah
bone	**l'osso**	**los**soa
bowels	**l'intestino**	leentay**stee**noa
breast	**il petto**	eel **peht**toa
chest	**il torace**	eel toa**raa**chay
ear	**l'orecchio**	loa**rayk**keeoa
eye(s)	**l'occhio (gli occhi)**	**lok**keeoa (lyee **ok**kee)
face	**il viso**	eel **vee**zoa
finger	**il dito della mano**	eel **dee**toa **dayl**lah **maa**noa
foot	**il piede**	eel pee**ay**day
genitals	**i genitali**	ee jaynee**taa**lee
gland	**la ghiandola**	lah gee**ahn**doalah
hand	**la mano**	lah **maa**noa
head	**la testa**	lah **teh**stah
heart	**il cuore**	eel **kwo**ray
intestines	**l'intestino**	leentay**stee**noa
jaw	**la mascella**	lah mah**shehl**lah
joint	**l'articolazione**	lahrteekoalahtsee**oa**nay
kidney	**il rene**	eel **rai**nay
knee	**il ginocchio**	eel jee**nok**keeoa
leg	**la gamba**	lah **gahm**bah
lip	**il labbro**	eel **lahb**broa
liver	**il fegato**	eel **fay**gahtoa
lung	**il polmone**	eel poal**moa**nay
mouth	**la bocca**	lah **boak**kah
muscle	**il muscolo**	eel **moo**skoaloa
neck	**il collo**	eel **kol**loa
nerve	**il nervo**	eel **nehr**voa
nervous system	**il sistema nervoso**	eel see**stai**mah nehr**voa**soa
nose	**il naso**	eel **naa**soa
rib	**la costola**	lah **ko**stoalah
shoulder	**la spalla**	lah **spahl**lah
skin	**la pelle**	lah **pehl**lay
spine	**la spina dorsale**	lah **spee**nah doar**saa**lay
stomach	**lo stomaco**	loa **sto**mahkoa
tendon	**il tendine**	eel **tehn**deenay
throat	**la gola**	lah **goa**lah
toe	**il dito del piede**	eel **dee**toa dayl pee**ay**day
tongue	**la lingua**	lah **leeng**gwah
tonsils	**le tonsille**	lay toan**seel**lay
vein	**la vena**	lah **vay**nah

Accident—Injury *Incidente—Ferita*

There has been an accident.	**C'è stato un incidente.**	chai **staa**toa oon eenchee**dayn**tay
My child has had a fall.	**Il mio bambino/ la mia bambina è caduto(a).**	eel **mee**oa bahm**bee**noa/ lah **mee**ah bahm**bee**nah ai kah**doo**toa(ah)
He/She has hurt his/ her head.	**Lui/Lei si è fatto(a) male alla testa.**	**loo**ee/**lay**ee see ai **faht**toa(ah) **maa**lay **ahl**lah **teh**stah
He's/She's unconscious.	**È svenuto(a).**	ai zvay**noo**toa(ah)
He's/She's bleeding heavily.	**Perde molto sangue.**	**payr**day **moal**toa **sahng**gooay
He's/She's (seriously) injured.	**È (gravemente) ferito(a).**	ai (grahvai**mayn**tay) fay**ree**toa(ah)
His/Her arm is broken.	**Si è rotto(a) il braccio.**	see ai **rot**toa(ah) eel **braht**choa
His/Her ankle is swollen.	**Ha la caviglia gonfia.**	ah lah kah**vee**lyah **goan**feeah
I've been stung.	**Sono stato punto.**	**soa**noa **staa**toa **poon**toa
I've got something in my eye.	**Ho qualcosa nell'occhio.**	oa kwahl**kaw**sah nehl**lok**keeoa
I've got a/an ...	**Ho ...**	oa
blister	**una vescica**	**oo**nah vay**shee**kah
boil	**un foruncolo**	oon foa**roong**koaloa
bruise	**una contusione**	**oo**nah koantoozee**oa**nay
burn	**una scottatura**	**oo**nah skottah**too**rah
cut	**un taglio**	oon **taa**lyoa
graze	**un'escoriazione**	oonayskoareeahtsee**oa**nay
insect bite	**una puntura d'insetto**	**oo**nah poon**too**rah deen**seht**toa
lump	**un bernoccolo**	oon bayr**nok**koaloa
rash	**un esantema**	oon ayzahn**teh**mah
sting	**una puntura**	**oo**nah poon**too**rah
swelling	**un gonfiore**	oon goanfee**oa**ray
wound	**una ferita**	**oo**nah fay**ree**tah
Could you have a look at it?	**Può esaminarlo?**	pwo ayzahmee**naar**loa
I can't move my ...	**Non posso muovere ...**	noan **pos**soa **mwo**vayray
It hurts.	**Mi fa male.**	mee fah **maa**lay

Dove fa male?	Where does it hurt?
Che genere di dolore è?	What kind of pain is it?
debole/acuto/lancinante costante/a intervalli	dull/sharp/throbbing constant/on and off
È ...	It's ...
rotto/distorto slogato/lacerato	broken/sprained dislocated/torn
Voglio che faccia una radiografia.	I want you to have an X-ray taken.
Sarà ingessato.	You'll get a plaster.
Ha fatto infezione.	It's infected.
È stato vaccinato(a) contro il tetano?	Have you been vaccinated against tetanus?
Le darò un antisettico/ un antinevralgico.	I'll give you an antiseptic/ a painkiller.

Illness *Malattia*

I'm not feeling well.	**Non mi sento bene.**	noan mee **sayn**toa **bai**nay
I'm ill.	**Mi sento male.**	mee **sayn**toa **maa**lay
I feel ...	**Mi sento ...**	mee **sayn**toa
dizzy nauseous shivery	**stordito(a) la nausea rabbrividire**	stoar**dee**toa(ah) lah **now**zayah rahbbreevee**dee**ray
I've got a fever.	**Ho la febbre.**	oa lah **fehb**bray
My temperature is 38 degrees.	**Ho la febbre a 38.**	oa lah **fehb**bray ah 38
I've been vomiting.	**Ho vomitato.**	oa voamee**taa**toa
I'm constipated/ I've got diarrhoea.	**Sono costipato(a)/ Ho la diarrea.**	**soa**noa koastee**paa**toa(ah)/ oa lah deeahr**ray**ah
My ... hurt(s).	**Ho male al/alla ...**	oa **maa**lay ahl/**ahl**lah
I have a nosebleed.	**Mi sanguina il naso.**	mee **sahng**gooeenah eel **naa**soa

NUMBERS, see page 147

I've got (a/an) ...	**Ho ...**	oa
asthma	**l'asma**	**lah**zmah
backache	**il mal di schiena**	eel mahl dee skee**ai**nah
cold	**il raffreddore**	eel rahffrayd**doa**ray
cough	**la tosse**	lah **tos**say
cramps	**i crampi**	ee **krahm**pee
earache	**il mal d'orecchi**	eel mahl doa**rayk**kee
hay fever	**la febbre del fieno**	lah **fehb**bray dayl fee**eh**noa
headache	**il mal di testa**	eel mahl dee **teh**stah
indigestion	**un'indigestione**	ooneendeejaystee**oa**nay
palpitations	**delle palpitazioni**	**dayl**lay pahlpeetahtsee**oa**nee
rheumatism	**i reumatismi**	ee rayoomah**tee**zmee
sore throat	**il mal di gola**	eel mahl dee **goa**lah
stiff neck	**il torcicollo**	eel torchee**kol**loa
stomach ache	**il mal di stomaco**	eel mahl dee **sto**mahkoa
sunstroke	**un colpo di sole**	oon **koal**poa dee **soa**lay
I have difficulties breathing.	**Ho difficoltà a respirare.**	oa deeffeekol**tah** ah rayspee**raa**ray
I have a pain in my chest.	**Ho un dolore nel torace.**	oa oon doa**loa**ray nehl toa**raa**chay
I had a heart attack ... years ago.	**Ho avuto un attacco cardiaco ... anni fa.**	oa ah**voo**toa oon aht**tahk**koa kahr**dee**ahkoa ... **ahn**nee fah
My blood pressure is too high/too low.	**La mia pressione è troppo alta/troppo bassa.**	lah **mee**ah prehssee**oa**nay ai **trop**poa **ahl**tah/**trop**poa **bahs**sah
I'm allergic to ...	**Sono allergico a ...**	**soa**noa ahl**layr**jeekoa ah
I'm a diabetic.	**Ho il diabete.**	oa eel deeah**beh**tay

Women's section *Sezione femminile*

I have period pains.	**Ho delle mestruazioni dolorose.**	oa **dayl**lay maystrooahtsee**oa**nee doaloa**raw**say
I have a vaginal infection.	**Ho un'infezione vaginale.**	oa ooneenfaytsee**oa**nay vahjee**naa**lay
I'm on the pill.	**Prendo la pillola.**	**prehn**doa lah **peel**loalah
I haven't had my period for 2 months.	**Non ho avuto le mestruazioni per 2 mesi.**	noan oa ah**voo**toa lay maystrooahtsee**oa**nee pair 2 **mai**see
I'm (3 months) pregnant.	**Sono incinta (di 3 mesi).**	**soa**noa een**cheen**tah (dee 3 **mai**see)

Da quanto tempo si sente così?	How long have you been feeling like this?
È la prima volta che ha questo disturbo?	Is this the first time you've had this?
Le misuro la pressione/ la febbre.	I'll take your blood pressure/ temperature.
Tiri su la manica.	Roll up your sleeve, please.
Si spogli (fino alla vita).	Please undress (down to the waist).
Per favore, si sdrai qui.	Please lie down over there.
Apra la bocca.	Open your mouth.
Respiri profondamente.	Breathe deeply.
Tossisca, prego.	Cough, please.
Dove sente il dolore?	Where do you feel the pain?
Lei ha ...	You've got (a/an) ...
l'appendicite	appendicitis
un avvelenamento da cibi	food poisoning
una cistite	cystitis
la gastrite	gastritis
un'infiammazione a ...	inflammation of ...
l'influenza	flu
l'itterizia	jaundice
una malattia venerea	venereal disease
il morbillo	measles
la polmonite	pneumonia
Le farò un'iniezione.	I'll give you an injection.
Desidero un campione del sangue/dell'urina/delle feci.	I want a specimen of your blood/urine/stools.
Deve restare a letto per ... giorni.	You must stay in bed for ... days.
Deve consultare uno specialista.	I want you to see a specialist.
Deve andare all'ospedale per un controllo generale.	I want you to go to the hospital for a general check-up.
Deve essere operato(a).	You'll have to have an operation.

Prescription—Treatment *Ricetta—Cura*

This is my usual medicine.	**Questa è la mia medicina abituale.**	koo**ay**stah ai lah **mee**ah maydee**chee**nah ahbeetoo**aa**lay
Can you give me a prescription for this?	**Può farmi una ricetta per questo?**	pwo **faar**mee **oo**nah ree**chay**ttah pair koo**ay**stoa
Can you prescribe a/an/some ...?	**Può prescrivermi ...?**	pwo pray**skree**vayrmee
antidepressant	**un antidepressivo**	oon ahnteedayprehs**see**voa
sleeping pills	**dei sonniferi**	**da**iee soan**nee**fayree
tranquillizer	**un tranquillante**	oon trahngkooeel**lahn**tay
I'm allergic to antibiotics/penicillin.	**Sono allergico(a) agli antibiotici/alla penicillina.**	**soa**noa ahl**layr**jeekoa(ah) **ah**lyee ahnteebee**oa**teechee/ **ahl**lah paineecheel**lee**nah
I don't want anything too strong.	**Non voglio qualcosa troppo forte.**	noan **vo**lyoa kwahl**kaw**sah **trop**poa **foar**tay
How many times a day should I take it?	**Quante volte al giorno devo prenderla?**	**kwahn**tay **vol**tay ahl **joar**noa **day**voa **prehn**dayrlah
Must I swallow them whole?	**Devo inghiottirle intere?**	**day**voa eenggeeoat**teer**lay een**tay**ray

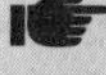

Che cura fa?	What treatment are you having?
Che medicine prende?	What medicine are you taking?
Per iniezioni o via orale?	By injection or orally?
Prenda ... cucchiaini di questa medicina ...	Take ... teaspoons of this medicine ...
Prenda una compressa con un bicchiere d'acqua ...	Take one pill with a glass of water ...
ogni ... ore	every ... hours
... volte al giorno	... times a day
prima/dopo ogni pasto	before/after each meal
al mattino/alla sera	in the morning/at night
in caso di dolore	if there is any pain
per ... giorni	for ... days

CHEMIST'S (PHARMACY), see page 108

Fee *Onorario*

How much do I owe you?	**Quanto le devo?**	kwahntoa lay dayvoa
May I have a receipt for my health insurance?	**Posso avere una ricevuta per la mia assicurazione malattia?**	possoa ahvayray oonah reechayvootah pair lah meeah asseekoorahtseeoanay mahlahtteeah
Can I have a medical certificate?	**Posso avere un certificato medico?**	possoa ahvayray oon chayrteefeekaatoa maideekoa
Would you fill in this health insurance form, please?	**Potrebbe compilare questo modulo per l'assicurazione malattie, per favore?**	potrehbbay koampeelaaray kooaystoa moadooloa pair lasseekoorahtseeoanay mahlahtteeay pair fahvoaray

Hospital *Ospedale*

What are the visiting hours?	**Quali sono gli orari di visita?**	kwahlee soanoa lyee oraaree dee veezeetah
When can I get up?	**Quando posso alzarmi?**	kwahndoa possoa ahltsaarmee
When will the doctor come?	**Quando verrà il dottore?**	kwahndoa vayrrah eel dottawray
I'm in pain.	**Ho male.**	oa maalay
I can't eat/I can't sleep.	**Non ho appetito/ Non riesco a dormire.**	noan oa ahppayteetoa/ noan reeehskoa ah doarmeeray
Can I have a painkiller/some sleeping pills?	**Posso avere un calmante/dei sonniferi?**	possoa ahvayray oon kahlmahntay/daiee soanneefayree
Where is the bell?	**Dov'è il campanello?**	doavai eel kahmpahnehlloa

nurse	**l'infermiera**	leenfayrmeeayrah
patient	**il/la paziente**	eel/lah pahtseeaintay
anaesthetic	**l'anestetico**	lahnaystayteekoa
blood transfusion	**la trasfusione di sangue**	lah trahsfoozeeoanay dee sahnggooay
injection	**l'iniezione**	leeneeaytseeoanay
operation	**l'operazione**	loapayrahtseeoanay
bed	**il letto**	eel lehttoa
bedpan	**la padella**	lah pahdehllah
thermometer	**il termometro**	eel tayrmomaytroa

Dentist *Dentista*

Can you recommend a good dentist?	**Può consigliarmi un buon dentista?**	pwo koanseel**yahr**mee oon bwawn dayn**tee**stah
Can I make an (urgent) appointment to see Dr . . .?	**Desidero un appuntamento (urgente) con il dottor/la dottoressa . . .**	day**zee**dayroa oon ahppoontah**mayn**toa (oor**jehn**tay) kon eel doat**toar**/lah doatoa**rehs**sah
Can't you possibly make it earlier than that?	**Non è possibile prima?**	noan ai poas**see**beelay **pree**mah
I have a broken tooth.	**Mi sono rotto un dente.**	mee **soa**noa **rot**toa oon **dehn**tay
I have a toothache.	**Ho mal di denti.**	oa mahl dee **dehn**tee
I have an abscess.	**Ho un ascesso.**	oa oon ah**shehs**soa
This tooth hurts.	**Mi fa male questo dente.**	mee fah **maa**lay koo**ay**stoa **dehn**tay
at the top	**in alto**	een **ahl**toa
at the bottom	**in basso**	een **bahs**soa
in the front	**davanti**	dah**vahn**tee
at the back	**dietro**	dee**eh**troa
Can you fix it temporarily?	**Può curarlo provvisoriamente?**	pwo koo**raar**loa proavvee-zoareeah**mayn**tay
I don't want it extracted.	**Non voglio un'estrazione.**	noan **vol**yoa oonaystrah-tsee**oa**nay
Could you give me an anaesthetic?	**Potrebbe farmi l'anestesia?**	po**trehb**bay **faar**mee lahnaystay**zee**ah
I've lost a filling.	**L'otturazione si è staccata.**	loattoorahtsee**oa**nay see ai stahk**kaa**tah
The gum . . .	**La gengiva . . .**	lah jayn**jee**vah
is very sore	**è infiammata**	ai eenfeeahm**maa**tah
is bleeding	**sanguina**	**sahng**gooeenah
I've broken this denture.	**Ho rotto questa dentiera.**	oa **roat**toa koo**ay**stah daynteee**eh**rah
Can you repair this denture?	**Può ripararmi questa dentiera?**	pwo reepah**raar**mee koo**ay**stah daynteee**eh**rah
When will it be ready?	**Quando sarà pronta?**	**kwahn**doa sah**rah** **proan**tah

Reference section

Where do you come from? *Da dove viene?*

Africa	**l'Africa**	**laa**freekah
Asia	**l'Asia**	**laa**zeeah
Australia	**l'Australia**	low**straa**leeah
Europe	**l'Europa**	layoo**ro**pah
North America	**l'America del Nord**	lah**mai**reekah dayl nord
South America	**l'America del Sud**	lah**mai**reekah dayl sood
Algeria	**l'Algeria**	lahljay**ree**ah
Austria	**l'Austria**	**low**streeah
Belgium	**il Belgio**	eel **behl**joa
Canada	**il Canada**	eel kahnah**dah**
China	**la Cina**	lah **chee**nah
Denmark	**la Danimarca**	lah dahnee**mahr**kah
England	**l'Inghilterra**	leengeel**teh**rrah
Finland	**la Finlandia**	lah feen**lahn**deeah
France	**la Francia**	lah **frahn**chah
Germany	**la Germania**	lah jayr**maa**neeah
Great Britain	**la Gran Bretagna**	lah grahn bray**taa**ñah
Greece	**la Grecia**	lah **grai**chah
India	**l'India**	**leen**deeah
Ireland	**l'Irlanda**	leer**lahn**dah
Israel	**Israele**	eesrah**ay**lay
Italy	**l'Italia**	lee**taa**leeah
Japan	**il Giappone**	eel jahp**poa**nay
Luxembourg	**il Lussemburgo**	eel loossaym**boor**goa
Morocco	**il Marocco**	eel mah**rok**koa
Netherlands	**l'Olanda**	lo**lahn**dah
New Zealand	**la Nuova Zelanda**	lah **nwaw**vah dzay**lahn**dah
Norway	**la Norvegia**	lah nor**vay**jah
Portugal	**il Portogallo**	eel porto**gahl**loa
Scotland	**la Scozia**	lah **skot**seeah
South Africa	**il Sudafrica**	eel soo**daa**freekah
Soviet Union	**l'Unione Sovietica**	looneeoanay soaveeehteekah
Spain	**la Spagna**	lah **spaa**ñah
Sweden	**la Svezia**	lah **sveh**tseeah
Switzerland	**la Svizzera**	lah **sveet**tsayrah
Tunisia	**la Tunisia**	lah tooneezeeah
Turkey	**la Turchia**	lah toorkeeah
United States	**gli Stati Uniti**	lyee **staa**tee oo**nee**tee
Wales	**il Galles**	eel **gahl**layss
Yugoslavia	**la Iugoslavia**	lah eeoogoa**slaa**veeah

Numbers *Numeri*

0	**zero**	**dzeh**roa
1	**uno**	**oo**noa
2	**due**	**doo**ay
3	**tre**	tray
4	**quattro**	**kwaht**troa
5	**cinque**	**cheeng**kooay
6	**sei**	**seh**ee
7	**sette**	**seht**tay
8	**otto**	**ot**toa
9	**nove**	**naw**vay
10	**dieci**	dee**ai**chee
11	**undici**	**oon**deechee
12	**dodici**	**doa**deechee
13	**tredici**	**tray**deechee
14	**quattordici**	kwaht**tor**deechee
15	**quindici**	koo**een**deechee
16	**sedici**	**say**deechee
17	**diciassette**	deechah**sseht**tay
18	**diciotto**	dee**chot**toa
19	**diciannove**	deechahn**naw**vay
20	**venti**	**vayn**tee
21	**ventuno**	vayn**too**noa
22	**ventidue**	vayntee**doo**ay
23	**ventitre**	vayntee**tray**
24	**ventiquattro**	vayntee**kwaht**troa
25	**venticinque**	vayntee**cheeng**kooay
26	**ventisei**	vayntee**seh**ee
27	**ventisette**	vayntee**seht**tay
28	**ventotto**	vayn**tot**toa
29	**ventinove**	vayntee**naw**vay
30	**trenta**	**trayn**tah
31	**trentuno**	trayn**too**noa
32	**trentadue**	trayntah**doo**ay
33	**trentatre**	traynta**tray**
40	**quaranta**	kwah**rahn**tah
41	**quarantuno**	kwahrahn**too**noa
42	**quarantadue**	kwahrahntah**doo**ay
43	**quarantatre**	kwahrahntah**tray**
50	**cinquanta**	cheeng**kwahn**tah
51	**cinquantuno**	cheengkwahn**too**noa
52	**cinquantadue**	cheengkwahntah**doo**ay
53	**cinquantatre**	cheengkwahntah**tray**
60	**sessanta**	say**ssahn**tah
61	**sessantuno**	sayssahn**too**noa
62	**sessantadue**	sayssahntah**doo**ay

63	**sessantatre**	sayssahntah**tray**
70	**settanta**	say**ttahn**tah
71	**settantuno**	sayttahn**too**noa
72	**settantadue**	sayttahntah**doo**ay
73	**settantatre**	sayttahntah**tray**
80	**ottanta**	o**ttahn**tah
81	**ottantuno**	ottahn**too**noa
82	**ottantadue**	ottahntah**doo**ay
83	**ottantatre**	ottahntah**tray**
90	**novanta**	noa**vahn**tah
91	**novantuno**	noavahn**too**noa
92	**novantadue**	noavahntah**doo**ay
93	**novantatre**	noavahntah**tray**
100	**cento**	**chehn**toa
101	**centouno**	chehntoa**oo**noa
102	**centodue**	chehntoa**doo**ay
110	**centodieci**	chehntoadee**ai**chee
120	**centoventi**	chehntoa**vayn**tee
130	**centotrenta**	chehntoa**trayn**tah
140	**centoquaranta**	chehntoakwah**rahn**tah
150	**centocinquanta**	chehntoacheeng**kwahn**tah
160	**centosessanta**	chehntoasays**sahn**tah
170	**centosettanta**	chehntoasay**ttahn**tah
180	**centottanta**	chehntot**tahn**tah
190	**centonovanta**	chehntoanoa**vahn**tah
200	**duecento**	dooay**chehn**toa
300	**trecento**	tray**chehn**toa
400	**quattrocento**	kwahttroa**chehn**toa
500	**cinquecento**	cheengkooay**chehn**toa
600	**seicento**	sehee**chehn**toa
700	**settecento**	sehttay**chehn**toa
800	**ottocento**	otto**chehn**toa
900	**novecento**	noavay**chehn**toa
1000	**mille**	**meel**lay
1100	**millecento**	meellay**chehn**toa
1200	**milleduecento**	meellaydooay**chehn**toa
2000	**duemila**	dooay**mee**lah
5000	**cinquemila**	cheengkooay**mee**lah
10,000	**diecimila**	deeaichee**mee**lah
50,000	**cinquantamila**	cheengkwahntah**mee**lah
100,000	**centomila**	chehntoa**mee**lah
1,000,000	**un milione**	oon mee**lyoa**nay
1,000,000,000	**un miliardo**	oon mee**lyahr**doa

first/second	**primo/secondo**	**pree**moa/say**koan**doa
third/fourth	**terzo/quarto**	**tehr**tsoa/**kwahr**toa
fifth/sixth	**quinto/sesto**	koo**een**toa/**seh**stoa
seventh/eighth	**settimo/ottavo**	**seht**teemoa/ott**aa**voa
ninth/tenth	**nono/decimo**	**no**noa/**deh**cheemoa
once	**una volta**	**oo**nah **vol**tah
twice	**due volte**	**doo**ay **vol**tay
three times	**tre volte**	tray **vol**tay
a half	**un mezzo**	oon **mehd**dzoa
half a ...	**mezzo ...**	**mehd**dzoa
half of ...	**metà di ...**	may**tah** dee
half (adj.)	**mezzo**	**mehd**dzoa
a quarter	**un quarto**	oon **kwahr**toa
one third	**un terzo**	oon **tehr**tsoa
a pair of	**un paio di**	oon **paa**eeoa dee
a dozen	**una dozzina**	**oo**nah doad**dzee**nah
one per cent	**uno per cento**	**oo**noa pair **chehn**toa
3.4%	**3,4%**	tray **veer**goalah **kwaht**troa pair **chehn**toa
1981	**millenovecentottantuno**	**meel**lay-noavay**chehnt**-ottahn**too**noa
1992	**millenovecento-novantadue**	**meel**lay-noavay**chehn**toa-noavahntah**doo**ay
2003	**duemilatre**	dooaymeelah**tray**

Year and age *Anno ed età*

year	**l'anno**	**lahn**noa
leap year	**l'anno bisestile**	**lahn**noa beesay**stee**lay
decade	**il decennio**	eel deh**chehn**neeoa
century	**il secolo**	eel **sai**koloa
this year	**quest'anno**	kooay**stahn**noa
last year	**l'anno scorso**	**lahn**noa **skoar**soa
next year	**l'anno prossimo**	**lahn**noa **pros**seemoa
each year	**ogni anno**	**o**ñee **ahn**noa
2 years ago	**2 anni fa**	2 **ahn**nee fah
in one year	**in un anno**	een oon **ahn**noa
in the eighties	**negli anni ottanta**	**nay**lyee **ahn**nee ott**ahn**tah
the 16th century	**il sedicesimo secolo**	eel sehdee**chay**zeemoa **sai**koloa
in the 20th century	**nel ventesimo secolo**	nayl vayn**tay**zeemoa **sai**koloa

How old are you?	**Quanti anni ha?**	kwahntee ahnnee ah
I'm 30 years old.	**Ho trent'anni.**	oa trayntahnnee
He/She was born in 1960.	**Lui/Lei è nato(a) nel millenovecento-sessanta.**	looee/laiee ai nahtoa(ah) nayl meellay-noavaychehn-toa-sayssahntah
What is his/her age?	**Quanti anni ha?**	kwahntee ahnnee ah
Children under 16 are not admitted.	**Vietato ai minori di sedici anni.**	veeaytaatoa ahee meenoa-ree dee saydeechee ahnnee

Seasons *Stagioni*

spring/summer	**la primavera/l'estate**	lah preemahvayrah/laystaatay
autumn/winter	**l'autunno/l'inverno**	lowtoonnoa/leenvehrnoa
in spring	**in primavera**	een preemahvayrah
during the summer	**durante l'estate**	doorahntay laystaatay
in autumn	**in autunno**	een owtoonnoa
during the winter	**durante l'inverno**	doorahntay leenvehrnoa
high season	**alta stagione**	ahltah stahjoanay
low season	**bassa stagione**	bahssah stahjoanay

Months *Mesi*

January	**gennaio***	jehnnaaeeoa
February	**febbraio**	fehbbraaeeoa
March	**marzo**	mahrtsoa
April	**aprile**	ahpreelay
May	**maggio**	mahdjoa
June	**giugno**	jooñoa
July	**luglio**	loolyoa
August	**agosto**	ahgoastoa
September	**settembre**	sayttehmbray
October	**ottobre**	oattoabray
November	**novembre**	noavehmbray
December	**dicembre**	deechehmbray
in September	**in settembre**	een sayttehmbray
since October	**da ottobre**	dah oattoabray
the beginning of January	**l'inizio di gennaio**	leeneetseeoa dee jehnnaaeeoa
the middle of February	**la metà di febbraio**	lah maytah dee fehbbraaeeoa
the end of March	**la fine di marzo**	lah feenay dee mahrtsoa

* The names of months aren't capitalized in Italian.

Days and Date *Giorni e data*

What day is it today?	**Che giorno è oggi?**	kay **joar**noa ai **o**djee
Sunday	**domenica***	doa**may**neekah
Monday	**lunedì**	loonay**dee**
Tuesday	**martedì**	mahrtay**dee**
Wednesday	**mercoledì**	mehrkoalay**dee**
Thursday	**giovedì**	joavay**dee**
Friday	**venerdì**	vaynayr**dee**
Saturday	**sabato**	**saa**bahtoa
It's ...	**È ...**	ai
July 1	**il primo luglio**	eel **pree**moa **loo**lyoa
March 10	**il 10 marzo**	eel dee**ai**chee **mahr**tsoa
in the morning	**al mattino**	ahl maht**tee**noa
during the day	**durante il giorno**	doo**rahn**tay eel **joar**noa
in the afternoon	**nel pomeriggio**	nayl poamay**ree**djoa
in the evening	**alla sera**	**ahl**lah **say**rah
at night	**la notte**	lah **not**tay
the day before yesterday	**ieri l'altro**	ee**ai**ree **lahl**troa
yesterday	**ieri**	ee**ai**ree
today	**oggi**	**o**djee
tomorrow	**domani**	doa**maa**nee
the day after tomorrow	**dopodomani**	dopoadoa**maa**nee
the day before	**il giorno prima**	eel **joar**noa **pree**mah
the next day	**il giorno seguente**	eel **joar**noa saygoo**ayn**tay
two days ago	**due giorni fa**	**doo**ay **joar**nee fah
in three days' time	**fra tre giorni**	frah tray **joar**nee
last week	**la settimana scorsa**	lah saytte**maa**nah **skoar**sah
next week	**la settimana prossima**	lah saytte**maa**nah **pros**seemah
for a fortnight (two weeks)	**per quindici giorni**	pair koo**een**deechee **joar**nee
birthday	**il compleanno**	eel koamplay**ahn**noa
day off	**il giorno di riposo**	eel **joar**noa dee ree**po**soa
holiday	**il giorno festivo**	eel **joar**noa fay**stee**voa
holidays/vacation	**le vacanze**	lay vah**kahn**tsay
week	**la settimana**	lah saytte**maa**nah
weekend	**il fine settimana**	eel **fee**nay saytte**maa**nah
working day	**il giorno feriale**	eel **joar**noa fayree**aa**lay

* The names of days aren't capitalized in Italian.

Public holidays *Giorni festivi*

While there may be additional regional holidays in Italy, only national holidays are cited below.

January 1	**Capodanno**	New Year's Day
January 6	**Epifania**	Epiphany
April 25	**Anniversario della Liberazione (1945)**	Liberation Day
May 1	**Festa del Lavoro**	Labour Day
August 15	**Ferragosto**	Assumption Day
November 1	**Ognissanti**	All Saints' Day
December 8	**L'Immacolata Concezione**	Immaculate Conception
December 25	**Natale**	Christmas Day
December 26	**Santo Stefano**	St. Stephen's Day
Movable date:	**Lunedì di Pasqua (Pasquetta)**	Easter Monday

Except for the 25th April, all the Italian holidays are celebrated in the Ticino, as well as the 19th March *(San Giuseppe),* 1st August (National Holiday), and the usual holidays *Ascensione* (Ascension Day), *Lunedì di Pentecoste* (Whit Monday) and *Corpus Domini.*

Greetings and wishes *Saluti e auguri*

Merry Christmas!	**Buon Natale!**	bwawn nah**taa**lay
Happy New Year!	**Buon anno!**	bwawn **ahn**noa
Happy Easter!	**Buona Pasqua!**	**bwaw**nah **pah**skwah
Happy birthday!	**Buon compleanno!**	bwawn koamplay**ahn**noa
Best wishes!	**Tanti auguri!**	**tahn**tee ahoo**goo**ree
Congratulations!	**Congratulazioni!**	koangrahtoolahtsee**oa**nee
Good luck/All the best!	**Buona fortuna!**	**bwaw**nah foar**too**nah
Have a good trip!	**Buon viaggio!**	bwawn vee**ah**djoa
Have a good holiday!	**Buone vacanze!**	**bwaw**nay vah**kahn**tsay
Best regards from ...	**I migliori saluti da ...**	ee meel**yoa**ree sah**loo**tee dah
My regards to ...	**I miei saluti a ...**	ee mee**ai**ee sah**loo**tee ah

What time is it? *Che ore sono?*

Excuse me. Can you tell me the time?	**Mi scusi. Può dirmi che ore sono?**	mee **skoo**zee. pwo **deer**mee kay **oa**ray **soa**noa
It's five past one.	**È l'una e cinque.**	ai **loo**nah ay **cheeng**kooay
It's ...	**Sono le ...**	**soa**noa lay
ten past two	**due e dieci**	**doo**ay ay dee**ai**chee
a quarter past three	**tre e un quarto**	tray ay oon **kwahr**toa
twenty past four	**quattro e venti**	**kwaht**troa ay **vayn**tee
twenty-five past five	**cinque e venticinque**	**cheeng**kooay ay vayntee-**cheeng**kooay
half past six	**sei e mezza**	**seh**ee ay **mehd**dzah
twenty-five to eight	**sette e trentacinque**	**seht**tay ay trayntah-**cheeng**kooay
twenty to eight	**otto meno venti**	**ot**toa **mai**noa **vayn**tee
a quarter to nine	**nove meno un quarto**	**naw**vay **mai**noa oon **kwahr**toa
ten to ten	**dieci meno dieci**	dee**ai**chee **mai**noa dee**ai**chee
five to eleven	**undici meno cinque**	**oon**deechee **mai**noa **cheeng**kooay
twelve o'clock (noon/midnight)	**dodici (mezzogiorno/ mezzanotte)**	**doa**deechee (mehdzoa**joar**noa/ mehdzah**not**tay)
in the morning	**del mattino**	dayl maht**tee**noa
in the afternoon	**del pomeriggio**	dayl poamay**reed**joa
in the evening	**della sera**	**dayl**lah **say**rah
The train leaves at ...	**Il treno parte alle ...**	eel **tray**noa **pahr**tay **ahl**lay
13.04 (1.04 p.m.)	**tredici e quattro***	**tray**deechee ay **kwaht**troa
0.40 (0.40 a.m.)	**zero e quaranta**	**dzeh**roa ay kwah**rahn**tah
in five minutes	**fra cinque minuti**	frah **cheeng**kooay mee**noo**tee
in a quarter of an hour	**fra un quarto d'ora**	frah oon **kwahr**toa **doa**rah
half an hour ago	**mezz'ora fa**	mehd**zoa**rah fah
about two hours	**circa due ore**	**cheer**kah **doo**ay **oa**ray
more than 10 minutes	**più di dieci minuti**	pe**eoo** dee dee**ai**chee mee**noo**tee
less than 30 seconds	**meno di trenta secondi**	**mai**noa dee **trayn**tah say**koan**dee
The clock is fast/ slow.	**L'orologio è avanti/ indietro.**	loaroa**lo**joa ai ah**vahn**tee/ eendee**ay**troa

* In ordinary conversation, time is expressed as shown above. However, official time uses a 24-hour clock which means that after noon hours are counted from 13 to 24.

Common abbreviations *Abbreviazioni correnti*

A.A.T.	**Azienda Autonoma di Soggiorno, Cura e Turismo**	local tourist board
a.	**arrivo**	arrival
ab.	**abitanti**	inhabitants, population
a.C.	**avanti Cristo**	B.C.
A.C.I.	**Automobile Club d'Italia**	Italian Automobile Association
a.D.	**anno Domini**	A.D.
A.G.I.P.	**Azienda Generale Italiana Petroli**	Italian National Oil Company
alt.	**altitudine**	altitude
C.I.T.	**Compagnia Italiana Turismo**	Italian Travel Agency
c.m.	**corrente mese**	of this month
C.P.	**casella postale**	post office box
C.so	**Corso**	avenue
d.C.	**dopo Cristo**	A.D.
ecc.	**eccetera**	etc.
E.N.I.T.	**Ente Nazionale italiano per il Turismo**	National Tourist Organization
F.F.S.	**Ferrovie Federali Svizzere**	Swiss Federal Railways
F.S.	**Ferrovie dello Stato**	Italian State Railways
I.V.A.	**Imposta sul Valore Aggiunto**	value added tax (sales tax)
Mil.	**militare**	military
p.	**partenza; pagina**	departure; page
P.T.	**Poste & Telecomunicazioni**	Post & Telecommunications
P.za	**Piazza**	square
R.A.I.	**Radio Audizioni Italiane**	Italian Broadcasting Company
Rep.	**Repubblica**	republic
sec.	**secolo**	century
Sig.	**Signor**	Mr.
Sig.a	**Signora**	Mrs.
Sig.na	**Signorina**	Miss
S.p.a.	**Società per azioni**	Ltd., Inc.
S.P.Q.R.	**Senatus Populusque Romanus**	The Senate and the People of Rome (Latin)
S.r.l.	**Società a responsabilità limitata**	limited liability company
S./S.ta	**San(to)/Santa**	Saint
S.S.	**Sua Santità**	His Holiness
T.C.I.	**Touring Club Italiano**	Italian Touring Association
V.le	**Viale**	avenue
V.U.	**Vigili Urbani**	city police

Signs and notices *Cartelli*

Affittasi	To let, for hire
Al completo	Full/No vacancies
Aperto da . . . a . . .	Open from . . . to . . .
Ascensore	Lift (elevator)
Attenti al cane	Beware of the dog
Caldo	Hot
Cassa	Cash desk
Chiudere la porta	Close the door
Chiuso	Closed
Chiuso per ferie/per riposo settimanale	Closed for holiday/Weekly closing day
Entrare senza bussare	Enter without knocking
Entrata	Entrance
Entrata libera	Free entrance
Freddo	Cold
Fuori servizio	Out of order
I trasgressori saranno puniti a norma di legge	Trespassers will be prosecuted
Informazioni	Information
In sciopero	On strike
In vendita	For sale
Libero	Vacant
Non disturbare	Do not disturb
Non toccare	Do not touch
Occupato	Occupied
Pericolo (di morte)	Danger (of death)
Pista per ciclisti	Path for cyclists
Pittura fresca	Wet paint
Privato	Private
Prudenza	Caution
Riservato	Reserved
Saldi	Sales
Signore	Ladies
Signori	Gentlemen
Spingere	Push
Strada privata	Private road
Suonare, per favore	Please ring
Svendita	Sales
Tirare	Pull
Uscita	Exit
Uscita di sicurezza	Emergency exit
Vietato . . .	. . . forbidden
Vietato fumare	No smoking
Vietato l'ingresso	No entrance
Vietato toccare	Do not touch

Emergency *Emergenza*

Call the police	**Chiami la polizia**	keeaamee lah poaleet**see**ah
DANGER	**PERICOLO**	pay**ree**koaloa
FIRE	**AL FUOCO**	ahl **fwaw**koa
Gas	**Gas**	gaz
Get a doctor	**Chiami un medico**	kee**aa**mee oon **mai**deekoa
Go away	**Se ne vada**	say nay **vaa**dah
HELP	**AIUTO**	ahee**oo**toa
Get help quickly	**Chiami aiuti, presto**	kee**aa**mee ahee**oo**tee **preh**stoa
I'm ill	**Mi sento male**	mee **sayn**toa **maa**lay
I'm lost	**Mi sono perso(a)**	mee **soa**noa **pehr**soa(ah)
Leave me alone	**Mi lasci in pace**	mee **laa**shee een **paa**chay
LOOK OUT	**ATTENZIONE**	ahttayntsee**oa**nay
Poison	**Veleno**	vay**lay**noa
POLICE	**POLIZIA**	poaleet**see**ah
Quick	**Presto**	**preh**stoa
STOP	**FERMATEVI**	fayr**maa**tayvee
Stop that man/ woman	**Fermate quell'uomo/ quella donna**	fayr**maa**tay kooayl**lwo**moa/ koo**ayl**lah **don**nah
STOP THIEF	**AL LADRO**	ahl **laa**droa

Emergency telephone numbers *Chiamate di emergenza*

Italy:	Police, all-purpose emergency number	113
	Road assistance (Automobile Club d'Italia)	116
Switzerland:	Police, all-purpose emergency number	117
	Fire	118

Lost! *In caso di perdite o di furti*

Where's the ...?	**Dov'è ...?**	doa**vai**
lost-property (lost and found) office	**l'ufficio oggetti smarriti**	looff**ee**choa oad**jeht**tee zmahr**ree**tee
police station	**il posto di polizia**	eel **poa**stoa dee poaleet**see**ah
I want to report a theft.	**Devo denunciare un furto.**	**day**voa daynoon**chaa**ray oon **foor**toa
My ... has been stolen.	**Mi hanno rubato ...**	mee **ahn**noa roo**baa**toa
I've lost my ...	**Ho perso ...**	oa **pehr**soa
handbag	**la mia borsetta**	lah **mee**ah boar**sayt**tah
passport	**il mio passaporto**	eel **mee**oa pahssah**poar**toa
wallet	**il mio portafogli**	eel **mee**oa portah**foa**lyee

CAR ACCIDENTS, see page 78

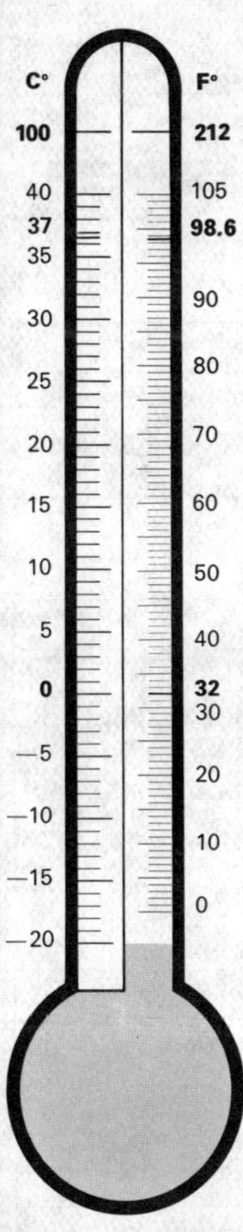

Conversion tables

Centimetres and inches

To change centimetres into inches, multiply by .39.

To change inches into centimetres, multiply by 2.54.

	in.	feet	yards
1 mm.	0.039	0.003	0.001
1 cm.	0.39	0.03	0.01
1 dm.	3.94	0.32	0.10
1 m.	39.40	3.28	1.09

	mm.	cm.	m.
1 in.	25.4	2.54	0.025
1 ft.	304.8	30.48	0.305
1 yd.	914.4	91.44	0.914

(32 metres = 35 yards)

Temperature

To convert centigrade into degrees Fahrenheit, multiply centigrade by 1.8 and add 32.

To convert degrees Fahrenheit into centigrade, subtract 32 from Fahrenheit and divide by 1.8.

Kilometres into miles

1 kilometre (km.) = 0.62 miles

km.	10	20	30	40	50	60	70	80	90	100	110	120	130
miles	6	12	19	25	31	37	44	50	56	62	68	75	81

Miles into kilometres

1 mile = 1.609 kilometres (km.)

miles	10	20	30	40	50	60	70	80	90	100
km.	16	32	48	64	80	97	113	129	145	161

Fluid measures

1 litre (l.) = 0.88 imp. quart or = 1.06 U.S. quart

1 imp. quart = 1.14 l.
1 imp. gallon = 4.55 l.

1 U.S. quart = 0.95 l.
1 U.S. gallon = 3.8 l.

litres	5	10	15	20	25	30	35	40	45	50
imp. gal.	1.1	2.2	3.3	4.4	5.5	6.6	7.7	8.8	9.9	11.0
U.S. gal.	1.3	2.6	3.9	5.2	6.5	7.8	9.1	10.4	11.7	13.0

Weights and measures

1 kilogram or kilo (kg.) = 1000 grams (g.)

100 g. = 3.5 oz.
200 g. = 7.0 oz.

½ kg. = 1.1 lb.
1 kg. = 2.2 lb.

1 oz. = 28.35 g.
1 lb. = 453.60 g.

CLOTHING SIZES, see page 115/YARDS AND INCHES, see page 112

A very basic grammar

Articles

There are two genders in Italian—masculine (masc.) and feminine (fem.).

1. Definite article (the):

	singular	plural
masc.	**l'** before a vowel	**gli**
	lo before **z** or **s + consonant**	**gli**
	il before all other consonants	**i**
	l'amico (the friend)	**gli amici** (the friends)
	lo studente (the student)	**gli studenti** (the students)
	il treno (the train)	**i treni** (the trains)
fem.	**l'** before a vowel	**le**
	la before a consonant	**le**
	l'arancia (the orange)	**le arance** (the oranges)
	la casa (the house)	**le case** (the houses)

2. Indefinite article (a/an):

masc. **un** (**uno** before **z** or **s + consonant***)

un piatto (a plate)
uno specchio (a mirror)

fem. **una** (**un'** before a vowel)

una strada (a street)
un'amica (a girl friend)

3. Partitive (some/any)

In affirmative sentences and some interrogatives, **some** and **any** are expressed by **di + definite article,** which has the following contracted forms:

masc.	**dell'** before a vowel	**degli**
	dello before **z** or **s + consonant**	**degli**
	del before other consonants	**dei**
fem.	**dell'** before a vowel	**delle**
	della before a consonant	**delle**

*When **s** is followed by a vowel, the masculine articles are **il/i** (definite) and **un** (indefinite).

For other contractions of preposition + definite article, see page 163.

Desidero del vino	I want some wine.
Vorrei delle sigarette.	I'd like some cigarettes.
Ha degli amici a Roma?	Have you any friends in Rome?

Nouns

Nouns ending in **o** are generally masculine. To form the plural, change **o** to **i**.

il tavolo (the table) — **i tavoli** (the tables)

Nouns ending in **a** are usually feminine. To form the plural, change **a** to **e**.

la casa (the house) — **le case** (the houses)

Nouns ending in **e**—no rule as to gender. Learn each noun individually. Plurals are formed by changing the **e** to **i**.

il piede (the foot)	**i piedi** (the feet)
la notte (the night)	**le notti** (the nights)

Adjectives

They agree with the noun they modify in number and gender. There are two basic types—ending in **o** and ending in **e**.

	singular	plural
masc.	**leggero** light (in weight)	**leggeri**
	grande big	**grandi**
fem.	**leggera**	**leggere**
	grande	**grandi**

They usually follow the noun but certain common adjectives precede the noun.

un caro amico (a dear friend)
una strada lunga (a long street)

Demonstratives

this	**questo/questa** (contracted to **quest'** before a vowel)
these	**questi/queste** (no contraction)
that	**quell', quello, quel** (masc.)/**quell', quella*** (fem.)
those	**quegli, quei** (masc.)/ **quelle** (fem.)

Possessive adjectives and pronouns

These agree in number and gender *with the nouns they modify* (or replace). They are almost always used with the definite article.

	masculine		feminine	
	singular	plural	singular	plural
my, mine	**il mio**	**i miei**	**la mia**	**le mie**
your, yours	**il tuo**	**i tuoi**	**la tua**	**le tue**
his, her, hers, its	**il suo**	**i suoi**	**la sua**	**le sue**
our, ours	**il nostro**	**i nostri**	**la nostra**	**le nostre**
your, yours	**il vostro**	**i vostri**	**la vostra**	**le vostre**
their, theirs	**il loro**	**i loro**	**la loro**	**le loro**
**your, yours (sing.)	**il suo**	**i suoi**	**la sua**	**le sue**
**your, yours (plur.)	**il loro**	**i loro**	**la loro**	**le loro**

Thus, depending on the context, **il suo cane** can mean *his, her* or *your dog,* **la sua casa,** *his, her* or *your house.*

Personal pronouns

	Subject	Direct Object	Indirect Object	After a Preposition
I	**io**	**mi**	**mi**	**me**
you	**tu**	**ti**	**ti**	**te**
he, it (masc.)	**lui/egli**	**lo**	**gli**	**lui**
she, it (fem.)	**lei/ella**	**la**	**le**	**lei**
we	**noi**	**ci**	**ci**	**noi**
you	**voi**	**vi**	**vi**	**voi**
they (masc.)	**loro/essi**	**li**	**loro**	**loro**
they (fem.)	**loro/esse**	**le**	**loro**	**loro**

* These forms follow the same system as **dell'/dello/della,** etc. (see p. 163).
** This is the formal form—used in addressing people you do not know well.

Note: There are two forms for "you" in Italian: **tu** (singular) is used when talking to relatives, close friends and children (and between young people); the plural of **tu** is **voi. Lei** (singular) and **Loro** (plural) are used in all other cases (with the 3rd person singular/plural of the verb).

Verbs

Here we are concerned only with the infinitive and the present tense.

Learn these two **auxiliary verbs:**

essere (to be)	**avere** (to have)
io* sono (I am)	**io* ho** (I have)
tu sei (you are)	**tu hai** (you have)
lui, lei è (he, she, it is)	**lui, lei ha** (he, she, it has)
lei è (you are)	**lei ha** (you have)
noi siamo (we are)	**noi abbiamo** (we have)
voi siete (you are)	**voi avete** (you have)
essi/esse sono (they are)	**essi/esse hanno** (they have)

C'è/Ci sono are equivalent to "there is/there are":

C'è una lettera per Lei.	There's a letter for you.
Ci sono due pacchi per lui.	There are two parcels for him.

Regular verbs follow one of three patterns (conjugations) depending on the ending of the infinitive.

	ends in **-are**	ends in **-ere**	ends in **-ire**
Infinitive:	**amare** (to love)	**vendere** (to sell)	**partire** (to leave)
io*	**amo**	**vendo**	**parto**
tu	**ami**	**vendi**	**parti**
lui, lei	**ama**	**vende**	**parte**
noi	**amiamo**	**vendiamo**	**partiamo**
voi	**amate**	**vendete**	**partite**
essi/esse	**amano**	**vendono**	**partono**

* The subject pronouns are seldom used except for emphasis.

Irregular verbs: As in all languages, these have to be learned. Here are four you'll find useful.

Infinitive:	andare (to go)	potere (to be able)	volere (to want)	fare (to make)
io	vado	posso	voglio	faccio
tu	vai	puoi	vuoi	fai
lui/lei	va	può	vuole	fa
noi	andiamo	possiamo	vogliamo	facciamo
voi	andate	potete	volete	fate
essi/esse	vanno	possono	vogliono	fanno

Negatives

Negatives are formed by putting **non** before the verb.

Non vado a Roma. I am not going to Rome.

Questions

In Italian, questions are often formed by simply changing the inflexion of your voice. Remember that the personal pronoun is rarely used, either in affirmative sentences or in questions.

Parlo italiano. I speak Italian.
Parla italiano? Do you speak Italian?

Prepositions

There is a list of prepositions on page 14. Note the following contractions:

Definite Article	a at, to	da by, from	di of	in in	su on	con with
+ il	al	dal	del	nel	sul	col
+ l'	all'	dall'	dell'	nell'	sull'	coll'
+ lo	allo	dallo	dello	nello	sullo	con lo
+ la	alla	dalla	della	nella	sulla	con la
+ i	ai	dai	dei	nei	sui	coi/con i
+ gli	agli	dagli	degli	negli	sugli	con gli
+ le	alle	dalle	delle	nelle	sulle	con le

Dictionary
and alphabetical index

English–Italian

f feminine   *m* masculine   *pl* plural

a un(a) 159
abbey abbazia *f* 81
abbreviation abbreviazione *f* 154
able, to be potere 163
about *(approximately)* circa 153
above sopra 15, 63
absces ascesso *m* 145
absorbent cotton cotone idrofilo *m* 109
accept, to accettare 62, 102
accessories accessori *m/pl* 116, 125
accident incidente *m* 78, 79, 139
accommodation alloggio *m* 22
account conto *m* 130, 131
ache dolore *m*, male *m* 141
adaptor presa multipla *f* 119
address indirizzo *m* 21, 31, 76, 79, 102
address book agenda per gli indirizzi *f* 104
adhesive adesivo(a) 105
admission entrata *f* 82, 89, 155
Africa Africa *f* 146
after dopo 14, 77
afternoon pomeriggio *m* 151, 153
after-shave lotion lozione dopobarba *f* 110
age età *f* 149; anni *m* 150
ago fa 149, 151
air conditioner condizionatore d'aria *m* 28
air conditioning aria condizionata *f* 23
airmail via aerea 133
airplane aereo *m* 65
airport aeroporto *m* 16, 21, 65
alabaster alabastro *m* 122
alarm clock sveglia *f* 121
alcohol alcool *m* 107
alcoholic alcolico(a) 59
Algeria Algeria *f* 146
allergic allergico(a) 141, 143
almond mandorla *f* 54
alphabet alfabeto *m* 8
also anche 15
amazing sorprendente 84
amber ambra *f* 122
ambulance ambulanza *f* 79
American americano(a) 93, 126
American plan pensione completa *f* 24
amethyst ametista *f* 122
amount importo *m* 62, 131
amplifier amplificatore *m* 119
anaesthetic anestetico *m* 144
analgesic analgesico *m* 109
anchovy acciuga *f* 41, 46
and e 15
animal animale *m* 85
ankle caviglia *f* 139
anorak giacca a vento *f* 116
another un(') altro(a) 123
answer, to rispondere 136
antibiotic antibiotico *m* 143
antidepressant antidepressivo *m* 143
antiques antichità *f/pl* 83
antique shop antiquario *m* 98
antiseptic antisettico(a) 109
antiseptic antisettico *m* 140
any del, della 14
anyone qualcuno(a) 11
anything qualcosa 17, 25, 113

aperitif aperitivo *m* 56
appendicitis appendicite *f* 142
appendix appendice *f* 138
appetizer antipasto *m* 41
apple mela *f* 54, 63
appliance apparecchio *m* 119
appointment appuntamento *m* 30, 131, 137, 145
apricot albicocca *f* 54
April aprile *m* 150
archaeology archeologia *f* 83
architect architetto *m* 83
area code prefisso *m* 134
arm braccio *m* 138, 139
arrival arrivo *m* 16, 65
arrive, to arrivare 65, 68, 130
art arte *f* 83
artery arteria *f* 138
art gallery galleria d'arte *f* 81, 98
artichoke carciofo *m* 41, 52
artificial artificiale 124
artist artista *m/f* 81, 83
ashtray portacenere *m* 27, 36
Asia Asia *f* 146
ask for, to chiedere 25, 61, 136
asparagus asparago *m* 52
aspirin aspirina *f* 109
assorted assortito(a) 41
asthma asma *f* 141
at a 14, 163
at least come minimo 24
at once subito 15; immediatamente 31
aubergine melanzana *f* 52
August agosto *m* 150
aunt zia *f* 93
Australia Australia *f* 146
Austria Austria *f* 146
automatic automatico(a) 20, 122, 124
autumn autunno *m* 150
average medio(a) 91
awful orribile 84

B

baby bambino *m* 24, 111; bebè *m* 111
baby food alimenti per bebè *m/pl* 111
babysitter babysitter *f* 27
back schiena *f* 138
backache mal di schiena *m* 141
bacon pancetta *f* 38
bacon and eggs uova e pancetta *m/pl* 38
bad cattivo(a) 13, 95
bag borsa *f* 18; sacchetto *m* 103
baggage bagagli *m/pl* 18, 26, 31, 71
baggage cart carrello portabagagli *m* 18, 71
baggage check deposito bagagli *m* 67, 71
baggage locker custodia automatica dei bagagli *f* 18, 67, 71
baked al forno 47, 50
baker's panetteria *f* 98
balance *(account)* bilancio *m* 131
balcony balcone *m* 23
ball *(inflated)* pallone *m* 128
ballet balletto *m* 88
ball-point pen biro *f* 104
banana banana *f* 54, 63
bandage benda *f* 109
Band-Aid cerotto *m* 109
bangle braccialetto *m* 121
bangs frangia *f* 30
bank *(finance)* banca *f* 98, 129
bank card carta d'identità bancaria *f* 130
banknote banconota *f* 130
bar bar *m* 33, 67; *(chocolate)* stecca *f* 64
barbecued alla graticola, alla griglia 50
barber's barbiere *m* 30, 98
basil basilico *m* 53
basketball pallacanestro *f* 89
bath *(hotel)* bagno *m* 23, 25, 27
bathing cap cuffia da bagno *f* 116
bathing hut cabina *f* 91
bathing suit costume da bagno *m* 116
bathrobe accappatoio *m* 116
bathroom bagno *m* 27
bath salts sali da bagno *m/pl* 110
bath towel asciugamano *m* 27
battery pila *f* 119, 121, 125; *(car)* batteria *f* 75, 78
be, to essere 162; trovarsi 11
beach spiaggia *f* 90
bean fagiolo *m* 52
beard barba *f* 31
beautiful bello(a) 13, 84
beauty salon istituto di bellezza *m* 30, 98
bed letto *m* 24, 144
bed and breakfast camera e colazione *f* 24
bedpan padella *f* 144
beef manzo *m* 48

beer birra *f* 59, 64

beet(root) barbabietola *f* 52

before *(place)* davanti a 14; *(time)* prima di 14, 151

begin, to iniziare 80, 88; incominciare 87

beginner principiante *m/f* 91

beginning inizio *m* 150

behind dietro 14, 77

beige beige 113

Belgium Belgio *m* 146

bell *(electric)* campanello *m* 144

bellboy fattorino *m* 26

below al di sotto 15; sotto 63

belt cintura *f* 117

bend *(road)* curva *f* 79

berth cuccetta *f* 69, 70, 71

best migliore 152

better migliore 13, 25, 101, 113

beware attento(a) 155

between tra, fra 15

bicycle bicicletta *f* 74

big grande 13, 101

bill conto *m* 31, 62, 102; *(banknote)* banconota *f* 130

billion *(Am.)* miliardo *m* 148

binoculars binocolo *m* 123

bird uccello *m* 85

birth nascita *f* 25

birthday compleanno *m* 151, 152

biscuit *(Br.)* biscotto *m* 64

bitter amaro(a) 61

black nero(a) 113

black and white bianco e nero 124, 125

blackberry mora *f* 54

blackcurrant ribes nero *m* 54

bladder vescica *f* 138

blanket coperta *f* 27

bleed, to perdere sangue 139; sanguinare 145

blind *(window)* persiana *f* 29

blister vescica *f* 139

block, to otturare 28

blood sangue *m* 142

blood pressure pressione *f* 141

blood transfusion trasfusione di sangue *f* 144

blouse blusa *f* 116

blow-dry asciugatura col fono *f* 30

blue blu, azzurro(a) 113

blueberry mirtillo *m* 54

boar *(wild)* cinghiale *m* 51

boarding house pensione *f* 19, 22

boat battello *m* 74

bobby pin molletta *f* 111

body corpo *m* 138

boil foruncolo *m* 139

boiled lesso(a) 47, 50

boiled egg uovo alla coque *m* 38

bone osso *m* 138

book libro *m* 11, 104

book, to prenotare 69

booking office ufficio prenotazioni *m* 19, 67

booklet blocchetto *m* 72

bookshop libreria *f* 98, 104

boot stivale *m* 118

born nato(a) 150

botanical gardens giardino botanico *m* 81

botany botanica *f* 83

bottle bottiglia *f* 17, 57

bottle-opener apribottiglia *m* 106

bottom basso *m* 145

bowels intestino *m* 138

bow tie cravatta a farfalla *f* 116

box scatola *f* 120

boxing pugilato *m* 89

boy *(child)* bambino *m* 112, 128

boyfriend ragazzo *m* 93

bra reggiseno *m* 116

bracelet braccialetto *m* 121

braces *(suspenders)* bretelle *f/pl* 116

braised brasato(a) 50

brake freno *m* 78

brake fluid olio dei freni *m* 75

brandy brandy *m* 59

bread pane *m* 36, 38, 64

break, to rompere 29, 119, 123, 145; rompersi 139, 145

break down, to avere un guasto 78

breakdown guasto *m* 78

breakdown van carro attrezzi *m* 78

breakfast colazione *f* 24, 34, 38

breast petto *m* 138

breathe, to respirare 141

bridge ponte *m* 85

briefs slip *m* 116

bring, to portare 12

bring down, to portare giù 31

British britannico(a) 93

broken rotto(a) 29, 119, 140

brooch spilla *f* 121

brother fratello *m* 93

brown marrone 113

bruise contusione *f* 139

brush spazzola f 111

Brussels sprouts cavolini di Bruxelles *m/pl* 52
bubble bath bagnoschiuma *m* 110
bucket secchio *m* 106; secchiello *m* 128
build, to costruire 83
building edificio *m* 81, 83
building blocks/bricks gioco di costruzioni *m* 128
bulb lampadina *f* 28, 75, 119
burn scottatura *f* 139
burn out, to *(bulb)* bruciare 28
bus autobus *m* 18, 19, 65, 72, 73; pullman *m* 72, 80
business affari *m/pl* 16, 131
business trip viaggio d'affari *m* 93
bus stop fermata dell'autobus *f* 72, 73
busy impegnato(a) 96
but ma, però 15
butane gas gas butano *m* 32, 106
butcher's macelleria *f* 98
butter burro *m* 36, 38, 64
button bottone *m* 29, 117
buy, to comprare 82, 104; acquistare 123

C

cabana cabina *f* 91
cabbage cavolo *m* 52
cabin *(ship)* cabina *f* 74
cable telegramma *m* 133
cable car funivia *f* 74
cable release scatto *m* 125
café caffè *m* 33
caffein-free decaffeinato 38, 60
cake dolce *m* 55; torta *f* 55, 64
cake shop pasticceria *f* 98
calculator calcolatrice *f* 105
calendar calendario *m* 104
call *(phone)* telefonata *f* 135, 136
call, to chiamare 11, 78, 156; telefonare 136
cambric tela battista *f* 114
camel-hair pelo di cammello *m* 114
camera macchina fotografica *f* 124, 125
camera case astuccio (per macchina fotografica) *m* 125
camera shop negozio di apparecchi fotografici *m* 98
camp, to campeggiare 32
campbed letto da campo *m* 106
camping campeggio *m* 32
camping equipment materiale da campeggio *m* 106
camp site campeggio *m* 32
can *(of peaches)* scatola *f* 120
can *(to be able)* potere 11, 12, 163
Canada Canada *m* 146
cancel, to annullare 65
candle candela *f* 106
candy caramella *f* 126
can opener apriscatole *m* 106
cap berretto *m* 116
caper cappero *m* 53
capital *(finance)* capitale *m* 131
car macchina *f* 19, 20, 75, 76, 78; automobile *f* 78
carafe caraffa *f* 57
carat carato *m* 121
caravan roulotte *f* 32
caraway cumino *m* 53
carbon paper carta carbone *f* 104
carburettor carburatore *m* 78
card carta *f* 93; *(visiting)* bigliettino *m* 131
card game carte da gioco *f/pl* 128
cardigan cardigan *m* 116
car hire autonoleggio *m* 19, 20
car park parcheggio *m* 77
car racing corsa automobilistica *f* 89
car radio autoradio *f* 119
car rental autonoleggio *m* 20
carrot carota *f* 52
carry, to portare 21
cart carrello *m* 18
carton *(of cigarettes)* stecca (di sigarette) *f* 17
cartridge *(camera)* rotolo *m* 124
case *(instance)* caso *m* 143; *(cigarettes etc)* astuccio *m* 123, 125
cash, to incassare 130; riscuotere 133
cash desk cassa *f* 103, 155
cashier cassiere(a) *m/f* 103
cassette cassetta *f* 119, 127
castle castello *m* 81
catacomb catacomba *f* 81
catalogue catalogo *m* 82
cathedral cattedrale *f* 81
Catholic cattolico(a) 84
cauliflower cavolfiore *m* 52
caution prudenza *f* 155
cave grotta *f* 81
celery sedano *m* 52
cellophane tape nastro adesivo *m* 104

cemetery cimitero *m* 81
centimetre centimetro *m* 112
centre centro *m* 19, 21, 76, 81
century secolo *m* 149
ceramics ceramica *f* 83, 127
cereal cereali *m/pl* 38
certificate certificato *m* 144
chain catena *f* 79
chain *(jewellery)* catenina *f* 121
chain bracelet braccialetto a catena *m* 121
chair sedia *f* 36, 106
chamber music musica da camera *f* 128
change *(money)* moneta *f* 77, 130; resto *m* 62
change, to cambiare 61, 65, 68, 73, 75, 123; *(money)* 18, 130
chapel cappella *f* 81
charcoal carbonella *f* 106
charge tariffa *f* 20; prezzo *m* 89; costo *m* 136
charge, to fare pagare 24; *(commission)* trattenere 130
charm *(trinket)* ciondolo *m* 121
charm bracelet braccialetto a ciondoli *m* 121
cheap buon mercato 13; economico(a) 101
check assegno *m* 130; *(restaurant)* conto *m* 62
check, to controllare 75, 123; *(luggage)* far registrare 71
check book libretto d'assegni *m* 131
check in, to *(airport)* presentarsi 65
check out, to partire 31
checkup *(medical)* controllo *m* 142
cheers! salute! cin-cin! 56
cheese formaggio *m* 53, 63, 64
chef chef *m* 40
chemist's farmacia *f* 98, 108
cheque assegno *m* 130
cheque book libretto d'assegni *m* 131
cherry ciliegia *f* 54
chess scacchi *m/pl* 93, 128
chest torace *m* 138, 141
chestnut castagna *f* 54
chewing gum gomma da masticare *f* 126
chicken pollo *m* 51, 63
chick-pea cece *m* 52
chicory indivia *f* 52; *(Am.)* cicoria *f* 52
chiffon chiffon *m* 114
child bambino(a) *m/f* 24, 61, 82, 93, 139
children's doctor pediatra *m/f* 137
China Cina *f* 146
chips patatine fritte *f/pl* 63, 64
chives cipollina *f* 53
chocolate cioccolato *m* 126, 127; *(hot)* cioccolata (calda) *f* 38, 60
chocolate bar stecca di cioccolato *f* 64
choice scelta *f* 40
chop braciola *f* 48
Christmas Natale *m* 152
church chiesa *f* 81, 84
cigar sigaro *m* 126
cigarette sigaretta *f* 17, 95, 126
cigarette case portasigarette *m* 121, 126
cigarette lighter accendino *m* 121
cine camera cinepresa *f* 124
cinema cinema *m* 86, 96
cinnamon cannella *f* 53
circle *(theatre)* galleria *f* 87
city città *f* 81
clam vongola *f* 45, 47
classical classico(a) 128
clean pulito(a) 61
clean, to pulire 29, 76
cleansing cream crema detergente *f* 110
cliff scogliera *f* 85
clip fermaglio *m* 121
clock orologio *m* 121, 153
clock-radio radio-sveglia *f* 119
close *(near)* vicino(a) 78, 98
close, to chiudere 11, 82, 108, 132
closed chiuso(a) 155
clothes abiti *m/pl* 29; indumenti *m/pl* 116
clothes peg molletta da bucato *f* 106
clothing abbigliamento *m* 112
cloud nuvola *f* 94
clove chiodo di garofano *m* 53
coach *(bus)* pullman *m* 72
coat cappotto *m* 116
coconut noce di cocco *f* 54
cod baccalà *m* 46, 47; *(fresh)* merluzzo *m* 46
coffee caffè *m* 38, 60, 64
coin moneta *f* 83
cold freddo(a) 13, 25, 61, 94, 155
cold *(illness)* raffreddore *m* 108, 141
cold cuts affettati *m/pl* 64
colour colore *m* 103, 112, 124, 125

colour chart tabella dei colori *f* 30
colour negative negativo a colori *m* 124
colour shampoo shampoo colorante *m* 111
colour slide diapositiva *f* 124
colour television *(set)* televisore a colori *m* 119
comb pettine *m* 111
come, to venire 36, 92, 95, 137, 146
comedy commedia *f* 86
commission commissione *f* 130
common *(frequent)* corrente 154
compact disc disco compatto *m* 127
compartment scompartimento *m* 70
compass bussola *f* 106
complaint reclamo *m* 61
concert concerto *m* 88
concert hall sala dei concerti *f* 81, 88
conductor *(orchestra)* maestro *m* 88
confectioner's pasticceria *f* 98
confirm, to confermare 65
confirmation conferma *f* 23
congratulations congratulazioni *f/pl* 152
connection *(train)* coincidenza *f* 65, 68
constant costante 140
constipated costipato(a) 140
contact lens lente a contatto *f* 123
contain, to contenere 37
contraceptive antifecondativo *m* 109
contract contratto *m* 131
control controllo *m* 16
convent convento *m* 81
cookie biscotto *m* 64
cool box ghiacciaia *f* 106
copper rame *m* 122
coral corallo *m* 122
corduroy velluto a coste *m* 114
cork tappo *m* 61
corkscrew cavatappi *m* 106
corner angolo *m* 21, 36, 77
corn plaster cerotto callifugo *m* 109
cost preventivo *m* 131
cost, to costare 10, 80, 133, 136
cotton cotone *m* 114
cotton wool cotone idrofilo *m* 109
cough tosse *f* 108, 141
cough, to tossire 142
cough drops pasticche per la tosse *f/pl* 109
counter sportello *m* 133
countryside campagna *f* 85
court house palazzo di giustizia *m* 81
cousin cugino(a) *m/f* 93
cover charge coperto *m* 62
crab granchio *m* 46
cramp crampo *m* 141
crayfish gambero *m* 46
crayon pastello *m* 104
cream panna *f* 55, 60; *(toiletry)* crema *f* 110
credit credito *m* 130
credit, to accreditare 130, 131
credit card carta di credito *f* 20, 31, 62, 102, 130
crockery stoviglie *f/pl* 107
crisps patatine fritte *f/pl* 64
cross croce *f* 121
crossing *(by sea)* traversata *f* 74
crossroads incrocio *m* 77
cruise crociera *f* 74
crystal cristallo *m* 122
cuckoo clock orologio a cucù *m* 121
cucumber cetriolo *m* 52
cuff link gemelli *m/pl* 121
cuisine cucina *f* 35
cup tazza *f* 36, 107
currency valuta *f* 129
currency exchange office ufficio cambio *m* 18, 67, 129
current corrente *f* 90
curtain tenda *f* 28
curve *(road)* curva *f* 79
custard crema *f* 55
customs dogana *f* 16, 122
cut *(wound)* taglio *m* 139
cut off, to *(phone)* interrompere 135
cut glass vetro tagliato *m* 122
cuticle remover prodotto per togliere le pellicine *m* 110
cutlery posate *f/pl* 107, 121
cuttlefish seppia *f* 47
cycling ciclismo *m* 89
cystitis cistite *f* 142

D

dairy latteria *f* 98
dance, to ballare 88, 96
danger pericolo *m* 155, 156
dangerous pericoloso(a) 90
dark buio(a) 25; scuro(a) 101, 112, 113
date data *f* 25, 151; *(fruit)* dattero *m* 54
daughter figlia *f* 93
day giorno *m* 16, 20, 24, 32, 80, 151

daylight luce naturale *f* 124
day off giorno di riposo *m* 151
death morte *f* 155
decade decennio *m* 149
December dicembre *m* 150
decision decisione *f* 25, 102
deck *(ship)* ponte *m* 74
deck-chair sedia a sdraio *f* 91
declare, to dichiarare 16, 17
deer cervo *m* 51
delay ritardo *m* 69
delicatessen salumeria *f* 98
delicious delizioso(a) 62
deliver, to consegnare 102
delivery consegna *f* 102
denim tela di cotone *f* 114
dentist dentista *m/f* 145
denture dentiera *f* 145
deodorant deodorante *m* 110
department *(museum, shop)* reparto *m* 83, 100
department store grande magazzino *m* 98
departure partenza *f* 65
deposit *(car hire)* cauzione *f* 20; *(bank)* deposito *m* 130
deposit, to *(bank)* depositare 130
dessert dessert *m* 40, 55; dolce *m* 39, 55
detour *(traffic)* deviazione *f* 79
develop, to sviluppare 124
diabetes diabete *m* 141
diabetic diabetico(a) *m/f* 37
dialling code prefisso *m* 134
diamond diamante *m* 122
diaper pannolino *m* 111
diarrhoea diarrea *f* 140
dictionary dizionario *m* 104
diet dieta *f* 37
difficult difficile 13
difficulty difficoltà *f* 28, 102, 141
digital digitale 122
dine, to cenare 94
dining-car carrozza ristorante *f* 66, 68, 71
dining-room sala da pranzo *f* 27
dinner cena *f* 31
direct diretto(a) 65
direct, to indicare 12
direction direzione *f* 76
director*(theatre)* regista *m* 86
directory *(phone)* elenco *m* 134
disabled andicappato(a) 82
disc disco *m* 77, 127
discotheque discoteca *f* 88, 96
disease malattia *f* 142
dish piatto *m* 36, 37, 40
dishwashing detergent detersivo per lavare i piatti *m* 106
disinfectant disinfettante *m* 109
dislocate, to slogare 140
dissatisfied scontento(a) 103
district *(town)* quartiere *m* 81
disturb, to disturbare 155
diversion *(traffic)* deviazione *f* 79
dizzy stordito(a) 140
do, to fare 163
doctor medico *m* 79, 137; dottore *m* (dottoressa *f*) 144, 145
doctor's office ambulatorio *m* 137
dog cane *m* 155
doll bambola *f* 127, 128
dollar dollaro *m* 18, 130
door porta *f* 155
double doppio(a) 59
double bed letto matrimoniale *m* 23
double room camera doppia *f* 19, 23
down giù 15
downstairs di sotto 15
down there laggiù 77
downtown centro *m* 81
dozen dozzina *f* 120, 149
draught beer birra alla spina *f* 59
drawing paper carta da disegno *f* 104
drawing pin puntina *f* 104
dress abito *m* 116
dressing gown vestaglia *f* 116
drink bevanda *f* 40, 56, 59, 60, 61; bicchiere *m* 95
drink, to bere 35, 36
drinking water acqua potabile *f* 32
drip, to *(tap)* sgocciolare 28
drive, to guidare, andare 21, 76
driving licence patente *f* 20
drop *(liquid)* goccia *f* 109
drugstore farmacia *f* 98, 108
dry secco(a) 30, 57, 111
dry cleaner's lavanderia a secco *f* 29, 98; tintoria *f* 38
dry shampoo shampoo secco *m* 111
duck anatra *f* 48
dull *(pain)* debole 140
dummy succhiotto *m* 111
during durante 14, 150, 151
duty *(customs)* dazio *m* 17
duty-free shop negozio duty-free *m* 19
dye tintura *f* 30, 111

E

each ogni 149
ear orecchio *m* 138
earache mal d'orecchi *m* 141
ear drops gocce per le orecchie *f/pl* 109
early presto 13, 31
earring orecchino *m* 121
east est *m* 77
Easter Pasqua *f* 152
easy facile 13
eat, to mangiare 36
eel anguilla *f* 44
egg uovo *m* (*pl* uova *f*) 38, 64
eggplant melanzana *f* 52
eight otto 147
eighteen diciotto 147
eighth ottavo(a) 149
eighty ottanta 148
elastic elastico(a) 109
elastic bandage benda elastica *f* 109
Elastoplast cerotto *m* 109
electrical elettrico(a) 119
electrical appliance apparecchio elettrico *m* 119
electrician elettricista *m* 98
electricity elettricità *f* 32
electronic elettronico(a) 125, 128
elevator ascensore *m* 27, 100
eleven undici 147
embark, to imbarcare 74
emerald smeraldo *m* 122
emergency emergenza *f* 156
emergency exit uscita di sicurezza *f* 27, 99, 155
emery board limetta per unghie *f* 110
empty vuoto(a) 13
enamel smalto *m* 122
end fine *f* 150
endive cicoria *f* 52; *(Am.)* indivia *f* 52
engagement ring anello di fidanzamento *m* 121
engine *(car)* motore *m* 78
England Inghilterra *f* 146
English inglese 11, 80, 82, 84, 104, 105, 126, 137
enjoyable piacevole 31
enjoy oneself, to divertirsi 96
enlarge, to ingrandire 125
enough abbastanza 14
enquiry informazione *f* 68
enter, to entrare 155
entrance entrata *f* 67, 99, 155
entrance fee entrata *f* 82
envelope busta *f* 27, 104
equipment equipaggiamento *m*, tenuta *f* 91; materiale *m* 106
eraser gomma *f* 104
escalator scala mobile *f* 100
escalope scaloppina *f* 49
Europe Europa *f* 146
evening sera *f* 87, 96, 151, 153; serata *f* 95, 96
evening dress abito da sera *m* 88, 116
everything tutto 31
examine, to esaminare 139
excellent eccellente 84
exchange, to cambiare 103
exchange rate corso del cambio *m* 18, 130
excursion gita *f* 80
excuse, to scusare 10
exercise book quaderno *m* 104
exhaust pipe tubo di scappamento *m* 78
exhibition esposizione *f* 81
exit uscita *f* 67, 99, 155
expect, to aspettare 130
expense spesa *f* 131
expensive caro(a) 13, 19, 24, 101
exposure *(photography)* posa *f* 124
exposure counter contatore di esposizioni *m* 125
express espresso 133
expression espressione *f* 9
expressway autostrada *f* 76
extension cord/lead prolunga *f* 119
extra supplemento *m* 40
extract, to *(tooth)* estrarre 145
eye occhio *m* (*pl* occhi) 138, 139
eye drops gocce per gli occhi *f/pl* 109
eye pencil matita per occhi *f* 110
eye shadow ombretto *m* 110
eyesight vista *f* 123
eye specialist oculista *m/f* 137

F

face viso *m* 138
face-pack maschera di bellezza *f* 30
face powder cipria *f* 110
factory fabbrica *f* 81
fair fiera *f* 81
fall caduta *f* 139; *(autumn)* autunno *m* 150
family famiglia *f* 93
fan ventilatore *m* 28

fan belt cinghia del ventilatore *f* 75
far lontano(a) 13
fare prezzo *m* 21
farm fattoria *f* 85
fast rapido(a) 124
fat *(meat)* grasso *m* 37
father padre *f* 93
faucet rubinetto *m* 28
February febbraio *m* 150
fee *(doctor)* onorario *m* 144
feeding bottle biberon *m* 111
feel, to *(physical state)* sentirsi 140
felt feltro *m* 114
felt-tip pen pennarello *m* 104
fennel finocchio *m* 52
ferry traghetto *m* 74
fever febbre *f* 140
few pochi(e) 14; *(a)* alcuni(e) 14
field campo *m* 85
fifteen quindici 147
fifth quinto(a) 149
fifty cinquanta 147
fig fico *m* 54
file *(tool)* lima *f* 110
fill in, to compilare 26, 144
fillet filetto *m* 48
filling *(tooth)* otturazione *f* 145
filling station stazione di rifornimento *f* 75
film *(movie)* film *m* 86; *(camera)* pellicola *f* 124, 125
filter filtro *m* 125
filter-tipped con filtro 126
find, to trovare 10, 11, 100, 137
fine *(OK)* bene 25
fine arts belle arti *f/pl* 83
finger dito *m* 138
fire fuoco *m* 156
first primo(a) 68, 73, 149
first-aid kit cassetta del pronto soccorso *f* 106
first class prima classe *f* 69
first course primo piatto *m* 40
first name nome *m* 25
fish pesce *m* 46
fish, to pescare 90
fishing pesca *f* 90
fishing tackle arnese da pesca *m* 106
fishmonger's pescheria *f* 98
fit, to andare bene 115
fitting room cabina di prova *f* 115
five cinque 147
fix, to riparare 75; curare 145
fizzy *(mineral water)* gasato(a) 60
flannel flanella *f* 114
flash *(photography)* flash *m* 125
flash attachment attaccatura del flash *f* 125
flashlight lampadina tascabile *f* 106
flask fiasco *m* 127
flat basso(a) 118
flat *(apartment)* appartamento *m* 22
flat tyre foratura *f* 75; gomma sgonfia *f* 78
flea market mercato delle pulci *m* 81
flight volo *m* 65
flight number numero del volo *m* 65
flippers pinne *f/pl* 128
floor piano *m* 27
floor show varietà *m* 88
florist's fiorista *m/f* 98
flour farina *f* 37
flower fiore *m* 85
flu influenza *f* 142
fog nebbia *f* 94
folding chair sedia pieghevole *f* 107
folding table tavola pieghevole *f* 107
folk music musica folcloristica *f* 128
food cibo *m* 37, 61; alimento *m* 111
food box contenitore per il cibo *m* 142
food poisoning avvelenamento da cibo *m* 142
foot piede *m* 138
football calcio *m* 89
foot cream crema per i piedi *f* 110
footpath sentiero *m* 85
for per 15, 143
forbid, to vietare 155
forecast previsione *f* 94
foreign straniero(a) 59
forest foresta *f* 85
fork forchetta *f* 36, 61, 107, 127
form *(document)* modulo *m* 133; scheda *f* 25, 26
fortnight quindici giorni *m/pl* 151
fortress fortezza *f* 81
forty quaranta 147
foundation cream fondo tinta *m* 110
fountain fontana *f* 81
fountain pen penna stilografica *f* 104
four quattro 147
fourteen quattordici 147
fourth quarto(a) 149
frame *(glasses)* montatura *f* 123
France Francia *f* 146
free libero(a) 13, 70, 82, 96, 155

French bean fagiolino *m* 52
French fries patatine fritte *f/pl* 63
fresh fresco(a) 54, 61
Friday venerdì *m* 151
fried fritto(a) 47, 50
fried egg uovo fritto *m* 38
friend amico(a) *m/f* 95
fringe frangia *f* 30
frock abito *m* 116
from da 14, 163
front davanti 75
fruit frutta *f* 54
fruit cocktail macedonia di frutta *f* 54
fruit juice succo di frutta *m* 38, 60
frying-pan padella *f* 106
full pieno(a) 13; completo(a) 155; intero(a) 80
full board pensione completa *f* 20
full insurance assicurazione completa *f* 20
furniture mobilio *m* 83
furrier's pellicceria *f* 98

G

gabardine gabardine *m* 114
gallery galleria *f* 81, 98
game gioco *m* 128; *(food)* cacciagione *f* 50
garage garage *m* 26, 78
garden giardino *m* 81, 85
garlic aglio *m* 53
gas gas *m* 156
gasoline benzina *f* 75, 78
gastritis gastrite *f* 142
gauze garza *f* 109
general generale 26, 100
general delivery fermo posta *m* 133
general practitioner medico generico *m* 137
genitals genitali *m/pl* 138
gentleman signore *m* 155
genuine vero(a) 118
geology geologia *f* 83
Germany Germania *f* 146
get, to *(find)* trovare 10, 21, 32; *(call)* chiamare 31, 137; *(obtain)* ottenere 134; procurarsi 89, 90
get back, to ritornare 80
get off, to scendere 73
get to, to andare a 19; arrivare a 70
get up, to alzarsi 144
gherkin cetriolino *m* 52, 64
gin and tonic gin e tonico *m* 60
girdle busto *m* 116
girl *(child)* bambina *f* 112, 128
girlfriend ragazza *f* 93
give, to dare 12, 123, 135
glad *(to know you)* piacere 92
gland ghiandola *f* 138
glass bicchiere *m* 36, 57, 60, 61, 143
glasses occhiali *m/pl* 123
glassware articolo di vetro *m* 127
gloomy malinconico(a) 84
glossy *(finish)* lucido(a) 125
glove guanto *m* 116
glue colla *f* 105
go, to andare 95, 96, 163
go away, to andarsene 156
gold oro *m* 121, 122
golden dorato(a) 113
gold plate placcato d'oro *m* 122
golf golf *m* 89
good buono(a) 13, 101
good-bye arrivederci 9
goods merci *f/pl* 16
goose oca *f* 51
gooseberry uva spina *f* 54
go out, to uscire 96
gram grammo *m* 120
grammar book grammatica *f* 105
grandfather nonno *m* 93
grandmother nonna *f* 93
grape uva *f* 54, 64
grapefruit pompelmo *m* 54
grapefruit juice succo di pompelmo *m* 38, 60
gray grigio(a) 113
graze escoriazione *f* 139
greasy grasso(a) 30, 111
Great Britain Gran Bretagna *f* 146
Greece Grecia *f* 146
green verde 113
green bean fagiolino *m* 52
greengrocer's negozio di frutta e verdura *m* 98
green salad insalata verde *f* 52
greeting saluto *m* 9, 152
grey grigio(a) 113
grilled alla griglia 47; ai ferri 50
grocery negozio di alimentari *m* 98, 120
group gruppo *m* 82
guide guida *f* 80
guidebook guida turistica *f* 82, 104, 105
gum *(teeth)* gengiva *f* 145
gynaecologist ginecologo(a) *m/f* 137

H

hair capelli *m/pl* 30, 111
hairbrush spazzola per capelli *f* 111
haircut taglio dei capelli *m* 30
hairdresser's parrucchiere *m* 27, 30, 98
hair dryer asciugacapelli *m* 119
hair lotion lozione per capelli *f* 111
hair slide fermaglio *m* 111
hairspray lacca *f* 30, 111
half metà *f*, mezzo *m* 149
half a day mezza giornata *f* 80
half a dozen mezza dozzina *f* 120
half an hour mezz'ora *f* 153
half board mezza pensione *f* 24
half price *(ticket)* metà tariffa *f* 69
hall *(large room)* sala *f* 81, 88
ham prosciutto *m* 41, 48, 63, 64
hammer martello *m* 106
hammock amaca *f* 106
hand mano *f* 138
handbag borsetta *f* 116, 156
hand cream crema per le mani *f* 110
handicrafts artigianato *m* 83
handkerchief fazzoletto *m* 116
handmade fatto(a) a mano 113
hanger attaccapanni *m* 27
hangover mal di testa *m* 108
happy felice, buon(a) 152
harbour porto *m* 81
hard duro(a) 123
hard-boiled egg uovo sodo *m* 38
hardware shop negozio di ferramenta *m* 99
hare lepre *f* 51
hat cappello *m* 116
have, to avere 162
hay fever febbre del fieno *f* 108, 141
hazelnut nocciola *f* 54
he egli, lui 161
head testa *f* 138, 139
headache mal di testa *m* 141
headlight faro *m* 79
headphones cuffia (d'ascolto) *f* 119
health salute *f* 56
health food shop negozio di cibi dietetici *m* 99
health insurance assicurazione malattie *f* 144
heart cuore *m* 138
heart attack attacco cardiaco *m* 141
heating riscaldamento *m* 23, 28
heavy pesante 13, 101
heel tacco *m* 118
height altitudine *f* 85
helicopter elicottero *m* 74
hello! *(phone)* pronto 135
help aiuto *m* 156
help, to aiutare 13, 21, 100, 134; *(oneself)* servirsi 120
her suo, sua (*pl* suoi, sue) 161
herbs odori *m/pl* 53
herb tea tisana *f* 60
here qui, ecco 13
herring aringa *f* 46
high alto(a) 90, 141
high season alta stagione *f* 150
high tide alta marea *f* 90
hill collina *f* 85
hire noleggio *m* 20, 74
hire, to noleggiare 19, 20, 74, 90, 91, 119; affittare 155
his suo, sua (*pl* suoi, sue) 161
history storia *f* 83
hitchhike, to fare l'autostop 74
hold on! *(phone)* resti in linea! 136
hole buco *m* 29
holiday giorno festivo *m* 151
holidays vacanze *f/pl* 151; ferie *f/pl* 155
home address domicilio *m* 25
honey miele *m* 38
hors d'oeuvre antipasto *m* 41
horse riding corsa di cavalli *f* 89
hospital ospedale *m* 144
hot caldo(a) 14, 25, 38, 94
hotel albergo *m* 19, 21, 22; hotel *m* 22, 80
hotel guide guida degli alberghi *f* 19
hotel reservation prenotazione d'albergo *f* 19
hot water acqua calda *f* 23, 28
hot-water bottle borsa dell'acqua calda *f* 27
hour ora *f* 153
house casa *f* 83, 85
how come 10
how far quanto dista 10, 76, 85, 100
how long quanto tempo 10, 24
how many quanti 10
how much quanto 10, 24
hundred cento 148
hungry, to be aver fame 12, 35
hurry *(to be in a)* avere fretta 21
hurt, to fare male 139, 145; *(oneself)* farsi male 139
husband marito *m* 93
hydrofoil aliscafo *m* 74

I

I io 161
ice ghiaccio *m* 94
ice-cream gelato *m* 55, 64
ice-cream parlour gelateria *f* 33
ice cube cubetto di ghiaccio *m* 27
iced coffee caffè freddo *m* 60
ice pack elemento refrigerante *m* 106
iced tea tè freddo *m* 60
ill malato(a) 140
illness malattia *f* 160
important importante 12
impressive impressionante 84
in in 13, 163
include, to comprendere 20, 24, 32, 62, 80; includere 31
India India *f* 146
indigestion indigestione *f* 141
indoor *(swimming pool)* coperto(a) 90
inexpensive economico(a) 35, 124
infection infezione *f* 141
inflammation infiammazione *f* 142
inflation inflazione *f* 131
inflation rate tasso d'inflazione *m* 131
influenza influenza *f* 142
information informazione *f* 67, 155
injection iniezione *f* 142, 144
injure, to ferire 139
injured ferito(a) 79, 139
injury ferita *f* 139
ink inchiostro *m* 105
inn locanda *f* 22, 33; osteria *f* 33
inquiry informazione *f* 68
insect bite puntura d'insetto *f* 108, 139
insect repellent crema contro gli insetti *f* 109
insect spray spray insetticida *m* 109
inside dentro 15
instead invece 37
instrumental *(music)* strumentale 128
insurance assicurazione *f* 20, 79, 144
interest interesse *m* 80, 131
interested, to be interessarsi 83, 96
interesting interessante 84
international internazionale 133, 134
interpreter interprete *m/f* 131
intersection incrocio *m* 77
introduce, to presentare 92
introduction presentazione *f* 92, 130
investment investimento *m* 131
invitation invito *m* 94
invite, to invitare 94
invoice fattura *f* 131
iodine tintura di iodio *f* 109
Ireland Irlanda *f* 146
iron *(laundry)* ferro da stiro *m* 119
iron, to stirare 29
ironmonger's negozio di ferramenta *m* 99
Israel Israele *m* 146
Italian italiano(a) 10, 11, 95, 104, 114
Italy Italia *f* 146
its suo, sua (*pl* suoi, sue) 161
ivory avorio *m* 122

J

jacket giacca *f* 116
jade giada *f* 122
jam marmellata *f* 38
jam, to incastrare 28; bloccare 125
January gennaio *m* 150
Japan Giappone *m* 146
jar vasetto *m* 120
jaundice itterizia *f* 142
jaw mascella *f* 138
jeans jeans *m/pl* 116
jersey maglietta *f* 116
jewel gioiello *m* 121
jeweller's gioielleria *f* 99, 121
jewellery gioielli *m/pl* 127
joint articolazione *f* 138
journey percorso *m* 72
juice succo *m* 38, 60
July luglio *m* 150
jumper *(sweater)* maglione *m* 116
June giugno *m* 116
just *(only)* soltanto 100

K

keep, to tenere 62
kerosene petrolio *m* 106
key chiave *f* 26
kidney rognone *m* 48; rene *m* 138
kilogram chilogrammo *m* 120
kilometre chilometro *m* 20
kind gentile 95
kind *(type)* genere *m* 140
knapsack zaino *m* 106
knee ginocchio *m* 138
kneesocks calzettoni *m/pl* 116
knife coltello *m* 36, 61, 107
knitwear maglieria *f* 127
knock, to bussare 155
know, to sapere 16; conoscere 96, 114

L

label etichetta *f* 105
lace pizzo *m* 114
lady signora *f* 155
lake lago *m* 81, 85, 90
lamb agnello *m* 48
lamp lampada *f* 46
landmark punto di riferimento *m* 85
landscape paesaggio *m* 92
lantern lanterna *f* 106
large grande 101, 118
lark allodola *f* 51
last ultimo(a) 13, 68, 73; scorso(a) 149, 151
last name cognome *m* 25
late tardi 13
later più tardi 135
laugh, to ridere 95
launderette lavanderia automatica *f* 99
laundry *(place)* lavanderia *f* 29, 99; *(clothes)* biancheria *f* 29
laundry service servizio di lavanderia *m* 23
laxative lassativo *m* 109
lead *(theatre)* ruolo principale *m* 86
lead piombo *m* 75
leap year anno bisestile *m* 149
leather pelle *f* 114, 118
leather goods pelletteria *f* 127
leave, to partire 31, 68, 74, 162; lasciare 156; *(deposit)* depositare 26, 71
leek porro *m* 52
left sinistro(a) 21, 63, 69, 77
left-luggage office deposito bagagli *m* 67, 71
leg gamba *f* 138
lemon limone *m* 37, 38, 54, 55, 60, 64
lemonade limonata *f* 60
lemon juice succo di limone *m* 60
lens *(glasses)* lente *f* 123; *(camera)* obiettivo *m* 125
lens cap cappuccio per obiettivo *m* 125
lentil lenticchia *f* 52
less meno 14
lesson lezione *f* 91
let, to *(hire out)* affittare 155
letter lettera *f* 132
letter box cassetta delle lettere *f* 132
letter of credit lettera di credito *f* 130
lettuce lattuga *f* 52
level crossing passaggio a livello *m* 79
library biblioteca *f* 81, 99
lie down, to sdraiarsi 142
life belt cintura di salvataggio *f* 74
life boat canotto di salvataggio *m* 74
lifeguard bagnino *m* 90
lift ascensore *m* 27, 100
light leggero(a) 13, 55, 57, 101, 128; *(colour)* chiaro(a) 101, 112, 113
light luce *f* 28, 124; *(cigarette)* fiammifero *m* 95
lighter accendino *m* 126
lighter fluid benzina per accendino *f* 126
lighter gas gas per accendino *m* 126
light meter esposimetro *m* 125
like, to volere 12, 20, 23; desiderare 103; piacere 25, 61, 92, 96, 102, 112
lime cedro *m* 54
line linea *f* 73, 136
linen *(cloth)* lino *m* 114
lip labbro *m* 138
lipsalve burro cacao *m* 110
lipstick rossetto *m* 110
liqueur liquore *m* 59
liquid liquido *m* 123
listen, to ascoltare 128
litre litro *m* 57, 75, 120
little *(a)* un po' 14
live, to vivere 83
liver fegato *m* 48, 138
lobster aragosta *f* 46
local locale 36, 60
London Londra *f* 130
long lungo(a) 115
long-sighted presbite 123
look, to guardare 123
look for, to cercare 12
look out! attenzione! 156
loose *(clothes)* largo(a) 115
lose, to perdere 123, 156
loss perdita *f* 131
lost perduto(a) 12; perso(a) 156
lost and found office ufficio oggetti smarriti *m* 67, 156
lost property office ufficio oggetti smarriti *m* 67, 156
lot *(a)* molto 14
lotion lozione *f* 110
loud *(voice)* forte 135
love, to amare 162

lovely bello(a) 94
low basso(a) 90, 141
lower inferiore 69, 70
low season bassa stagione *f* 150
low tide bassa marea *f* 90
luck fortuna *f* 152
luggage bagagli *m/pl* 18, 26, 31, 71
luggage locker custodia automatica dei bagagli *f* 18, 67, 71
luggage trolley carrello portabagagli *m* 18, 71
lump *(bump)* bernoccolo *m* 139
lunch pranzo *m* 34, 80, 94
lung polmone *m* 138

M

mackerel sgombro *m* 47
magazine rivista *f* 105
magnificent magnifico(a) 84
maid cameriera *f* 26
mail, to spedire 28
mail posta *f* 28, 133
mailbox cassetta delle lettere *f* 132
main principale 80
make, to fare 131, 163
make up, to rifare 28; preparare 108
make-up remover pad tampone per togliere il trucco *m* 110
man uomo *m* (*pl* uomini) 115
manager direttore *m* 26
manicure manicure *f* 30
many molti(e) 14
map carta geografica *f* 76, 105; pianta *f* 105
March marzo *m* 150
marinated marinato(a) 47
marjoram maggiorana *f* 63
market mercato *m* 81, 99
marmalade marmellata d'arance *f* 38
married sposato(a) 93
marrow midollo *m* 48
mass *(church)* messa *f* 84
mat *(finish)* opaco(a) 125
match fiammifero *m* 106, 126; *(sport)* partita *f*, incontro *m* 89
match, to *(colour)* ravvivare 112
material *(cloth)* tessuto *m* 113
matinée spettacolo del pomeriggio *m* 87
mattress materasso *m* 106
mauve lilla 113
May maggio *m* 150
may *(can)* potere 11, 12, 163
meadow prato *m* 85
meal pasto *m* 24, 34, 62, 143
mean, to significare 10, 25
means mezzo *m* 74
measles morbillo *m* 142
measure, to prendere le misure 114
meat carne *f* 48, 49, 61
meatball polpetta *f* 48
mechanic meccanico *m* 78
mechanical pencil portamine *m* 105
medical medico(a) 144
medicine medicina *f* 83, 143
medium *(meat)* a puntino 50
meet, to incontrare 96
melon melone *m* 54
mend, to riparare 75; *(clothes)* rammendare 29
menthol *(cigarettes)* mentolo *m* 126
menu menù *m* 36, 39, 40
message messaggio *m* 28, 136
methylated spirits alcool metilico *m* 106
metre metro *m* 112
mezzanine *(theatre)* galleria *f* 87
middle mezzo *m* 69; metà *f* 87, 150
midnight mezzanotte *f* 153
mileage chilometraggio *m* 20
milk latte *m* 38, 60, 64
milkshake frullato di latte *m* 60
million milione *m* 148
mineral water acqua minerale *f* 60
minister *(religion)* pastore *m* 84
minute minuto *m* 153
mirror specchio *m* 115, 123
miscellaneous diverso(a) 127
Miss Signorina *f* 9
miss, to mancare 18, 29, 61
mistake errore *m* 31, 61, 62
mixed misto(a) 55
moccasin mocassino *m* 118
modified American plan mezza pensione *f* 24
moisturizing cream crema idratante *f* 110
moment momento *m* 136
monastery monastero *m* 81
Monday lunedì *m* 151
money denaro *m* 129, 130
money order vaglia *m* 133
month mese *m* 16, 150
monument monumento *m* 81
moon luna *f* 94
moped motorino *m* 74
more più 14

morning mattino *m* 151, 153
mortgage ipoteca *f* 131
mosque moschea *f* 84
mosquito net zanzariera *f* 106
motel motel *m* 22
mother madre *f* 93
motorbike moto *f* 74
motorboat barca a motore *f* 91
motorway autostrada *f* 76
mountain montagna *f* 85
moustache baffi *m/pl* 31
mouth bocca *f* 138
mouthwash gargarismo *m* 109
move, to muovere 139
movie film *m* 86
movie camera cinepresa *f* 124
movies cinema *m* 86, 96
Mr. Signor *m* 9
Mrs. Signora *f* 9
much molto(a) 14
mug boccale *m* 107
muscle muscolo *m* 138
museum museo *m* 81
mushroom fungo *m* 52
music musica *f* 83, 128
musical commedia musicale *f* 86
mussel cozza *f* 46
must, to dovere 23, 31, 37, 61, 95
mustard senape *f* 37, 64
my mio, mia (*pl* miei, mie) 161

N

nail *(human)* unghia *f* 110
nail file lima da unghie *f* 110
nail polish smalto *m* 110
nail polish remover solvente per le unghie *m* 110
nail scissors forbicine per le unghie *f/pl* 110
name nome *m* 23, 25, 79; cognome *m* 25
napkin tovagliolo *m* 36, 105, 106
nappy pannolino *m* 111
narrow stretto(a) 118
nationality cittadinanza *f* 25; nazionalità *f* 92
natural naturale 83
natural history storia naturale *f* 83
nausea nausea *f* 140
near vicino(a) 13; vicino a 14
nearby qui vicino 77, 84
nearest il (la) più vicino(a) 78, 98
neat *(drink)* liscio(a) 56, 59
neck collo *m* 30, 138
necklace collana *f* 121
need, to aver bisogno 29, 118; essere necessario 90; servire 118
needle ago *m* 27
needlework ricamo *m* 127
negative negativo *m* 125
nephew nipote *m* 93
nerve nervo *m* 138
nervous nervoso(a) 138
never mai 15
new nuovo(a) 13
newsagent's giornalaio *m* 99
newspaper giornale *m* 104, 105
newsstand edicola *f* 19, 67, 99, 104
New Year Capodanno *m* 152
New Zealand Nuova Zelanda *f* 146
next prossimo(a) 65, 68, 73, 76, 149; seguente 151
next to accanto a 14, 77
niece nipote *f* 93
night notte *f* 24, 151
nightclub night-club *m* 88
night cream crema da notte *f* 110
nightdress camicia da notte *f* 116
nine nove 147
nineteen diciannove 147
ninety novanta 148
ninth nono(a) 149
no no 9
noisy rumoroso(a) 25
nonalcoholic analcolico(a) 60
none nessuno(a) 15
nonsmoker non fumatori *m/pl* 36, 70
noon mezzogiorno *m* 31, 153
normal normale 30
north nord *m* 77
North America America del Nord *f* 140
nose naso *m* 138
nosebleed emorragia nasale *f* 140
nose drops gocce nasali *f/pl* 109
not non 15, 163
note *(banknote)* banconota *f* 130
notebook taccuino *m* 105
note paper carta da lettere *m* 105
nothing nulla 15, 17; niente 15
notice *(sign)* cartello *m* 155
November novembre *m* 150
now adesso 15
number numero *m* 26, 65, 135, 136, 147
nurse infermiera *f* 144
nutmeg noce moscata *f* 53

O

occupied occupato(a) 13, 155
October ottobre *m* 150
octopus polpo *m* 46
offer, to offrire 95
office ufficio *m* 19, 67, 99, 132, 133, 156
oil olio *m* 37, 64, 75, 111
oily grasso(a) 30, 111
old vecchio(a), anziano(a) 13
old town città vecchia *f* 81
olive oliva *f* 41
omelet frittata *f* 42
on su 14, 163
once una volta 149
one uno(a) 147
one-way *(ticket)* andata *f* 69
on foot a piedi 76
onion cipolla *f* 52
only soltanto 15, 80
on request a richiesta 73
on time in orario 68
onyx onice *m* 122
open aperto(a) 13, 82, 155
open, to aprire 10, 17, 82, 108, 131, 132, 142
open-air all'aperto 90
opera opera *f* 88
opera house teatro dell'opera *m* 81, 88
operation operazione *f* 144
operator centralinista *m/f* 134
operetta operetta *f* 88
opposite di fronte 77
optician ottico *m* 99, 123
or o 15
oral orale 143
orange arancio 113
orange arancia *f* 54, 64
orange juice succo d'arancia *m* 38, 60
orangeade aranciata *f* 60
orchestra orchestra *f* 88; *(seats)* poltrona *f* 87
orchestral music musica sinfonica *f* 128
order *(goods, meal)* ordinazione *f* 40, 102
order, to *(goods, meal)* ordinare 61, 102, 103
oregano origano *m* 53
ornithology ornitologia *f* 83
our nostro(a) 161
out of order fuori servizio 155
out of stock esaurito(a) 103
outlet *(electric)* presa *f* 27
outside fuori 15; all'aperto 36
oval ovale 101
over there laggiù 69
overalls tuta *f* 116
overdone troppo cotto(a) 61
overheat, to *(engine)* surriscaldare 78
overtake, to sorpassare 79
owe, to dovere 144
overwhelming sbalorditivo(a) 84
oyster ostrica *f* 41, 46

P

pacifier succhiotto *m* 111
packet pacchetto *m* 120, 126
page pagina *f* 77
page *(hotel)* fattorino *m* 26
pail secchio *m* 106; secchiello *m* 128
pain dolore *m* 140, 141; male *m* 144
painkiller antinevralgico *m* 140; calmante *m* 144
paint pittura *f* 155
paint, to dipingere 83
paintbox scatola di colori *f* 105
painter pittore *m* 83
painting pittura *f* 83
pair paio *m* 116, 118, 149
pajamas pigiama *m* 117
palace palazzo *m* 81
palpitation palpitazione *f* 141
panties slip *m* 116
pants *(trousers)* pantaloni *m/pl* 116
panty girdle guaina *f* 116
panty hose collant *m* 116
paper carta *f* 105
paperback libro tascabile *m* 105
paper napkin tovagliolo di carta *m* 107
paraffin *(fuel)* petrolio *m* 106
parcel pacco *m* 132
pardon? prego? 10
parents genitori *m/pl* 93
park parco *m* 81
park, to parcheggiare 26, 77
parking parcheggio *m* 77, 79
parking disc disco di sosta *m* 77
parking meter parchimetro *m* 77
parliament parlamento *m* 81
parsley prezzemolo *m* 53
part parte *f* 138
partridge pernice *f* 51

party *(social gathering)* ricevimento *m* 95
pass *(mountain)* passo *m* 85
pass, to *(car)* sorpassare 79
passport passaporto *m* 16, 17, 25, 26, 156
passport photo fotografia d'identità *f* 124
pass through, to essere di passaggio 16
pasta pasta *f* 44
paste *(glue)* colla *f* 105
pastry pasticcino *m* 64
pastry shop pasticceria *f* 99
patch, to *(clothes)* rappezzare 29
path sentiero *m* 85; pista *f* 155
patient paziente *m/f* 144
pay, to pagare 31, 62, 102
payment pagamento *m* 102, 131
pea pisello *m* 52
peach pesca *f* 54
peak picco *m* 85
peanut arachide *f* 54
pear pera *f* 54
pearl perla *f* 122
pedestrian pedonale 79
peg *(tent)* picchetto *m* 107
pen penna *f* 105
pencil matita *f* 105
pencil sharpener temperamatite *m* 105
pendant pendente *m* 121
penicillin penicillina *f* 143
penknife temperino *m* 107
pensioner pensionato *m* 82
people gente *f* 93
pepper pepe *m* 37; *(sweet)* peperone *m* 52
per cent per cento 149
percentage percentuale *f* 131
perch pesce persico *m* 46
per day per un giorno 20, 89; al giorno 32
perform, to *(theatre)* rappresentare 86
perfume profumo *m* 110
perfume shop profumeria *f* 100
perhaps forse 15
per hour all'ora 77; per un'ora 89
period *(monthly)* mestruazioni *f/pl* 141
period pains mestruazioni dolorose *f/pl* 141
permanent wave permanente *f* 30
permit permesso *m* 90
per night per una notte 24
per person per persona 32
person persona *f* 32
personal personale 17
personal call telefonata con preavviso *f* 135
personal cheque assegno personale *m* 130
person-to-person call telefonata con preavviso *f* 135
per week per una settimana 20, 24
petrol benzina *f* 75, 78
pewter peltro *m* 122
pheasant fagiano *m* 51
photo fotografia *f* 82, 124, 125
photocopy fotocopia *f* 131
photograph, to fotografare, fare delle fotografie 82
photographer fotografo *m* 99
photography fotografia *f* 124
phrase espressione *f* 11
pick up, to prendere 80, 96
pickles sottaceti *m/pl* 41, 64
picnic picnic *m* 63
picnic basket cestino da picnic *m* 107
picture quadro *m* 83; *(photo)* fotografia *f* 82
piece pezzo *m* 120
pig porcellino *m*, porchetta *f* 46
pigeon piccione *m* 51
pill pillola *f* 141; compressa *f* 143
pillow guanciale *m* 27
pin spillo *m* 111, 122
pineapple ananas *m* 54
pink rosa 113
pipe pipa *f* 126
pipe cleaner nettapipe *m* 126
pipe tobacco tabacco da pipa *m* 126
pipe tool curapipe *m* 126
pizza pizza *f* 42, 63
pizza parlour pizzeria *f* 33
place luogo *m* 25; posto *m* 76
place of birth luogo di nascita *m* 25
plane aereo *m* 65
planetarium planetario *m* 81
plaster, to ingessare 140
plastic plastica *f* 107
plastic bag sacchetto di plastica *m* 107
plate piatto *m* 36, 61, 107
platform *(station)* binario *m* 67, 68, 69, 70
platinum platino *m* 122

play *(theatre)* commedia *f* 86
play, to interpretare 86; suonare 88; giocare 89, 93
playground parco giochi *m* 32
playing card carte da gioco *f/pl* 105
please per favore, per piacere 9
plimsolls scarpe da tennis *f/pl* 118
plug *(electric)* spina *f* 28
plum prugna *f* 54, 64
pneumonia polmonite *f* 142
poached affogato(a) 47
pocket tasca *f* 117
pocket watch orologio da tasca *m* 121
point punto *m* 80
point, to *(show)* indicare 11
poison veleno *m* 156
poisoning avvelenamento *m* 142
pole *(ski)* bastone *m* 91
police polizia *f* 78, 156
police station posto di polizia *m* 99, 156
polish *(nails)* smalto *m* 110
pond stagno *m* 85
pop music musica pop *f* 28
poplin popeline *m* 114
porcelain porcellana *f* 127
pork maiale *m* 48
port porto *m* 74; *(wine)* porto *m* 59
portable portatile 119
porter facchino *m* 18, 26, 71
portion porzione *f* 37, 61
Portugal Portogallo *m* 146
possible possibile 137
post *(letters)* posta *f* 28, 133
post, to spedire 28
postage affrancatura *f* 132
postage stamp francobollo *m* 28, 126, 132
postcard cartolina *f* 105, 126, 132
poste restante fermo posta *m* 133
post office ufficio postale *m* 99, 132
potato patata *f* 52
pottery terracotta *f* 83
poultry pollame *m* 50
pound *(money)* sterlina *f* 18, 130; *(weight)* libbra *f* 120
powder cipria *f* 110
powder compact portacipria *m* 121
prawns scampi *m/pl* 47
preference preferenza *f* 101
pregnant incinta 141
premium *(gasoline)* super 75
prescribe, to prescrivere 143
prescription ricetta *f* 108, 143
press, to *(iron)* stirare a vapore 29
press stud bottone a pressione *m* 117
pressure pressione *f* 75, 142
price prezzo *m* 24
priest prete *m* 84
print *(photo)* stampa *f* 125
private privato(a) 80, 91, 155
processing *(photo)* sviluppo *m* 124
profession professione *f* 25
profit profitto *m* 131
programme programma *m* 87
prohibit, to vietare 79, 91, 155
pronunciation pronuncia *f* 6
propelling pencil portamine *m* 105
Protestant protestante 84
provide, to procurare 131
prune prugna secca *f* 54
public holiday giorno festivo *m* 152
pull, to tirare 155
pullover pullover *m* 117
pumpkin zucca *f* 52
puncture foratura *f* 75
purchase acquisto *m* 131
pure puro(a) 114
purple viola 113
push, to spingere 155
put, to mettere 24
pyjamas pigiama *m* 117

Q

quail quaglia *f* 51
quality qualità *f* 103, 113
quantity quantità *f* 14, 103
quarter quarto *m* 149; *(part of town)* quartiere *m* 81
quarter of an hour quarto d'ora *m* 153
quartz quarzo *m* 122
question domanda *f* 10, 163
quick rapido(a) 13; presto 156
quickly presto 137, 156
quiet tranquillo(a) 23, 25
quince cotogna *f* 54

R

rabbi rabbino *m* 84
rabbit coniglio *m* 51
race course/track ippodromo *m* 90
racket *(sport)* racchetta *f* 90
radiator radiatore *m* 78
radio *(set)* radio *f* 23, 28, 119
radish ravanello *m* 52

railroad crossing passaggio a livello *m* 79
railway ferrovia *f* 154
railway station stazione *f* 19, 21, 67, 70
rain pioggia *f* 94
rain, to piovere 94
raincoat impermeabile *m* 117
raisin uva passa *f* 54
rangefinder telemetro *m* 125
rare *(meat)* al sangue 50, 61
rash esantema *m* 139
raspberry lampone *m* 54
rate tariffa *f* 20; tasso *m* 131
razor rasoio *m* 110
razor blade lametta *f* 110
reading-lamp lampada *f* 27
ready pronto(a) 29, 118, 123, 125, 145
real vero(a) 121
rear dietro 75
receipt ricevuta *f* 103, 144
reception ricevimento *m* 23
receptionist capo ricevimento *m* 26
recommend, to consigliare 35, 36, 40, 80, 86, 88, 137, 145
record *(disc)* disco *m* 127, 128
record player giradischi *m* 119
rectangular rettangolare 101
red rosso(a) 57, 113
redcurrant ribes *m* 54
red mullet triglia *f* 46
reduction riduzione *f* 24, 82
refill ricambio *m* 105
refund, to rimborsare 103
regards saluti *m/pl* 152
register, to *(luggage)* far registrare 71
registered mail raccomandato(a) 133
registration registrazione *f* 25
registration form scheda *f* 25, 26
regular *(petrol)* normale 75
religion religione *f* 83
religious service funzione religiosa *f* 84
rent, to noleggiare 19, 20, 74, 89, 91, 119; affittare 155
rental noleggio *m* 20, 74
repair riparazione *f* 125
repair, to riparare 29, 118, 119, 121, 123, 125, 145
repeat, to ripetere 11
report, to denunciare 156
reservation prenotazione *f* 19, 23, 65, 69
reservations office ufficio prenotazioni *m* 19, 67
reserve, to prenotare 19, 23, 87; riservare 36
restaurant ristorante *m* 19, 32, 33, 35, 67
return *(ticket)* andata e ritorno 69
return, to *(give back)* rendere 103
reverse the charges, to telefonare a carico del destinatario 135
rheumatism reumatismo *m* 141
rib costola *f* 48, 138
ribbon nastro *m* 105
rice riso *m* 45
right destro(a) 63, 69, 77; *(correct)* giusto 13, 70
ring *(on finger)* anello *m* 121
ring, to suonare 155
river fiume *m* 85, 90
road strada *f* 76, 77, 85
road assistance assistenza stradale *f* 78
road map carta stradale *f* 105
road sign segnale stradale *m* 79
roast arrosto 48, 50
roast beef rosbif *m* 48
rock masso *m* 79
roll *(bread)* panino *m* 38, 64
roller skates pattini a rotelle *m/pl* 128
roll film bobina *f* 124
roll-neck a collo alto 117
room camera *f* 19, 23, 24, 25, 28; *(space)* posto *m* 32
room number numero della stanza *m* 26
room service servizio nella stanza *m* 23
rope corda *f* 107
rosary rosario *m* 122
rosé rosatello 57
rosemary rosmarino *m* 53
rouge fard *m* 110
round rotondo(a) 101
round-neck a girocollo 117
roundtrip *(ticket)* andata e ritorno 69
rowing-boat barca a remi *f* 91
royal reale 82
rubber gomma *f* 105, 118
ruby rubino *m* 122
rucksack zaino *m* 107
ruin rovina *f* 82
ruler *(for measuring)* riga *f* 105
rum rum *m* 60
running water acqua corrente *f* 23

S

safe *(not dangerous)* sicuro(a), senza pericolo 90
safe cassaforte *f* 26
safety pin spillo di sicurezza *m* 111
saffron zafferano *m* 53
sage salvia *f* 53
sailing-boat barca a vela *f* 91
salad insalata *f* 52, 64
salami salame *m* 41, 63, 64
sale vendita *f* 131; *(bargains)* saldi *m/pl* 100, svendita *f* 155
sales tax I.V.A. *f* 24, 102
salmon salmone *m* 41, 46
salt sale *m* 37, 64
salty salato(a) 61
sand sabbia *f* 90
sandal sandalo *m* 118
sandwich panino imbottito *m* 63
sanitary towel/napkin assorbente igienico *m* 109
sardine sardina *f* 41, 47
satin raso *m* 114
Saturday sabato *m* 151
sauce salsa *f* 44
saucepan casseruola *f* 107
saucer piattino *m* 107
sausage salsiccia *f* 48, 64
scallop arsella *f* 46
scarf sciarpa *f* 117
scenic route strada panoramica *f* 85
scissors forbici *f/pl* 107; forbicine *f/pl* 110
scooter motoretta *f* 74
Scotland Scozia *f* 146
Scottish scozzese 93
scrambled eggs uova strapazzate *f/pl* 38
screwdriver cacciavite *m* 107
sculptor scultore *m* 83
sculpture scultura *f* 83
sea mare *m* 23, 85,
sea bass spigola *f* 47
sea bream orata *f* 46
seafood frutti di mare *m/pl* 46
season stagione *f* 40, 150
seasoning condimento *m* 37
seat posto *m* 69, 70, 87
seat belt cintura di sicurezza *f* 75
second secondo 149
second secondo *m* 153
second class seconda classe *f* 69
second hand lancetta dei secondi *f* 122
second-hand d'occasione 104
secretary segretaria *f* 27, 131
see, to guardare 11
sell, to vendere 162
send, to mandare 31, 78, 102, 103; spedire 132; inviare 133
send up, to portare su 26
separately separatamente 62
September settembre *m* 150
seriously *(wounded)* gravemente 139
service servizio *m* 24, 62, 98, 100; *(religion)* funzione *f* 84
serviette tovagliolo *m* 36
set *(hair)* messa in piega *f* 30
set menu menù (a prezzo fisso) *m* 36, 40
setting lotion fissatore *m* 30; lozione fissativa *f* 111
seven sette 147
seventeen diciassette 147
seventh settimo 149
seventy settanta 148
sew, to attaccare 29
shade *(colour)* tonalità *f* 112
shampoo shampoo *m* 30, 111
shape forma *f* 103
share *(finance)* azione *f* 131
sharp *(pain)* acuto(a) 140
shave, to radere 31
shaver rasoio (elettrico) *m* 27, 119
shaving cream crema da barba *f* 111
she ella, lei 161
shelf scaffale *m* 100, 120
ship nave *f* 74
shirt camicia *f* 117
shiver, to rabbrividire 140
shoe scarpa *f* 118
shoelace laccio *m* 118
shoemaker's calzolaio *m* 99
shoe polish lucido *m* 118
shoe shop negozio di scarpe *m* 99
shop negozio *m* 98
shopping acquisti *m/pl* 97
shopping area zona dei negozi *f* 19, 82, 100
short corto(a) 30, 115,
shorts short *m* 117
short-sighted miope 123
shoulder spalla *f* 138
shovel paletta *f* 49, 128
show spettacolo *m* 86, 87
show, to mostrare 11, 12, 100, 101, 103, 119

shower doccia *f* 23, 32
shrimp gamberetto *m* 41, 46
shrink, to restringersi 114
shut chiuso(a) 13
shutter *(window)* imposta *f* 29; *(camera)* otturatore *m* 125
sick, to be *(ill)* sentirsi male 140, 156
sickness *(illness)* malattia *f* 140
side lato *m* 30
sideboards/burns basette *f/pl* 31
sightseeing visita turistica *f* 80
sightseeing tour giro turistico *m* 80
sign *(notice)* cartello *m* 155; *(road)* segnale *m* 79
sign, to firmare 26, 131
signature firma *f* 25
signet ring anello con stemma *m* 122
silk seta *f* 114, 127
silver argentato(a) 113
silver argento *m* 121, 122
silver plate placcato d'argento 122
silverware argenteria *f* 122
simple semplice 124
since da 15, 150
sing, to cantare 88
single scapolo *m*, nubile *f* 93
single *(ticket)* andata 69
single room camera singola *f* 19, 23
sister sorella *f* 93
sit down, to sedersi 95
six sei 147
sixteen sedici 147
sixth sesto 149
sixty sessanta 147
size formato *m* 124; *(clothes)* taglia *f*, misura *f* 114, 115; *(shoes)* numero *m* 118
skates pattini *m/pl* 91
skating rink pista di pattinaggio *f* 91
ski sci *m* 91
ski, to sciare 91
ski boot scarpone da sci *m* 91
skier sciatore *m* (sciatrice *f*) 91
skiing sci *m* 89, 91
ski lift sciovia *m* 91
skin pelle *f* 138
skirt gonna *f* 117
ski run pista di sci *f* 91
sky cielo *m* 94
sled slitta *f* 91
sleep, to dormire 144
sleeping bag sacco a pelo *m* 107
sleeping-car vagone letto *m* 66, 68, 69, 70
sleeping pill sonnifero *m* 109, 143, 144
sleeve manica *f* 117
slice fetta *f* 55, 63, 120
slide *(photo)* diapositiva *f* 124
slip sottoveste *f* 117
slipper pantofola *f* 118
slow lento(a) 13
slow down, to rallentare 79
slowly lentamente 11, 21, 135
small piccolo(a) 13, 25, 101, 118
smoke, to fumare 95
smoked affumicato(a) 41, 47
smoker *(compartment)* fumatori *m/pl* 70
snack spuntino *m* 63
snack bar snack bar *m* 67
snail lumaca *f* 46
snap fastener bottone a pressione *m* 117
sneakers scarpe da tennis *f/pl* 118
snorkel maschera da subacqueo *f* 128
snow neve *f* 94
snow, to nevicare 94
soap saponetta *f* 27, 111
soccer calcio *m* 89
sock calzino *m* 117
socket *(outlet)* presa *f* 27
soft morbido(a) 123
soft drink bibita *f* 64
soft-boiled *(egg)* molle 38
sold out *(theatre)* esaurito 87
sole suola *f* 118; *(fish)* sogliola *f* 47
soloist solista *m/f* 88
some del, della (*pl* dei, delle) 14
someone qualcuno 95
something qualcosa 36, 55, 108, 112, 113, 139
son figlio *m* 93
song canzone *f* 128
soon presto 15
sore *(painful)* infiammato(a) 145
sore throat mal di gola *m* 141
sorry *(I'm)* mi dispiace 11, 16
sort genere *m* 86
sound-and-light show spettacolo suoni e luci *m* 86
soup minestra *f*, zuppa *f* 43
south sud *m* 77
South Africa Sudafrica *m* 146
South America America del Sud *f* 146
souvenir oggetto ricordo *m* 127
souvenir shop negozio di ricordi *m* 99
Soviet Union Unione Sovietica *f* 146

spade paletta *f* 128
Spain Spagna *f* 146
spare tyre ruota di scorta *f* 75
spark(ing) plug candela *f* 76
sparkling *(wine)* spumante 57
speak, to parlare 11, 135
speaker *(loudspeaker)* altoparlante *f*
specialist specialista *m/f* 142
speciality specialità *f* 40, 60
specimen *(medical)* campione *m* 142
spectacle case astuccio per occhiali *m* 123
spell, to sillabare 11
spend, to spendere 101
spice spezia *f* 53
spinach spinacio *m* 52
spine spina dorsale *f* 138
spiny lobster aragosta *f* 46
spit-roasted allo spiedo 50
spoon cucchiaio *m* 36, 61, 107
sport sport *m* 89
sporting goods shop negozio di articoli sportivi *m* 99
sprain, to distorcere 140
spring *(season)* primavera *f* 150; *(water)* sorgente *f* 85
square piazza *f* 82
squid calamaro *m* 46
stadium stadio *m* 82
staff personale *m* 26
stain macchia *f* 29
stainless steel acciaio inossidabile *m* 107, 122
stalls *(theatre)* poltrona *f* 87
stamp *(postage)* francobollo *m* 28, 126, 132
staple graffetta *f* 105
star stella *f* 94
start, to iniziare 80, 88; *(car)* partire '78
starter antipasto *m* 41
station stazione *f* 19, 21, 67, 70, 73
stationer's cartoleria *f* 99, 104
statue statua *f* 82
stay soggiorno *m* 31, 92
stay, to restare 16, 24; trattenersi 26; soggiornare 93
steak bistecca *f* 48
steal, to rubare 156
steamed cotto(a) a vapore 47
stew spezzatino *m* 49
stewed in umido 50
stiff neck torcicollo *m* 141
still *(mineral water)* naturale 60
sting puntura *f* 139
sting, to pungere 139
stitch, to *(clothes)* cucire 29; *(shoes)* attaccare 118
stock exchange borsa valori *f* 82
stocking calza da donna *f* 117
stomach stomaco *m* 138
stomach ache mal di stomaco *m* 141
stools feci *f/pl* 142
stop *(bus)* fermata *f* 72, 73
stop! fermatevi! 156
stop, to fermarsi 21, 68, 70, 72
stop thief! al ladro! 156
store negozio *m* 98
straight *(drink)* liscio 56, 59
straight ahead diritto 21, 77
strange strano 84
strawberry fragola *f* 54, 55
street strada *f* 25
streetcar tram *m* 72
street map pianta della città *f* 19, 105
strike sciopero *m* 155
string spago *m* 105
strong forte 143
student studente(essa) *m* 82, 93
stuffed farcito(a) 50
subway *(railway)* metropolitana *f* 73
suede renna *f* 114; camoscio *m* 118
sugar zucchero *m* 37, 64
suit *(man)* completo *m* 117; *(woman)* tailleur *m* 117
suitcase valigia *f* 18
summer estate *f* 150
sun sole *m* 94
sunburn scottatura solare *f* 108
Sunday domenica *f* 151
sunglasses occhiali da sole *m/pl* 123
sunshade *(beach)* ombrellone *m* 91
sunstroke colpo di sole *m* 141
sun-tan cream crema solare *f* 111
sun-tan oil olio solare *m* 111
super *(petrol)* super 75
superb superbo 84
supermarket supermercato *m* 99
suppository supposta *f* 109
surfboard sandolino *m* 91
surgery *(consulting room)* ambulatorio *m* 137
surname cognome *m* 25
suspenders *(Am.)* bretelle *f/pl* 117
swallow, to inghiottire 143
sweater maglione *m* 117

sweatshirt blusa *f* 117
Sweden Svezia *f* 146
sweet dolce 57, 61
sweet caramella *f* 126
sweetener dolcificante *m* 37
swell, to gonfiare 139
swelling gonfiore *m* 139
swim, to nuotare 90
swimming nuoto *m* 89; balneazione *f* 91
swimming pool piscina *f* 32, 90
swimming trunks costume da bagno *m* 117
swimsuit costume da bagno *m* 117
Swiss svizzero(a) 18
switch interruttore *m* 29
switchboard operator centralinista *m/f* 26
switch on, to *(light)* accendere 79
Switzerland Svizzera *f* 146
swollen gonfio(a) 139
swordfish pesce spada *m* 46
synagogue sinagoga *f* 84
synthetic sintetico 114
system sistema *m* 138

T

table tavolo *m* 36; tavola *f* 107
tablet pastiglia *f* 109
tailor's sartoria *f* 99
take, to prendere 18, 25, 73, 102; durare 72; portare 114
take away, to *(carry)* portare via 63, 102
talcum powder talco *m* 111
tampon tampone igienico *m* 109
tangerine mandarino *m* 54
tap *(water)* rubinetto *m* 28
tape recorder registratore *m* 119
tax tassa *f* 32; I.V.A. *f* 24, 102
taxi taxi *m* 19, 21, 31
tea tè *m* 38, 60, 64
tear, to lacerare 140
tearoom sala da tè *f* 34
teaspoon cucchiaino *m* 107, 143
telegram telegramma *m* 133
telegraph office ufficio telegrafico *m* 133
telephone telefono *m* 28, 78, 79, 134
telephone, to telefonare 134
telephone booth cabina telefonica *f* 134
telephone call telefonata *f* 135, 136
telephone directory elenco telefonico *m* 134
telephone number numero di telefono *m* 96, 135, 136
telephoto lens teleobiettivo *m* 125
television *(set)* televisore *m* 23, 28, 119
telex telex *m* 133
telex, to mandare un telex 130
tell, to dire 12, 73, 76, 136, 153
temperature temperatura *f* 90; *(fever)* febbre *f* 140, 142
temporary provvisoriamente 145
ten dieci 147
tendon tendine *m* 138
tennis tennis *m* 89
tennis court campo da tennis *m* 89
tennis racket racchetta da tennis *f* 89
tent tenda *f* 32, 107
tenth decimo 149
tent peg picchetto per tenda *m* 107
tent pole palo per tenda *m* 107
term *(word)* termine *m* 131
terrace terrazza *f* 36
terrifying terrificante 84
terrycloth tessuto di spugna *m* 114
tetanus tetano *m* 140
than di 14
thank you grazie 9
that quello, quella 10, 100, 161
the il, lo, la (*pl* i, gli, le) 159
theatre teatro *m* 82, 86
theft furto *m* 156
their il, la loro (*pl* i, le loro) 161
then poi, in seguito 15
there là 13; ecco 13
thermometer termometro *m* 109, 144
these questi, queste 63, 160
they essi, loro 161
thief ladro *m* 156
thin fine 113
think, to pensare 62, 94
third terzo 149
third terzo *m* 149
thirsty, to be aver sete 12
thirteen tredici 147
thirty trenta 147
this questo, questa 10, 100, 160
those quegli, quei, quelle 160; quelli, quelle 63, 120
thousand mille 148
thread filo *m* 27

three tre 147
throat gola *f* 138, 141
throat lozenge pasticca per la gola *f* 109
through train treno diretto *m* 68, 69
thumbtack puntina *f* 105
thunder tuono *m* 94
thunderstorm temporale *m* 94
Thursday giovedì *m* 151
thyme timo *m* 53
ticket biglietto *m* 65, 69, 72, 87, 89
ticket office biglietteria *f* 67
tide marea *f* 90
tie cravatta *f* 117
tie clip fermacravatte *m* 122
tie pin spillo per cravatta *m* 122
tight *(clothes)* stretto(a) 115
tights collant *m* 117
time tempo *m* 80; *(clock)* ora *f* 137, 153; *(occasion)* volta *f* 143
timetable orario ferroviario *m* 68
tin *(can)* scatola *f* 120
tinfoil foglio d'alluminio *m* 107
tin opener apriscatole *m* 107
tint sfumatura *f* 111
tinted colorato(a) 123
tip mancia *f* 62
tire ruota *f* 75; gomma *f* 76
tired stanco(a) 12
tissue *(handkerchief)* fazzoletto di carta *m* 111
to a 14, 163
toast pane tostato *m* 38
tobacco tabacco *m* 126
tobacconist's tabaccheria *f* 99, 126
today oggi 29, 151
toe dito del piede *m* 138
toilet paper carta igienica *f* 111
toiletry articoli da toilette *m/pl* 110
toilets gabinetti *m/pl* 27, 32, 37, 67
token *(telephone)* gettone *m* 134
toll pedaggio *m* 75
tomato pomodoro *m* 52
tomato juice succo di pomodoro *m* 60
tomb tomba *f* 82
tomorrow domani 29, 151
tongue lingua *f* 48, 138
tonic water acqua tonica *f* 60
tonight stasera 29, 96; questa sera 86, 87
tonsil tonsilla *f* 138
too troppo(a) 14; *(also)* anche 15
tooth dente *m* 145
toothache mal di denti *m* 145
toothbrush spazzolino da denti *m* 111, 119
toothpaste dentifricio *m* 111
top cima *f* 30; alto *m* 145
topaz topazio *m* 122
torch *(flashlight)* lampadina tascabile *f* 107
torn lacerato(a) 140
touch, to toccare 155
tough duro(a) 61
tourist office ufficio turistico *m*, azienda di promozione turistica *f* 22, 80
tourist tax tassa di soggiorno *f* 32
towards verso 14
towel asciugamano *m* 27
towelling tessuto di spugna *m* 114
town città *f* 19, 76
town hall municipio *m* 82
tow truck carro attrezzi *m* 78
toy giocattolo *m* 128
toy shop negozio di giocattoli *m* 99
tracksuit tuta sportiva *f* 117
traffic traffico *m* 76
traffic light semaforo *m* 77
trailer roulotte *f* 32
train treno *m* 66, 68, 69, 70, 73
tram tram *m* 72
tranquillizer tranquillante *m* 109, 143
transfer *(bank)* trasferimento *m* 131
transformer trasformatore *m* 119
translate, to tradurre 11
transport trasporto *m* 74
travel, to viaggiare 92
travel agency agenzia di viaggi *f* 99
travel guide guida turistica *f* 105
traveller's cheque traveller's cheque *m* 18, 62, 102, 130
travel sickness mal d'auto *m* 108
treatment cura *f* 143
tree albero *m* 85
tremendous fantastico(a) 84
trim, to *(beard)* spuntare 31
trip viaggio *m* 93, 152; percorso *m* 72
tripe trippe *f/pl* 49
trousers pantaloni *m/pl* 117
trout trota *f* 47
truffle tartufo *m* 52
try, to provare 115; *(sample)* assaggiare 60
T-shirt maglietta di cotone *f* 117
tube tubetto *m* 120
Tuesday martedì *m* 151
tuna tonno *m* 41, 47

Tunisia Tunisia *f* 146
tunnel galleria *f* 79
tunny tonno *m* 41, 47
turbot rombo *m* 46
Turkey Turchia *f* 146
turkey tacchino *m* 51
turn, to *(change direction)* girare 21, 77
turquoise turchese 113
turquoise turchese *m* 122
turtleneck a collo alto 117
tweezers pinzette *f/pl* 111
twelve dodici 147
twenty venti 147
twice due volte 149
twin bed due letti *m/pl* 23
two due 147
typewriter macchina per scrivere *f* 27, 105
typewriter ribbon nastro per macchina da scrivere *m* 105
typing paper carta per macchina da scrivere *f* 105
tyre ruota *f* 75; gomma *f* 76

U

ugly brutto(a) 13, 84
umbrella ombrello *m* 117; *(beach)* ombrellone *m* 91
uncle zio *m* 93
unconscious svenuto(a) 139
under sotto 15
underdone *(meat)* al sangue 50; poco cotto(a) 61
underground *(railway)* metropolitana *f* 73
underpants mutande *f/pl*, slip *m* 117
undershirt canottiera *f* 117
understand, to capire 11, 16
undress, to spogliare 142
United States Stati Uniti *m/pl* 146
university università *f* 82
unleaded senza piombo 75
until fino a 14
up su, in alto 15
upper superiore 69
upset stomach mal di stomaco *m* 108
upstairs di sopra 15
urgent urgente 12, 145
urine urina *f* 142
use uso *m* 17
use, to usare 78, 134
useful utile 15
usual abituale 143

V

vacancy camera libera *f* 23
vacant libero 13, 155
vacation vacanze *f/pl* 151
vaccinate, to vaccinare 140
vacuum flask thermos *m* 107
vaginal vaginale 141
valley valle *f* 85
value valore *m* 131
value-added tax I.V.A. *f* 24, 102, 154
vanilla vaniglia *f* 55
VAT *(sales tax)* I.V.A. *f* 24, 102, 154
veal vitello *m* 48
vegetable verdura *f* 52
vegetable store negozio di frutta e verdura *m* 99
vegetarian vegetariano *m* 37
vein vena *f* 138
velvet velluto *m* 114
velveteen velluto di cotone *m* 114
venereal disease malattia venerea *f* 142
venison selvaggina *f* 51
vermouth vermouth *m* 59
very molto 15
vest canottiera *f* 117; *(Am.)* panciotto *m* 117
video cassette video cassetta *f* 119, 124, 127
video recorder video ıagistratore *m* 119
view vista *f* 23, 25
village villaggio *m* 76, 85; paese *m* 85
vinegar aceto *m* 37
vineyard vigna *f* 85
visit, to visitare 84
visiting hours orari di visita *m/pl* 144
vitamin pills vitamine *f/pl* 109
V-neck con scollatura a punta 117
volleyball pallavolo *f* 89
voltage voltaggio *m* 27, 119
vomit, to vomitare 140

W

waistcoat panciotto *m* 117
wait, to aspettare 21, 95
waiter cameriere *m* 26, 36
waiting-room sala d'aspetto *f* 67
waitress cameriera *f* 26, 36
wake, to svegliare 26
Wales Galles *m* 146
walk, to camminare 74; andare a piedi 85
wall muro *m* 85

wallet portafogli *m* 156
walnut noce *f* 54
want, to volere 18, 35, 163; *(wish)* desiderare 12
warm caldo(a) 94
wash, to lavare 29, 114
wash-basin lavabo *m* 28
washing powder detersivo *m* 107
watch orologio *m* 122, 127
watchmaker's orologiaio *m* 99; orologeria *f* 121
watchstrap cinturino per orologio *m* 122
water acqua *f* 23, 28, 32, 38, 75, 90
waterfall cascata *f* 85
water flask borraccia *f* 107
watermelon anguria *f* 54, cocomero *m* 54
water-ski sci nautico *m* 91
way strada *f* 76
we noi 161
weather tempo *m* 93
weather forecast previsioni del tempo *f/pl* 94
wedding ring fede nuziale *f* 122
Wednesday mercoledì *m* 151
week settimana *f* 16, 24, 80, 151
weekend fine settimana *m* 151
well pozzo 85; *(healthy)* bene 9, 140
well-done *(meat)* ben cotto(a) 50
west ovest *m* 77
what che cosa 10, 12; quanto 20; quale 20, 21
wheel ruota *f* 78
when quando, a che ora 10
where dove 10
which quale 10
whipped cream panna montata *f* 55
whisky whisky *m* 17, 59
white bianco(a) 57, 113
whiting merlano *m* 46
who chi 10
why perchè 10
wick stoppino *m* 126
wide largo(a) 118
wide-angle lens grandangolare *m* 125
wife moglie *f* 93
wild boar cinghiale *m* 51
wind vento *m* 94
window finestra *f* 28, 36; *(train)* finestrino *m* 69; *(shop)* vetrina *f* 100, 112
windscreen/shield parabrezza *m* 76
wine vino *m* 56, 57, 61
wine list lista dei vini *f* 57
wine merchant vinaio *m* 99
winter inverno *m* 150
winter sports sport invernali *m/pl* 91
wipers tergicristalli *m/pl* 76
wish augurio *m* 152
with con 14, 163
withdraw, to *(bank)* prelevare 131
without senza 14
woman donna *f* 115
wonderful magnifico(a) 96
wood bosco *m* 85
wood alcohol alcool metilico *m* 107
woodwork lavoro in legno *m* 127
woodcock beccaccia *f* 51
wool lana *f* 114
word parola *f* 11, 15, 133
work lavoro *m* 79
work, to *(function)* funzionare 28, 119
working day giorno feriale *m* 151
worse peggiore 13
wound ferita *f* 139
wrinkle resistant ingualcibile 114
wristwatch orologio braccialetto *m* 122
write, to scrivere 11, 101
writing pad blocco per appunti *m* 105
writing-paper carta da lettere *f* 27
wrong sbagliato(a) 13, 135

X

X-ray *(photo)* radiografia *f* 140

Y

year anno *m* 149
yellow giallo 113
yes sì 9
yesterday ieri 151
yet ancora 15
yoghurt yogurt *m* 64
you tu, voi 161
young giovane 13
your tuo(a) (*pl* tuoi, tue) 161; vostro(a) (*pl* vostri(e)) 161
youth hostel ostello della gioventù *m* 22, 32
Yugoslavia Iugoslavia *f* 146

Z

zero zero *m* 147
zip(per) cerniera *f* 117
zoo zoo *m* 82
zoology zoologia *f* 83

Indice italiano

AUSTRIA
SWITZERLAND
HUNGARY
ALTO ADIGE
Trento
TRENTINO
Udine
Trieste
Aosta
LOMBARDIA
Venezia
PIEMONTE
Milano
VENETO
Torino
EMILIA-
ROMAGNA
FRANCE
Genova
LIGURIA
Bologna
YUGOSLAVIA
Firenze
Ancona
TOSCANA
Perugia
MARCHE
UMBRIA
ADRIATIC
Isola d'Elba
L'Aquila
LAZIO
ABRUZZI
Corsica
MOLISE
Roma
Campobasso
Bari
Ischia
Napoli
CAMPANIA
PUGLIA
Potenza
Capri
LUCANIA
SARDEGNA
Cagliari
CALABRIA
Lipari
Catanzaro
MEDITERRANEAN
Egadi
Palermo
SICILIA
Catania
N
ALGERIA
TUNISIA